THE GUINNESS GUIDE TO
WATER SKIING

THE GUINNESS GUIDE TO
WATER SKIING

DAVID NATIONS/KEVIN DESMOND

GUINNESS SUPERLATIVES LIMITED
2 CECIL COURT, LONDON ROAD, ENFIELD, MIDDLESEX

797.85
NAT

797.176

For Elaine

(12/8/94)

T 213771

Foreword

by Admiral of the Fleet
the Right Honourable the Earl Mountbatten of Burma
KG, GCB, OM, GCSI, GCIE, GCVO, DSO

In 1932, just before I left the Mediterranean Fleet, I acquired my first pair of water-skis. Two years later, in 1934, I returned to the Mediterranean, this time in command of the destroyer HMS DARING, and had an opportunity of greatly improving my skill and enjoyment of this exhilarating sport. Thirty years later my younger daughter, Pamela, became one of the many hundreds who learned to water-ski on Ruislip Lido with David Nations.

Since then I have heard much about David Nations' tireless efforts and total dedication to the sport; indeed I believe he has come to be known as the "Father" of water-skiing. I admire his consistent ability to produce championship talent and it is very apt that the title page of this book bears his name.

A worldwide history of waterskiing has long been needed and this book comes at a time when the sport is going from strength to strength. Indeed, as I write this foreword I have heard the splendid news that Britain's foremost champion water-skier, Mike Hazelwood, has won at the Moomba Masters Water-Ski Tournament in Melbourne, beating world championship class skiers from both America and Australia. This is the first time in the fourteen years history of this classic competition that a British skier has won and will give tremendous encouragement to the sport in this country.

I am sure that all water-skiers, whether they be beginners, experts, men or women, young or old, will find this history of the sport fascinating.

Mountbatten of Burma

Preface

The life of a sport is in its very playing, from moment to moment. A history merely attempts to celebrate the best of those moments gone by.

During some thirty years spent with the sport of water-skiing David Nations realised that a time might come when he would have to put down on paper a record of the agonies and the ecstasies of his life as competitor, coach, innovator and judge. Various publishers approached him with this challenge, but on each occasion he had felt that the time was not right, and did not proceed.

One day in the Spring of 1975, however, another young man approached him with a proposal to write a definitive work on the sport. Again the reply was in the negative. But Kevin Desmond would not take no for an answer. Impressed by Desmond's determination and sincerity, it was decided that indeed the time was now ripe for such a book incorporating a history of water-skiing around the world, including Nations' many entertaining personal recollections and, not least, his expert technical advice on the sport.

A mountain of work lay ahead of them to record accurately the first worldwide history in more detail than had ever been attempted before. When Nations' unique collection of photos became coupled with Desmond's extensive researches into the ancient origins of the sport, they had documentation from 57 different countries sufficient for five books. Then followed that rigorous process of selection and rejection, with the overriding aim of doing justice to skiers all over the world who have enthusiastically helped to make this book into a fascinating saga of what is a comparatively new sport.

Sport has always suffered from the curse of talented, but under-privileged, young people whose opportunities have not equalled those less talented but better provided for. Owing to coaches and enthusiasts like David Nations, water-skiing broke through that barrier. In a period of nearly twenty years no pupil had more or less attention given him – whether he be the son of a caretaker or of a multi-millionaire. Nations passionately believes that as long as the talent is there, and that there are boys and girls in this country who will train through all the rigours of our traditionally incredible climate of 'ten months winter and two months bad weather', then his task is worthwhile.

For the last six years David Nations has been Chairman of the Water Recreation Division of the Central Council of Physical Education. Other important positions and offices he holds are: Founder and member of the Group 2 Technical Committee of the World Water Ski Union, President of the Group 2 Commission for Disabled Waterskiers of the World Water Ski Union; Founder Member and Vice-Chairman, Chairman of Tournament Division, National Coach of the British Water Ski Federation; Chairman of Sponsors of Sport Committee of the Central Council of Physical Recreation; Commissioner of the Water Space Amenity Commission; Governor of the Sports Aid Foundation; Vice-Chairman of the Hillingdon Borough Sports Advisory Council; Vice-Chairman of the Three Rivers Sports Council; Chairman of the Ruislip Water Ski Club; Chairman of the Rickmansworth Water Ski Club.

Declaration and Appeal

The Authors and Publishers do not claim that this history is complete: Fifty-seven countries can make up only thirty per cent of the territorial divisions of the world.

We would therefore welcome any facts, reports and illustrations about the origin and growth of 'walking on the water' – ancient and modern. This may include any point located by Time and Space in the Universe, of which our Solar System is only a tiny speck . . .

The authors wish to acknowledge the following to whom they are indebted: Sid Adraensen, Jean Ander, Antonio Agcaoli, George Athans, Liliane Aubenneau, P. J. Barck, Reg Barnes, Geoff Burgess, James Carne, Maria Vittoria Carrasco, Alan Clark, Claude de Clercq, William D. Clifford, André Coutau, Dick Cowell, Alan Crompton, Taghi Emami, David Emery, J. J. Finsterwald, L. F. de Groot, L. Griffin, Wayne Grimditch, Pierre Haddad, Thomas C. Hardman, Isla Henderson, John Horder, Hsu Te-Tsin, Thomas Hsueh, Felix Hulsemann, Clive F. Jenkins, Jan H. Johannessen, Masanori Komorimya, Lady Cooper-Key, Jim Laversuch, Colin McLeod, Lance Macklin, Ron Marks, Andi Matalata, The Earl Mountbatten of Burma, Billy Moyes, Jean Marie Muller, Odette Muller, Miklavz Music, Ladislav Nemes, Rene Daumas Nemoz, David Niven, Boris Olshevsky, Yoko Ozawa, Christos Papageorgiou, Mayme Ober Peak, Peter Pearl, Jon Pertwee, Emil Petersen, Dick Pope Sr and Jr, Sandy Primo, The 6th Earl of Ranfurly, Dr K. Rauchenwald, Isidro Oliveras de la Riva, Jack Rutherford, Ralph Samuelson, Roy Saint, Paul Seaton, Liz Allan Shetter, Artur Starewicz, Franz Stevens, Malcolm King Stewart, Freddy Strasser, Alan Taylor, Monty Tolkin, Niels Vinding, Bianca Vitali, John Whatnall, Christer Widing, Yugoslav National Tourist Offices.

Special thanks are due to Jeannette Williamson (*née* Stewart-Wood) and Paul Adlington, Assistant British National Coach, for their help in the preparation of the Technique Section; to Wallace Schulberg for the Specific Weight Training Section; to Raymond Thatcher, who for over a decade has been taking such fine water-ski photographs, so very many examples of his work appearing in this book; to Joel Martin for his photographic contribution, with respect to his son, Patrice; to Pat Gibbon for the line illustrations; and to Aubrey Sheena, for the loan of his superb collection of water-ski stamps.

Contents

History

1 The beginning: walking upon the water

Illustration from *The Life of Christ* commissioned by Ludolphus of Saxony. An illuminated manuscript of the 15th century, carefully preserved in the British Library. (British Library/British Museum)

At a private audience after the 1964 European Water-skiing Championships, His Holiness Pope Paul VI received some 40 skiers and officials who had been competing in the shadow of his summer residence at Castel Gandolfo. Along with his blessing, he told them smilingly that: 'You are special people, very holy and blessed, because you are like Jesus, who walked on the water.' He was referring to the Gospel According to St Mark, Chapter 6, Verse 49: 'But when they saw him walking upon the sea, they supposed it had been a spirit, and cried out.' More than a millennium passed before there was any other reference to walking on the water.

14th Century: In Alphonse Faussaire's *Les Histoires des Sorciers Anciens* (Paris 1843), reference is made to Eliseo of Tarentum, a mid-14th century, green-eyed, green-haired sorcerer thus:

'In the name of the Underworld. Behold Eliseo of Tarentum. A Jew. A Sorcerer of Thunderbolts and A

Water Diviner. He sings the Devil's Songs, then in the dusk of the Sun and the Full Moon, he walks and dances over the water.'

1511: In Signor Renati's *Vier Bücher von der Rytteschaft*, there is a woodcut illustration by K. Knappen, of a pair of large double-skin air-boots, designed to render the wearer's body so buoyant that he could walk in, or almost *upon the water*.

1643: A pamphlet was published which stated: 'A Most Certain, Strange and True Discovery of a Witch, being taken by some Parliament Forces, as she was standing on a small planck-board and sayling it over the River of Newbury.' The unfortunate woman was executed for her sorcery.

1670: In this year was published: *Naturall and Artificiall Conclusions . . . Englyshed and set forth by Thomas Hill, Londoner, whose own Experiments in this kind were held most excellant . . . to recreat wits withall at vacant times.*

The Witch of Newbury, 1643.

One of its brittle pages reads: 'Take two little Timbrels, and bind them under the soles of thy feet, and at thy stave's end fasten another; and with these thou may'st walk on the water, unto the wonder of all such as shall see the same; if so be you often exercise the same, with a certain boldness, and lightness of the body.'

1690: Johannes Christopher Wagenseil, of Nuremberg, who had been carefully observing the swimming of geese and of ducks, decided that it should be possible for men to imitate them. So he invented 'the Hydrapsis, or Water-Shield: A Machine by the Help of Which a Person May Walk upon the Water without Fear of Sinking.' It is reported that the King of Denmark himself tried the Hydrapsis and went more than a mile with it on, in the open sea.

THE HYDRAPSIS, OR WATER-SHIELD.
A MACHINE BY THE HELP OF WHICH A PERSON MAY WALK ON THE WATER WITHOUT FEAR OF SINKING.

Johannes Christopher Wagenseil of Nuremberg, came up with this skilful contraption in 1690 which he called the Hydrapsis.

1783: Backed by the French Government, Monsieur Lionnait pulled on *his* shoes and attempted to walk upon the waters of the River Seine – only to tumble backwards, his head beneath and his feet above the water. As local boatmen went to the rescue, the cry went forth that it was impossible to walk upon the water. But then Señor Perez from Spain, arrived with his 'Sabots Elastiques':

Señor Perez, after overcoming some initial difficulties with his Sabots Elastiques in the late 18th century.

SABOTS ELASTIQUES, AN APPARATUS FOR WALKING ON WATER.

'My first obstacle was to discover some method to prevent an upset and after diverse experiments I found that some kind of ballast or counterpoise was indispensable.

'I made many essays based upon theory, but without success. At length I placed four slender supports, two under the forepart and two in the rear, furnished with a fork of iron at their extremities, which touched the bottom of the water and offered resistance when the machine was not too rapid; and I have traversed the Seine several times without much opposition.'

1821: His Majesty King George IV visited Ireland. On the day of his departure from the harbour then called Dunleary, but henceforth known as Kingstown, near Dublin, there were several ships of war in attendance on the Royal Yacht. In 'The Royal Visit' one reads how: 'Mr Kent, on his *marine velocipede*, contributed not a little to amuse the people during the day, firing shots, waving a flag, and going through the sword exercise. To those on land he appeared to be walking on the water. After the King embarked, he went round the yacht several times, with his hat off, bowing, to the great amusement of His Majesty.'

This reproduction of an old print of about 1870, adorning the title page of the memorial volume of the 50th anniversary of the Royal Dutch Rowing Federation in 1969, shows part of the Amstel river at Amsterdam, Holland.

Water-skiing in Denmark: 1898.

1838: Brussels newspapers gave an account of Monsieur Teissier who 'walked upright in the water, dressed as Neptune, and carried in his hand a trident of the fabled god,' and who, 'having advanced slowly to the centre of the lake, remained there motionless for the space of twenty minutes'. A few years later, on the River Neva in Russia – and in Dresden and Magdeburg in Germany, people were being entertained by similar feats.

1845: Two young men – a Swede and a Norwegian – exhibited at Hanover, the exploit of *running* on the water. According to the Continental news-sheets, they had derived the idea from 'the gear called *skies,* by aid of which the inhabitants of the Northern regions traverse the snow-filled valleys and ravines without sinking'.

1858: Mr Ochoner won a wager by ascending the Rhine, from Rotterdam to Cologne, standing erect on his 'podoscaphs' and propelling himself by paddling with a long pole, flattened at the end; the 'podoscaphs' were only 4·57 m *15 ft* long!

1859: Saturday, 8 October: Mr Hickock, a well-known resident of Toronto, Canada, used the same method to tackle the fast-flowing River Don; his 1·22 m *4 ft* long shoes were made out of tin.

1902: Captain Grossman of Cologne trekked along

the River Danube from Linz to Vienna. His 3·96 m *13 ft* water-shoes were basically aluminium cylinders and 'the wearer propels himself by a treading movement, which causes four oar-shaped wings to revolve'. During the 160 km *100 mile* journey, Grossman towed his wife, who was sitting in a boat behind, for the whole two days.

1906: A Cornell University undergraduate tested out his sea-boots on Lake Cayuga, and is stated to have 'walked' with no apparent difficulty. His ambition – to pioneer the sport of 'water-lacrosse'!

1916: In the presence of Ministers of the various Allied powers and of a numerous public, Doctor G. Galansimo demonstrated his Hydro-Ski Risso on a lake in the Bois de Boulogne. By swinging his feet, Galansimo turned the blades of a water-vane at the back of two adjacent floats, so propelling himself forwards at speeds of 5–12 km/h *3–7 mph*. The Hydro-Ski Risso supported a weight of 200 kg *441 lb*, folded up easily, could be assembled in under three minutes – and not only served a sporting use, but potentially a military one: whole armies might use it to cross a river. But somehow the idea never caught on – maybe because it would have turned an Allied soldier into a 'sitting duck'.

1928: 'Walking on the Water' was re-invented. A young Viennese student and amateur snow skier named Joseph Krupka, observing a long-legged waterfly racing over the surface of a rain-barrel, got the idea of skiing over water as he had done over snow. That night, Krupka sketched out a light and portable water-ski and within a few days had realised his design in 2·40 m *8 ft* long light skeleton frames with waterproof covers – similar to unusually long Eskimo kayaks. Krupka pioneered the 'new' game on a tiny pond in Ober-Saint-Veit, near Vienna, helping himself forward with double-bladed paddles, like poles used by snow-skiers.

Aleksander Wozniak getting his water-walking practice on the Bridgewater Canal at Monton in Lancashire in 1950. (*Daily Mirror*)

The popularity of Krupka's game was instant. A group of young people organised themselves to learn its technique, and were delighted to find that many principles learned in snow-skiing could be adapted. From the Danube, they took their game to Alpine lakes and streams, learned to run rapids and to enjoy the excitement of 'water skijoring' behind fast motorboats. Several rapids-runners developed the physical strength to tie a rope to a bridge, weir or whatever, lowering themselves into the water, 'paying out' the rope a few yards and then staying still with the rapids rushing underneath them!

1930: Some Austrian students demonstrated the game in England and France, and before long it reached Scandinavia, where Arne Borg, Sweden's multi-record-breaking swimmer, got the bug. There were contests between Finland and Estonia and a 64 km *40 miles* trip was made from Helsinki to Tallinn. Ironically, the game did not catch on in the United States of America.

1953: Aleksander Wozniak, a 30-year-old Polish draughtsman from Dagenham, Essex 'walked' for 28 km *12·5 miles* down the River Thames. Three years later, Wozniak challenged the English Channel. Leaving the favourable conditions inside Dover Harbour, he soon met with broken water and capsized, ignominiously to be brought back by a motorboat.

1970: The last of the 'Water-Walkers', Wozniak trekked the Thames once again, to raise funds for charity – only to be booked by a policeman for landing without authority at Westminster Bridge!

The 'game of the twin canoes' never attained the popularity it might have done. It was overshadowed by a much more exciting, exhilarating and challenging variation of 'walking upon the water'.

Dr Galansimo's Hydro-Ski Risso – 1916.

2 Birth of water skiing

Real water-skiing originated from two traditional sports: Snow-skiing and surfboarding.

Snow-skis go back to 2500 BC in Scandinavia, the modern downhill ski evolving from the long, narrow 'Nordic' type. Snow-skiing as a sport dates from 1868 in Norway, when Sondre Nordheim had developed a ski with re-designed binding of heel and instep strap, enabling him to jump and to perform a series of 'S' turns on steep slopes; by 1895, Norwegian ski-sportsmen had carried the Telemark style and ski design throughout the world.

Surfboards go back to the ancient Polynesians of such island groups as Tahiti and Hawaii. In 1777, Captain James Cook concluded his description of a Tahitian surfer with the remark: 'I could not help concluding that this man felt the most supreme pleasure while he was driven on so fast and smoothly by the sea.'

Dr John H. Ball in his *Scrapbook of Surfriding and Beach Stuff*, states that George Freeth revived 'the lost art of *standing up while riding*' in 1900, when he was only sixteen, at Waikiki Beach, Hawaii. In 1910 Alexander Hume Ford promoted the Outrigger Canoe Club in Waikiki Beach, with the stated purpose of advancing 'the almost forgotten arts of surfriding with boards and canoes'. At this time, Freeth could be seen at Redondo Beach, Southern California, heading an aquatic display.

While snow-skiers had always been able to gain added excitement in their sport by 'skijoring' – (skiing behind a galloping horse, while holding on to its lengthened harness) – the surfboarder was left helpless if his waves deserted him. Then the motor-launch came along.

While steamboats had been plying rivers and lakes of the world since the middle of the 19th century, it was not until 1885 that Herr Gottlieb Daimler produced a petrol-engined launch that could travel at 10 km/h *6 mph*. By the 1890s motor-launches with Daimler engines were being distributed throughout Europe and the United States; they now had a turn of speed up to 24 km/h *15 mph*.

Now, not 160 km *100 miles* down the Pacific Coast from Redondo Beach – where George Freeth's surfboarding had caught on in a big way – was Coronado Beach. Sometime in the early 1900s – the exact date is lost – Captain J. L. LeRoy, then manager of the Coronado boathouses, took a party of young people from the fashionable Coronado Hotel out on a deep-sea fishing excursion to the local islands in his motor-launch, *Neptune*.

After a good day's fishing the party enjoyed some swimming in mid-ocean. One of the young men, reluctant to leave the water, declared that to get him home, they

'The ever-increasing army of outdoor girls have flocked to the Aquaplane.' (*Harpers Weekly*)

would have to tow him. Whereupon the ingenious Captain heaved over a heavy fish box cover, with a rope attached, and the return trip was triumphantly started.

It was not long before the swimmer – anxious to make good his threat – found he could stand on the impromptu 'life saver' for a few minutes at a time. Calling for another line, he rigged up reins and then was able to maintain an erect position.

It did not take such a stretch of the marine imagination to fit a line of hemp to the curved end of a 2·43 m *8 ft* redwood surfboard and tow it behind a motor-launch – why wait for waves, when you could ride for as long as you liked through the surf of the Pacific?

'Aeroplanes! Hydroplanes! Hydro-aeroplanes! Aero-hydroplanes! So why not . . . why not Aqua-planes? That's it, Aquaplaning!'

As the sport developed, the old *Neptune* proved too slow, and when Captain LeRoy died and the management of the boathouses was taken over by Captain W. B. Perkins, a speedier launch, the *Glorietta* was constructed, principally for aquaplaning and ocean outing parties. Captain Perkins designed and built new aquaplane boards and, before long, athletically inclined guests had become very skilful in their use and were doing all sorts of 'trick riding':

'That daring young man on his aquaplane boards
As he rides through the surf, letting go of his cords!'

A company was duly formed in Chicago to manufacture an aquaplane, 3·6 m *12 ft* long and 30 cm *1 ft* wide, marked to show where to stand at various speeds. The project folded because motorboat owners discovered how easy it was to make and colour their own 'water sprites'.

Before long Europe was doing it. On 15 July 1914, a regatta of aquatic sports was held at the famous health spa of Scarborough in Yorkshire, England. The *Weekly Post* recorded:

'100 yards planking or plank-gliding race. The new craze. Competitors to stand on loose plank attached to motor boat while going at full speed. First Prize Value 10s 6d. Second 7s 6d; Third 5s.' The competition was won by Mr H. Storry, followed by Mr J. Dixey and Mr W. Shaw.

Although the Great War put an end to the sport in Europe, during 1915 aquaplaning contests were included in hundreds of US motorboat regattas. In August and September alone, aquaplaners competed at Long Island, the Thousand Islands on the St Lawrence, the New Jersey, Massachusetts and Maine coasts, Chicago, the Mississippi valley, the Pacific coast, Florida and Texas. These contests were judged on the merits of the stunts performed and as the magazine, *Harper's Weekly* pointed out:

'The ever-increasing army of outdoor girls have flocked to the aquaplane. It provides them with the thrills that seem to be necessary to the modern girl; and it is the best possible exercise that they could get.'

In the winter of 1917, one of the first newsreel-men ever seen in central Florida, shot a film of a stunt man cutting fancy capers on an aquaplane. This was the first film record of the sport and the stunt man's name is worth remembering – Dick Pope.

After the 1918 Armistice, aquaplaning was resumed at speeds around 19–32 km/h *12–20 mph*, even though by this time the maximum speed of a racing hydroplane was over 96 km/h *60 mph*.

Lord Louis Mountbatten, uncle to His Royal Highness Prince Philip, Duke of Edinburgh, has recalled that he was staying with Brigadier-General and Mrs Cornelius Van der Bilt on board their yacht the *Polar Star*, during Cowes Week in August 1921. King George V was there on board the *Victoria and Albert*, the Royal Yacht. His second son, Prince Albert had just been made Duke of York, the year before. Albert came over and Lord Louis

A plank-gliding race at the Aquatic Sports Regatta in Scarborough 1914. Mr H. Storry winning first prize.

showed him an aquaplane that had been made up from descriptions, and which was towed behind a fast motorboat owned by the Van der Bilts. Prince Albert was shown how to do it and they went aquaplaning round the Royal Yacht and the anchorage. King George V was told that there was this disgraceful behaviour going on, so he came on deck – by which time, the Duke of York was now standing on the aquaplane.

As he went round the Royal Yacht, the King remarked on that young fellow Dicky Mountbatten, playing the fool. Whereupon Sir Charles Custs, his Naval Equerry said, 'I'm sorry sir, that's your own son – that's the Duke of York who's aquaplaning!'

In contrast, the Cockney lightermen thought nothing of 'boarding' behind their barges along the River Thames between the Pool of London and Rotherhithe Docks, providing the tide was right.

With time, it was perhaps logical that aquaplanes should be developed – or to put it more accurately, *divided*, to give the rider more manoeuvrability. It was perhaps inevitable that a number of men – on both sides of the Atlantic – claimed to have been the 'first' to do it. In fact there are three 'known' claimants.

One of these was the colourful Count Maximilian Pulaski, founder of the famed Côte d'Azur Yacht Club in the South of France; this exclusive club was open solely to the nobility of the continent. The story goes that the Count was aquaplaning with a French girl behind a Despujols motorboat at Juan-les-Pins, on the Riviera. Suddenly the girl fell off and her riderless aquaplane kept bumping into the Count's board. To avoid trouble, Pulaski put one foot on the other aquaplane to keep the two apart and, to his amazement, managed to straddle both boards and ride them quite easily. The Count and his friends soon built two narrow aquaplanes 1·83 m *6 ft* long and 30 cm *1 ft* wide, added rubber bands to anchor his feet, and inspired a new technique that spread like wildfire at the famed French playground. This was in 1929.

Now follows the testimony of a Norwegian snow-skier called Emil Petersen, who in 1932 was consultant for a company building a wintersport resort in the Alpes Maritimes near Nice:

'I began by having a rope tied from the boat to the skis, as well as a supporting rope from the skis to my hands. This was 3 August 1932 in the Golfe Juan. A large powerful Chris-Craft pulled me and the experiment was a success. A photographer and journalist from *L'Eclaireur De Nice* (the Riviera's largest newspaper) came along. The day after, the newspaper carried the story with pictures on the first page. The same picture was also carried by the largest illustrated newspaper in France at that time, *L'Illustration* of September 1932 (Issue no 3, page 32). It was a sensation! Many people were watching, and coming ashore I was approached by an English gentleman who had the same idea. He was as far as I remember an Army officer, some years older than me, perhaps 40 (I don't remember his name . . . Major Howard, I think). We went to the villa where he lived and he showed me into his small workroom where he was designing water-skis.' During the days that followed, they made lighter, better skis, and they experimented by being pulled directly from the boat by hands and rope. That worked very well and they both skied at the same time, going criss-cross past one another.

Emil Petersen experimenting in the Golfe Juan in 1932.

Shortly afterwards there was a big maritime week in Cannes, 'La Semaine Nautique de Cannes' which included regattas, water polo, etc. Petersen was asked by the organising committee to give a water-skiing exhibition, which he did with his English friend. They had a big new motorboat to pull them at top speed before large crowds on the quay and along the beach. It was an enormous success! One of the big Paris newspapers, possibly *Paris Soir*, had its own plane which flew over taking pictures the whole time. He never met his English friend again. Since neither of them was interested in anything else in water-skiing than having fun, they lost contact.

Later in the autumn of that same year Petersen thought it must be possible to jump, so he made a ramp of boards held up by a gasoline barrel. The slope was about one metre high at the outer end. He put soap on the planks hoping that it would make a slippery surface and tried this at a beach in Nice before a crowd of onlookers. It was not successful – he lost speed due to the ineffectiveness of the soap but he managed to slide over and hop one metre *3 ft*.

During the autumn he was moved up to the mountains, so his adventure with water-skiing was 'put on ice' until the following spring. That summer, 1933, he returned to Norway for good.

17

It was that summer that the sport began to spread among many who had seen him the year before on the Riviera. The jump was prepared and someone in Juan-les-Pins made a new one constructed with rollers in which there were ballbearings. When one had good speed and came in for the jump the speed increased and gave a jumping distance of 15 m *49 ft*. But at that time, that type of jump was too expensive for him.

At home in Norway he had fun showing his friends the new sport, one of whom, Sverre Østbye, made a pair of skis and they had great fun at Larkollen and Fornebu. It was that summer, 1933, that the committee which arranged 'Oslofjorden Rundt', a regatta with small outboard motorboats, asked him to demonstrate the new sport. He went out to Bunnefjorden near Nesodden where he went in the water with the skis, and drove at top speed to Ingierstrand which was full of spectators watching the incoming boats from the regatta. *Aftenposten* carried the story and pictures of the event and with that water-skiing began in Norway.

Almost ten years before, on 22 August 1924, Mr Fred Waller, a 38-year-old, bespectacled inventor from Huntington, Long Island, New York, filed a patent for a twin aquaplane system. Two months later he was granted US Patent No 1559390 and soon he had begun to market them through William H. Young & Co. (a New York sales agency for motorboats and marine equipment) as *Dolphin Akwa-Skees*.

Fred Waller's original patent.

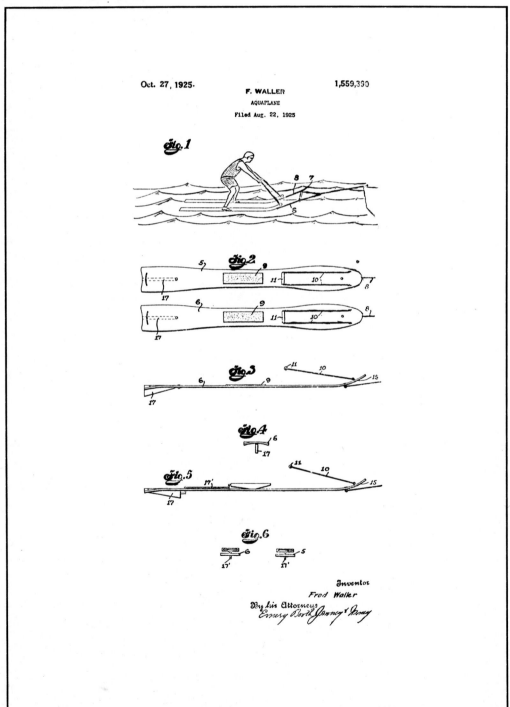

A keen sportsman, Waller had worked on his Akwa-Skees, testing them out himself in Long Island Sound for a considerable time before he was granted that patent. Basically, each 2·43 m *8 ft* Skee was attached to a rope connected with a bridle that in turn was pulled by a boat. A hand rope was attached to the bow end of each Skee. A steadying keel was used on the bottom, designed so that the Skees would run parallel and would not side-swipe each other. Only the best materials were used – straight-grain kiln-dried mahogany, best spar varnish, best grade heavy cotton rope, bronze, brass, copper and rubber. With each pair of Akwa-Skees, came an instruction manual.

Of the stunts listed for Akwa-Skees – including stemming a sharp curve and a double-S turn – perhaps the most remarkable was a Skee Charleston!

An early pair of Akwa-Skees was introduced into Europe by the Swiss sportsman, Frederick Firmenich of Geneva.

At Miami Beach, in 1928, Dick Pope and his brother Malcolm were the newsreel stars for new water sports. Dick had once organised an association of professional golf players. Then he turned to the more thrilling activity of performing hair-raising, daredevil stunts in boats, on aquaplanes and on Akwa-Skees for the 'movie men'. Dick was the first one to make a clear leap out of the water with a surfboard. His 20-year-old brother, Malcolm, drove to nineteen outboard victories in 32 races during one season. In the eyes of young Americans, Malcolm was the star performer with an outboard. Always wearing their black swimsuits, he and his brother invented stunts and the rest of the fans of America would take them up as new water games.

Here Dick Pope instructs his fans on Akwa-Skee jumping: 'When you are jumping you should have the towing boat as close as is possible. As it nears the platform, the rider should pull his board over to the side and get his feet as far forward as possible. Then just before he hits the jump he should take hold on each of the lines and hang on for all he is worth as he goes up into the air.

'Really the trick when landing in the water is to keep the eyes and mouth closed tight so that the spray and splash do not bother and then to keep pulling as hard as possible on the ropes. If you are bounced away over to one side so that the arm and face are in the water, you will come back all right if you keep on pulling on the ropes.'

A contemporary magazine noted that many games had been introduced for those who walk on water with skis. At some beaches the girls rode in small boats, tossing hoops out on to the water. 'These float upright because they are weighted in one part and boys riding on skis behind swift boats, spear the hoops, using long wooden lances. Each player has a quota of six, but the one who spears the most hoops wins the tournament.'

In 1929, on the shores of Lake Howard, in Winter Haven, Florida, Marilyn Mores Hughes received the first trophy for Akwa-Skeeing; there were five contestants and the boat driver was Malcolm Pope.

Dick Pope Sr jumping on Akwa-Skees over a wooden ramp at Miami Beach in 1928. Distance 7·62 m *25 ft*

When he died in 1954, Fred Waller had over 50 patented inventions to his name, including Cinerama, and the development of water-skis from his original Akwa-Skee equipment. Indeed right up until 1965, he continued to be heralded as the 'Father of Water-skiing'. But it was in that year that he was deposed by Ralph W. Samuelson, who claimed to have developed his skills, back in 1922 (two years before Waller).

Ralph Samuelson was born and brought up in Lake City, Minnesota, east of the snow-capped Rocky Mountains and overlooking Lake Pepin. He recalls that: 'I was eighteen in 1922, and believe me, if there was anything new or dangerous I could figure out, I wanted to try it. I decided that, if you could ski on snow, you could ski on water. I first got the idea after I had used boards to surfboard behind a boat. My brother and dad had boats, so I was around the water all the time.'

So when he was not fishing for walleye in the clear Minnesota lakes, Samuelson set out to prove his theory, with his brother driving their 24 hp, 7·30 m *24 ft* fishing launch as a towboat. Holding onto a 30 m *100 ft* sash cord with a rubber-wrapped metal ring, Ralph first tried barrel staves – with near disastrous results. He next tried 2·13 m *7 ft* snow skis, but found them too thin for use on water.

Then he went to the lumber yard and bought two long pine boards for $1 each, and cut them down to 2·70 m *8 ft 9 in*. He curved them at the tips by steaming them in his mother's old copper boiler for three hours. He also placed a simple leather footstrap halfway along the skis. 'I started in deep water: for two weeks I didn't realise that I had to lift my tips from the water; I swallowed a lot of water that way.' When these 'water skis' (as he chose to call them) broke under strain, he went back to the lumber yard, and repeated the process. But this time, he added sections of rubber floor treading for footing and added an iron strap for reinforcement at the point at which the 6·8 kg *15 lb* skis curved up. He also moved the leather footstraps forward to put more weight of the skis in the back.

'It took me at least three weeks and 25 tries before I mastered it. Everyone, of course, thought I was completely nuts.'

Ben Simons, a native of Lake City, has recalled: 'I was one of the many young punks who went down to the lake to watch. Everyone in town thought it was a kind of joke. No one thought he could get up, and even if he did, we figured that the water would hold him back. Because we all thought the idea was so impossible, it was really a thrill when he finally did get up and go.'

Samuelson continues, 'I was as strong as a bull in those days and got so I could hold on with one hand and swing abreast of the boat. To keep up speed, I had to criss-cross constantly. That first boat would only go about 32 km/h *20 mph*.'

Admitting he was somewhat of a playboy and showman at the time, each Fall, Samuelson stashed his skis in a fancy yellow roadster and took off for Palm Beach, Florida, to stage his one-man water shows. He also 'barnstormed' throughout Minnesota and Michigan, including Detroit. It was at these venues that he had the chance to be pulled by 9 m *30 ft* boats with 200 horsepower motors at speeds up to 56 km/h *35 mph*.

'The wake had a trough about 1·22 m *4 ft* deep and you had to hit it just right or you'd be sure of a spill. In

A description of Samuelson's ride behind the Curtiss flying-boat from the Wabasha County Leader.

1924, during an exhibition in Florida, one of my ski straps broke – so I just kept on criss-crossing on one ski.'

It was in 1925 that Samuelson got another idea. If he tipped down one end of a 1·52 m *5 ft* floating dock, why shouldn't he jump from it?

'But I didn't think of wetting it down,' and he left his skis at the top of the dock when the bindings ripped out, and he sailed over. 'So I took a pound of lard – you know how slippery lard is – greased the dock, and started going over like a shot.' His jumps, which stunned spectators, were 15–18 m *50–60 ft* in length.

'My reputation as an eccentric really grew when I started skiing behind a boat with a World War I airplane propeller. You could hear it for 16 km *10 miles* around, and it would go about 80–96 km/h *50–60 mph*. One time it caught fire and everybody nearly went crazy.'

This was in 1925 when Walter Bullock, one of the Northwest Airline's first pilots went to Lake City with his Curtiss MF flying boat, a World War I surplus boat with wings. 'Bullock and I got together as two nuts, I guess. He'd take passengers for a ride and then pull me for a show. Naturally I was plastered with oil from the engine.'

Samuelson, almost air borne, travelling behind the Curtiss flying-boat at about 130 km/h *80 mph* at Lake City, 1925.

Samuelson, in 1925, going over the first water-ski jump at 1·2 m *4 ft* wide and which was greased with lard to make it slippery.

The 220 hp winged boat pulled Samuelson as fast as 128 km/h *80 mph* when it began to rise off the water. 'The front half of the skis would be out of the water entirely for all of the ride; you can imagine the endurance it took to hold on. I felt as if my arms were going to be pulled right out.' He was towed behind the flying boat with a 61 m *200 ft* sash cord and the usual rubber-wrapped ring.

For all his shows, Samuelson declined to accept any payment, except for petrol expenses for the boat. 'I never made a dime out of it.' Most of the admission charges went towards the purchase of more land for the Lake City harbour and park area.

In 1937 he sustained a compression fracture of his back in an accident while assisting with the building of a speedboat livery in Palm Beach, Florida. This injury, plus another in which he fell from a light pole and broke his collar bone and wrist in five places, put an abrupt end to Samuelson's activities.

Over the next 33 years, Ralph Samuelson became a prosperous and retiring turkey farmer in Minnesota, who would occasionally smile quietly to himself when he recalled the daredevil days of his youth.

At Lake Washington in 1928, a certain Don Ibsen, ignorant of both Waller and Samuelson, had built his first 'water-skis' by steaming a couple of cedar boards over a 5-gallon can of boiling water, with the end of a telephone pole serving as a bending form, then equipping them with tennis-shoe bindings. By 1931, Ibsen was beginning to be regarded as a character around Lake Washington. Not owning a boat, he was forced to 'hitchhike' and it was not unusual to see him standing on shore, frantically waving at passing boat drivers. Soon afterwards Don and his wife, Dorothy, began a small business, making water-skis; Ibsen has since been regarded as the founder of water-skiing in the West.

Now we must look again to Europe – to Lake Annecy, South-west France. A group of French troops, the Chasseurs Alpins of the 11th Regiment of Annecy, shock troops excelling in mountain-climbing and snow-skiing, were sunbathing and swimming in the lake, when they noticed a speedboat with *Rapide I* painted on its bows, roaring round the lake. One of the favourite pastimes of the Chasseurs Alpins was to skijore behind fast horses and the story goes that one of them made the joking suggestion that they try skijoring behind *Rapide I*. Soon the joke became a challenge. As with Samuelson, the first attempt was a failure because the regular snow-skis were too narrow. So they widened and shortened the skis, using boots for foot-binders – and succeeded in water-skiing. Inevitably, for decades to come, the Chasseurs Alpins were to be promoted – especially by the French – as the true founders of water-skiing.

But historians appear to differ as to the exact year in which this chance occurrence took place. Some say 1912, others 1922, and still others 1929. Moreover, Monsieur André Coutau of Geneva has cast doubts on the whole story. Being from that area and having relatives in that town, he verified that the boats at that time were indeed called *Rapide I* and *II*, but their maximum speed was only 24 km/h *15 mph*. He suggests that it is a fable for anyone to have water-skied at this speed and with snow-skis. But he does not dismiss the possibility that the attempts did take place.

What is certain is that at the turn of the decade, the process of development from aquaplanes and snow-skis was virtually over, while the extravagant era of vintage water-skiing was just beginning.

Samuelson water-skiing in 1922. Notice his bathing costume and the rubber-wrapped metal ring tied to the sash cord.

3 Evolution: The Thirties

1977: reunion at the AWSA's new headquarters for (*from left*) Julie Pope, Betty Sligh, Dick Pope, Chuck Sligh, Ralph Samuelson, Don Ibsen, Dottie Ibsen and Lee Sutherland.

In the early 1920s Florida had had a land boom. One of the many land salesmen was Dick Pope, who – together with his brother Malcolm – promoted his father's real estate business by staging newsreel boat and Akwa-Skee stunts (previously mentioned) to attract attention to their land developments.

When the financial crash hit Florida, Dick Pope went to Chicago to become a promotion consultant. His first client was Johnson Motors, and he was back in the business of promoting boat racing. Dick had offices in New York, Chicago and Philadelphia.

It was in 1932 that Dick and his wife Julie first looked upon an eerie, yet fascinating maze of tropical growth along the banks of Lake Eloise, most beautiful of some 100 spring-fed lakes in the valley highlands area of Winter Haven, Florida. Centuries-old cypress trees, shrouded in silken wisps of Spanish moss, towered majestically above the lake, admiring their shaggy hair-dos in the mirrored waters below. The Popes realised that if they could beautify a spot on this lake – with flowered islands and sylvan lagoons – they could show potential customers how beautiful lakefront property could be.

But it was not easy and the land for Cypress Gardens was acquired piece by piece in small lots at a time, as it was still the Depression and money was tight. But eventually they were to acquire a headquarters in the 100 Lakes Yacht Club, which had had to close through lack of money. Cypress Gardens was to grow to 220 acres of beauty, spreading out from Lake Eloise towards the shores of Lake Summit.

To continue the publicity, Dick kept motorboating and performing Akwa-Skeeing stunts, going for the newsreels so that cinema audiences would be tempted by the backcloth of the Gardens.

In 1932 Bob Eastman took his International Nautical Stunt Team to make a motion picture among the cypresses. Bob Eastman acted as the World Champion Akwa-Skee rider, leading a team of young athletes who put on a spectacular show of ultra ski-riding and jumping on an inclined platform of 90 degrees, the skiers sometimes sailing through the air for 12–15 m *40–50 ft*, while staging an exciting pillow fight.

Two years later the team left Winter Haven for Chicago, where they put on a show at the Century of Progress Exhibition. Among the thousands of spectators who saw this show was a young Swiss civil engineer named André Coutau from Lake Geneva. Coutau was so impressed by what he saw that before returning to Europe he had bought a Garwood sports runabout with a 95 hp Chrysler engine, plus a pair of water-skis, with the intention of teaching himself to water-ski when he got home. 'Our beginnings were not easy because we hadn't the least idea of the way to do it, especially how to move off.' But as will be seen later, those beginnings were to be profoundly significant.

In 1932, Lord Louis Mountbatten was Fleet Wireless Officer for the Mediterranean Fleet, on board the battleship HMS *Queen Elizabeth*, and he remembers that:

'One day I was driving along the front, and I distinctly remember seeing a man going very fast on what I thought was a freeboard. Then I saw that he seemed to have two freeboards. When he turned, he turned quite differently to a freeboard, and I suddenly realised that he was on skis. This excited me very much, but my time in the *Queen Elizabeth* was just up, and I was going back to England to come out again next spring in command of a destroyer.

'So I got all the particulars I could, including a photograph of a Socialite with a double-barrelled name, which I now forget, water-skiing in the South of France. I told my friend, Robert Neville, the Captain of the Royal Marines on board the Aircraft Carrier *Glorious*, who was also the back of my Navy Polo team which did so well in the Inter-Regimental Competition – and he promised to get some skis made.'

Major-General Sir Robert Neville RM recalls that in the *Glorious* he had a great friend called Squadron Leader Cedric Hall RAF (at that time the RAF manned the aircraft in the carriers). All they could see of the skis in the photograph was the tips sticking out of the water but they determined, however, that they must ski this way – both of them were already snow skiers.

They proposed to get the skis made in the *Glorious*. The ship's carpenter produced a pair of skis 2·13 m *7 ft* long and 15 cm *6 in* wide which together gave roughly the same area as a freeboard. There were two 3·8 cm *1½ in* × 61 cm *2 ft* long pieces of wood, with slots cut in them to take the feet, which were screwed on to the skis. As they were ignorant of where one should stand on the skis, they imagined it would be the same as for a freeboard; that is about one-third of the length from the after end of the skis.

'In actual fact you need the feet holds well ahead of the centre of the skis but we swallowed half the Mediterranean learning this as we only dared move the feet holds forward about 4 in at a time until we got it right.'

Lord Mountbatten notes that when it came to getting up on the skis they did a very ingenious thing. They made a little sort of breakwater, which they called a cleet – that is to say, across the front, 15 cm *6 in* from the foot slots, they put a strip of wood across, quite thick, curved back so that underneath it one could put the stick of the towing rope. It had the effect of holding the two skis as though it was a single board, firmly. 'What happened was that when the boat started up, you would lie back as

you did on a freeboard until the skis came out and sat on top of the water. Then with infinite care you moved first one foot in, then the other foot in, then you lifted up and out – a most laborious way, but that's the way they did it.'

Sir Robert Neville recalls: 'When we did get it right I think I was the first individual in the Mediterranean Fleet to water-ski. We had marvellous fun skiing in perfect conditions all around the Adriatic and the Greek Islands and in Alexandria. When I left the *Glorious*, on promotion, I gave the skis to Admiral Mountbatten.'

Lord Mountbatten continues the story: 'In the spring of 1934, I went out in command of the new destroyer, HMS *Daring*, and Captain Neville left me the skis which he'd built at my suggestion. I quickly improved on them and soon found that you did not have to put this cleet in, and I made the discovery quite early on that you could sit at the end of a gangway and be pulled straight off – with a small boat going very fast, it just jerked you out of your seat.

'Well, the next thing was that I began to get rather good at this game – I innovated a lot. I used to go out to dinner on water-skis. If I was invited out to dine in another destroyer, I would put on my mess undress uniform and then roll up my trousers to the knee, take off my shoes and socks, put the socks inside the shoes, tie the shoes together with their shoe-laces and hang them round my neck. Then I sat on the end of the gangway and an officer – in those days we were very particular – usually my first lieutenant, would pull me off. If it was a dark night, all the signalmen in the flotilla would turn on their shore-lights to illuminate the way down. On arrival at my host's ship, I would let go at the precise moment to be able to hold on to his gangway, the accommodation ladder; there was always a sort of wire stay that held it up. Holding on to the end of it as one went by, one could swing oneself straight up, leaving the skis behind. Then the boat picked up the skis, while I came on deck with nothing more than my ankles wet – if that.

'Now this became quite a legendary story in 1934, when skis were virtually unknown in the Fleet.

'Much later, when I was First Sea Lord, I was having a dinner party with all the senior Admirals. They were pulling my leg about whether the story was really true that I used to ski to dinner in mess undress. Before I could answer, the Commander-in-Chief at Plymouth, Admiral Sir Richard Onslow, interrupted "One moment, I'd like to answer that question. I was his First Lieutenant on the *Daring* and I was the wretched chap that had to drive the boat for him!"'

As another stunt, his Lordship skied in and out of the 36 destroyers of the Mediterranean Fleet – a kind of primitive slalom course.

It was in this same year, 1934, that Jack Andresen, a New York engineer, was beginning to experiment with acrobatics while water-skiing. One year later, George Ducros, a 29-year-old Frenchman, whose Spanish was said to be better than his French, arrived in New York to begin his one-man tour of a chain of American motorboat regattas as European Water-Skiing Champion of three years' standing. As part of Ducros' routine there were dance-steps, 9 m *10 yd* jumps, and one-ski stands – holding one ski above the head while swinging the free leg back and forth. Such routines were eventually to result in the ski-discipline of 'Tricks' – also known as 'Figures'.

In 1936, a Captain d'Arcy Rutherford, sports manager at both the Société de Bains de la Mer in Monte Carlo and the Corviglia Winter Sports Club in St Moritz, arrived back in London to promote water-skiing. The suave, moustachioed Captain approached Lillywhites, the well-known London sports outfitters, stating that as the World Water Ski Champion, he had developed a type of water-ski, measuring 8 ft 10 in by 6 in wide, which if they would be prepared to market, he would be prepared to demonstrate on the Thames as a promotion stunt.

Captain Rutherford's colourful career is best recalled by his brother, Major Jack Rutherford, who recalled that D'Arcy was an Irish name; their maternal great-great-grandfather was first Lord Lieutenant of Ireland. The Rutherford came from their father, who was a Scottish ship-owner and coal-exporter. He married in Wales and that was where they were born, by the sea at a little village called Mumbles, near Swansea. D'Arcy and Jack took an interest in the water from the very start – always swimming.

During the First World War, they both served on the Western Front. Jack transferred to the RFC, while d'Arcy was in the Brigade of Guards and also fought at Gallipoli. He came out of the War as a Captain, resigned his commission and joined the financial department of Crosse & Blackwell in the City. Between the Wars, Jack's business was producing films, but the extrovert d'Arcy went on to bigger things.

In the late 1920s, he was living in style at Gloucester House in London's Park Lane – a popular member of both the Royal St George Golf Club in Sandwich, IOW and the Sunningdale Club. Then news came through that Aix-les-Bains was to be re-vamped as a world-famous watering place. The Lac du Bourget at the 'Petit Port' was to be given a lavish new plage, from which High Society would be able to enjoy 'Les Plaisirs Nautiques' together with a round of golf. D'Arcy was offered the job of sports manager out there and in 1929 readily accepted.

He bought a 5–18 m *17 ft* Chris-Craft runabout, which he not only used to aquaplane across the Channel, but also launched into the Lac du Bourget with the intention of teaching visitors to enjoy the sport of aquaplaning. It was also at this period that d'Arcy took to snow-skiing and became Secretary of the Corviglia Club in St Moritz. He was quite tough, but a great host with enormous charm and a great flair for meeting people and socialising. One of his prize pupils at Aix was the Princess Achille Murat.

In 'The Town: Men and Intimacies', a column by 'Autolycus' in *The Sunday Times* of January 1930, one reads: 'Mr d'Arcy Rutherford . . . has yet to meet a serious rival at "planking". This is the comparatively new amusement that everyone struggles to master along the Mediterranean shores during the summer season . . . Those who get so far can then indulge in "stunts", one of the hardest being to pluck a floating chair out of the sea, place it on the plank, and then stand on the chair, all the while proceeding at a really smart pace.'

Not long after this, d'Arcy had left Aix-les-Bains for a new post – the Sports Manager of the Société de Bains de la Mer in Monte Carlo. It was here that, according to one magazine article:

'The final step was when someone – either Captain d'Arcy Rutherford of London or George Ducros of

Above: Captain d'Arcy Rutherford holding his well used water skis in the 1930s.

Below: Start position: Rutherford style.

Below: Skiing position: Rutherford style.

Below: d'Arcy Rutherford and his brother, Jack, skiing at Monte Carlo.

Paris, or likely both at the same time – had a pair of aquaplanes made in the shape of snow skis, but slightly longer and wider, and rode them holding directly to the towline.'

In his recent book, *Bring on the Empty Horses*, the film star David Niven tells how Errol Flynn had read somewhere that a man named d'Arcy Rutherford had invented a new sport in the South of France – water-skiing – and had showed him pictures of Rutherford skimming along behind a speedboat off Eden Roc.

'Look, Sport,' said Flynn, 'we've got to try that' and designed a pair of very painful heavy wooden skis which the studio carpenter knocked together for them. The following weekend, Niven remembers, 'we tried them out off Catalina Island – and they worked. There is no record to prove it but I am pretty sure that on that day in the mid-30s Flynn and I introduced water-skiing to California, and maybe even to the US.'

Sir Thomas Danill Knox, KC, MG, The 6th Earl of Ranfurly, Viscount Northland and Baron Welles, has also recalled that there were two- or three-dozen British people who used to ski in Monte Carlo in 1933/34. They taught each other to a large extent. He remembers that he and d'Arcy skied together on one occasion for Monte Carlo against a French team from Cannes, although he cannot recall who won.

But to return to d'Arcy Rutherford's plans to demonstrate his design of water-skis on the Thames in London. The Chairman of Lillywhites in 1936 was Major Foster Gretton, who was an old member of Hurlingham Rowing Club. He was able to persuade his fellow members that it would be a splendid idea to put on a show. He obtained permission from the Port of London Authority to close off that particular area.

Thus it was, on an afternoon in August 1936, the gallant Captain d'Arcy Rutherford demonstrated the new sport to Hurlingham Club members and to the public watching from the other bank. First of all he showed them how to make a deep water start naturally, he had to put one hand across his 2·43 m *8 ft* skis at the back simply to hold them down underneath the water; he then went into a crouching position. After skiing up and down several times, the Captain demonstrated skiing on one ski and slalom on a very short course.

Then to show the public that anyone could learn it, d'Arcy Rutherford introduced two young Lillywhites employees as two people who had never set foot on skis before – Mr Colin McLeod and Miss Bunnie Coast. Mr McLeod has recalled: 'I got off to a ramp start the very first time and I think I was on skis for ten minutes before I was brought back to the ramp again and sank in the water – it was pure luck! But it was first class for the demonstration. Then Bunnie Coast got on and she flopped all over the place, but after trying for ten minutes, she did get up and went for 45–55 m *50–60 yd* – cheered on by the excited spectators – before she fell off! I think it was the very fact that they were such long, wide skis which enabled us to get up as soon as we did.'

For the next three years, Lillywhites were marketing d'Arcy Rutherford-designed skis, built by Murray & Baldwins Ltd of Bath, Somerset. They sold at 4 guineas (£4·20), plus 10s 6d (52½p) for the tow rope and toggle. Over 700 enthusiasts were to learn on this model alone.

In 1937, during the Paris Exhibition, members of the International Nautical Stunt Team, were invited to come over from Florida as guests of the French Government, to give a water-skiing demonstration on the lake in the Bois de Boulogne, Paris (where over twenty years before, Doctor G. Galansimo had demonstrated his Hydro-Ski Risso). Skiing with Madame Maggy Savard and Monsieur Langlois, they were watched by no less than 80 000

From the Lillywhites' catalogue, published in London in 1939.

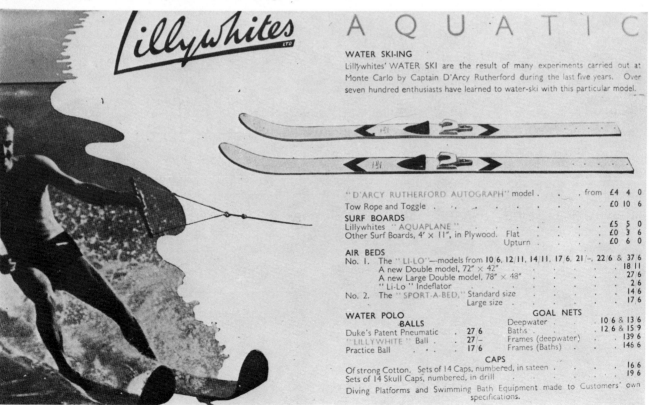

Lillywhites LTD

AQUATIC

WATER SKI-ING
Lillywhites' WATER SKI are the result of many experiments carried out at Monte Carlo by Captain D'Arcy Rutherford during the last five years. Over seven hundred enthusiasts have learned to water-ski with this particular model.

"D'ARCY RUTHERFORD AUTOGRAPH" model			from £4 4 0
Tow Rope and Toggle			£0 10 6
SURF BOARDS			
Lillywhites "AQUAPLANE"			£5 5 0
Other Surf Boards, 4' × 11", in Plywood. Flat			£0 3 6
Upturn			£0 6 0
AIR BEDS			
No. 1. The "LI-LO"—models from 10 6, 12 11, 14 11, 17 6, 21 -, 22 6 & 37 6			
A new Double model, 72" × 42"			18 11
A new Large Double model, 78" × 48"			27 6
"Li-Lo" Indeflator			2 6
No. 2. The "SPORT-A-BED," Standard size			14 6
Large size			17 6
WATER POLO		**GOAL NETS**	
BALLS		Deepwater	10 6 & 13 6
Duke's Patent Pneumatic	27 6	Baths	12 6 & 15 9
"LILLYWHITE" Ball	27 -	Frames (deepwater)	139 6
Practice Ball	17 6	Frames (Baths)	146 6
		CAPS	
Of strong Cotton. Sets of 14 Caps, numbered, in sateen			16 6
Sets of 14 Skull Caps, numbered, in drill			19 6

Diving Platforms and Swimming Bath Equipment made to Customers' own specifications.

people, including the President of France. The Sports and Tourist Commissions of France greeted the Americans as real heroes and said that their performance started the renaissance of *jeux nautiques* in Europe.

But by 1937, sea-skiing in the Mediterranean was already a flourishing concern, on the Spanish and French Rivieras, and down along the Italian coast as far as the romantic isle of Capri.

One example was the Club Nautique at Juan-les-Pins, sponsored by the wealthy American railroad heir, Mr Frank Jay Gould, brilliantly managed by Mademoiselle Madeleine Homo, and with Monsieur Leo Roman as 'professeur du ski nautique' for many hundreds of European skiers. While Mademoiselle Homo was, by her untiring love of the sport, to acquire the reputation as the great mother figure of water-skiing to all European enthusiasts (and later champions), in 1935 it was Madame Jay Gould who took the initiative of organising an Association of water-skiing clubs. Alongside her own Club Nautique there was the Côte d'Azur Motor Yacht Club and the Club Nautique of the Val d'Esquières, with Robert Baltié as coach. Although the Rhone Yacht Club, founded by Gilbert Dumas in 1935, was keen on water-skiing, motorboating and sailing, for some reason it was not included in this the world's very first national water-ski Federation.

Also at Juan-les-Pins, there were some furniture makers with a boatbuilding and repair shop, who shrewdly judged that as water-skiing had come to stay, it might profit them to make pairs of skis on a regular basis to sell alongside their aquaplanes. Their names were Toche et Lahuppe. One family that took a pair of these skis home with them were the De Clercqs of Belgium. Claude de Clercq has recently recalled that Every year his parents liked to spend four weeks on the Côte d'Azur. His father had always been a great fan of water sports, motorboating with a 24 hp Evinrude outboard and aquaplaning across the waves of the Mediterranean. In 1937 he returned to the Belgian coast on the North Sea with his first pair of water-skis. He always wanted his five sons to be more active in sports than he had been himself. Claude and his twin brother Guy were always playing

sport together, always competing with each other in a friendly way to see who was better – be it javelin-throwing, tennis or water-skiing.

On their first attempts to ski, they had absolutely no idea as to how it was supposed to be done. The skis were enormous, about 3·35 m *11 ft* long, with leather bindings fixed to the skis by wooden strips – so raising a ski above the head was almost impossible because of the weight. 'Tricks' were reduced to their most simple expression of lifting one foot, taking off a ski with one hand and putting it back on again. As de Clercq remembers: the main problem was that the motorboat engine was continually breaking down and the largest part of our training came in changing the sparking plugs. The first take-offs were attempted underwater, swallowing litres of the North Sea, or being pulled along the sand. It was only after numerous attempts they discovered that by sitting on the jetty with the ski-tips out of the water, they could make a successful take-off and enjoy a ski-run. Thus it was that sea-skiing came to Belgium, via a family from Bruges.

Also in Belgium, Paul Mingelbier was pioneering a water-ski demonstration team on the River Meuse, using virtually the same equipment, wearing pullovers and greasing legs against the cold. In fact, it was during the Fêtes de Wallonie, on the last Sunday of 1938, that the Mingelbier group held the first unofficial Belgian Championships – more of an exhibition than a competition, but easily won by Monsieur Mingelbier.

In Europe, Belgium had started rather later than Italy, where the sport had been going for three years on Lake Viverone near Biella in Northern Italy, while it had been in 1935 that a Doctor Machard of Vienna had brought a pair of water-skis to the Worthersee in Austria. Herr Santner, director of the Werzer-Astoria Hotel in Portschach became one of the first Austrians to ski on the Worthersee, setting an example that was soon followed in Velden. Water-skiers had also been seen on the Dutch lakes, among whom His Royal Highness Prince Bernhard must have been one of the very first.

Water-skiing in Switzerland had begun with André Coutau's return from Chicago to Geneva in 1934, with his American water-skis and Garwood runabout. Together with his brother Henri, Frederick Firmenich (who had been 'Akwa-Skeeing' behind his own Garwood boat for several years), and Henri Guisan (son of a famous Swiss General), Coutau organised weekend skiing on Lake Geneva.

Before long, this small group from Geneva had begun to consider the possibility and advantages of creating a club. Marcel Pahud, representing the Nautical Society, A. Bernard, representing the Geneva Snow Ski Club, Marc Cougnard, representing Geneva's tourists interests, and the lawyer and sportsman, Edmond Desert, were all keen to assist André Coutau in the organisation of this prototype. Coutau shrewdly stated this when inviting the Geneva Press together with several influential and wealthy Genevans (General Guisan, Marshall Clyde, Frederick Firmenich) to a meeting in late 1937.

The Belgian pioneer, Claude de Clercq recalls:

'The first competition that I saw took place in Monte Carlo Harbour in June/July 1939. They had set up a slalom, marked out rather like a snow-ski course with three buoys to the left of the boat and three buoys to the right. You rode on two skis, leaving the first buoy to the left, the second on the inside of the wake and continued as with snow-skiing. The speed was left to each skier's judgement and by the greatest of miracles I completed the course and won that event.

'In the jumping where long skis were less of a handicap, one could achieve more. The speed was again left to the judgement of the skier and those who could obtain the fastest boats jumped the farthest. Besides it was not difficult to find a fast boat, because the owners were very happy to demonstrate the performance of their boats and proud to tow the skiers. A French boy called Jules le Billon jumped 27 m *88¼ ft* behind a fast inboard runabout doing 80–85 km/h *50–52 mph*.'

De Clercq was 16-years-old then, and had never dreamt that simply by putting one's feet on two planks one could so amaze a crowd. But at that contest there were as many as 30000 people lining the shores of Monte Carlo Harbour to watch four or five dare-devils jumping and making the first attempts at a slalom run.

The only other pre-War competition he knew of, took place in Brussels. 'It was organised by our first patron of sports, Major Crombez, veteran pilot of the 1914–18 War, and moreover personal pilot to King Albert when he surveyed the Western Front during the years 1917 and 1918. This man not only offered his magnificent 150-hp Chris Craft inboard but had paid for a jumping ramp to be constructed with teak rollers, which were supposed to turn when the skier mounted the ramp. These, however, proved useless but did not stop me, in front of large crowds, making jumps of 14–17 m *46–55 ft* which assured me of an easy victory in that event. Monsieur Mingelbier won the tricks, while Mr Libert from Kortrijk won the slalom.'

Meanwhile in Norway, Mr Tomm Murstad had been among those who saw his compatriot Emil Petersen's exhibition, and at once became interested in the sport, skiing on the Riviera from 1936 to 1938. In the autumn of 1938, having competed in a jumping contest at Juan-le-Pins (himself landing at 25·5 m *83½ ft*), Murstad had a similar roller-bearing ramp constructed in Hvalstran Bay on Oslo Fjord, sponsored by one of the largest tobacco companies in Norway. It was used in a show, but soon after a class of schoolboys climbed on to it and it sank under the extreme weight (and is presumably still on the bottom).

About 160 km *100 miles* to the south-west of Oslo, a Swedish photographer named Sjöstedt had returned to Gothenburg from a holiday in the USA with a pair of skis and became the first Swede to ski in Sweden.

In August 1939 Miss Lorna Harmsworth (now Lady Cooper-Key), the attractive daughter of the Honourable Esmond Harmsworth (now Viscount Rothermere, owner of the *Daily Mail* and other newspapers) was staying at Monte Carlo. Lady Cooper-Key, who was taught to ski by Captain d'Arcy Rutherford on a pair of Lillywhites skis, recalls that: 'Once a week, there was a Gala Night at the Summer Sporting Club with a ski display around the harbour. D'Arcy and myself were always among those skiers. We used to leave the Gala after dinner, go and change into bathing costumes, then slip into the water just before the flares were lit. One night, there was a swell when we were just about to start and d'Arcy had just had his flare lit. The boat didn't get away quickly enough and I drifted into d'Arcy's skis and put his fire out!'

One Society magazine reported that: '700 notable personalities, entertained by Prince Rainier of Monaco, the sporting and handsome young grandson of the ruling Prince, attended the wonderful Gala on Friday August 11th, during the course of which, besides two sketches presented by the alluring Monte Carlo girls, and a couple of attractive exhibition turns, three well-known and much admired water-skis specialists – lovely Lorna Harmsworth, handsome Captain d'Arcy Rutherford, the snow and sea-ski expert, and athletic Vladimir Lanau, demonstrated to the full their daring skill in this particular branch of the sport. Applause which unfortunately could not reach their ears was showered on them in no half-hearted manner.'

Also in June of that year, at the New York World's Fair, a group of French water-skiers, including Mlle

28

André Coutau at the start of a ski run on Lake Geneva in 1938. (*L'Echo Illustré*)

Monte Carlo Harbour in the 1930s: perhaps the first painting of a water skier.

Maggy Savard, were invited to give daily demonstrations in front of Billy Rose's Aquacade and the Florida building. Because passport regulations held up the French team for a week, members of the newly formed American Water Ski Association stood in for them.

The AWSA, which had beaten the Swiss to be the first national organisation for water-skiing, had been incorporated in the State of New Jersey by Dan B. Hains only weeks before with a small but enthusiastic group of friends as founder-members. Herbert Welsh was elected as their first President.

On 22 June the *New York Times* reported: 'Ski Stars Furnish Thrills on Water: A new wrinkle in skiing was introduced here yesterday when the newly formed AWSA presented a spectacular program on the choppy waters outside the World's Fair Boat Basin in Flushing Bay.

'A talented group of men and women, as well as 13-year-old Dan P. Hains, son of one of the Association officials, gave thrilling exhibitions of what could be interpreted as "snow ploughing", "stem turning" and "wake jumping" on wooden runners that in most instances were almost half the weight of ordinary skis.'

After their exhibitions had been filmed by newsreel men and photographers, the participants took part in a competition in which, as President Welsh stated, the winners would be eligible for the first National Championships to be held at Jones Beach State Park on Long Island in one month's time. While the snow-skier Mikkelsen won the trick-riding event, the slalom and the wake jumping was won by a strong, husky-voiced skier, who had been teaching water-skiing on Jones Beach since 1937. His name was Bruce Parker.

By winning the World's Fair competition, Parker had automatically qualified for the Nationals Tournament.

At 3 pm on 22 July 1939, the first US National Championships took place at the Marine Stadium, Jones Beach. More than thirty men and women competed and the Long Island State Park Commission did not charge for admission. The late Dan Hains recalled:

'It was a bit presumptuous to call this a "national" tournament since it was made up largely of local talent. In this first tournament the three basic championship events of Slalom, Jumping and Tricks were inaugurated. The slalom buoys were in a straight line rather closely spaced. The jump was at 1·5 m *5 ft* with a surface of 5 cm *2 in* diameter wood rollers spaced about 20 cm *8 in* apart – quite a dangerous contraption.'

Jack Schiess of Bayville, Long Island won the jumping by being the only man not to fall on landing after all three jumps. Trick riding was a bit primitive. The winning trick was the familiar removing one ski, placing the tow bar on the instep, then replacing the ski. By winning both tricks and slalom, Bruce Parker won the Over-all, while Esther Yates won the women's slalom and Over-all but there were neither tricks nor jumping events for women.

Back in Europe, the outbreak of the Second World War brought an abrupt halt to the development of water-skiing. Even though Switzerland was neutral, she was unable to continue skiing on a national basis through the simple fact that there was no more petrol with which to run the Garwood runabouts waiting on the shores of Lake Geneva.

Captain d'Arcy Rutherford had returned to London

from France and done his best to join up, only to be told that he was too old. 'Well,' he replied, 'you know where you can find me. I shall be in Nassau. I'm joining Sir Harold Christie on real estate business.'

Once out there, he set about introducing water-skiing to the Bahamas and by March 1940 had organised the first Bahamian Ladies' Water Ski Championship, won by Whitney Borr Griffiths. When the Duke of Windsor arrived as Governor of the Bahamas, d'Arcy was re-commissioned and became his ADC. At this period, he also gave his first exhibition of water-skiing to Canadian High Society at Baron Louis Empain's 'Domaine d'Esterel' in the Laurentians. A photograph was taken of d'Arcy with a group of skiers performing together, from which a Bahamas postage stamp was struck – possibly the very first postage stamp depicting water-skiing.

In August 1940, the second US National Championships were held, again at Jones Beach. This tournament marked the appearance of Charles R. Sligh, a furniture maker from Holland, Michigan. 'Chuck' Sligh had been staging aquaplaning shows in various parts of Michigan in 1936–37, and in 1939, using a pair of skis bought at the Marshall Field store in Chicago, had returned to Holland, to become the first person to ski 'west of the Alleghenies and east of the Rockies'.

Also competing for the first time was Jack Andresen, the New York engineer who had been working on his particular brand of water-skiing – trick-riding.

But once again Bruce Parker won both Tricks and Jumping to take the Over-all Championship for 1940. The *New York Times* commented that 'while most of the field were far superior to those of the previous summer, they experienced difficulty in negotiating the 1·22 m *4 ft* high-jumping ramp, except the defending champion who took it in his stride, showing absolute confidence and assurance in his leaps out of the surface . . . (in the Slalom) Parker again dominated his rivals with a clean-cut performance, his elongated runners just clipping the obstacles by the narrowest of margins.' Chuck Sligh tied for second place in the Slalom, while Jack Andresen became the first American to do 180-degree turnarounds on his short, double-ended skis. In the Ladies events, Virginia Pfaff won Tricks, Slalom and Over-all.

The 1941 Nationals sponsored by Chuck Sligh at Macatawa Park, Holland, Michigan, were the last to be held before America's entry into the War, with Chuck winning the Jumping and the Over-all.

With the American entry into the War in December 1941, water-skiing probably ceased throughout the World. But with US PT boats cruising about in the warm waters of the Pacific, and the British MTB's and motor-gunboats and German E-boats speeding around the Atlantic and Mediterranean, it would have been possible for aquaplaning or even water-skiing to occur during any break in hostilities. However, as far as the writers are aware water-skis were never actually used for warfare purposes.

4 Towards a world championship

The years immediately following the War were to see a strong worldwide growth of water-skiing as an exhilarating form of relaxation. On both sides of the Atlantic the sport was also beginning to develop as a serious competitive discipline, and would culminate in the first World Championships held at Juan-les-Pins in 1949. Many new countries began to make their presence felt in the sport.

Back in 1930 a few Japanese had been aquaplaning with inboard motorboats powered by Chrysler or Universal engines in the waters off Tokyo and Yokohama. But the Sino-Japanese War had put a stop to that, as all fuel was utilised for military purposes and motorboating was prohibited. In the summer of 1946 some US soldiers began water-skiing on lakes, watched by a few curious Japanese spectators. Before long they had taught their Japanese friends to ski and formed a Club – Tokyo Monozuki. American sports magazines told the Japanese more about it, but there were no shops selling water-skiing equipment in Japan. In 1948, a shipyard in Hakono, a seaside resort 60 miles north of Tokyo, began buying up second-hand motorboats from America. Also from the Americans, the motorboat pilots learnt how to water-ski. More or less the same thing happened at Lake Biwa in Western Japan and elsewhere on other lakes. It was only a year later, in 1949, that a future star performer, Masanori Komorimya began water-skiing on the Sumida River, Tokyo.

In 1936, Carl Atkinson had 'scootered' across Darwin Harbour, Australia, on a pair of skis – he attempted Sydney Harbour the same year but fell foul of the police. Then in 1938 Reg Johnson put on a detached pair of skis bought in America, and paraded round Sydney Harbour. Thus Australian water-skiing was born.

It was resumed after the War when 'Charlie' Atkinson introduced the sport to well-known car trials drivers 'Wild Bill' McLachlan of Darwin and 'Gelignite Jack' Murray, and a Sydney doctor. It was in 1946 that they tried out their home-made water-skis behind their hand-built motorboats at Tizana, near Sackville on the Hawkesbury River, New South Wales.

Jack Murray's nickname of 'Gelignite' stemmed from the days when he was in the famous Redex car reliability trials around Australia, for if another driver came too close to Jack in these trials, he used to throw a stick of gelignite out of the back of his car. 'Gelignite Jack's' stamina was fantastic. He was reputed to eat crocodiles for breakfast, to always wash himself in Salvol (the mechanics' very abrasive soap) and not to have smoked in twenty years! He brought his rough-shod, dynamic approach to water-skiing.

The Hawkesbury River always was ideal for water-skiing. Starting in the Blue Mountains (about 120 km *75 miles* west of Sydney), the Hawkesbury heads all the

The first person to water-ski in Australia 1938–39, Reg Johnson.

way down until it turns saltwater with an estuary to the sea, giving 96 km *60 miles* of skiable river. At that time there were only four boats on the river – belonging to 'Wild Bill' McLachlan, Ray Leighton, Alan Clark and the Purnell family. These pioneers virtually had the 96 km *60 miles* to themselves – 'bloody glorious!'.

Alan Clark ('Clarkie'), an ex-fighter/bomber pilot has recalled:

Above: The first jump in Australia! (*left to right*) Bill McLachlan, Ann Hookham, Jack Murray: 1949–50.

Left: Bruck Wheeler, Bruce Hope, Bill McLachlan and Gordon McLennan: 1950–51.

Left: Barry Snowball (*left*) and Alan Clark in 1952–53.

Below: John Kumm and Betty Leighton, Australia's first competitors at the World Championships in 1954. John Kumm later became the Australian Association President and Betty Leighton became a judge at the World Championships in 1969, 1971 and 1973.

'We used to make our own skis – just any old chunks of wood. I was a bit luckier; my father was in the timber business, so I had a cedar boat which was something out of this world in those days. Bloody thing fell to pieces in no time, wasn't very well made; but for two years it was the best boat on the Hawkesbury River.'

An old wrestling pal of 'Gelignite Jack's' was John Primo, a man very much involved in the surfing, swimming and water polo world. Primo's daughter, Sandy, remembers that they went down to Tamworth NSW, where a big dam had just been built across the Namoi River, creating an enormous artificial lake, about twice the size of Sydney Harbour. Not only did the Namoi run into this Keepit Dam, but a lot of smaller mountain rivers as well. The 'cockies' (or Aussie property-owners) had fashioned successful home-made water-skis and good motorboats with marinised car engines. Now the sport had reached the Outback.

Alan Clark recalls that it was two years before they discovered 'that you had to put fins on the bottom of the bloody things!' One day Jack Murray rang him up to tell him that there was a film at one of the newsreel theatre-ettes, which included a shot of a guy skiing on one ski! Not believing such a thing possible Alan, Bill, and Jack sat through the newsreel for the whole day, until about eleven o'clock at night, ignoring most of it, waiting for that particular shot. Eventually they bribed the operator to run it through again and try and slow it down and they saw the skier was on one ski, jumping the wash, and that he had something sticking out of the bottom of the ski. The film was slowed down even more and they realised that there was a small fin there. Though it was then about one o'clock in the morning, Clark raced down to his factory, cut up bits of sheet metal and fixed fins on the back of his skis. At six o'clock on the following morning they were up the Hawkesbury River, trying it out. 'We were still on two skis, but, Oh boy, this made it so much easier.'

For jumping they built the first ramp in Australia in about three days in the backyard of Clark's factory. It was slatted with 3.8×2.5 cm *1½ × 1 in* timbers, but there was about a 15 cm *6 in* gap between each piece of timber, but running crosswise, not vertical! Nobody had ever jumped before and of the 20 or so skiers it was a woman who was the only one to remain upright. 'I don't think she ever skied again – frightened the hell out of herself. The fins of our skis had only been made out of tin, so as they went up the slatted ramp, they buckled – so no wonder none of us males landed properly. But those were the fun days of it!'

After a while, John Primo sold his hotels in the Bush and his family went back to the big city, Sydney. There, Jack Murray taught Sandy to mono-ski. He got her up on to one ski in the most alarming way, just supporting her up with her arm. 'I didn't even touch the water,' remembers Sandy 'when I came out, I was just like in the air. He said "Now I'm going to put you back on the water" and I said "What do you mean on the water? What am I doing in the air?" His only instructions to her were "Keep your head up and stick your fanny out!"' And such advice was yelled at her all the way down the Hawkesbury until eventually she was skiing on one ski.

In 1950, The Sackville Water Skiing Club was formed, and the Australian Water Ski Association quickly fol-lowed. An attempt was made to stage Australian Championships at Sackville, or 'Sexville', as it was irreverently referred to in 1951, but these were not officially recognised. The first sanctioned Nationals were held at Penrith in 1952 on the River Nepean, at the top of the Hawkesbury.

Over the water in New Zealand, aquaplaning was practised by a few hardy enthusiasts in the late 1940s. The early water-skiers lacked a knowledge of suitable equipment and most appear to have manufactured their own from slightly bent 'planks' with a pair of plimsolls nailed on. Similarly take-off technique was sadly lacking and many claim to have started off the beach, some 9–18 m *10–20 yd* up the sand. Driving standards were also low with consequent bruises and abrasions to the skiers. Geographically speaking, it could be said that Auckland, with its magnificent harbour and sub-tropical climate, led the way in water-skiing, but enthusiasts in the South Island with its uncounted lakes and waterways was not far behind.

Skis made their first appearance in Makassar, Indonesia soon after the War on the feet of an athletic Lieutenant-Colonel in the Indonesian Army named Andi Matalata. The Colonel, a descendant of the local aristocracy, commander of the Hasanuddin Regiment and war administrator of the South and South-East Celebes, introduced water-skiing to the officers on his staff. Matalata, a small but indefatigable skier, would fuel his speedboat, the *Red Arrow*, and explore the coastal waters around Makassar; once taking a 100 km *60-mile* jaunt to say hello to some of his troops in Pare-Pare. Before long a dozen pairs of skis and about fifteen outboard speedboats had been acquired and the Popsa Water Ski Club had been formed.

In 1945, Dr W. S. Reid of Manitoba, Canada, had ordered some scarce waterproof plywood with which to construct an aquaplane. He went to collect it only to find that two other residents of Lac du Bonnet had 'absconded with the wood'. These two men made the first pair of skis used in Manitoba with this plywood. The skis were constructed of 6 mm *¼ in* plywood over a 2·54 cm *1 in* thick frame. They were 2·13 m *7 ft* long by 30 cm *12 in* wide. A pair of size 5 shoe-rubbers were used for the foot bindings. The maker of these skis stated that the rubbers, 'created quite a suction on my size 10 feet and were fine until one took a spill and ended upside down with a pair of very buoyant skis on one's feet'.

But the sport became more widely known in Canada when Mr George Duthie, Chairman of the Sports Commission, made arrangements to have a ski show at the 1948 Canadian National Exhibition in Toronto. It was here that 40 000–50 000 spectators saw Miss Johnette Kirkpatrick climb aloft on to the shoulders of Miss Katy Turner and Miss Joan Ryan to build the first all-girl ski pyramid. These girls, and the other star performers came from an increasingly popular ski-show that was put on four times a day around the central Floridan Lake Eloise – at Cypress Gardens.

In the early autumn of 1942, Dick Pope had enlisted in the US Army, leaving his wife Julie with the responsibility of running Cypress Gardens. Because of petrol rationing, and the resulting restriction on tourists, the only admission income came from soldiers at nearby camps. They seemed to have plenty of time on their hands during these vists, and Julie Pope thought it would be a good idea to have a regular water-ski show every afternoon. She sent a publicity handout to all the State newspapers, advertising the show. The *Orlando Sentinel* ran the story in its Monday edition and that same afternoon a lieutenant, two sergeants and one corporal passed through the Garden gates. The show was put on by eleven-year-old Dick Pope Jr, eight-year-old Adrienne Pope, with their schoolmates Katy Turner and Buddy Boyle, and with fifteen-year-old Trammel Pickett driving the boat.

The following Sunday a convoy of 800 soldiers rolled up at the Gardens entrance, bringing along a five-gallon can of petrol for the boat which had been appropriated from the US Army Air Corps under the heading of 'Entertainment'. The shows continued, most put on by High and Junior High School girls and boys, not regularly scheduled, but only when convoys of soldiers arrived. Before long, the servicemen themselves were taught by the young skiers of Cypress Gardens.

Cypress Gardens in the 1940s.

When the War was over, and Dick Pope Sr had been demobbed, three regular ski shows a day were put on, opening with a girls' routine and winding up with a clown act. The boys had a great finish in the jumping act – upon highballing into the shore wide open, they skied up a low jump on to the grassy lawn and slid up to and through the gardenia bed a hundred feet away. This was the beginning of 'The Greatest Show on Water'.

It was in 1947 that Willa Worthington became part of that Show. From the Far West, near Oregon City, Oregon, she had learnt to ski on Lake Oswego in 1945 when she was only fifteen. Within two years, she was not only skiing backwards but, with her great love of ballet, Willa had originated the graceful but difficult backward swan. In July 1946 she competed for and won her first US National Championships – the first of seven.

This tournament had been revived and sponsored by Chuck Sligh at Lake Macatawa, Holland in Michigan. This time, although Chuck won the Jumping event with 10·6 m *35 ft*, Lewis Withey III of Grand Rapids, won the Over-all with second places in the Slalom, Jumping and 'optional events' (tricks). Willa Worthington won the Over-all title from Irene Boer of Holland, with victories in Slalom and 'optional events' and a second in Jumping.

Her tricks consisted of a deepwater start on two skis backward, riding one ski backward, and the backward swan. The best trick done by her closest competitor was the front toe-hold, free ski overhead. Her skis were 1·98 m *6½ ft* long with tennis shoes attached to a wooden shoeplate and bolted to Don Ibsen bevel-bottomed specials. Slalom was run on two skis then, and, as for Jumping, 'we were lucky to make a jump with good form,

The wonderful Pope family (*left to right*) Dick Sr, Adrienne, Julie, Dick Jr.

never mind counting distance'. First in Jumping was Kate Turner of Cypress Gardens, who may well have introduced Willa Worthington to Cypress Gardens.

By 1947, water-skiing in the USA was firmly establishing itself as a popular recreation. With the advent of lightweight but powerful outboard and small inboard motors, such as Evinrude and Johnson were turning out, the many owners of outboard boats were always volunteering to teach their friends or the neighbourhood kids. Thus literally thousands of new skiers were launched.

The year also saw two memorable American tournaments. As well as their three shows a day, the Popes decided to hold a Dixie Water-Ski Meet at the Gardens. It was at this competition that the height of the jumping ramp was fixed at 1·80 m *6 ft* for men and 1·50 m *5 ft* for women, and during which Chuck Sligh set the first official long-distance jumping record – 14·93 m *49 ft*!

For the third and last time, the US Nationals were held on Lake Macatawa. The slalom course was laid out by trial and error and guesswork. Bud Leach arrived from California ostensibly to show the Easterners how to slalom on one ski. However, he was forced into a run-

off with Dick Pope Jr in the finals. The guesswork on the slalom seemed to turn out pretty good in practice, so President Dan Hains and officials went out in a rowboat with some light cord and made some primitive measurements. This then was how the length from the entry gate to the first buoy was fixed at 41 m *45 yd*.

Willa Worthington demonstrated the backward swan on a single ski but also had a run-off before winning the Tricks from Dotty Mae Anderson of Santa Monica. Also interesting was a mixed doubles match (à la tennis) which was won by Bob Sligh and Irene Boer.

But perhaps the most exciting part of the 1947 Nationals was the jumping duel between two young Cypress Gardens skiers, Tram Pickett and Buddy Boyle. 'Form be darned' was their motto as they employed untested talents in the fight for distance. Tactics included pulling the rope in hand-over-hand fashion as they went over the ramp. This pulled them through space and took up all the slack. Sometimes it even looked as if they were actually pulling the boat back to them. This was extremely dangerous since there was a chance of getting tangled up in the rope in the event of a fall. They eventually tied with a jump of 18·60 m *61 ft* each.

A skiing double at Cypress Gardens:
Alfredo Mendoza and Joan Faye.

At this time, the AWSA was charging Club Active membership at $1·00 a year and $5·00 for Life Membership. They were having to fight against splinter groups trying to form rival associations, and associated problems such as standardising on minimum and maximum ski equipment and designs. Their aim was to recognise the ability of the man and not the speed of the boat or trick equipment.

It was also in this year that the Florida Southern College at Lakeland began to offer water-skiing as a course in physical recreation – the first of many colleges to do so.

But perhaps most significant for the AWSA in 1948 was its affiliation to the International Water-Ski Union based at Geneva with Chuck Sligh's son Bob crossing the Atlantic to compete at the European Championships on Lake Geneva, where for the past two years water-skiing had been developing on a completely separate, if uncertain basis.

In 1945, the original ten-year-old French Association of water-skiing clubs formed by Mrs Frank Jay Gould as President, without ever being dissolved, was replaced by a new Federation created by Madame Maggy Savard and Jean Bladinaire. With its embryonic five clubs, this second French Federation had a constitutional form sufficient to take in the 130 clubs that were to grow up in later years. That same year the first French National Championships took place at Evian.

In Switzerland, although his attempts to form a National Water Ski Federation had been delayed by the Second World War, by 1945 André Coutau of Geneva was working with renewed enthusiasm towards the establishment of a world organisation for water-skiing. Someone had once described André Coutau as 'very Swiss, very charming and as correct and directive as the movements of a Swiss watch'.

The first steps were taken in July 1946 during a three-day Motorboat Meeting at Geneva, organised by the Nautical Society of that town. The Society invited some skiers to give exhibitions between each motorboat race. Watched and applauded by an estimated 10 000 spectators were Maggy Savard and Jean Bladinaire from France, Monsieur Mingelbier from Belgium and Monsieur Haering of Switzerland. The demonstrations were so successful that on 27 July, the wealthy Marshall Clyde, a resident of Geneva, invited the participants to a reception on his yacht, moored at the Mont Blanc quay. Here it was that André Coutau and Albert Schmidt (Switzerland) together with the representatives of Belgium and France created the Union Internationale de Ski Nautique (International Water Skiing Union). The first statutes of the USIN specified in particular:

(a) To establish a friendly and fair co-operation between all members for the profit of the water-ski sport in the whole world.

(d) To examine, ratify and register European and World Records.

These founder members then decided to meet together before the end of the year at Brussels, on the occasion of the General Assembly of the International Motornautical Union (UIM), to draw up the first Constitution. That November, Belgium, with Messieurs du Roy, de Blicky, Mingelbier, Gerard, de Backer and Claude de Clercq, hosted Maggy Savard and Jean Bladinaire from France, and Messieurs Coutau and Schmidt from Switzerland with Albert Schmidt also having the authority to represent Italy.

To repeat, at this stage they had no contact with the AWSA, and so they had to create technical rules and regulations from scratch. But if they intended to hold the

The 1948 US Nationals, Martin Lagoon, Middle River, Maryland.

first European Championships the following summer, they had to make a start somewhere. Therefore the following was decided:

'The type of towing is left to the choice of skier (outboards, dinghies, slides, *aeroplanes*). Each skier is free to have his means of towing and his personal pilot. Each tow-craft must be equipped with a boat hook, a buoy and a ladder . . . The Union allows the shapes of skis in whatever material they might be, in order to permit research into the best material and shapes to use.'

There were to be *four* disciplines: Jump, Slalom, Style and Speed.

The Slalom course would comprise 12 buoys in line with different spacings: 5–6–10 m *16–19–32 ft*, which the skier would have to take as quickly as possible.

In the 'Style', the competitors would be called to make two runs, regulated in neither time, length nor speed. The first run required four recognised tricks in order:

1 The Christiana Godilée (zig-zag);
2 The advance on one foot (the other slightly lifted from the water);
3 The skater's step (lifting alternately one ski, then the other, while keeping it parallel to the water);
4 The jump of the wave.

The second run required four free tricks, which were left to the competitor's choice so long as they were not the same as the first four.

André Coutau has recalled: 'We really had problems when we started to build the first jumping ramp. We had no idea of the dimensions needed and had to improvise before anything could possibly become official. So we decided on a ramp that was 2 m *6½ ft* wide, with its surface formed by wooden rollers of a diameter of 8 cm *3·1 in* turning on fixed axis.'

Claude and Guy de Clercq from Belgium mono skiing at Cypress Gardens. Claude won several European titles during 1947–52, while Guy won two world titles.

On Monsieur Clyde's yacht at the creation of the International Water Ski Union on 28 July 1946.

As a try-out on 29 June 1947, the first Swiss National Water Ski Championships were held at Geneva, following a motorboat regatta, as part of the Geneva Games. By winning both Style and Slalom, Albert Firmenich, son of Frederick, won the Over-all.

The very first European Championships were organised and held at Evian in July 1947 by the Swiss Federation of Automobile Navigation, again during an international motorboat meeting. Four ladies and thirteen men participated. The competition could only be held on Lake Geneva in the early morning and early evening, because at other times there was too much wind and rough water.

The Slalom was won by Mademoiselle Beday of France and Monsieur Michel H. Vuilleti for Switzerland. 'Style' was won by Maggy Savard of France and Monsieur Haering of Switzerland. Haering's winning trick – that of lifting one ski vertically and travelling forwards with one arm lifted free above his head – created a sensation among the other skiers. While Maggy Savard won the Ladies' Over-all for France, the Men's Over-all was won by the young Belgian who had 'competed' at Monte Carlo before the War – Claude de Clercq.

Claude has recalled: 'In 1945 we returned to our property which had been requisitioned by the Nazis to find that by a miracle our Chris-Craft had been left undisturbed in the garage and so we could ski again.

'In 1946, I was with my father on the Côte d'Azur and I decided to cut my skis; they were a beautiful pair, fashioned by Toshe et Lahuppe out of hickory wood. When people noticed me using the saw at first they thought I was mad, while my father found it shameful to ruin such good material. But after demonstrating how much easier it was to ski on 1·80 m *5 ft 11 in* planks, other skiers began to follow my initiative.

'I was invited to the European Championships personally because there was neither a Federation nor a Club in Belgium. The only organisation that had anything to do with our sport at that time was the Royal Belgian Yachting Association, where a water-skiing section was planned with Monsieur Mingelbier as Secretary-General.

'At Evian I met the French and Swiss teams and perhaps an Italian or two. In trick-riding, there was one compulsory item; all tricks had to include helicopters on one foot!

'The speed event offered a first prize of a Sèvres Vase presented by the President of the French Republic, Monsieur Vincent Auriol. This competition consisted of letting yourself be pulled by the fastest boat on Lake Leman. If I won, it was because, like everyone else, I asked for the maximum speed, but I took care to cut the fins of my skis and to coat their base with paraffin oil. I was completely bent over flat in the water and in this "foetal" position I gained the vital few seconds over the others, behind a boat that was reaching 80–90 km/h *50–56 mph* – it was idiotic.

'I believe I also won the Jump with 15 m *49 ft* and in the end, I won the Over-all by one point over a hundred, followed very closely by a Swiss boy living in the Argentine, Michel Vuilletis (who did a lot to publicise water-skiing in South America and was later towed by an aeroplane at 150 km/h *93 mph*!).'

When he returned to Belgium there were small paragraphs in the newspapers, referring to 'A Great Cham-

pion of Water-skiing in Europe'. But it was still early days as they had virtually improvised the rules on the spot. It was after his victory that he met Philippe de Backer who soon became the pillar of water-skiing in that country.

In 1948, the AWSA was informed of the existence of the International Water Skiing Union and Dan B. Hains came in as President for North and South America. Bob Sligh was invited to represent the USA at the Second European Championships at Geneva, and arrived early to put in some practice. Claude de Clercq has recalled:

'Some friends and I made the trip to Geneva to watch Bob in training and to find out about his methods of skiing. We spent the day with him, lunched with him, and as with all Americans, sure enough, he told us all he knew. For the very first time in Europe, we saw someone slaloming *on a single ski* and doing turnabouts of 180°. We already knew about fins and had already fitted them, but with Bob we saw the importance of one leg behind the other and how it was necessary to have a distribution of weight on the wood.'

Lanfranco Colombo (Italy) and David Nations (GB) about to put on a ski show somewhere in the South of France.

The main regulations for these championships were largely based on those used by the AWSA. For the first time, the buoys of the slalom course had been placed criss-cross, with two gates; there were five judges; all falls, with the exception of those due to motorboat breakdown or damaged equipment were from now on eliminatory; the height of the jumping ramp was put up to 1·50 m *5 ft*.

As had perhaps been expected, Bob Sligh won all three disciplines in spectacular style, with a points score of 39 500, followed by Claude de Clercq with 36 450 points. But as Claude explains:

'The Union had ruled that the dimensions for trick skis must be 1·22 m *4 ft* long and 18 cm *7 in* wide. The first turnabout of 180° that I made from front to back, was considered impossible by everybody. But with skis of such a ridiculous length, even I had a thousand falls before succeeding! Certainly, this American had made his mark on European skiing.'

At about this time a young man called Leon Lambert from Luxembourg built himself a small motorboat and fashioned a pair of skis. Regardless of derision, Lambert began water-skiing on the Moselle, the frontier river of Luxembourg and Germany. Slowly but surely, the Sunday trippers who walked along the banks of the river, began to go to Ehnen to watch the free and unusual spectacle of the lone water-skier. Before long other sportsmen had got in touch with Lambert.

In northern Italy, at Viverone, for a bet, several Biellesi skied behind a small seaplane, while farther south on the Po and on the Naviglio, other fanatics could be seen towed behind cars. The first Italian Press interest was in 1948 when the names of Franco Bettoni, Nelio Ronchi and Lanfranco Colombo were mentioned as leaders of water-skiing in their country. Lanfranco Colombo was also pulled behind a helicopter at 120–125 km/h *75–78 mph*.

'It was much easier than with a motorboat, in as much as there were no waves. I remember that I was left with sore legs for two days from the spray.'

The 'Grand Old Man' of Finnish water-skiing was Kauko Kolma, who had seen one of these Italian demonstrations, returned to Finland and began the sport by being towed by a motorboat, then graduated to 160 km/h *100 mph* behind a hydroplane. He then attempted to ski the 354 km *220 miles* from Helsinki to Stockholm, but failed because of engine trouble.

In Stockholm, Sweden, 52-year-old Ragnar Frunck had already put in one season of self-taught skiing, together with his daughter Marie-Louise and a colleague Gert Vellner. It had all begun in 1947 with a phone-call from a friend on the west coast of Sweden, asking Ragnar if he might be interested in water-skiing. Despite the leather bindings, the 2 m *6½ ft* skis, and the mistake of starting with a rope length of 10 m *33 ft* instead of an easier 7 m *23 ft* it was not long before Ragnar Frunck was using his friend's skis to demonstrate and promote the sport in Sweden; he too was later acknowledged as the pioneer of the sport in Sweden.

An article 'Water-Ski-Man Thrills Durban' in South Africa's *National Mercury* of Tuesday, 9 March 1948, reads: 'Many of Durban's week-end picknicers at Fynnland are treated to a rare thrill when it is high tide and weather conditions are calm. They gather in a long line on the water's edge to watch Mr Eddie Schultz skim on the surface of the Bay, as if he were on the soles of his feet, behind a speedboat travelling at more than 48 km/h *30 mph*.'

Ragnar Frunck, the Swedish 'father of water-skiing', seen here in Stockholm demonstrating a backward swan position.

In March 1948 Eddie Schultz became the first man to ski in South Africa.

'Mr Schultz is the only man in the Union who enjoys the water-ski sport . . . The crowds applaud Mr Schultz's daring as he whizzes past in a cloud of spray.' In that same year in the 1948 US Nationals, held at Martin Lagoon, Middle River, Maryland, Dick Pope Jr won the Men's Over-all, while Willa Worthington took the Women's Over-all and Tricks. Bud Leach, Bob Sligh, Buddy Boyle, Dottie Mae Andreson and Johnette Kirkpatrick also won trophies.

The year 1949 was to be even more memorable for competitive water-skiing. Beginning with the Dixie Water Ski Meet at Cypress Gardens, USA, Buddy Boyle increased the official jumping record to 20·72 m *68 ft* before going on to win the Men's Jumping at the US Nationals, being held for the second time at the lagoon adjoining the Glenn L. Martin aircraft plant near Baltimore, Maryland.

It was at this tournament that jump meters, engineered by Martin personnel were used for the first time. Charles Tilger Jr of Long Island and Don Ibsen of Bellvue, Washington, alternated as chief judge. The two star performers were Dick Pope Jr and Willa McGuire (*née* Worthington), building on the endless practise which they had gained at Cypress Gardens. At the end of the meet, Chuck Sligh became the second President of the AWSA, now made up of a few hundred members. One of Sligh's contributions was to start up a little magazine called *The Water Skier*, for which his secretary, Isabel Howe, was the first editor.

Once again Cypress Gardens sent a troupe to the Canadian National Exhibition at Toronto, where George N. Duthie had sponsored the 'First Canadian Open and Canadian Closed Water Ski Championships, 26 and 27 August 1949.' The Cypress Gardens skiers entered the Open contest and helped with the judging, while AWSA President Chuck Sligh was 'on mike' along with Dave Prince of CBC. At the closing dinner and prize-giving, the Canadian Water Ski Association was founded, with Duthie as its first President.

In the meantime, the Europeans had been preparing for the first World Championships, to be held at Juan-les-Pins in front of the Hotel Provençal. Particularly in Belgium, where as Claude de Clercq recounts: 'We had one lake in the suburbs of Brussels where we could train – at the 120-acre Hofstade ("The Cradle"). With bad weather we did not ski for pleasure or relaxation, but for achievement. With our friend Philippe de Backer, my brother Guy and myself used to leave the office in time to arrive at Hofstade for just one hour's skiing, before having to return to the office again.

'My speciality was trick-riding, while my brother Guy became the specialist in jumping. He was above all of a daring nature, but rather lazy, nonchalant and always relaxed. He did a little slalom because he had to do as well as the others, but he always refused to do tricks because they bored him, they were idiotic, a waste of time. But he was a born jumper and the first to understand that to attack the ramp, he must present himself to it with his legs almost stretched, instead of conventionally crouching and springing in the air, which was absurd. He was also the first to propel himself forward using the front of the cord and thanks to this technique, he increased jumping distances from 15·24 m *50½ ft* to 25 m *82 ft*.'

In 1949, the first official Belgian Championships were held at Hofstade and Claude de Clercq made a clean sweep to win the Over-all while Major Crombez's daughter, Anny, did the same in the Women's Division. Then on 2 June 1949, he became one of the founder members (representing Brussels) of the Belgian Water Ski Federation together with:

M. Roland du Roy de Blicquy (President)
M. Philippe de Backer (Secretary)
M. Georges Van Pelt (of Antwerp)
M. Fernand de Langhe (of La Hulpe/Genval)
M. Paul Mingelbier (of Liège).

Now they could send an official team to Juan-les-Pins for the World Championships.

For the World Championships, the technical regulations were more complete and better studied. Even if limited, a more correct list of tricks had been established, seventeen in all, including 'Dangerous Jump in front', 'Backward Swan', 'Reverse turn on one ski with double-handles', not to mention 'Take off one ski, hold over the head, put it back on the foot holding on to the tow-bar all the time'.

The skiing took place that August in Angels Bay, Juan-les-Pins. Representing the USA were Dick Pope Jr, and Willa Worthington. The Ladies' Over-all was won by the American girl with victories in Slalom and Jumping. The Men's Over-all was a tie between Jourdan of France and Guy de Clercq of Belgium. Guy de Clercq came first in Jumping, while Claude was second in Tricks and third in Slalom and Jumping – both men using skis made by Monsieur Poncelet. Dick Pope Jr was only able to win third place in Tricks – although he had noticed the contrast between European and American rules, he made no comment. Normally a brilliant slalomer, he was used to a shorter rope than the European regulation, but the judges refused to make exceptions. There was also the rule that competitors must slalom on two skis. Because it was bad weather on the day of the slalom, Dick Pope fell and Jourdan won. Pope used the hand-over-hand method to set a new World Record. However, he lost his balance and fell before he could get out of the course and the record was not accredited.

It was at these championships that the International Water Ski Union grew to nine-strong: Switzerland, Belgium, France, USA, were now joined by Canada,

Monaco, Mexico, Italy and Great Britain. It was perhaps inevitable that after seeing so much pre-War skiing at Monte Carlo, that Monaco should join.

In Mexico, sometime during 1949, the owner of the Proal Hotel in Tequesquitengo, brought a pair of skis to the place and immediately people living near the lake began to build and use home-made skis. Among these were Samuel and Catalina Zamudio and their brood of children, Toribio and Carlos Dorantes, Quirino Ramirez and a young man called Alfredo Mendoza. Mendoza had originally wanted to become a bullfighter but changed his mind when he saw a film about Cypress Gardens.

Great Britain was represented at the championships by a lone skier with a farsighted enthusiasm for promoting water-skiing in a coldwater country – his name was David Nations.

Below: David Nations with, on his right, Lester Piggott, learning to ski at Ruislip Lido. Piggott, one of the greatest jockeys of all time, went on to win the Derby in 1954, the year after this photograph was taken.

5 Cold water challenge

David Nations water-skiing in Golfe Juan in the early 1950s.

In looking at the career of a man who has totally devoted his life to a single cause with an unquenchable enthusiasm, it is always interesting to discover exactly what sparked it off. With David Nations, this is simple:

'We'd had a war and sport was not of first importance in our life. It was to re-build our homes, our industries and to re-establish a proper way of life. I had spent six years in the Army. Early in 1945, with my Passing-Out Gratuity, I decided to give myself a good holiday before I went back into my profession as a pattern-cutter and designer in the fashion trade. So I bought a small car

with the intention of driving through post-War Europe to see how it looked. I had heard so much about the South of France, and in particular the fashionable Juan-les-Pins, where the Hollywood film stars such as Charlie Chaplin and Douglas Fairbanks had stayed before the War.

'After travelling all night, I drove on to the front, parked my car with my bags in the back, and sat back to relax. Then I saw something that amazed me – two people being pulled across the water on two lines behind one boat. I could not believe it – that people were actually

Other British pioneers engaged in a water-ski tug-of-war.
Left to right: Eddie Arida, Peter Felix and Simon Khoury.

walking on the water! I was so fascinated that I left my things in the car, sat down on the beach and watched them from early morning to the middle of the afternoon; before long I was talking to the local ski instructor of the Hotel Provençal, Professeur Roman. He told me how popular water-skiing and aquaplaning had been along the South of France before the War. At the end of the day, I had plucked up enough courage to ask for a lesson. The skis were 2·75 m *9 ft* long and they had metal heel-binders so that if you put your foot hard on that metal you could get a nasty cut. The worst thing in the world happened – I was able to stand up on my first attempt! The exhilaration hooked me.

'I only had a certain amount of money and had originally been planning on a three-week holiday. On finding out the cost of a ski lesson, I worked out that if I did so much skiing a day, it would cost more than the hotel bill. So I decided to stay less days, so I could ski as often as possible. It was during those nine days that I met and made friends with the de Clercq family and went out skiing with the twins from their father's yacht.

'By post-War standards, I was getting paid well, so I saved every penny I could and returned to Juan later that year so as to continue skiing, meet skiers who were better than I, and get as much expertise and knowledge about the sport, which I was now firmly convinced was going to play a big part in my life. It took all of my time and attention and I dreamed of nothing else.

'These were the days before regular disciplines, and we got up to some pretty riotous games. One was to ski out while holding a stick with a nail on the end and see how many balloons we could stab in a given run. Another game was to be towed behind the same boat by ropes of the same length and at a given signal to make each other fall by every possible honest means. Yet again there was the 'Suitcase Game' where there were as many suitcases as competitors and before starting each competitor had to choose a suitcase, which during a timed run he or she must open and dress themselves in whatever clothes happened to be inside!

'I knew that a Monsieur Coutau of Switzerland and his friends had formed the nucleus of an International Water Skiing Union, and I returned to England determined to get Britain into this sport. Recreation for the nation had to recommence and I had met several other Englishmen skiing at Juan – Ted Tresise, David De Young and Edward Van den Bergh – and Professeur Roman had kindly given me several other names to contact. I wanted to arrange a meeting with all the people who had ever gone skiing, because at that time we had nothing going in Britain at all.

'The Central Council for Physical Recreation had been the pre-War body for all recreationalists with offices at No. 6 Bedford Square, Bloomsbury, London. I rang the secretary and obtained permission to use their hall, then wrote to all these people inviting them to meet at Bedford Square. As Secretary-General, I took on the working job but at the same time decided that we needed a figurehead, if we were going to get anywhere. I knew a very interesting man, who had been in the Olympics and was the President of the Amateur Rowing Association – Sir Eugene Millington-Drake. I wrote to him and asked him if he would become President of this first Water Ski Association. He declined but accepted the Vice-Presidency. Perhaps my most enthusiastic contact was Ted Tresise from Burton-on-Trent, and he took the chair at this first meeting.'

Also among those present were Edward Van den Bergh, Pete Halford, Colin McLeod of Lillywhites and Monsieur Marcour from Belgium. It was at this historic meeting that a resolution was passed establishing a British Water Ski Club – embryo of the British Water Ski Federation, with the intention of finding a good stretch of water for club activities as soon as possible. But this was not to be so easy as David Nations recalls:

'Wherever I went it was a closed door. Leased to Sailing, Fishing, and Rowing Clubs, reservoirs and private lakes simply did not wish to know about motorboats let alone water-skiing. I searched all over London where the most obvious possibility – the Welsh Harp – was at that time exclusive for sailing. Gravel pits were extremely difficult to find then and a year went by and we still had not found a site. Then I tried Ruislip Lido.'

By a coincidence, at the time when David Nations arrived at the Lido, the Ruislip and Northwood District Council were negotiating to take it over as a recreation area. 'The manager was very sympathetic and suggested that I write to the Council. With amazing foresight, Mr Saywell, the Town Clerk asked me to go and see him. "Well," he said to me, "I can't believe it – people walking on the water – but I'll put it in front of the Council."'

Nations had to wait impatiently but eventually he received a letter, saying that they would be very glad to see him on 23 October early in the morning. It was in the middle of the week and it was mid-winter, but the opportunity simply could not be missed.

The enthusiasts had the 2·43 m *8 ft* skis but they needed a boat. As no new small motorboats were yet on the market, they had to find something pre-War. Ted Tresise knew of a Nottingham Club which owned several pre-War Derby-Class motorboats, a couple of which were still in working order. The Club Secretary told them that his Derby boats could still do a good 40–50 km/h *26 mph* and so one was hired out. The difficulties of getting it towed down to London were incredible. But this was their one opportunity and it could not be missed even though a great deal of time was spent on getting the engine going.

Finally, on that bitterly cold October morning in 1949, the councillors arrived at the Lido wearing thick overcoats and mufflers, and the women among them in fur coats and scarves. They looked at the skiers as if they were mad, because they wore nothing but swimsuits. Praying that the boat would work, Ted Tresise drove it while Nations skied, then they changed places. The councillors said 'This shi-ing – quite remarkable – never seen shi-ing like this before!'

But soon after, a letter was received from the Council stating that: 'If you are brave enough to attempt this, we feel we should give you the opportunity and you will be allowed to use a roped-off area at the north end of the Lido.'

The area they had been given was noticeably short, but it was the only chance to be had, and at least it would be possible to teach people to get up on two skis.

After returning the Derby boat, David Nations bought a Simmons boat with a 6-cylinder Ford Consul engine, from his friend David Brown of Aston Martin's. 'David and I had thought of going into the boatbuilding industry to produce a proper boat for British skiing but sadly, this never happened, because we were unable to get together with the man who owned the Simmons design patent.'

All that could be done was to get the skier in the water, get him up on two skis, then stop by the boundary rope, turn the boat round and repeat the process in the opposite direction. Literally, the word 'Ruislip' means 'the wet place where the rushes grow' and there were plenty of those: they even had to change in the woods, leaving their clothes in the boots of cars. Two years were spent like that, during which the British Water Ski Club grew in number to about twelve people, including Mr and Mrs Carl Erhardt, Ernie Ramus, Bobby Panton, Pete Halford, David De Young, Edward Van den Bergh, the actor Jon Pertwee and a sculptor named Emile Hartmann. In time, the Council realised that they were more responsible than had been originally thought, and they were allowed to use a small stone hut as a clubhouse. It was a full season but in a limited area.

'In those days,' remembers Nations, 'I would go to work at 5.30 am, work until midday and then come to Ruislip. We had no drivers, so during his lunch-hour I would give the foreman, Jimmy Murphy, a drink and look after him, in return for him towing me; there was no one else who would give time and come out to drive during the week.

'For this sport to become popular, I had made my own personal decision that it would have to be practised with a great deal of self-control, to live and co-operate fully with other water users and the local Authority. As the water was so scarce my total consideration was towards the time factor.'

Before long, the membership of the British Water Ski Club had doubled to 24, and it was now time to diversify. At the end of the season, there was a meeting in which several members of the BWSC – Pete Halford, Bobby Panton, Carl Erhardt and Ernie Ramus – decided to leave Ruislip and go in search of a more unrestricted stretch of water. It was to take them two years before they found their own permanent base. They decided that anywhere within a 48 km *30-mile* radius of London would do, and they looked up and down the Thames Valley – but again to be met with 'Leased to Sailing/Fishing'.

Water boards refused because of the pollution aspect. One weekend out of two, they went searching for water, while on the other weekends, they travelled around the South Coast with an unofficial Water Ski Road Show. Carl Erhardt now had his own Albatross boat and they put on demonstrations at St Neots in Cambridge, on the River Hamble, the River Arun near Littlehampton, on the Solent and even on the Thames. There was a great call for demonstrations of skiing as part of any pageant or show which was by the water. Their star performer was Jon Pertwee who says:

'In those days, I made water-skiing a bit fancier than most other people. I don't think they bothered as much about tricks as I did.

'I would be towed with the bar behind the neck, which was considered to be very silly because if you fell, you'd have your neck pulled out of its socket. Towing by holding the rope in my teeth at the knot where it joined the bar, then slaloming quite a bit – not too far over because my head would have come off. Retournaments and trail-toe out of the water. I was one of the earliest people to do

Four British pioneers: Robert Panton, David Nations, Jack May and Edward Van den Bergh.

46

retournaments, but I didn't do them on skis, I did them on discs and on a chair. Then I did my tin bath trick, which was so made that the water went in one end and shot out of the other like a shower, when towed behind the boat. On one occasion, the bath hit the bank with an outward swing of 64 km/h *40 mph*, which took me out of the water. Then again towing between the knees, which didn't look all that pretty but in fact was one of the hardest to do, to get the point of balance.

'But perhaps my most spectacular trick was the motor-cycle and sidecar routine. You went off with a slalom ski on your right foot, an ordinary ski on your left foot, a single rope, with a single bar on your right hand. You'd then kick off your left ski and pick it up out of the water and hold it in your left arm. You'd then put the rope round the top of your left foot which you stretched out straight ahead of you – then down on the right knee so that you were towing on your right on a slalom ski, your left foot forward, holding you, with the rope pulling on the top of your foot (I used a little loop with canvas padding round it), take your left hand and put that in the foot piece and put that out on the water. Then lie right back, the whole body straight back and hold like this for half a minute in good water conditions. Then the only way to break it off was to sit up, let go the rope off your foot so that you got that out of your way, and do a forward front – you usually came up against your skis.'

Nor was the 'British Water Ski Club' the only group to ski outside Ruislip. With David Nations' help, Ted Tresise had gone up to found the Midland Water Ski Club, and there was also a Yorkshire Water Ski Club being developed by a bank clerk named George Adlington.

Meanwhile the Ruislip Water Ski Club, as David Nations had now re-named his pioneer group, was continuing to enjoy its skiing up and down the Lido, being joined by several new members who were to play a sizable part in British competitive skiing – Peter Felix, who in 1929 had enjoyed aquaplaning as a boy in Austria and was a keen snow-skier, and Eddie Arida from the Lebanon, who had a British passport and was studying at Cambridge. The wealthy Arida family had been among the first to water-ski in the Lebanon in St George's Bay, Beirut. Eddie has recalled 'Our first boat was an American Higgins and the skis were very long with very funny bindings. The first time I skied was in the harbour: it was full of jelly-fish, which is probably the reason why I stayed up!'

Two other members were ex-fighter pilot Jack May, and Geoffrey Eker.

In 1953, Dick Pope Jr invited David Nations to Cypress Gardens: 'I went to America, because I was so burning with desire to enhance my knowledge. I met all of the early skiers there – Willa Worthington, Alfredo Mendoza, Scotty Scott, Dick Binette, Red McGuire, Busta McCalla and also one of the younger skiers called Jimmy Jackson, nicknamed "Flea" because he was so small. I was to go back to Cypress Gardens three years running as a family guest of Julie and Dick Pope, gaining more and more information and technical knowledge.'

That same year, David Nations, Edward Van den Bergh and Eddie Arida competed at the European Championships on the Wertersee in Austria. They did not do at all well, Van den Bergh entering the slalom course on two skis, taking alternate buoys and then falling ignominiously.

Despite amateurish performances, the British team from Ruislip determined to improve before they returned to European contests. During the winter of 1953–54, they put in some hard practise on their makeshift slalom course and Heath Robinson-type ramp. On measuring the slalom course, using ropes and bits of plywood floating on the water, they soon found out how difficult and deceptive it was to check distances on the water. They had built the jumping ramp with 15 cm *6 in* mahogany slats, securing each slat to the understructure by six screws. Moving it from behind the 'clubhouse', they launched it into the Lido. Recalling his experiences in France, David Nations was the first to try out Britain's inaugural jumping ramp. With his tuition, and after several painful attempts, the others also managed to stand up, jumping 4·5–6 m *15–20 ft*. But the screws soon came loose and as a skier went up over the ramp the fins of his skis would rattle like machine-gun fire. When René Giraud, the French water-skiing champion of Europe came to Ruislip and saw this hair-raising style of jumping, he is said to have remarked, 'Now I know why you British build the jump like this with space between your slats – to let the blood run through!'

Later that year the first National Championship was held at Ruislip. Competitors were Eddy Arida, David Nations, Geoffrey Eker, Jack May, Ken Roberts and Peter Felix. It lasted half an hour. The Slalom took about five minutes, and they scribbled the buoy score on a scrap of paper. In Jumping, Geoffrey Eker managed about 15–18 m *50–60 ft*, while David Nations fell and broke his ribs. When it came to trick-skiing, Eddy Arida could just about go from front to back and front again – thus it was he who won the over-all competition, and the prize – which he shared with the others – was a smoked salmon sandwich!

The British Water Ski Federation, with its new Constitution, could now boast four clubs – Ruislip, Yorkshire, Midlands and Princes – and it was clear that there would be more to come.

However, the poor British performance at the 1954 European Championships at Milan, was accurately summed up by the Dane, Bent Stig Møller when he asked 'Is this the *British* style?'

Among other things, 1955 was to be a year of spectacular shows to popularise British interest in water-skiing at home and abroad. As David Nations says: 'In 1951, I had been able to create good publicity during the Festival of Britain. I'd met someone from the *Daily Mirror*, who told me that the Festival was to include the opening of a brand new concert hall on the Embankment. Within a water festival, I thought that it would be a nice idea to put on the first International Skiing Show in the UK and I invited the de Clercq twins from Belgium, Marc Flachard from France, and Princess Doris Pignatelli with Lanfranco Colombo from Italy. We had neither a slalom course nor a jumping ramp, but even so it was still a spectacle. It was a terrible day with a lot of wind. Of the 90 motorboats which had entered the racing event, only three finished – the timber debris in the river took toll of the others. Then I led the water-skiing parade, holding a British flag, avoiding large logs of wood like grim death, while the other skiers, mischievously waited to see me fall. That was the most arduous effort I ever had in my life – to stay afloat with the Union Jack. I didn't crash but my legs were like rubber for a long time afterwards.'

It was in 1954 that he had arranged the first 'live' television show for the Ruislip skiers with the BBC, based on ideas which had been taken from Cypress Gardens. The pioneer concept of stage-managing a live television show with 'ballet-dancing' girls was met by the BBC Producer, John Vernon, with the remark 'My God, I don't understand anything about this. I'll go down to the pub and have a drink. You organise everything, tell my cameramen what to do, then I'll come back, we'll have a run-through, but I leave it all to you.' It worked out fine, except that as Nations was being towed along, reading a newspaper, on a chair, balanced on a disc, the boat driver accelerated too suddenly and he became an involuntary mermaid!

With one eye on the 1955 World Championships, the British trained doggedly. As part of their training, they performed again before the critical eyes of the BBC audience. There was also a match against the Italians – the first International ever held in this country. Bent Stig Møller, who took an almost affectionate interest in the British water-skiers, sent over a most attractive lady water-skier from Copenhagen – actress Annette Stroyberg, who later became the second Mme Roger Vadim. While on the subject of charming ladies, Doris Pignatelli, who skied with the Italian team in the televised match, received 23 proposals of marriage after her appearance on the small screen.

In 1955 Donald Campbell broke the World Water Speed Record in his *Bluebird K7* jet hydroplane at speeds well over 320 km/h *200 mph*. Don was a keen water-ski enthusiast at Ruislip and he and David Nations formed a close friendship that was to last for over ten years. That year they both went over to Cypress Gardens as guests of the Pope family. In fact, they even performed in 'The Greatest Show on Water' as 'I-say-old-boy' English gentlemen, and created quite a sensation.

Also during that summer, they gave two exhibitions outside Ruislip and joined forces with George Adlington and the Yorkshire Water Ski Club to give the first display to the North at Waterloo Lake, Roundhay Park, Leeds. Some 50000 people who lined the banks saw Peter Felix thrown heavily into a boundary wall after his ski struck a rock which somersaulted him into the water. During the slalom contest, despite badly gashed hands and abrasions from shoulder to ankle, Peter insisted on taking part in a comedy and tricks routine with Geoffrey Eker. René Ast from Switzerland had been invited and he gave the crowds a spectacular jumping display.

Then on 7 July a display was given in the Inner Basin of the Royal Harbour, Ramsgate, Kent, assisted by Annette Stroyberg from the Danish Ski Club, who was billed as 'Annette on one ski'. The skiing was at dusk, watched by 10000 people, and just as darkness fell, thousands of lights on every ship in the harbour were switched on and batteries of coloured floodlights suddenly blazed. The demonstration finished by skiing with flares, followed by a mammoth firework display.

But as Peter Felix remembers: 'We found out the hard way that if you go over a jump at night, carrying a torch, you get a down draught and your hand gets burnt! We had a lot of fun experimenting with double-jumping and triple-jumping until I found out – like famous Alphonse –

that it doesn't pay to be in the middle when you don't know much about it, because as I landed, the two outside men came down and scraped my skin!'

Also in 1955, to aid practice, a more powerful Albatross with a Coventry Climax engine was obtained. The jump was re-surfaced, though not yet fitted with a cow-catcher. Yorkshire and Cambridge sent competitors that year to the National Championships, held at Ruislip, but David Nations swept the board by winning all events, and also set the first National Jumping Record of 21·33 m *70 ft.*

As yet, the Record Books did not show a Ladies' Champion. That was soon to be rectified.

Scotland became involved with water-skiing in 1956, thanks to Isla Henderson ('the first lady of British water-skiing'). As she recalls:

'I first became involved with water-skiing when I met David Nations and Edward Van den Bergh in the South of France in 1950 and became one of the first members of the then British Water Ski Club. For the first couple of years, Ruth Erhardt and myself were the only two females skiing at Ruislip.

'Then in 1953, I went home to teach at a little Highland village school in Inverness-shire, where there are so many beautiful lochs. I used to drive around the countryside, seeing beautiful places, which no one was using. My thoughts immediately went to Ruislip – which was the best we could get, but it wasn't really as big as these huge lochs with their obvious potential.

'I spoke to several people about this but couldn't get anyone interested, until I met Jock Kerr-Hunter, the Senior Technical Adviser to the Scottish Council for Physical Recreation. He arranged all sorts of courses and pony trekking – and he immediately became interested in this. I contacted David Nations and put those two in touch with one another.'

The owner of the Lochearnhead Hotel, overlooking six miles of Loch Earn in Perthshire, was Ewan Cameron, a former Scottish Highland Games Heavyweight Champion, standing 1·93 m *6 ft 4 in*, weighing 139 kg *22 stone*, who competed in such feats as tossing the caber and putting the shot.

Jock Kerr-Hunter and David Nations approached him to see if he would be interested in forming Scotland's first water-ski school. He was.

Opposite: **Donald Campbell (*left*) and David Nations doing a 'terribly English' routine at Cypress Gardens.**

David Nations persuaded Cameron to come as his guest to Ruislip with his wife, the Steels, and Dr Penicuik, and they spent a week at the Lido learning the techniques of skiing. 'Ewan was so big that when we put him behind an Albatross and he was three-quarters of the way round the Lido, the tops of his skis still had not emerged from the water. It was the first time we ever had to hitch two Albatrosses in tandem to get someone up out of the water,' Nations recalls. When the lesson was over he suggested to Cameron that he could get skiing started in Scotland. After all, Ewan had an hotel and the sport had a great future in tourism. All he needed was a boat. Back came the rejoinder:

'Auch! I thought there was a catch in it!'

However, an Albatross was duly despatched to Perthshire, followed by David Nations and Edward Van den Bergh, who gave the first demonstration of water-skiing across Loch Earn, assisted by Isla Henderson. Soon after, the Lochearnhead Water Ski Club was formed with an initial membership of 25 – all Scots.

It was also on one cold September's day in 1956 that a shy little girl arrived with her mother at Ruislip and asked to ski. She was thin and only ten years old, but determined to try because she had seen somebody enjoying it that summer, while holidaying in Alassio, Italy. 'It was a cold, wet day. Patti Morgan and Danny Chamoun (son of the then President of the Lebanon) were there. I think I got up on the second pull. But I went back on odd weekends because I'd enjoyed it, and I gradually became more and more involved.'

David Nations recalls the first time he gave this little girl a ski lesson: 'There was an instant recognition, an easy translation of what I wanted her to do, by motions of my hand, raising of my finger, a pointing – it was reflected and it was so terribly unusual to find such wonderful acceptance of instruction from the boat.'

This girl was to become World Champion and a legend in her own lifetime. Her name was Jeannette Stewart-Wood. Before looking at her career, it is worthwhile examining what had been happening to the sport overseas since those first World Championships at Juan in 1949.

6 International growth

During the 1950s water-skiing continued to spread worldwide. In 1950, a Russian engineer called Grigori Malinovsky built himself a pair of skis, modified a motor-boat, and tested them out on the Istra Reservoir in the suburbs of Moscow – the beginning of the sport in the USSR.

Denmark had already progressed to having a Federation. As far back as 1932, a Danish engineer called O Begtrup-Hansen had gone aquaplaning on the Silkeborg lakes behind a boat called *Flying Chris Craft*. Then in 1945, the 23-year-old Danish Snow Ski Champion, Bent Stig Møller had gone on a trip to Southern Europe and purchased his first pair of water-skis – 2·43 m *8 ft* long with very primitive leather bindings. Back in Denmark he tried them out:

'Unfortunately, I did not have a boat at the time, but my family had a swimming pool in the garden. It didn't take me long to figure out that a lot of learning could be done with me at one side of the pool on one end of a tow-line. On the other side of the pool and the other end of the line were two or three helpful assistants running like mad across the lawn. In September of that year, I tried it for the first time behind a boat – an easy job when you've already had hours of slow skiing across a pond.'

In 1947 he got his own boat – a small outboard, powered by a 16-hp Johnson on which most of the time was spent in pulling the starting rope. But a new 34 hp Evinrude gave a much better performance. Unfortunately Møller had to leave Denmark a month or two later, to go to the USA on behalf of his firm. From then until the spring of 1950, he only skied three times – on the muddy River Ohio, near Cincinnati.

Back in Denmark again in July 1950, Møller received a phone-call from the Sales Manager of Scandinavian Airlines, who announced that Michel Vuilletis, World Water Ski Speed Record holder, was coming to Copenhagen. They wanted to sponsor a Water Ski Show at Bellevue Beach and asked if he, Møller, would do something along with the champion.

Later that month the two of them, plus a helicopter, put on a spectacular show. A demonstration had already been seen in June 1947 at Skovshoved Harbour, north of Copenhagen, but on this occasion more than 10000 spectators turned up to watch stunts, such as mono-skiing with the other ski held above Møller's head. Vuilletis had painted 'S.A.S.' on the skis he held up in the air, so Møller 'tried to think of something else to write on my ski'. He finally adopted a friend's suggestion, and created great amusement when he skied after Vuil-

The Danish water-ski pioneer, Bent Stig Møller, using the twin-handle method of water-skiing.

letis holding up his ski, which bore the message, 'It is not at all difficult.'

Through Vuilletis, Møller contacted the IWSU in Geneva, and a month later, on 14 August 1950, he founded the Danish Water Ski Association, along with two friends, M. C. Dahl and Hans Schrøder, with the latter as first President. There were 25 members initially.

Meanwhile in Italy, four clubs: Sci Club Nautico Milano, Circolo Sciatori Nautico Como, Sci Club 18 di Roma and the Water-skiing Section of the Milan Nautical Association, gave birth, on 12 November 1950, to the Italian Water-skiing Union, under the control of the Italian Motornautical Federation.

In the same year a water-ski school was set up at Santa Margherita Ligure, with its premises near the Grand Hotel Miramare. The Italian Waterskiing Union showed its dynamism immediately under President Fortunato Poletti. Through such enthusiastic pioneers as Franco Bettoni, Vittorio Baldoni, Nelio Ronchi, Lanfranco Colombo, Pippi Olivi and Franco Cantaluppi, and with their athletic demonstrations to the Press, the reputation of water-skiing was spread even farther. In subsequent years, through the vice-Presidency and then Presidency of Doctor Gianni Fustinoni, the

Union was transformed into the Italian Water Ski Association with its centre in Milan, officially recognised by the IWSU.

Back in Belgium, as Claude de Clercq recalls: 'Access to our training lake of Hofstade was forbidden us. We were politically outnumbered by the local fishermen. So we rejoined a group of skiers who were installed on a little lake of 36 acres at Genval, 25 km *15½ miles* south-east of Brussels. The water was not very deep (about 1·50 m *5 ft*) and it was easy to lay out a slalom, to position a ramp and for several years we had ideal training facilities.'

Many thousands of miles away, in the Delta of the River Paraná, Argentina, a group of skiers enjoyed themselves in the waters of the Sarmiento and the Capitan. Among them were Oscar Rumy, Alarice Martinez, Aldo de Micheli, Alfredo Castelnuovo, Rogelio Gamba, Jorge Tresca, Adela y Clara Elortondo, particularly helped by Luis de Ridder and his wife May Parkins.

The Second World Championships were held at Cypress Gardens with about a dozen countries and 30 competitors taking part.

Claude de Clercq further recalls: 'When we went to Cypress Gardens in December 1950, we had not had the slightest training since the end of September. The tricks event was held on an icy cold day. I remember that in the car parks all radiators were switched on and they had fires everywhere in the Gardens so that the exotic plants would not perish.'

Although Dick Pope, with a dazzling Slalom, won the Over-all, he was closely followed by Claude de Clercq, while Guy de Clercq 'showed the Americans how to jump', by setting a new World Record of 25·6 m *84 ft*, followed very closely by Dick Pope and Jake McQuire.

Guy and Dick jumped about the same distance, and it was decided that in the case of such a small difference, the film of the event would be used to decide on the winner. A light plane took the film to be developed in Winterhaven, and some hours afterwards Claude de Clercq was invited, as Captain of the European team, to witness the projection.

'I was very astonished to be alone to see this, with as sole witness the projectionist; not one American representative was there. In Europe, I would have had at least ten people alongside me looking with a magnifying-glass to see whose was the longest jump and the discussion would have gone on for hours. The issue was settled in several minutes, the American projectionist came out of the tent and shouted to the officials "It's the Belgian boy who has won!" and no questions were asked.'

The exquisite Willa Worthington won the Tricks and Over-all titles, performing the 'swivel swan' she had already successfully used both in the US Nationals and also for her water-ski ballet sequences. This trick depended on a swivel binder and before long had been outlawed from tournaments on the grounds that it was a gadget inaccessible to ordinary skiers since it was not commercially available.

Unfortunately it was at these first World Championships that the young International Waterskiing Union was almost destroyed. During the Congress of 25 November, serious differences of opinion arose concerning the general organisation of the Union. The American Association withdrew, inviting other federations to join

them. They were followed by Canada, Mexico and the Argentine. These four countries created a new world organisation which was called the World Water Ski Federation.

However, on the resignation of President Albert Schmidt from the IWSU in January 1951, European federations began to resume friendly relations with countries in the WWSF, and the lengthy process of re-unification began.

In July 1951, a Danish national team participated for the first time in an international championship in Lausanne, Switzerland. It comprised Fleur Dahl, Bent Stig Møller and Axel Ottesen. To quote Møller:

'I shall never forget the first day of practise in Geneva. When we came down to the dock with our skis, we were asked what we wanted to do. Little knowing that water-skiing was divided up into three events, we answered that we would like to water-ski.'

In a few days they learnt more than ever before about water-skiing. Up to that time they had never seen a slalom ski – yet Møller was placed sixth in slalom. 'I remember how everyone gasped at Lausanne when Bernard Coliere did a back-swan – one of the first in Europe.' The Danish Association, which was actually only a club, grew larger, although membership had to be limited owing to the lack of a club boat. In Stockholm, Ragnar Frunck had started the Swedish Water Ski Club and began ski-training.

Italy held its first national championships that year, divided into three heats held at Stresa, at Santa Margherita and at Menaggio, with 30 skiers competing. After its success the Italian Federation held the first of a series of International contests, organised by the Santa Margherita Club for the Miramare Trophy. Italian skiers fell short of the skills attained by the Belgians, French and Swiss, although in defeat they learnt a great deal.

Guido Colnaghi is the athlete who certainly merits mention as the first supreme Italian champion. He was instructor at the Santa Margherita School, where with the collaboration of Luciano Mosti, Piatti, Baldoni, Ansbacher, Bettoni and others, he succeeded in creating a group of young, well-trained skiers capable of succeeding abroad.

There was a similar situation in France, where the members of two large clubs had begun to dominate national water-skiing and to shine in European competition. These clubs were the Nautical Club of Juan-les-Pins and the Rhône Yacht Club and future French champions always came from either of these clubs.

Also in 1951, when the well-known American show-skier Jeanette Burr spent a considerable time skiing in Anschluss at Grossglockner-Skirennen in Velden, a number of Austrians became fascinated by the sport.

Liesl Schuh-Feichtinger, Karl Fischer, Rudi Kreuzhuber in Velden, Frau Felder de Rook and Robert Mureny in Reifnitz, Bibi Grossl, Erwin Lang, Bruno Pich, Walter and Max Schludermann, Prof Knobloch and H. Brauchart in Portschach became the pioneers in Austria. Bibi Grossl, some friends and the boat-builder Wunder got together to produce skis, taking the design and methods directly from the French and the Belgians. Bruno Pich made a binding, in which he fitted tennis shoes on to a 2 m *6½ ft* plank, 0·5 m *1·6 ft* wide.

With the first clubs formed in Velden, on the Worthersee, and in Portschach, the Austrian Water Ski Federa-

The Swiss Marina Doria demonstrating the two ski side-slide (see page 54).

tion was then created by Messrs von Fodermayer, Maurizio and Schuh in Velden.

In the United States, Willa Worthington won the Slalom, Tricks and Jumping events, and the Over-all title for the sixth consecutive time at the US Nationals held on Lake Placid, New York. Her winning trick speciality was the 180° Swan. Dick Pope won the Men's Tricks, Skillman Suydam, the National Junior Boys' Champion in 1949 and 1950, won the Men's Slalom and Over-all, and the Junior Boys title was a walkover for Suydam's former rival, Emilio Zamudio of Mexico. The following year, Zamudio himself won all the Men's events, except for the Jump, which was won by a Mexican skier, who instead of heading straight for the ramp, cut across from the right and accelerated towards it – this innovator was Alfredo Mendoza.

The year also saw the start of water-skiing in Colombia, South America, particularly in the towns of Bogotá and Barrancabermeja. Los Lagartos ('Lizards') Lake in

Bogotá and Del Miedo ('Fear') Lake in Barrancabermeja saw pioneers such as Oscar Boza, Daniel D'Costa and Eduardo Lemon enjoying themselves on skis.

In 1952, the American Water Ski Association extended control of the sport across the United States, when its President Chuck Sligh Jr directed his six Regional Vice-Presidents to 'keep in touch with all water-skiing activities in the area which they represent, authorise AWSA sanction of local events where they deem it desirable and within the aims of the AWSA, assist in all sanctioned events and make recommendations for any necessary action by the Board'. Perhaps this was the first concerted attempt to tackle growth problems on a scale which was to appear in most other nations in later years.

The following year witnessed the appearance of a beautiful Swiss lady – Marina Doria. Marina's father, René, was a long-time member of the Geneva Swimming Club, and his daughter became a pupil of Monsieur Krebec at the first Swiss school of water-skiing. She made her début at the 1953 European Championships, held at Portschach in Austria, not only winning Tricks and jumping, and coming fourth in slalom, but winning the Women's Over-all title. Guy Vermeersch of Belgium won the Men's Over-all, although Luciano Mosti created a controversy in slalom. After persuading the judges that although it might be the fashion to mono-ski, there was nothing in the rules which forbade the use of *two* skis, the Italian put on his novel small narrow skis with fins and executed a couple of skilful runs to tie with Simon Khoury for the same number of buoys. In the exciting run-off, Khoury went first, and Mosti, when he came back from his attempt, went up to his rival and exclaimed, 'Is you who are the winner, Simon! I do the split leg going over one buoy!' But the judges had decided otherwise; and the title was awarded to Luciano – Simon was a very distressed and upset Lebanese skier.

Following this, Jean-Pierre Galtier won Tricks for France, and Jumping was won by a skier who had trained with Robert Baltié at the Yacht Club du Rhône called Marc Flachard.

Marc Flachard of France, European jumping champion 1953–55.

In the US Nationals, Willa Worthington made a comeback by winning Women's Jumping and (for the seventh time) Tricks, although Leah Maria Rawls won Slalom and the Over-all. The Men's Slalom, Tricks and Over-all were won by a brilliant 19-year-old, lanky schoolteacher from Troy, New York, named Warren Witherall. Witherall brought to skiing the approach of a US Football pro and was to break many a towline in his prime.

That year the World Jumping Record had climbed past the 27·43 m *90 ft* barrier. After Bob Nathey of Cypress Gardens hit the 27·43 m *90 ft* mark at the Lakeland Tournament, Alfredo Mendoza followed with 27·74 m *91 ft*, Warren Witherall with 29·26 m *96 ft*, and again – at the US Nationals – Alfredo Mendoza with 29·56 m *97 ft*.

The Golden Age of Mexican water-skiing had now dawned. With Tequesquitengo, Acapulco, Merida and Chihuahua as the principal sites, Alfredo Mendoza, Emilio Zamudio, Carlos Elias and Quirino Ramirez became the best in the world and, with Miguel Cobo and Raymundo Villegas, they travelled all over the world teaching and training people in competition water-skiing.

Also in 1953, Mr Nakajima became Chairman of the very first official water-ski club in Japan – the Hakone Ashinoko Club. The first Japanese contest was held on Lake Ashinoko with eighteen skiers competing.

Austrian water-skiing which by now had seen its first two Nationals at Velden, had spread – thanks to Otto Fischer, Ing. Donner and Herr Brauchart of the Portschach WSC – on to the Salzkammergut-See, to Seewalchen on the Attersee, in St Gilgen on the Wolgangsee and in Gmunden on the Traunsee.

Despite the continuing rift between the IWSU and the WWSF, the fact that many countries were members of both organisations enabled the World Championships to be held that September at Toronto, Canada, as part of the Canadian National Exhibition. It was at this tournament that Alfredo Mendoza made his revolutionary double cut to jump 27·80 m *91 ft* and win the Jumping and Over-all titles.

It was about this time that throughout the world, the general public was being introduced to the glamorous and spectacular side of water-skiing by way of two films.

Not long after his Akwa-Skees had stopped selling in the 1930s, that 'tinkering genius' Fred Waller had become deeply involved in pioneering a new 3-D cinema technique. Twenty years later, on 30 September 1952, the fruits of Waller's experiments were revealed when 'This is Cinerama' opened in a Broadway theatre. Produced by Merion C. Cooper and narrated by journalist-broadcaster Lowell Thomas, the idea was to present the familiar through the '3-D Sensation', Niagara Falls, the Grand Canyon, flying shots across country, a ride on a roller-coaster and – as might have been expected from Fred Waller's friendship with the Pope brothers – a visit to Cypress Gardens to see the 'Greatest Show on Water'.

The significance for water-skiing is that 'This is Cinerama' ran on Broadway for nearly two-and-a-half years, breaking all box office records. It did the same in cities across the US and round the world. It grossed some thirty million dollars at a time when motion pictures were in a deep depression because of the television boom. Fred Waller died on 18 May 1954, hailed as the 'Father of Water Skiing' and the 'Inventor of Cinerama'.

The inimitable Willa Worthington, water-ski ballet innovator.

Emilio Zamudio, one of Mexico's champion skiers during the 1950s.

At the time of his death, yet another film, also shot in Technicolor at Cypress Gardens, was running in ordinary cinemas throughout the world. Metro-Goldwyn-Mayer's 2½-million-dollar production of the musical comedy 'Easy to Love' was made to commemorate the famous Hollywood company's Thirtieth Anniversary. With their glamorous and daring aqua-stunt queen, Esther Williams, MGM had hit on a formula for success – Esther had starred in some seventeen pictures since 1942, and with her eighteenth, director Charles Walters placed her, Van Johnson, Tony Martin and the countless and elegant Busby Berkeley Chorus Girls in the glamorous setting of Florida's Cypress Gardens, with songs by Cole Porter.

Esther Williams in a sequence in the film *Easy to Love* showing her learning to ski.

Together, 'Easy to Love' and 'This is Cinerama' not only provided some of the most spectacular and sensational water carnival scenes ever shot, but well and truly placed water-skiing on the map.

That year 1954 also saw the 'Swan Song' of the Belgian de Clercq twins. Claude recalls: 'Guy and I left water-skiing when we were 31 years old; there was nothing left for us to prove. We had developed equipment and techniques, and we had totted up all the titles from 1948 to 1952. In fact I had beaten Guy at the Belgian Championships, while each time at the European and World Championships, he had beaten me.'

Right: Under the expert choreography of Willa Worthington the water-ski ballet at Cypress Gardens soon become a superbly co-ordinated spectacle.

Below: A water-skiing first at Cypress Gardens in 1960. There are seven Johnson-engined motor boats and – 50 skiers!

In addition to the loss of the de Clercqs, the Belgians were now denied the use of Genval as a training base – again by the irate local fishermen. However, there were three other water-skiing centres in the country: the Royal Yachting Club of Ghent at Langerbrugge; the Neptunus Club at Baarode; and the Antwerp Waterski Club, while later on there was the Skianna, also at Antwerp. For the next twenty years, Skianna was to be the foremost club in Belgium with champions de Kinder, Stevens and Salik. During the first decade an exception was Jean-Pierre Delcuve from Profondeville.

In Argentina, the first public demonstrations took place on the Luján river, including tricks, humorous numbers and a ski-ballet with choreography and costumes by the indefatigable Mrs Luis de Ridder (*née* Parkins).

The late summer of 1954 saw three Slovenians – Marjan Magusar, Milan Bernik and Max Zavrsnik – water-skiing across the artificial lake created by a 2-year-old hydro-electric dam, near the village of Zbilje, not far from Medvode in Yugoslavia.

Marjan Magusar, Yugoslavia's water-skiing pioneer who first skied in 1954.

Although the Gusar Club had done some pre-war aquaplaning on the River Sava in Zagreb (tying the aquaplane to a bridge on a long rope and using the strong flowing current as a substitute for a motorboat), it was not until 1950 that Max Zavrsnik, functionary of the Enotnost snow-skiing club in Ljubljana, came across the idea that water-skiing would be a good form of training for Alpine skiing. As they were only amateurs at the time, they had difficulties in buying a motorboat. Help eventually came from Kalman Hodoscek, who was employed at the Jozef Stefan Institute in Ljubljana, and who provided them with a Volkswagen motor from an old German boat which he re-installed into a wooden boat which he had himself manufactured. Skis were obtained through the help of Rudi Finzgar, former Director of the Elan factory which manufactured prototype water-skis.

They were later faced with difficulties in getting their old worn-out Volkswagen unit both to start up and then to continue during a ski run, but it was in such circumstances that water-skiing was begun in Yugoslavia.

Water-skiing now appeared around Hong Kong Harbour where some expatriate businessmen bought ski boats and kept them alongside their pleasure junks and, with a pair of skis, were ready to entertain customers and visitors from overseas.

Italian water-skiing continued to grow, particularly in the South, after the success of a National Championships heat held at Anzio, which drew great interest from Naples, Capri and other centres in that tourist zone. A Juniors contest was also held by the Santa Margherita Ligure Club, won by Franco Carraro and Piera Castelvetri who, along with Doris Pignatelli, were to become the new champions from Italy. But above all, this country was honoured with the responsibility of holding the 1954 European Championships in Milan.

Since 1951, much discussion had gone on between the International Water Ski Union and the World Water Ski Federation, to reach general agreement. On 12 April 1955, after many meetings held at Cypress Gardens, Sarasota and New York, the principals in the Union and the Federation finally agreed to a fusion. On that day the World Water Ski Union (WWSU) was formed. Dan Hains, President of the WWSF and his secretary, on the one hand, and André Coutau as Secretary-General of the IWSU on the other hand, signed the protocol of this memorable agreement. William Geneux of Switzerland, was appointed as first president of the WWSU.

The most difficult task was to decide on the fundamental principles for drawing up a new constitution, giving satisfaction to both sides, especially concerning the organisation of the groups and of their roles in the various committees. A committee was set up to prepare provisional statutes. Some 21 National Federations were recognised by the WWSU. A committee of five members: Charles Sligh Jr, Dick Pope Sr and Jr, Simon Khoury and André Coutau, was formed to prepare temporary regulations immediately after the fusion, taking into consideration the wishes of the two former bodies. The problem of the technical rules was also checked in readiness for the next World Championships, due to be held in the Lebanon.

The Union divided the world into a series of five geographical groups, one for each continent. For immediate purposes, three were organised straight away:

Group 1: North, South and Central America
Group 2: Europe, Africa, Near East and Middle East
Group 3: Australia, Japan, the Pacific and Far East.

Other groups were to be formed as the need arose.

The South African Water Ski Association joined Group 2 in 1955, through the enthusiastic efforts of Monty Tolkin, the Association's first President. Tolkin recalls that the inaugural meeting of the SAWSA was held in Johannesburg with Claude Cartoon, Harvey Flowers, Jimmy Hall, Ken Campbell, Claude Warne, Andy Willox, Max Bohm, Martin Cohen, several others and himself. This group, forming the Riviera Aquatic Club in the Transvaal, organised the first South African Water Ski Championships. 'We set about building a ramp to WWSU specifications. We did not know how to measure distances so the judging was based primarily on general form and approach. In slalom, we arrived at our champion by increasing boat speed by 2 mph for each successful run from a starting speed of approximately 26 mph. In those early years there were about 10 to 12 men and 3 to 4 lady competitors.'

In 1955, they were asked as a National Body to send a team to give a skiing demonstration, including ramp jump show, at the Livingstone Centenary Celebrations in Rhodesia. The Regatta which embraced powerboat racing, canoeing and rowing between Rhodesia and South Africa, included a water-ski demonstration. Since there were either no skiers in Rhodesia or none who were prepared to ski on the Zambesi, the South Africans filled the gap. At Livingstone, some four miles from the Victoria Falls, the Zambesi River flows at about 10 knots. Shortly before they went skiing, a Rhodesian very kindly (and possibly maliciously) showed them the *crocodile farm* some several hundred yards from the venue and told them that due to the noise of the powerboats, all crocodiles and hippo in the vicinity would be well away!

'We went ahead with our various little acts with great trepidation and bulging eyes,' remembers Tolkin. 'Harvey Flowers and myself had the misfortune to fall off our skis. Harvey fell while doing a slalom and was taken from the water almost out of his wits, as the boat which was towing him took about a minute to come back to him due to engine failure.

'My fall can also be substantiated since it was witnessed by the then Governor-General of Rhodesia, together with a crowd of some 4000 persons who were in the Grand Stand overlooking the ramp. As South African Champion and Ramp Jump Champion, I had the privilege of being asked to do the first ramp jump off a 4 ft floating ramp, about 6 ft wide, which we had asked the Rhodesians to construct. What they did do, however, was to make it 3·60 m *12 ft* wide and at least 5·56 m *18 ft* of surface in length which created a very unsuitable ramp.

'Just as I was about to take off, a local resident jocularly remarked that, despite all assurances given that there would be no crocodiles, "Old George", was still bound to be around, since he lived in a cave very near the ramp and was some 30 ft long – definitely not scared of powerboat noises!

'Suffice it to say that before I had time to run away I was pulled off and heading for the ramp which was liberally coated with engine oil. I lined up as perfectly as I could and would feel quite happy just to get over and land on two feet. But as I hit the bottom of the ramp, I felt my skis start to turn sideways. I there and then made up my mind that there was no way I was going to land at all even on my backside.

'As I came over the top, I somehow managed to come off my skis and was facing back in the direction of the ramp and swimming in the air even before I hit the water. They tell me that not even Johnny ("Tarzan") Weismuller could have out-raced me as I swam back towards the ramp and leapt on to it like a man possessed. The crowd was quite delighted with what had happened as they had got what they came to see, and I sat shivering on the ramp like a bloody fool.

'Something told me that if I did not try again, I would never be able to come to terms with myself and accordingly I then successfully jumped the ramp a further three times.'

When shown in Japan, the film 'This is Cinerama' had stimulated an increase in the number of skiers on the beaches of Itoh and Hakone, to the point where in June 1955 a Japanese Association was founded. Mr Tsunenori Kaya was elected President, and Mr Tsunayoshi Harada, an old hand at motorboating, was made General Manager. The officials of the Skating Association and the Snow Ski Association were elected as officials of this new water-ski association, which held its first championships on 28 August 1955 on the Motor Boat Racing course of the Tama River, on the outskirts of Tokyo. Thirty-seven skiers participated, including Chinese and Americans – four being women. The competition included Slalom on twin skis and Tricks, limited to swan flights and jumps across the wash. The records were announced irrespective of sex and Mr T. Sakata succeeded in a 180° turn after removing the fins from his skis.

In Yugoslavia, the Volkswagen engine had become so bad towing the Slovenian skiers across Lake Zbilje, that Milan Bernik and Marjan Magusar decided to give up promotional demonstrations. Notwithstanding, elsewhere in Slovenia, in Maribor, Franc Vizjak and Lipokotic, members of the Sidro Club, took up the sport. It was here, not far from the Austrian border, that waterskiing behind fast boats was introduced by the Austrians, who used to come to the Drava River on Maribor Isle and participate in motorboat contests organised by the Sidro Club; at the end of these contests, they demonstrated their skiing skills to the Slovenians, who soon followed their example.

Both the European (Group 2) and World Championships, held on the open sea at St George's Bay, Beirut, Lebanon, were limited by the simple fact that with a strong Mediterranean wind, the waves prevented anyone from performing at their best. Indeed, at the beginning of the World Championships, there was such a swell – with waves 1·22 m *4 ft* high – that a competitor could be invisible because he was down in the trough, and all the boat judge could see was the tow-rope coming out from the other side of a wave. Indeed, the first four skiers in jumping were taken to hospital in ambulances which had been standing by, just in case!

With the trick runs, a competitor was allowed 100 m *328 ft*. Without a fixed time, it was possible for a competitor to do as many tricks as a slow motorboat speed would let him. Thus US skier Scotty Scott took his time to gain the most Trick points. For the rest, Alfredo Mendoza won Slalom, jumped 33·33 m *109·35 ft* and took the title of World Champion. Following the announcement of his victory in a Lebanese newspaper, a whole family of Arabian aunts, uncles and nephews, grand-parents and great-grandparents came down from the mountainside, claiming that they were Alfredo Mendoza's long-lost family and that he was no longer Mexican but Lebanese. Over-all second to Mendoza was a true Lebanese, Simon Khoury, who won Slalom, Tricks and Over-all in the Group 2 (European) Championships at Beirut. Khoury had been studying medicine in Switzerland when he had his first ski on Lake Geneva. In 1952 he had abandoned his studies and gone out to Cypress Gardens where he became a professional skier and one of the most brilliant slalomers of his era – he was also to spend many challenging years running the Cypress Gardens Ski Show.

It was also in Beirut in those unsettled waves that ravishing Marina Doria and sculptural Willa McGuire came face to face for the first and only time. Although conflicting reports state that Willa and Marina had each become the first woman competitor to do a 360° toe-turn on one ski, the record books show that although Willa won the Slalom with six buoys and Jumping with 18 m *59 ft*, it was Marina who won the Tricks. In addition Marina Doria won all three events in the Group 2 Championships, tying for Slalom with Jacqueline Keller (France) and Lisilotte Schuh (Austria). It was after these

Serge Nader, Serge Tcheky and Simon Khoury, pioneer Lebanese skiers.

Championships that Willa McGuire (*née* Worthington) gracefully retired as one of the living legends of competitive water-skiing: 'My great thrill in competitive years' she was to recall, 'was doing something in tricks that had never been done before. I was the first one to go over the jump on one ski – and make it. The backward jump on two skis was the one that really put my heart in my mouth. Everyone said I was a fool even to try it because it couldn't be done. I made it on my seventh try. Other tricks I remember being first with, were the backward swan, the swivel swan, the 180° toe-turn and the 360° toe-turn. It was a lot of fun, I had a great time.'

With the coming of 1956 Dick Pope Jr was elected second President of the World Water Ski Union and he devoted much of his time and energy over the next two years in helping to propagate the sport. One of his main aims concerned a more standard set of rules and regulations for worldwide acceptance.

It was also in 1956 that two multi-million dollar water-skiing 'Gardens', largely based on the Popes' successful ideas were opened up for shows and competition purposes.

The 109-acre horticultural wonderland that comprised Sunshine Springs and Gardens, on the outskirts of Sarasota, Florida, had been transformed from a jungle-like ranch, with pigs rooting in the underbush, in less than a year. A water stage, 274 m *900 ft* long and 152 m *500 ft* wide, made a fine setting for water-ski ballets, or three jumpers taking off from a 2·43 m *8 ft* ramp simultaneously and criss-crossing through the air. One of the Sunshine showmen was a nineteen-year-old Sarasotan who was to make a name for himself in future years – Joe Cash.

The second centre was Callaway Gardens and its 65-acre Robin Lake at the foot of Pine Mountain in South-West Georgia. Back in the 1940s the enterprising Cason

60

Four great skiers going over the same jump at Callaway Gardens. *Left to right:* Billy Spencer, Jimmy Jackson, Chuck Stearns and Ken White.

J. Callaway ('Mr Cason') created a family vacation mecca when he turned thousands of acres of eroded, farmed-out land on the northern slopes of Pine Mountain into a chain of twelve lakes. Howard H. ('Bo') Callaway, his son, joined him in the operation of the gardens in 1953. A West Pointer, the younger Callaway had served as an infantry platoon officer in the Korean War.

As an excellent snow-skier and keen water-skier 'Bo' brought a ski show to Callaway Gardens in 1954 for a weekend exhibition under the direction of Glenn Kirkpatrick. It attracted so much attention that he enlarged the show the following season, and in 1956 benefitting from the organisational and judging expertise of William D. Clifford of the AWSA hosted the first Robin Lake water-ski tournament, the Georgia Invitational. In time, Callaway Gardens was to become one of the finest tournament sites in the world.

The year also saw further stirrings in South America. An Argentinian Water Ski Club was formed and planned to build a jumping ramp in the Este Canal, while a Venezuelan Federation of Watersports was formed in Caracas including water-skiing as one of those sports.

In South Africa trick skiing was introduced in the second year of the South African Championships. In this second year, a number of entries came from Natal to the Riviera Aquatic Club. The Western Province only came to light in the fourth year of competition and, whilst the Transvaal dominated the scene in the men's section for the first two years, Natal took over thereafter through Alf Korving and then Mike Plotz. Subsequently, Western Province skiers came to the fore by leaps and bounds and names to be remembered from that source were Fred Leighton and Chonky Hampson – in the Transvaal the top skiers were Claude Cartoon, Harvey Flowers, Vic de la Porte and, of course, Monty Tolkin. Among the ladies there was really only one outstanding skier who gained Springbok Colours – Barbara Drimie of the Transvaal.

Back in Europe, in Finland, the first Watersports Club was started in Valkeakoski. The skiers from this club went out to Cypress Gardens to train and also received a visit from the Cypress Gardens skiing troupe on a world tour.

Athanasious Diakakis, president of the Nautical Club of Vouliagmeni Beach, near Athens, Greece, introduced the sport to his country, and was soon joined by the Ioannides brothers, former fencing champion Elias Lypiterakos, Alexandros Bouxinos, Spiro Diakakis, Aggelos Stathatos, John Stathatos, Aggelos Lembesis and the other members of the Vouliagmeni Club.

Danish water-skiing 'grew up' in 1956 when the European (Group 2) Championships were held in Denmark, at Bagsvaerd Lake, under the leadership of the new federation president, Ole Vollmond. The Italian, Franco Carraro, won the Slalom through a course marked out for the first time in Europe by buoys made out of rubber. Frenchman Michel Kandelaft won the Jumping and sixteen-year-old Jean Marie Muller won the Tricks.

Muller's father had begun water-skiing in 1929 and Jean Marie followed suit for fun twenty years later, aged 9, at the Yacht Club du Rhône. Taught by René Giraud and Marc Flachard, he became quite proficient in tricks and not long after the Group 2 contest, Jean swallowed a great deal of water, innovating toe side-slide, for which he was given an official citation by the World Water Ski Union.

The rapidly growing water-skiing fraternity of 1957 were unaware that 50 years previously at California's Coronado Beach, people first began to enjoy a novel game called aquaplaning.

In West Germany (although there had been a pre-war ski manufacturer. based in Munich), pioneers such as Griasch, Nolte, Lieser, Appel, Jacke, Freiling and Nordmann, representing the Frankfurt WSC, the Hann Münden WSC and the Kassel WSC came together to found the Deutscher Wasserski Verband, with their first President Doktor Bergmann, and so plan their very first Nationals for 1958.

The founding during 1957, of the Milan Water-Skiing Club with 21 members, was to have considerable significance for both Italian and world skiers in the following two years. Away in Japan, televised winter water-ski contests and competitions took place between the students of Keio and Waseda Universities and after many attempts, Japan became a member of the WWSU at the invitation of Dick Pope.

In the Netherlands, the representatives of three newly-born water-ski clubs decided to organise their first unofficial National Championships, and to found the Nederlandse Waterski Bond. Among the founders were Anton Berg, Ge Roerade and Lakens Douwes, the latter being chosen as the NWB's first president and the Netherlands was welcomed into the WWSU.

The 1957 WWSU Championships were hosted by President Dick Pope Jr at Cypress Gardens. Contestants came from 29 countries and a special DC-6 was chartered to fly over the European and Middle Eastern entries. When it landed at Tampa Airport, contestants were greeted with flags flying, a brass band playing, and the sign 'Welcome Y'All World Ski Champions'. Three

Prize-giving at the 1957 World Championships. *From left to right:* Marina Doria (Switzerland), Simon Khoury (Lebanon), Leah Maria Atkins (USA), Joe Cash (USA), Piera Castelvetri (Italy), Emilio Zamudio (Mexico).

separate training areas were placed at their disposal during the ten-day training period, but they were warned about Lake Eloise's resident crocodiles, led by 'George', and also of the poisonous water moccasins lurking in the vicinity of the jump!

The championships opened with a parade of national flags, while a giant Hammond organ played excerpts from the various national anthems.

Perhaps the most exciting and spectacular battle took place between Simon Khoury and Joe Cash for the Men's Slalom, watched by millions of television viewers. In the fourth and final run-off, Khoury tagged seven buoys, while Cash tagged a winning eight. After three exciting run-offs Marina Doria just beat Piera Castelvetri in the Women's Slalom.

Joe Cash on the Robin Lake Slalom Course at Callaway Gardens. He was killed in a tragic accident in the summer of 1967.

The Swiss World Team. Marina Doria encircled by her team-mates.

The Italian World team.

Since the World Championships at Beirut in 1955, a new technical rule had come into force, for Tricks. Instead of the two 100 m *109 yd* runs, the Union calculated at a given speed that for 100 m the time should be 20 sec. So at Cypress Gardens the imposition was one of time instead of distance.

At first, the judges had given Mexican Carlos Elias, the unofficial first in Tricks, placing France's Jean Marie Muller second and Mike Amsbry of Orange, California, third. But after figuring the complicated scoring all night and well into the following day, the judges gave first to Amsbry and third to Elias while Muller retained second place. It was in this tournament that Muller had executed, for the first time in world competition a side-slide toe-hold, which he had to hold for three seconds. Again Marina Doria only just beat Piera Castelvetri in Tricks. The 'Jumpin' Joes' – Cash of Sarasota and Mueller of McQueeny (Texas) – fought it out over the ramp, with Mueller making the winning 37·80 m *124 ft*, and Cash spilling on landing. Jean Marie Muller took a spectacular fall in jumping – 'I nearly killed myself, to the great joy of American TV, who wanted me to do it again'.

Nancie Rideout soared gracefully to 23·50 m *77 ft* for the Women's title, with Scarlet Voris of Honolulu coming third. The Over-all champions were Joe Cash and Marina Doria.

Among other things, the following year 1958 saw the publication of one of the classic books on the sport. Published by Prentice Hall Inc. *Water Skiing* had been written by the Popes, father and son, and 'all of us here at Cypress Gardens', with an Introduction by Cinerama-famous Lowell Thomas and the Preface by TV's Ed Sullivan. It served as both instruction-manual and selected history. Despite its mistaken instruction methods and slightly inaccurate history section, parts of it are well worth quoting to show the contemporary state of worldwide water-skiing at that time.

The first paragraph, dramatically ghost-written by Al McFadye, reads: 'If the pilot of a fast jet plane could race the sun around the globe, he would look down on countless thousands of happy people enjoying the exciting sport of water-skiing on the lakes, bays, rivers, lagoons, gulfs, coves, inlets, bayous and oceans of many continents.'

It continues: '. . . skiing is enjoyed throughout Brazil, Argentina, Peru and Chile. On our recent tour through South America, my wife and I found country after country where enthusiasm for water-skiing was just fantastic. In Brazil, Peru, Colombia and Uruguay we found bodies of water teeming with water skiers. They have a series of lakes 86 miles long in São Paulo, Brazil, where skiers enjoy the sport twelve months of the year . . . water-skiing is catching on even in Singapore and Malaya, according to Lionel Horety, president of the Malayan Water Ski Association. The sport is at fever pitch and skiing is a year round activity in the Singapore area. It is found throughout Malaya, Sarawak in North Borneo, and Brunei. Horety further attested to skiing in Djakarta, Indonesia, and on a not too desirable river in Bangkok, Siam.'

During the year of publication, Pope Sr and his wife, Julie, flew on a 75-day circumnavigation of the globe. Writing of their journey in *The Water Skier* magazine, Dick Pope Sr stated: 'Our first stop was Hawaii where the Kaiser Interests have built at the Hawaiian Village a beautiful sleepy lagoon perfect for tournament purposes . . . Japan was next where they have a federation consisting of 5500 members. Believe me, over there is Banzai water-skiing. They are great water-skiing fans and can they eat with chop sticks! . . . In Hong Kong after the big gala show they gave us, the headlines in the daily newspaper said, "Deep Water Bay takes on Cypress Gardens Appearance." Here are perhaps the most expert skiers in the Far East led by Rick Remedios and Luigi Roza. This big club with their President, S. M. Churn, and Commodore Tseng, the godfather of water-skiing in Hong Kong, is planning many big tournaments in the future . . .

'In Manila most of the skiing is done by the Americans who are in the Service. Tommy Bartlett's Show gave them a great push forward when they toured there.

'Singapore with its new president Bryan Blakeborough and a transplanted Australian, Lionel Horety, staged another special show for us and on the Fourth of July had a terrific crowd out to see their annual water-ski spectacular.

'In Thailand we missed the skiing King who had left Bangkok on a three-week vacation but the Princess "Chumphot" is one of the better skiers and Dr Oei (pronounced Wee) has a rabid crew who have beautiful waters to ski on . . . In Iran we were with the Shah at his summer palace, Shenran. He has a group of skiers with a club on the Caspian Sea. We saw no skiing in Egypt and only two people skiing in the Bosporus which separates Asia and Europe at Istanbul.'

One place which Dick Pope did not visit was the Soviet Union, where in 1958, the first water-skiing competition took place inshore from the Baltic Sea, at Riga in the Latvian Republic. Although the best jumps were no further than 15 m *49·2 ft* at least it was a beginning.

In Spain, the first championships of Catalonia were held on Lake Banolas with such pioneer Spaniards as Victor Ivanow, Mariano Puig, Andres Morros, Gregory, Pujol and Monjo competing. Spain's first National Championships came the following year.

There was also a beginning in Alaska, where members of the Arctic Aqua Club introduced water-skiing to the Eskimos, and at the 1958 Americas' Cup in Miami, a Venezuelan team was able to observe at close-hand, competitive quality skiing over an official ramp, and through a slalom and trick course. They returned to Caracas with something to aim at.

At the Group 2 Championships of 1958, France continued to win everything in Europe. Maxime Vazeille of the Juan-les-Pins Club won the Tricks and Over-all, while Jean Marie Muller won Slalom and Jumping. Second in Tricks was a promising 16-year-old French newcomer to competition, called Philippe Logut.

Logut's father had first put him on water-skis in 1946 when he was only four years old. With almost exclusive use of his father's speedboat, Philippe had been skiing for ten years when he was 'noticed' by Mademoiselle Homo at Juan-les-Pins, who gave him the virtual freedom of the club. Maxime Vazeille and Jacqueline Keller, members of the Provençal Club, had further encouraged him. In 1956, very taken by the graceful ease of Marina Doria's style, he began to concentrate on tricks. A keen gymnast, Logut soon turned the springiness in his style into a deceptive and elegant lightness and he appeared to have a promising future.

Also in the 1958 Group 2 Championships, Piera Castelvetri beat Marina Doria in Tricks, Slalom and Over-all, leaving Renate Hansluwska to win the jumping. This was the final time that Marina Doria appeared in International competition. It is a story rather like a fairy tale, as for some time Crown Prince Umberto of Italy had been courting this beautiful water-ballerina, until she finally accepted him, to become a Princess of water-skiing. She is still the only European to have won three European titles in succession and in her career she took 23 championships back to Switzerland.

The year 1959 saw the first of what was to be an epic and annual competition in Georgia. The Ida Cason Callaway Gardens Invitational Tournament (so named after Bo's grandmother, and from the following year onwards called the US Masters after the famous Georgian Golf Tournament) took place on 27 and 28 June. Some of the rules were practically rewritten to eliminate several time-consuming delays in an effort to make the sport faster and more interesting for spectators without affecting competition. About 16000 spectators gathered at Robin Lake Beach to see among other things, blonde tomboy, Barbara Cooper, leave even skiers breathless with a 27·74 m *91 ft* leap to take first place in the girl's division and set the girls' record even higher than the women's World mark of 27·13 m *89 ft* held by Nancie Rideout.

The US Nationals, watched by 30000 spectators, were held on Lake Opeechee, Laconia, New Hampshire and saw Over-all victories for Yankee Mike Osborn, Nancie Rideout, Fred Pendlebury, Vicki Van Hook and Henry Holmes ('Paul Bunyan of the South') in the various categories. Athletic Mike Osborn's 43·30 m *142 ft* jumping mark tied with the record that Joe Cash had set at Fort Myers earlier in the season.

Both the Group 2 Championships and the World Championships were held that year just outside Milan, Northern Italy, at the Idroscalo.

The World Championships had 100 contestants representing 22 countries (including South Africa and Japan) competing in front of five judges.

Former World Champion, Joe Cash, had injured his leg jumping in the Nationals and voluntarily withdrew from the US team. Thus 'Flea', Chuck, Buster and the two 'Mikes' (Osborn and Amsbry), accompanied by Nancie Rideout, Vicki Van Hook and Janelle Kirtley, flew over to successfully defend their world title, winning six out of the eight Gold Medals, in spectacular style.

The weather conditions during the tournament were unseasonable with chilly temperatures, overcast skies, and even rain and rough water during the Men's Slalom, when Chuck Stearns had the final run-off with Jean Marie Muller. In the Women's Slalom – rubber buoys were now obligatory for safety reasons – 15-year-old Vicki Van Hook of San Diego, California, gave the best performance of her skiing career, to beat Piera Castelvetri.

Buster McCalla 38·70 m *127 ft* and Nancie Rideout 25·30 m *83 ft* made successful double-cuts to win the Jumping titles, although Jean Marie Muller came a close second.

Milan's Idroscalo, site of the 1959 World Championships.

But the real turn-up for the record books came during the trick-riding events, when the almost entirely European audience went mad with cheering and applause to see Piera Castelvetri and Philippe Logut tricking with supreme elegance and swiftness to well-earned victories. The World Rules recognised air tricks on the one condition that they at least cleared the wake of the towboat – and Castelvetri and Logut used these to great advantage.

Although Chuck Stearns won the Over-all, *Jr Girl* Vicki Van Hook went past Nancie Rideout to win the Women's Over-all, with Piera Castelvetri second. The Japanese contestant, Masanori Komorimya managed to jump 18·90 m *62 ft* and came 39th over-all.

Perhaps the hairiest incident came during the Slalom, when one contestant in the Men's Division stretched hard for the sixth buoy and just made it by inches. As he zoomed past the buoy, he lost the rope and at a good speed sailed up over the ramp, which was situated outside the slalom course!

The WWSU Congress was held by Lake Como, where William Geneux was again elected as third President over the 30 Federations and technical rules were finalised and printed.

Soon after this, some newsreel films of the Milan Championship were seen by a group of Czechoslovakians. They were sufficiently impressed to take out the only available 30-year-old Johnson outboard-engined motorboats and home-made skis on the upper reaches of the Ultava River and established the first official water-ski club in the ČSSR with Jaroslav Malik as its president. Malik was very effective as both publicist and instructor in the years to come.

In South America on 1 September 1959, the first Colombian Nationals were sponsored by a company called Ecopetrol on the lake of San Silvestre, near Barrancabermeja with the Ecopetrol, Medellin and Santa Marta clubs taking part.

Elsewhere, the New Zealand Water Ski Association was formed, and in January 1960, held their first Nationals at sun-drenched Marlborough Sound, South Island, with the fullest co-operation of the Harbour Board there – even to the extent of diverting an ocean-going vessel to allow uninterrupted running of the championship – with victors coming from the Rotorua Water Ski Club, and their training base on Blue Lake.

Meanwhile, back at Cypress Gardens, the Popes once again came up with a photographic water-skiing 'First', when with a complex system of tow-ropes and seven brand-new Johnson outboards, a massive V-formation of pennant-carrying skiers combed across Lake Eloise.

Within the various national structures 1960 was a boom year for the growth of the sport. In France, there were ten Leagues, made up of one or more Academies – Brittany, Champagne, Central South-east, Dauphine-Savoie, Île de France, Midi-Pyrenees, Mediterranean Côte D'Azur, East, Loire Valley and South-west. The ever-increasing clubs installed on the geographic territory of these Academies were obliged to belong to the Regional League, on which they depended. In Switzerland the centre of water-skiing interest had shifted away from Geneva, and now there were fourteen clubs belonging to the Swiss Federation, including Zurich, Chillon Viznau, and Montreux – where for over twenty years an International tournament had been held annually.

It was also in 1960 that Joseph Ben David and his friends, formed a club called PEP (Pilgrims Exodus Pyramid) in Israel, with plans for developing Lake Tiberias (the Sea of Galilee) into a water playground for Israelis and tourists who could go water-skiing from the Degania Kibbutz at the end of the warm, calm lake.

Meanwhile, one of Australia's younger skiers, Ron Marks had begun to carve a niche for himself in the national record books. Marks has recalled:
'In the early 1950s, the gods of Senior competitive water-skiing in Australia were Ray Leighton and Bill Grenfell, together with guys like Jimmy Roder, George Baynon and Wally Smith. Bill Grenfell was a policeman and was revered as a trick skier in Australia, as the only person capable of Wake Turnarounds 180°. If you could do a side-slide, a 180 and a 360, you were pretty damned

good. Grenfell was the only guy that had ever done this in a tournament. The girl champions at that period were Betty Leighton, who had won the Nationals hat-trick three times, and Beverly Bauman.

'I didn't ski in a tournament at all until I was fourteen, in 1958, which was the first year they introduced Junior events into the Nationals, held at a disused reservoir called Manley Dam, near Sydney.

'There were only two events. It was the first time I had seen a slalom course and I had the rules explained to me on the beach, just prior to going out. Even when a kid I was always interested in anything to do with balance and speed – such as motor-racing – and slalom skiing's nothing else but getting from one buoy to another in the fastest possible time. It was pretty interesting but straightforward because the speeds were quite low and I came second in the Junior Division.

'I also won Tricks. On the Hawkesbury River, which is very tidal, it was impossible to put down a slalom course, or even a jump, and of course there were regulations laid down by the Maritime Services Board, which prohibited the implanting of any solid obstacle in the waterway. So I specialised in Tricks. At that stage in Australia there were no Junior jumping competitions, and I was unable to win the Over-all, but, at least I had been noticed.'

Surfers Paradise Gardens, on the southern coast of Queensland, on the eastern shores of Australia, had been born at Christmas-tide 1955 as a water-ski school. From an idea nurtured by the dynamic Keith Williams, came the conviction that here existed an opportunity to create an Australian equivalent of Cypress Gardens. Since this time Nature had not provided any ready-made wonderlands, it was decided that the ideal location was a 200-acre tract in rural country with three-quarters of a mile bordering on the Nerang River. Before long, Williams was managing a 1½-hour daily Water Ski Revue, sometimes put on by floodlights at night – and Surfers Paradise had become a leading resort on Queensland's Gold Coast.

Ron Marks recalls: 'By 1959 Surfers Paradise Gardens was well under way and you had a very close-knit group of people skiing on the Nerang River. There were the five members of the Birmingham family (including Colin, Jack and Kevin), who were crash-hot skiers with a farm opposite the Gardens. It was here that we skied during the 1959 Nationals.

'It was also in the same year that I skied on Melbourne's Yarra River – we reckon it's the only river that runs upside down! – at the very first Moomba Masters tournament. Rex Carnegie, the managing director of Sports Marine (concessionaires for the Mercury outboard engine in Australia) came up with the idea of running a contest on the Yarra River, offering substantial prizes for each event. The prizes were products of his company – ie an outboard engine or a fibre-glass boat. The contest coincided with the City of Melbourne's Moomba Festival and the skiing was watched by a public holiday crowd of 200 000 riverside spectators, not to mention millions of nationwide TV viewers. Therefore it captured everybody's imagination, and came to be repeated each year – as the Moomba Masters in emulation of the US Masters.

'The 1960 Nationals were also held on the Yarra River; it was my first year in the Senior Division and I don't think some of the Seniors – being somewhat

parochial – were too impressed when I won Tricks, Slalom and Over-all. It was comments made by other people that just made me decide to go for water-skiing as a career and do better at it than anybody ever had in Australia.'

Apart from regular tournaments, 1961 saw two new and interesting championships for the sport and a hard fought World Championship, almost taken from the United States.

For some time, Group 2 had realised that training in the warm waters of the Mediterranean gave France and Italy an unfair advantage over the remaining 'coldwater' countries. At the suggestion of Philippe deBacker of Belgium, himself an experienced WWSU judge, half a dozen countries above the Nordic Belt, formed the Northern European Federation, with deBacker as first president.

One of the NEF countries was the Netherlands, where Gé Roerade had been undisputed national champion for the past four years.

Another was Norway, which had suffered badly from post-War growing pains. In 1947, the first attempt to form a water-ski club had been made by Tomm Murstad, together with Konrad Bryde and Stein Eriksen (1952 Winter Olympics Slalom Champion). But the club had to be disbanded due to restrictions from the authorities on speed limits and safety. In 1950, Murstad had become trainer of the Norwegian Olympic Team, and put on shows with them around Norway. It was not until 1 March 1961, that Vannskiklubben-61 (Water-Ski Club – 61) was formed by Knut Hauge, Leif-Jørgen Ulleberg and Bjorne Arentz, who had learnt the sport during a stay in the United States. Simultaneously the Norwegian Water-ski Federation was formed and affiliated to the WWSU two months later.

Finland also came into NEF and in 1961, Mr Rikkonen, the chairman of Valkeakoski and Mr Penti Barck from Jyvaskyla decided to arrange a National Championship in Valkeakoski in September. There were eight women and fifteen men skiers. Events were Slalom and Jumping with the rules taken partly from the WWSU and partly set by the Finnish judges. After the competition the Finnish Water-ski Association was established and members came from Valkeakoski, Pori, Helsinki, Hanko and Jyvaskyla. The first President was Mr Rikkonen and Vice-President Mr Barck.

Other NEF countries were Britain, Denmark, Sweden and Belgium and the first championships were held that July at Stilling, Denmark, with Jean-Pierre Delcuve, Belgian airline pilot and national champion, winning the Men's Over-all from Mike Cooper-Simpson of Britain.

It was also in 1961 that the very first West Indies Water-Skiing Championships were held in front of the Arawak Hotel in Ochi Rios, Jamaica. The story of how this tournament came to be is worth telling. In 1958, Richard Cowell and David Nations were on a jet-set tour, buying up property on the islands. Nations recalls: 'Dick and I soon saw the possibility of drumming up interest in water-skiing in the Caribbean. So while Dick concentrated on Jamaica, Anguilla, Antigua and Barbuda, I went to Trinidad and Tobago, and then on to stay in Barbados at the newly opened Sandy Lane Hotel. There I asked the manager, who was ex-Claridges (London), if he'd mind my putting a little note in the local newspaper to the effect: "Visitor to Sandy Lane Hotel, David

Nations, the National Coach, is giving a cocktail party for anyone on the island interested in water-skiing." Quite a number of enthusiasts turned up, among them a consultant surgeon called Jack Leacock, and Lord Beaverbrook's daughter, the Honourable Janet Kidd. In no time at all I was teaching them to ski and they had elected me to be President of the Barbados Water Ski Association. The following year I went back, and after organising a slalom course in Holetown Bay, we had a jump built, which was anchored in the bay alongside the Barbados Yacht Club, just opposite the Government buildings. Every day, on their way home, huge crowds of Barbadians would stop to watch us jumping with great awe and much applause. A wonderful new sport had come to this holiday island. The following year I moved to Trinidad, to set up the Trinidadian Water Ski Association.'

For the first International and the first West Indies Water-Ski Championships combined – held at Ochi Rios, Dick Cowell brought over Joe Cash, Mike Osborn, Simon Khoury and Al Tyll, and David Nations invited Jean Marie Muller and Jean Pierre Delcuve from Europe in addition to the people that they had trained throughout the Islands – Walter ('Gillie') Byles, Jennifer Stephenson, Ernest Smatt, 'Peanuts' Diverti, André Tomas, and the son of a Canadian banker working in Kingston, Jamaica, named Pete Brady (later a BBC Disc Jockey).

World Champion, Jean Marie Muller.

Larry Penacho of the USA and one of the sport's more colourful jumpers. In the tournaments of the sixties he gave fellow Californian, Chuck Stearns, a run for his money and set national records of 150 and 155 ft in 1961 and 1962.

The European contingent that competed and officiated at the 1961 World Championships, Long Beach, California.

Unfortunately the competition was extremely difficult to hold because of choppy seas, but nevertheless the 10 000 West Indians on the beach loved it and they screamed and yelled practically every time a skier did a 180° turn, let alone a 360°. But probably more fun was had with a car pulling the skiers in a swimming pool and the jumpers doing helicopters off the top board on jumping skis! Nevertheless, the outcome was that Cowell was able to take a West Indian team to the VIIth World Water Ski Championships, held at Long Beach, California.

For the water-sport events of the 1932 Olympic Games, the City of Long Beach had carved from the many picturesque bays along its coast, a mile and a quarter marine stadium, with seating accommodation for about 12 000 spectators. The WWSU now comprised 33 nations (including Turkey), and nineteen of these felt sufficiently confident to send more than 60 competitors in an attempt to wrest the titles away from the United States at the stadium.

Indeed, the US team only managed to retain the Women's Slalom (Janelle Kirtley), the Men's Jumping (Larry Penacho) and the Team title. Otherwise, under refreshing ocean breezes and sometimes dazzling sunshine, Bruno Zaccardi slalomed to victory and also took the Men's Over-all back to Italy, while Sylvie Hulsemann's Tricks score was over 500 points ahead of other competitors, and her placings in Jumping (2nd) and Slalom (3rd), qualified her to take the Women's Over-all. Deservedly, Jean Marie Muller took the Tricks back to France, and Renate Hansluwska jumped to victory for Austria. It is interesting to note that placed 13th, 14th, 15th and 16th in the team standings were the West Indies, Japan, Morocco and Peru respectively.

7 The making of a champion

From left to right: David Spyer (GB), Jean Bladinaire (France), Peter Felix (GB), Simon Khoury (Lebanon), Lance Callingham (GB), Piera Castelvetri (Italy), Johnny Morris (GB), David Nations (GB), Franco Carrero (Italy), Anna Gerber (GB), Alberto Pederzani (Italy), Leo Roman (France).

By 1958 new blood had begun filtering into the 'old' club at Ruislip. It included thin 11-year-old Jeannette Stewart-Wood, gaining confidence in herself by learning to wake-jump and to slalom, Anna Gerber, and a dark young man, Lance Callingham, somewhat of a celebrity being the son of the fabulously wealthy Sir Bernard and Lady Docker. David Nations recalls that:

'I'd often seen the Docker's *Shemara* anchored off Cannes and Monte Carlo – the showpiece and jewel of all the Mediterranean luxury yachts. In about 1954, we were sunbathing on the beach at Juan les Pins, when all eyes were turned to a very trim-looking launch tying up at the pier, with a very smartly dressed officer enquiring as to my whereabouts. He invited me to go on board the *Shemara* to meet Sir Bernard and Lady Norah Docker. On board, they introduced me to their 14-year-old son Lance, and asked me if, as National Coach, I would train him. In those days, Lance was a thin, pimply-faced kid, and I felt sorry for him, because he really needed something to fight for – he had everything he could ever need. He was very sincere in his enjoyment of skiing, often going out six

times a day for twenty minutes at a time, to enjoy the waters of Capri, Theoule, Beaulieu, or Juan. But he wanted to learn to ski competitively. So whilst I was there, I taught him the rudiments of slalom, toe-holds and some other tricks.

'As I was leaving, he said, "Well what do I do when you go away – what could I learn?" And I don't know what made me say this, but there was a slalom course at Juan, so as a joke I said "Well why don't you ski *backwards* on a slalom ski through the course?" But Lance took me seriously.

'"How do you ski backwards?"

'"Simple, just reverse your binders," I replied, continuing to tease him.

'"When are you coming back here?"

'"Well, I expect to be back in a couple of months' time," and I let him know the date. Two months later, no sooner had I arrived than I was greeted by, "I've done it! I've done it!"

'"You've done what?"

'"I'm skiing backwards on a slalom ski."

Jeannette Stewart-Wood slaloming in the 1960s.

Lance Callingham, son of Sir Bernard and Lady Docker, with Jilly Morris and Anna Gerber during a demonstration at Roundhay Park in the 1950s.

'We went out with the boat, and as large as life, he was taking those buoys poised in reverse. I've never since seen it done by anybody else and I don't suppose I ever shall. Lance had worked so hard and I think he was rather disappointed and could not believe that it was not part of proper competition.'

Later, in 1958, Lance joined the Ruislip Water Ski Club. He was working on a two-day shift behind the scenes in television, so he could devote the rest of his time to skiing. Under the auspices of David Nations, he found that due to his solid Mediterranean grounding he was quick to learn new things. Thus the first time he jumped, he fell; but he kept his balance on both the second and third attempts and his subsequent progress was unusually steady.

One hot day before the 1958 British Championships, held at Lochearnhead, Lance was driving the Albatross for a fellow skier when the engine cover flew off. Quite badly burned, he refused to scratch from the competition and managed to take part, wearing a bulky frogman's suit all day long to protect his burned skin from the wind and water. Not only did he enter, but he also gave Peter Felix a tremendous run for his money in the Slalom.

At about this period David Nations was instrumental in the setting up of two water-skiing clubs in widely differing centres. The son of wealthy Industrialist, Charles Colson (of 'Hoover' fame), who was a Cambridge University undergraduate, invited Nations to give a lecture on the sport at Trinity College to an audience of over 400 undergraduates. This resulted in the formation of a club at the University.

This Cambridge University Water Ski Club, with all the enthusiasm but impecunity of Varsity youth, had· a water pit just big enough to allow for a four-buoy slalom, so they did not at first distinguish themselves in that competition event. As compensation, the extra practice they therefore put in on their jump, brought them splendid competitive dividends. To augment their scanty finances, the Cambridge boys – Rubin, Cooper-Simpson, Paul Catlin – approached seaside councils during the summer holidays, with offers to stage displays to entertain the holiday visitors, and the money they received in this way helped to keep the club solvent. One of their displays helped revive water-skiing at Scarborough.

The other place where interest was stimulated was Ireland.

In the summer of 1957, a pair of water-skis was left by a guest at the Lakeside Hotel, Killaloe – and before long several Irishmen had made the first – if somewhat tentative attempts – to water-ski at the Killaloe Regatta in August of that year. It was just over a year after this, that a legendary demonstration took place on the River Liffey, Dublin.

David Nations recalls that:

'I had a phone-call from a Dublin jeweller, Desmond West, asking me to help start skiing in Southern Ireland. I asked him if he had any skiers, and he said, "No."'

The intention was to ski on the River Shannon, Lough Derg. West offered to pick up Nations at Dublin and get him to Killaloe. West told him: 'It's 100 miles in a 100 minutes – I have a fast Rolls Royce.'

It was a most hair-raising journey but it took 120 minutes. Nations was introduced to Hector Noonan, who ran a little old hotel at Killaloe. It was in a beautiful area with surrounding hills, and would make the ideal site.

Back in Dublin, he was introduced to an official of the Irish Tourist Board, who asked him if he would put on a show as one of the highlights of the Catering Exhibition in Dublin. David was a trifle doubtful when it was pointed out that not only was it to be in October, but also at night under floodlights. Also there was one condition – that Irish skiers be part of the show. 'But you don't have any –'

'Well, that's the idea – you'll be teaching them!'

'But it's already August – we haven't got much time. Look, I'll only do it one way. Jacques Cousteau has invented some rubber diving suits for the French Navy. If you will put your Irish skiers in these, with lifejackets, then I'd feel happy to help.'

So Desmond West flew to France, bought eight suits and they taught fourteen Irishmen (and women) to ski. Some experts were invited, including Max Salik from Belgium, world champion Marina Doria, as well as Peter Felix, Johnny and Jilly Morris and David Nations.

The placards read: 'Tonight, Water Skiing by Floodlight on the River Liffey at 8.15 p.m. For the first time ever, water-skiing and jumping will take place. Come and see this spectacular free show.'

David Nations continues the story: 'For our take-off point, we stationed ourselves in the Guinness Brewery – that was our first mistake: We'd taught these people to ski and they were to go down, carrying Irish flags, in front of the star performers. There was a remarkable crowd of 50000 lining the river, even though it was winter. The parade started, multi-coloured rockets were fired, and off they went. There was about half a mile of darkness and bridges before they came into the limelight, but when the boats appeared, there was not a single Irishman to be seen. They'd had such a wonderful reception at the Guinness Brewery before the start, that they'd fallen off! So we had to turn the boats round and direct the searchlights to find them. A Limerick dentist, "Red" McDonnell, who was wearing a chef's tall white cap and tunic, had sunk while negotiating a difficult turn just above O'Connell Bridge – he was to sink again before reaching Metal Bridge.'

Then came the jumping. They had found it impossible to moor the jump in the middle of the swift-flowing River Liffey, so rather than cancel that most exciting part of the show, it was moored against a wall. This made the approach rather terrifying as a sideslip would hurl the jumper straight into that wall. Luckily, there were no accidents and Irish skiing had been helped a great deal.

It was not too long before Southern Ireland, in particular the Killaloe Water Ski Club, the Balscadden Bay Ski Club and the Sandycove Water Ski Club – with such brave skiers as Gerry Doyle and Declan White – was ready to hold its first Nationals.

David Nations, acting as coach-judge, has recalled: 'One chap was absolutely convinced that he should be awarded points for a new trick – juggling three golf balls!'

Later, the Irish were to have a fine water-ski competitor in Alan Dagg of the Golden Falls WSC. Between 1967 and 1973, Alan reigned six times as National Champion, also winning two Irish Open titles in 1971–72.

About this time, David Nations had decided to retire from competition: 'I'd been skiing for over ten years, so I decided that this was the time to retire and dedicate myself to teaching and organisation. I was embittered by being a "good British loser" in the international field, and thought that I could help the sport in the British Isles, by passing on some of the hard lessons from my own experience.'

Jeannette Stewart-Wood was now a boarder at Headington School, Oxford, but in the Easter and Summer holidays she became even more involved in improving her skiing at Ruislip Lido – it would not be long before she would be ready to go over the jump.

That year, Nations invited Frenchman Philippe Logut to Ruislip. 'He had seen me the previous year at Juan-les-Pins and said he would like to come over and ski. Noting that we did not have an experienced boat driver he suggested that it would be a good idea if he brought his boat driver from Golfe Juan to Ruislip.' The suggestion was enthusiastically received and it was agreed to employ Titou, who was quite well known as a driver in Golfe Juan. They trained and worked together for a whole season – Logut only went back to France to compete for a place in the French team, subsequently going to Milan and becoming Champion of the World in Tricks.

It was also back in 1960 that organised water-skiing began in Wales. Clive Jenkins has written: 'My earliest recollection of the sport in the Principality was seeing a group of Americans from a local US-owned factory skiing in the wide sweep of Oxwich Bay, on the Gower coast, in the summer of 1958. Within two years, there were sufficient numbers of local enthusiasts to consider the formation of a ski club at Mumbles, a holiday village between Oxwich Bay and Swansea. This was closely followed by the Penarth WSC near Cardiff in the following season.'

It is interesting to note that Mumbles had also been the childhood home of the pioneer Captain d'Arcy Rutherford.

Meanwhile, 13-year-old Jeannette Stewart-Wood had her first experience of the ramp at Ruislip: 'My learning to jump was a terrible experience. I had never seen anyone of my age learning to jump before. I'm a very determined, resilient sort of person, but I'm also very nervous. It took me ages to land off the jump, simply because I was scared out of my mind – this great big plank of wood in front of you! I don't know how long it took me to have my first landing, but I do remember that I didn't have a rubber suit and I was perishing cold. If you ask me one of the reasons why I wanted to jump, I think probably – like most people in early childhood – I wanted to fly.'

She spent years just practising over the jump until she could go over steady and land safely. Learning was taken slowly. In those days the great ambition of men like Lance Callingham was to jump 30·48 m *100 ft* and become the first British member of the Century Club, while the women were just jumping 13·72 m *45 ft*.

'I still stood enormously in awe of other European skiers because Britain was really not seen as a country that did anything at all abroad. Instead, Britain looked up to all the rest of the world then, because we had never achieved anything – and I was very aware of this.'

In the summer of 1961, with her headmistress's permission, she went to the Junior European Cup at Aix-les-Bains, France, with Mrs Elaine Nations as chaperone and confidante. There she won the jumping event and brought back the first international gold medal Britain had ever won abroad. The four years' hard training that she and Nations had undertaken, the heartaches that

Elaine had helped them through – had all been worthwhile and from then on, along with Great Britain, they never looked back.

Lanfranco Colombo, at this period Secretary-General of the WWSU, wrote her offering congratulations on her success at the first Coup d'Europe des Jeunes, and hoping that it would induce her to go on into the higher class with the same enthusiasm.

At about the same time, at the repeated insistence of his wife, David Nations gave his close attention to a 16-year-old lad from the Norwich Ski Club, who having just left school, intended to join a merchant ship and work his way round the world. Recognising his potential Nations asked him to come and work at the Ruislip Club and undertake serious training. 'I'd never done this before, but I recognised the need and the talent. Robin Beckett became my first serious protégé in the world of trained skiers. Skiing became his life.'

It was also during this period that Pamela Mountbatten, the daughter of Lord Louis, joined the Ruislip club and – like her father had thirty years before – thoroughly enjoyed the sport.

The growth of British water-skiing continued and by the end of 1962 there were 50 clubs affiliated to the British Water Ski Federation with another 30 clubs in the process of formation. With 30000 skiers, this made it the second largest Federation in the World Water Ski Union. But as Chairman Arnold Mainprize stated, there was still the need 'to take water-skiing out of the gossip columns and into serious sporting debate'. A positive move towards this end was made when Princess Margaret and the Earl of Snowdon learned to ski, and soon afterwards the Earl agreed to become Patron of the Federation, thus giving the sport the recognition it deserved.

While on the subject of the Royal Family, Philip, Duke of Edinburgh, already knew how to ski, having done so while serving in HMS *Magpie* with the Mediterranean Fleet, but it was to be several years before Prince Charles (the present-day Prince of Wales) would put on the pair of Royal skis. (**See photograph below.**)

One weekend in January 1963, there was a very heavy frost at Ruislip, so that the Lido was frozen over with 7–10 cm *3–4 in* of solid ice. Some of the Ruislip skiers, including Aubrey Sheena, Peter Pearl and Jean Pierre Delcuve, the Northern European champion, fitted the Club Land Rover with chains and began skiing on the frozen Lido! While Ruislip skiers were content with jumping skis, Delcuve used trick skis and was performing 'stepovers' until one of them snapped on the ice. This was only the prelude to a year of extraordinary feats executed on the Lido.

It continued when James William 'Flea' Jackson came to Ruislip for three months. As David Nations recalls: 'I had been visiting Cypress Gardens each year and become very friendly with all concerned. By inviting Jimmy Jackson to come to the Lido as my guest, I thought that if we could rub off some of his expertise in slalom and jumping and he could help us with out training, it would work well for British water-skiing abroad.'

When it was suggested he wear a wetsuit, Jimmy Jackson (who had once been a weak 44 kg *97 lb* youth threatened with tuberculosis) originally declined. But when he had felt the coldwater tingle, he decided to wear one after all. Coming from Cypress Gardens, 'Flea' tended to be a somewhat spectacular clown and practical joker, rather fond of putting jokes from the comic magazines he read so avidly, into practice. As Peter Pearl recalls: 'I've seen him put on a slalom ski and go through that course both ways at 55 km/h *34 mph*, with his front foot in the binder and the other behind his knee. I've seen him put a pair of skis on the water, hold the handle and say to the driver "Go!" and he skied a little way then jumped straight out of his binders and was away barefoot. We also had all the photographers in a boat by the jump, as Jimmy comes thundering up, waiting for him to come over the other side. But Jimmy throws away the handle, skids round the ramp, picks up the handle again – and they're still there, waiting for him to appear over the ramp. Then again the boat-driver might be towing him and suddenly he'd walk along the rope and climb into the boat. The driver would turn round and there he was, sitting in the boat with him, grinning.'

But behind this façade, he worked hard and took his skiing seriously showing the British skiers that the impossible was possible, particularly when he jumped in the 40–45 m *140 ft* region. And as Jeannette Stewart-Wood recalls:

'I think everyone's got to have an inspiration and for a time I had nothing really to copy in my jumping. Then Jimmy arrived and I saw how he had this kind of lift and this beautiful graceful flight; and I had something to aspire to. Jimmy was my idol really.'

Jimmy's influence paid off in Jeannette's competitive achievements that year, beginning with the British Championships, held that year at the Lido. She won the Slalom and had a winning jump 23·56 m *77 ft 4 in* to take the Ladies' Over-all title.

Then again at the Junior European Cup contest at Bañolas, Spain, she jumped a winning 24·68 m *81 ft* and scored a total of 44·5 buoys, narrowly failing to beat Austria's Gitti Boss. Miss Boss prophesied that Jeannette would be the champion the next year and world champion by the time she was twenty.

When the World Championships took place at Vichy,

Jimmy 'The Flea' Jackson at Ruislip Lido, London.

France, Jeannette was the reserve at 17-years-old, and was able to watch her idol in competition jumping a winning 40 m *131 ft* on the River Allier's 244 m *800 ft* wide by 4 km *2½ mile* long Olympic basin.

The IXth World Championships were a triumph for American youth, especially for two of Joe Cash's protégés from Sarasota, 14-year-old Billy Spencer and 16-year-old Jeannette Brown. In a thrilling Slalom climax, Spencer got home by one buoy from Jimmy Jackson and Bruno Zaccardi. Unfortunately, Jean Marie Muller, faced with rain and unpleasant conditions, fell on each of his trick runs to come 29th, while little Billy Spencer tricked his way to victory.

US skiers at Callaway Gardens. *From left to right:* Billy Spencer, Jimmy Jackson, Jeannette Brown, Dicksie Ann Hoyt, Chuck Stearns, Ken White.

In the Women's Tricks, the French girl Dany Duflot, was left bobbing helplessly semi-conscious in the water for many agonising moments after a nasty fall. Her team-mate, European Trick champion for 1963, Guyonne Dalle, went on to win the World title while Jeannette Brown won the Women's Slalom. Renate Hansluwska won the Jumping with a decisive leap of 25·85 m *84 ft 10 in.* Although Dany Duflot, with her knee heavily strapped, courageously managed to leap 25·90 m *85 ft,* the judges simply did not rate her style very highly. It was note-worthy that Jeannette's Junior jump had only been 1·22 m *4 ft* away from the World standard.

Also competing at Vichy was a West Indies team, whom David Nations had trained at Ruislip – Peter Brady and Gilly Byles (Jamaica) and David de Verteuil (Trinidad). Other entries included South African Deirdre Barnard, the 13-year-old daughter of a young and then-unknown heart research-worker, Dr Christiaan Barnard, and a 13-year-old Mexican lad in the tradition of Alfredo Mendoza, named Adolfo ('Tito') Antunano. Alongside Jeannette, both these skiers showed promise as future world champions.

It was at these Championships that David Nations was faced with an unusual judging problem: 'One of my jobs was to qualify the Japanese team, because we didn't really know what their performance was like. I was worried that if I had to disqualify them, it would be a terrible blow to national pride. It was the most unusual awful weather for that time, freezing cold, but at six o'clock in the morning, I had these four boys and two girls from Japan, whom I had to judge in Tricks. I said they would have four runs, with the best runs added up and if they made the minimum points criteria, I would qualify them.

The West Indies Team training at Ruislip Lido for the World Championships at Vichy. *From left to right:* Peter (Ince) Brady, David de Verteuil (Trinidad), David Nations, Gilly Byles (Jamaica).

'But I took pity on them. I should have seen a certain number of tricks on one run, but they did some in one run and fell, then they did some more in another run and fell again. So I used my "poetic judgement" and added the two lots of points together. When it was all over they stood their waiting – in their special track-suits from the Land of the Rising Sun. I announced to the team captain that they were all qualified. Then in one motion, the six of them together said "Thank you honourable judge. Thank you honourable judge."'

Meanwhile Jeannette stayed in England to train for the 1964 season. Ever since she had started skiing, she had been more and more financially backed by her dynamic father, mushroom-grower and ace pilot, Mr John Stewart-Wood. During the coming year, one of the problems which Jeannette – like every young skier – would increasingly face, was the amount of time she should be devoting to her academic studies.

Nevertheless, she seemed to find the right balance, and this showed itself at the Group 2 Championships, held on Lake Albano, near Rome, Italy, in the shadow of the Pope's summer residence at Castel Gandolfo.

With only sixth place in Tricks, Jeannette came third Over-all – unprecedented in British water-skiing. The Union Jack was unfurled and the National Anthem played for the first time after an international competition. Europe began to sit up and take notice, even though in team positions Britain was still sixth.

After the Championships, Pope Paul VI received the 40 skiers and officials at the Castel Gandolfo. As David Nations recalls: 'His Holiness was wonderful because he spoke in English, French and Italian. In good English he told us "You are special people, very holy and blessed people, because you are like Jesus, who walked on the water." He said this with a very nice smile, adding that he was sad Italy had not done better. With his blessing, he gave us Consideration and a special Medal of Audience which those who were present, have and cherish to the present day.'

There were still two more tournaments to be dealt with that season.

The Northern European Championships for the Philippe de Backer Challenge Trophy, had now been running for three years with the Belgian Jean Pierre Delcuve doing the hat-trick to win the Men's Over-all all three times. In 1962, at Amsterdam, Holland's Connie Dane won the Women's Over-all, while in 1963 at Lochearnhead in Scotland the victor was Luxembourg's Sylvie Hulsemann. Nevertheless, in both those years, the team trophy had been won from eleven other countries by England. In this competition the British home countries compete as separate entities.

The 1964 Championships were again held on the Bosbaan Canal, Amsterdam, location of the world-famous rowing course, and considered by many as one of the best water-skiing venues in Europe. Connie Dane and Sylvie Hulsemann did not compete this time. With Germany's Ralph Edelmann out of action, his country-man, Karl Benzinger cleared 32·61 m *107 ft* to win the Men's Jumping, alongside the Slalom victory of his fellow team member George Nolte. Tricks were won by Belgium's Lucien Servais. Once again the English women put their male team mates to shame. Anne Wilton won Slalom, while Jeannette won Tricks and jumped a winning 25·90 m *85 ft*, so that England again successfully

His Holiness Pope Paul VI gave an audience to the water-ski officials at the 1964 European Championships at Castelgandolfo. Here he talks to Philippe de Backer of Belgium.

defended their team title for the third successive year.

It was also in this year that the first water-ski contest in Wales was held, at Mumbles, with David Nations officiating as Chief Judge, assisted by such stalwarts as Aubrey Sheena, Peter Pearl and Ronnie Emmanuel. This was the first Welsh Inter-Club competition, very low in skiing standards, but high in enthusiasm. With an incredible and rare 15–18 m *50–60 ft* rise in the tidal water, tricks took place on enormous swells, following a Force 8 gale, and the jumping was almost wrecked by the storm. Nations recalls:

'The incredible thing was that while I was officiating and recording the distances, I was also having to shout instructions while they were jumping in competition – "Keep your hand down! Keep your head up!" It was the only way.'

By 1965, a Welsh Water Ski Committee was formed. It had been originally proposed by William Eynon and Clive Jenkins, who had felt it was time a Welsh team was organised to take its place beside those of the other three UK countries.

Following an approach to members of the Penarth Club, Arthur Dawe, Major Gwyn Davies and Viv Perry agreed to help set up the committee. The first aim was to raise funds to help train and equip a team to enter the next Northern European tournament, at Trier, in 1965. To raise these funds a Welsh Open Water Ski Championships was organised. With sponsorship from W. D. & H. O. Wills and enthusiastic help from the Director of Parks, of Cardiff City Council, Mr Nehues, the competition was set up in Roath Park Lake in the heart of Cardiff.

A new steel-framed ramp was built and transported from Swansea to Cardiff and the committee members layed the slalom course from rowing boats using 3·66 m *12 ft* long stakes and a floating line to measure between the buoys. After the late arrival of the ramp at the lakeside, the mobile crane which lifted the ramp into the water almost toppled on to the ramp, which was saved only by the weight of the ramp being taken as it touched the water. Unfortunately the ramp then settled into the soft mud bottom and this took several nerve-wracking hours to free, tow into position and moor at the required angle.

With visiting skiers of the calibre of Robin Beckett, Jeanette Stewart-Wood, Philippe Logut, Guy Robinet and Jean Marie Muller, the Welsh Committee was naturally anxious to catch up on lost time and practise sessions were hurriedly begun.

As soon as skiing was under way, they found to their horror that the stone walls bordering the lake were creating an acute backwash problem, making skiing conditions treacherous. Robin Beckett was only able to win Slalom, while Philippe Logut (part of a French team invited over) won Jumping and Peter Rubin won Tricks with Paul Adlington a close second. Jeanette made a clean sweep of the women's events.

The funds had been raised and the Welsh team was formed, with members David Lynn of the Llangorse Club, John Morse, Maurice Nash, William Eynon and Clive Jenkins, all from the Mumbles Club. Although they did enter the Northern European Championships a number of times, as Clive Jenkins has said: 'The Red Dragon has been something of an "also ran" and I am sorry to say that – due to the lack of a suitable inland lake – we never managed to provide much opposition to the other teams, at least not on the water!'

Five years before, it had been the British men who had been aiming for the Century Jumping Club. Now this became Jeannette's burning ambition – to jump beyond the 30·48 m *100 ft* mark by the time of the 1965 World Championships due to be held in Australia.

Her devotion to training in 1964 had taken its toll on her studies: 'I nearly had a breakdown at "A" levels. The times my mother said she wasn't going to let me ski any more; I was such a nervous wreck, she had to threaten to stop me. David, and particularly Elaine, also bore the brunt of this tension. Elaine gave so much of herself by listening to me, sharing my problems and consoling me.

'I had to give up history – a subject I wanted – only three days before the exam. But I took English and Latin and got Distinctions – and became a "School scholar", awarded a place at Westfield College, London University, reading Medieval English – but at a great sacrifice.

'But I began to achieve what I wanted to achieve in terms of jumping style, when I took a year off between school and University and skied all winter. It was my first opportunity for working non-stop; I had no one to copy – I was very much on my own.'

She practised at Rickmansworth Aquadrome ('Ricky'), near Ruislip and often arrived in the morning to find the course frozen over. With Robin Beckett, she used to take a boat out and break the ice. Sometimes even that didn't work. The course was often frozen solid and at such times, when it was so cold, not much could be accomplished as after ten minutes on the water, they had to go inside.

But as David Nations recalls: 'She rarely missed a day, and neither did I. She did a lot of skipping and running around the lake, and a lot of circuit training. By using imagination and projecting herself towards her own concept of an ideal jump, we worked out the fine detail, like the position of her toes and feet in the binders and the complete and total control of her skis in flight and on landing. When, later on, she was to be acknowledged by the other top skiers as one of the greatest stylists in jumping ever, this control became her hallmark.'

By April 1965, after intensive training, Jeannette Stewart-Wood had broken through the 30·48 m *100 ft* barrier, skiing behind the Boesch boat at 46 km/h *28 mph*.

Then came a setback, when while training she felt a sharp spasm of pain in her right ankle – recalling a 1962 netball injury – and wisely decided to rest before her European battles. The ligament seemed to have re-healed for the International Jump Competition in Holte, Denmark, where she landed a safe but winning 29·26 m *96 ft*, which was ratified as a new European record.

The Group 2 Championships were held on Lake Bañolas, Spain. But as Jeannette remembers: 'One of the difficulties of sport is that you do tend to go on and off form. By this time I think I'd just over-skied and lost about 10 ft; it was very sad.'

Then came the Northern European Championships held near Trier on the River Moselle, West Germany. Despite the ultra-long river barges creating extensive delays, England again retained first place in the team title, with Scotland sixth, Ireland ninth and Wales last of the coldwater countries. Robin Beckett won Slalom in superb style. To her disappointment, Jeannette's winning jump was only 27·43 m *90 ft*. If she were going to have any chance against the American girls at the next World Championships at Surfer's Paradise Gardens in Australia, she would have to regain that extra 3·05 m *10 ft* from the ramp.

'In the end I went into a sort of depression. I'd go out, and come back thinking that perhaps it would be all right next time. But it never seemed to be. I just lost heart.'

But before chronicling that story, it is necessary to bring the rest of the world, and particularly the achievements of some American girls, up to date from 1961.

Interlude

In 1962, André Coutau, the then President of the WWSU might well have wondered how much larger his 16-year-old organisation, with its 34 Federations, would grow.

In Sweden, for example, ten clubs came together to form the Swedish Water Ski Federation, 'Svenska Vattenskidforbundet' with millionaire Sigurd Hallstrom as the President and one from each club on the board. The SVF also became a member of the Riksidrottsforbundet, Swedish Sport Association, and the sport was accepted.

Elsewhere, in Jordan, His Majesty King Hussein, together with Simon Khoury and Pierre Haddad, went skiing for the first time in the Gulf of Aqaba with the intention of promoting the sport throughout the Hashemite Kingdom and ultimately becoming affiliated to the WWSU.

Across the Atlantic, among the countless organised tournaments in the USA, the Nationals, now in their 22nd year, were again held at Callaway Gardens. Chuck Stearns ('the world's winningest skier') won the Slalom and Men's Over-all for the fourth time since 1957, although Larry Penacho, who during the year created a new Jumping Record of 47·24 m *155* ft, won the Jumping. That year, and for the next three years running, the Men's Tricks were won by Al Tyll of Bantam, Connecticut.

Tyll was born in Troy, New York, the son of athletic-minded German-born parents, who brought him up with the Healthy Body/Sound Mind philosophy. Al first skied in 1954, when aged 22. In 1959, by this time a Connecticut court reporter, he saw his first Nationals, and the following year he qualified to enter and placed tenth in Men's Tricks. In 1961 a torn cartilage prevented him from entering, but his formidable achievement was that, even though he could only ski part-time due to his job, Al Tyll was 30 when he first became National Men's Tricks champion.

Jenny Hodges, who won Women's Slalom, Tricks and Over-all, and Cecele Campbell who won Jumping, came and went too quickly. But in strong contrast, the Junior Division saw the appearance of three youngsters who were to carve great niches for themselves in water-skiing history. Winning the Slalom, Jumping and Over-all, was 13-year-old 'Billy the Kid' Spencer. The Tricks winner was Ricky Joe McCormick, whose victorious figures were scored so quickly and by such a small boy, that the judges found difficulty in seeing them.

Ricky Joe (later nicknamed 'Tricky Ricky') of Independence, Missouri, had begun skiing when he was five years old. In fact, not long after he had been exposed to a pair of miniature slats, Ricky actually water-skied behind a swimmer – Allen Brown, a 1·88 m *6 ft 2 in*, 95 kg *210 lb* athlete, wearing swim fins, managed to 'plane' the 91 cm *3 ft* Ricky, who was hanging on to a 3·66 m *12 ft* towline. He was five years old when he entered his first tournament, the Omaha Open – to win Tricks, come second in Jumping and third in Slalom. Incidentally, apart from his skiing abilities, Ricky was also a Junior Boy judo champion under the instructions of Wey Seng Kim. The 1962 Nationals victory was the first important rung on the ladder, in which Ricky was always helped by his brothers Jim and Terry on the Lake of Ozarks, where Jim had a water-ski school. Coincidentally, Ricky's idol was also 'Flea' Jackson.

Winning the Junior Girls' Slalom and Jumping in the 1962 Nationals was the third promising newcomer, 12-year-old Elizabeth Christine Allan. In 1955 her father, Colonel William D. Allan of the US Army Corps of Engineers, was demobbed and returned from West Germany to settle in Winter Park, Florida. In America, anyone who lives by a lake, usually has a boat and before long – aged only five – she was fun-skiing behind her father's boat, soon joined by her sister Susan. When she was ten she joined a water-ski club in Orlando and started training on Lake Killarney. Although her father could not ski, everything she learned, he taught her. As she has recalled: 'He just studied and he watched me. He knew me, he knew my attitudes, my thoughts, my enthusiasm, my tomboyishness! In 1961, I entered the Florida State Tournament and came second in Slalom and fourth in Tricks. Later that year, I finally convinced boat drivers that I was big enough to go over the ramp and before long I was practising the double wake cut.'

As with Ricky McCormick, Liz Allan's career had only just begun. One of her greatest opponents was to be blonde 'Babs' Cooper Clack, who in 1962 had lifted the Women's World Jump record to 28·03 m *92 ft* at the Lakeland Tournament, to tie with Judy Rosch.

By 1963, the Canadian Water Ski Association had extended to most provinces – Quebec, Manitoba, British Columbia and more recently, the Maritime Provinces (with the exception of Newfoundland) and Saskatchewan. Under the Presidency of David McMyllan, it became a pattern that the Canadian Championships (called the Canadian Closed) be alternated from east to west in succeeding years. It was customary for a strong delegation to be sent from the east when the tournament was held in the west and the reverse held true when the tournament was in the east. It also became a custom at this point to hold a Canadian Open Championships as

Marc Cloutier. One of Canada's champion skiers.

well as the Closed. Thus, in a year when the 'Closed' was held in the east, the 'Open' would be held in the west. The 'Open' was also an attempt to attract skiers from other countries and, in particular, the US. It eventually became very confusing as to who was champion of what and the dual tournament format was later dropped. In 1961, the new CWSA President, Lloyd Gilbert, encouraged further development to the point where ten sanctioned tournaments were held – five in Ontario and five in Quebec.

Also, in 1963, Australian Ron Marks became the first non-American ever to be invited to the US Masters at Callaway Gardens; he has recalled:

'As the younger generation in Australia moved successfully into National and State Tournaments, the pedantic and parochial attitude which had existed before, was replaced by a spirit of genuine sportsmanship and mutual co-operation. Three or four of us would decide that we'd go to such-and-such a location and train together. I skied an awful lot with Rosemary and Ken Margan. We never adopted the attitude that we would only ski at State or National level championships. We competed in all the rinky-dink tournaments throughout the country – Forbes, Newcastle, Berry, Bendigo, Bridgewater, Bort, Swanhill and so on – and we would gladly pass on information to anybody.

'At the US Masters, I skied nowheresville, because it was held off-season as far as I was concerned. But it was a great feather in my cap to be there.'

The same year, Oscar Botero Mejia, devoted South American sportsman, organised the Colombia Water Ski Association, not long after Andrés Botero had come fifth in an International contest at Acapulco, Mexico and Colombians had begun to compete outside their own country. WWSU Vice-President Frau Brigitte Felder de Rook arranged not only for Colombia's affiliation to the Union, but also for that of the Yacht Club Argentino, who had just held a most successful Slalom championship in the Parque 3 Lake.

On the initiative of the Naftikos Omilos Vouliagmenis (Nautical Club of Vouliagmeni), five clubs were assembled to form the Greek Federation. The first administrative council was constituted with Athanasious Diakakis as President and George Papadakis as Vice-President.

Through the energies of Paul Lieser of the Trier WSC, together with Werner and Marianne Kolb in West Germany, after consultation with Felix Hulsemann from Luxembourg about World Class judging, a water-ski contest was organised at Trier between Germany and Luxembourg. This saw a fine performance by the up-and-coming German skier, Karl-Heinz Benzinger, who was to be so consistently and brilliantly successful during the coming decade of competitive water-skiing, winning the only medal ever taken away from a World Championship (Bañolas 1971) by a German skier, an achievement looked up to by all other German water-skiers.

From 1963 the French Federation began to work with, and to be sponsored by, the Ministry of Sport, which awarded State Diplomas to Instructors and Assistant Instructors, based on very serious examinations about general knowledge of sport.

In 1964, a Federation was set up in the Union of Soviet Socialist Republics, on the initiative of the legendary Cosmonaut Yuriy Gagarin (the first man to orbit the Earth), who headed its technical commission. By this time there were water-skiing clubs in 30 cities of the USSR with an aggregate membership running into tens of thousands of young people. The organisation con-

Skiing behind an outboard engine – Soviet style.

sisted of a Government Department with a Minister under whom a Sports Committee controlled the sport. Each federation – Karelia, Estonia, Latvia, Lithuania, White Russia, Ukraine, RSFSR, Armenia, Georgia, etc. was represented on this committee. Once a sport is officially recognised in the USSR, it receives assistance from the State, including the provision of paid coaches.

In Czechoslovakia, there were five clubs, with 200 members, and the State Committee for Physical Education endowed the SPOFA PRAHA club with two new 50 hp and 70 hp Mercury-engined boats. It was here that a 14-year-old named Frantisek Stehno was just learning to ski at the Pardubice Water Ski Club, east of Prague – with, as so very often happens, his father as his first trainer.

Two water-skiing centres were progressing in Turkey, one at Kadiköy-Moda, a suburb of Istanbul on the Marmara Sea, and the other at Antalya on the Mediterranean.

In Iran, following a Royal Decree by His Imperial Majesty Shahanshah Aryamehr, the Iranian Water Ski Federation was founded and no effort was to be spared to bring the sport up to international standards.

Summer is the season for this sport in Iran and the lake at Amir Kabir Dam, some 70 km *45 miles* from Tehran, became the centre of attraction for the enthusiasts. Multitudes of people from the capital, and locals, would head towards this spot, and water-ski under the supervision of coaches and Federation authorities. Apart from the Federation, the Army, the Air Force, the Navy and some private groups all made their headquarters at the lake. The sport also came to be practised in other parts of the country, particularly on the lakes of the various dams – Darius in Shiraz, Shah Abbas in Isfahan, Tarik in Guilan, Mohammed Reza Shah in Khuzestan – and at the Caspian Coast stretching for some 992 km *616 miles*.

Perhaps the most interesting men's match to take place in 1964 was the United States versus the Rest of the World at Callaway Gardens that April. David Nations recalls:

'I had a call from "Bo" Callaway, asking me if I would choose a team to represent the Rest of the World. This had never been done before and was to be broadcast on ABC Television. I was rather taken aback with being

Cosmonaut Yuriy Alekseyevich Gagarin. In 1964 he headed the Technical Commission of the newly-formed Soviet Water-Ski Federation.

Above: The Shah of Iran skiing at the Amir Kabir Dam.

Below: His Imperial Majesty Shahanshah Armehr and the Shareena.

singled out for this signal honour of picking such a team; so after informing "Bo" Callaway, I invited André Coutau to come with me.'

David tried to balance the team by picking all-rounders or specialists – four against four. He picked Ron Marks, Australian National champion for several years and a great slalom skier, then Jean Marie Muller, among the best trick skiers of all time. Also invited was Switzerland's ace jumper Pierre Clerc, and Gerhardt Rainer of Austria, another good jumper, and Italy's Bruno Zaccardi, an excellent all-rounder. With the exception of Ron Marks, these skiers were at the beginning of their season, while the Americans – Billy Spencer, Chuck Stearns, Jimmy Jackson, Ken White – had been training through their warm winter.

Although 'Bo' Callaway put all equipment at their disposal, wind and rain prevented them from carrying out a full training programme. The sportsmanship between the two teams was marvellous, sharing their precious ropes, life-jackets, rubber-suits and – unbelievably – even their skis. White even offered his jumping skis to Zaccardi who had the bad luck to break his own during practice. The contest was to be held in three rounds over two days.

These young, high-spirited skiers wanted to go out to Le Grange, a nearby Southern town where there was some swinging night life, and this caused some concern. Nations was asked to lead the team, and trained them up to the eve of the event, when he had to relinquish his training position and take on a position as a judge. As judge, he then had to find a captain for the Rest of the World team – he appointed his wife, Elaine. She took her duties so seriously that, to stop the boys from getting to Le Grange, she had André Coutáu guard the exit of one end of their chalets at the Holiday Inn, Callaway Gardens, because in the end they even tried to get out with their clothes over their pyjamas!

At the start of the competition, there was one very amusing incident. Because there was very little distance between the starting dock and the slalom course entrance, when Bruno Zaccardi had to get his back foot in his binder, there was not sufficient time and he had to throw away his handle. David Nations was one of the boat judges and they had to circle round and pick him up again; but still Bruno could not get it in. By this time the boat was making wave-circles, not allowing time for the wash to subside before they towed him off again.

'What are you doing to my skier! It's not fair to Zaccardi! What about the waves then?' the conscientious Rest of the World team captain was gesticulating like crazy and shouting. 'I'm going to protest!'

Also in the boat was an American judge, who did not know the Europeans. He looked at Nations and enquired:

'Er, excuse me, Mr Nations, but who is that lady?' Back came that well-known punch line – 'That's no lady – that's my wife!'

But it was a brilliant and hard-fought battle. Although the Americans won handsomely, with 'Flea' Jackson executing a superb 45·72 m *150 ft*, Pierre Clerc set up a new European jumping record with 43·28 m *142 ft*. Unfortunately Gerhardt Rainer cracked a rib while jumping, which handicapped him rather seriously. In a superb slalom duel, Billy Spencer beat Ron Marks. At the end, the score was: USA – 22 300 points, Rest of the World – 19 600 points.

The story is continued by David Nations:

'I could not understand how a 14-year-old could become Champion of the World. So when the team went back to Europe, Elaine and I took a week's holiday and went to Sarasota to try and see the phenomenal Billy Spencer, watching him train and learning of his background. Apparently Billy's mother had not been well and they had moved from the North down to a warmer climate. Billy had begun skiing at five years old – living on the side of a lake he practically skied everywhere. From five to fourteen years old Billy the Kid had done more skiing than the professionals at Cypress Gardens.

'But this was still not the whole story. So when I was invited back to judge the Masters, the first non-American to be asked to do so, I went again to Sarasota. I realised that he had had more opportunity to ski than anybody I had known in the world. He had his own jump and his own slalom course right outside his house and he did nothing else. What he'd crammed into seven years would have taken an older skier twice as long. His power and strength had overcome his immaturity.' 'Flea' Jackson put it in a nutshell when he said:

'You just wind him up and then shout "Go on Billy! Go out there and beat 'em, Kid!" And when he's won he comes back and asks "Who's got my comic?"'

At the Masters Nations was able to see Barbara Cooper Clack and Dicksie Ann Hoyt going through their jumping paces around the 30·48 m *100 ft* mark, and he realised that this was the goal that Jeannette Stewart-Wood should be aiming for by the time of the World Championships at Surfers Paradise, Australia.

That October, the British team captain, Peter Felix took his youngish team, among them a very uncertain

Howard H. 'Bo' Callaway.

Jeannette, out to Brisbane and on to Surfers Paradise, where 19 other countries and over 60 skiers had assembled to do battle, and make friends. They had problems getting used to the complete reversal of day and night and acclimatizing themselves to the weather after a bitterly cold British September. Now, for the first time, Jeannette would come face to face with Barbara Cooper Clack and Liz Allan. For Jeannette 'competitions were always purgatory'.

After the opening parade of flags, came the Women's Jumping. Jeannette competed fourth – and startled the crowd with two soaring and glorious leaps of 30·51 m *100 ft 1 in*, receiving a great ovation when her distance was announced, particularly from the wild British contingent. When Mrs Cooper Clack's jumps failed to reach even the 27·43 m *90 ft* mark, the tension mounted. Then 15-year-old Deirdre Barnard of South Africa, surprised the crowd again with two leaps of 28·34 m *93 ft* and 30·17 m *99 ft* and the tension got worse. Jeannette was so near a World Championship Gold.

It was then that Liz Allan, after some final words with her father/trainer 'Colonel Bill', went out on to the River Nerang. On her first pass, Liz delayed her cut so long that she had to pass up the first jump of her three. On her second attempt, she committed herself a fraction of a second sooner and flew off the ramp at top speed, landing 31·00 m *101 ft 8 in* away. Under the new World Rules, instead of the average of jumps, the best one of two jumps counted. Liz and the Colonel didn't know until they had returned to the States what distance she made on her third and final pass – only 24·38 m *80 ft*! If the old rule had been applied, Jeannette would have been a world champion. It was a bitter disappointment after so much training.

In 1964 David Nations was invited to judge the US Masters – the first European official ever to be given this honour. He is sitting on the left in the front row, with the tall figure of Bill Clifford standing behind him.

For the rest, the Xth World Championships saw yet another pretty decisive victory for the United States. Tournament driver Billy Tucker of Australia pulled 198 consecutive slalom runs without a re-run or protest, on tidal water at that! Roland Hillier won the Men's Slalom, as well as the Over-all – Billy Spencer had by now retired from water-skiing in favour of scholastic American football. Barbara Cooper Clack won the Women's Slalom, setting up a record of five buoys at 58 km/h *36 mph* on a 3·66 m *12 ft* shortened rope. In this Jeannette tied with Anne Wilton for sixth place. Larry Penacho won the Jumping from team captain Chuck Stearns, with 45·11 m *148 ft*, while 15-year-old Tito Antunano of Mexico came fourth. Ken White of Winterhaven performed his trick wizardry, and with Liz Allan taking the Over-all, the only event not won by the Americans was the Women's Tricks, gracefully executed by France's superb Dany Duflot (Jeannette again came sixth). In the team positions, second to the US was France – Britain came ninth.

At the WWSU Congress following the Championships, there was a reorganisation on the lines of the US Masters, with three days put aside for elimination and a final day of competition. Manila and linen lines, which surely must have been used since water-skiing began, were ruled out of World tournaments in favour of 'single-braided, monofilament line of olefin plastic material'. (Twin handles had gone out of fashion in the late 1950s.)

There were now 42 Federations affiliated to the Union and Italy's Franco Carraro was elected its seventh President.

8 Winning golds

As evidence of the continuing spread of interest in the sport, not only did champions come and go but even the sport's traditional 'Grand Old Man', the late Fred Waller of Long Island, was now deposed.

In the summer of 1965, Margaret Crimmins, a writer for the *Pioneer Press* had been on holiday in Lake City, Minnesota, when she stumbled across a pair of long, very strange-looking skis on display in the Municipal Bathhouse:

'I asked the manager, Ben Simon, if I could try them out for a story for the *Pioneer Press*. He agreed and said they were the first ever – belonged to a man called Samuelson – but no one had done anything about making any claims.'

Ralph Samuelson holding his original 'pine boards'. See page 20 et seq.

So she rode on them and it was a wild experience! She plopped twice but got up on the third try behind a 40-horsepower rig. The skis were really difficult to hold together because of their length. Two teen-age boys went out with her. One got up and skied for a short distance (about a hundred yards, just as she had done) but the other never did make it.

The column she did for the St Paul paper led to the discovery of Ralph Samuelson, then in his sixties, at his home in Pine Island. Before long, the whole city was excited, and Samuelson was brought in for a sort of impromptu celebration.

On 9 December 1965, the Lake City Chamber of Commerce wrote to the AWSA: 'Gentlemen. We understand you are checking out the origin of water-skiing. In 1922, a young daredevil of Lake City skied on Lake Pepin for the first time so far as any of us know . . . We are happy to have the signatures below of Lake City Men who remember and are glad to testify . . . Sincerely, Lake City Chamber of Commerce.'

On 22 April 1966, William D. Clifford, Executive Manager of the AWSA since 1958 wrote: 'Dear Mr Samuelson. One of the most significant developments in organised water-skiing for many years has been the "rediscovery" of your pioneering activities in the sport . . . It is my real pleasure to recognise you as the first water-skier of record known to the American Water Ski Association and to salute you in the name of a sport that now attracts more than 9 000 000 participants each year in America alone.'

Since then, Samuelson has become a cult figure, often in the limelight of the world mass media, helping above all to promote tourism in Minnesota. When asked his reaction to watching water skiers today, Ralph comments: 'It's funny, I almost worry about them until I think about how much more dangerous my own skiing was. I can't help but get a rather warm feeling that I had a part in starting it.'

Meanwhile, 'the most growing sport in the world' continued to expand.

In Yugoslavia, now a WWSU member, the first National Championships were organised in July 1965 by the Sidro Club on Maribor Isle, the competitors arriving from Maribor, Ljubljana, Belgrade and Austria. The first heat was held on Maribor Isle in ice-cold water clogged with driftwood, and won by Mr Pukelj on beginner's skis and by Miss Milena Soss. The second heat was cancelled because the sea at Porec was too rough. The third heat, a slalom contest in Belgrade, behind a badly leaking 40 hp boat saw a dozen competitors; although the winner was Blaz Gornik of Ljubljana, it was by being placed second in this that Mr Pukelj of Maribor was made Over-all National Champion, together with Milena Soss in the Ladies' Division. Ironically, Mr Pukelj was an invalid.

Soon after this the Ljubljana competitors set up the first Yugoslav slalom track at Saladinki near Porec, began training there, and subsequently founded, in Ljubljana, the first specialised 'Vodno smucarski klub Ljubljana' (Ljubljana WSC). After this clubs were established in Belgrade, Begunj, Zagreb, Skopje and so the sport's popularity spread in that country.

In Austria, the great era of Renate Hansluwska, Bernd and Stefan Rauchenwald and Gerhard Rainer had ended with their retirement and the era of Juniors such as Eva Maria Fritsch, Egon Brunner, Wolfgang Loscher, Werner Schicher, Miki Rauchenwald and Franz Oberleitner was just beginning. Their problem was that nowhere in Austria was there water calm enough and traffic-free enough for these promising newcomers to train.

The reign of Jean-Pierre Delcuve as Belgian National Champion came to an end, and Messrs Servais, Roothaert, Depoorter and Adriaensen came to the fore, to be superseded in a matter of three years by the unrivalled Frank Dedecker, winning the coveted 'Diamond Ski' Trophy.

The Spanish Federation of Waterskiing had been created and its champions, Victor Palomo, Isidro Oliveras, Ira Ferrer and Ivon Sala competed in such tournaments as the Ricardo Sans Memorial Trophy.

In Sweden, the sport had grown rapidly since the formation of its Federation in 1962, backed by its President, Sigurd Hallstrom. The federation was a member of the Swedish Sports Federation and by 1966 could boast 27 member clubs, from Malmö in the south to Ostersun in the north. With training from two American skiers, Lynn Vermuellen and Larry Penacho, Swedes such as Lars Bjork of Stockholm were to reach top class European standards competing with Finns like Heiki and Hannu Olamo, the Norwegians such as Bjorn Erland Rustad and the Danish skiers Mikel and Finn Grabowski in the Scandinavian Championships.

Also in 1965 the Buenos Aires Water Ski Club had hosted the first Argentine Nationals and by 1966 the Federacion Argentina de Esqui Acuatico (FADEA) was formed.

Even St Helena, in the middle of the South Atlantic Ocean, had seen its first water-skiing from Dr Mackay, an overseas medical officer. He owned a 14-ft dory equipped with a 40-hp Johnson outboard, together with a pair of skis, and he showed the island inhabitants that in reality this sport simply has no boundaries so long as there is good skiable water. There will never be any water-skiing on Ascension Island, for example, because 'the large waves – a phenomenon locally known as "Rollers" – the rocky shore and the dangerous predatory fish in deeper water would make it a very unsafe sport here' writes the Administrator of that island.

In Australia, after Rex Carnegie had closed down his Sports Marine concern, the Victoria Water Ski Association took up the organisation of the Moomba Masters and successfully continued the task of getting financial sponsorship for the contest – mostly from Quantas Airlines. At the 1965 Moomba Masters, America's Chuck Stearns took the Men's Over-all from Bruno Zaccardi to win a trip round the world.

Mexico's Tito Antunano won the Tricks title, while South Africa's Deirdre Barnard won the Women's Jumping and Tricks and took second in Slalom for an Over-all victory.

Opposite: **Lars Bjork, one of Sweden's foremost skiers. This picture was taken in 1969.**

Again Royalty acknowledges the sport. Ragnar Frunck, the 'father' of Swedish water-skiing, shows his ski to King Gustav VI.

Ron Marks. One of Australia's great skiers.

By this time Ron Marks had decided to retire. He had won an Australian title – one or other of the three events – every year for eight consecutive years and ended up with thirteen National titles. At the time he retired, he had been the Over-all champion for the three previous consecutive years and the slalom champion for the four previous years, 'not a bad record, I guess'.

As an Australian champion bowed out, a Canadian skier made his international début. He was George Athans, who had only been four years old when he first planed on the water. He recalls:

'My mother had this old ironing-board and my father used to pull me along the shore of Okanaga Lake. That's in Kelowna, British Columbia, where my family lives. Our proximity to the lake and the fact that both my parents were champions in water sport made it natural for me to start water-skiing.'

Athans' father, Dr George Athans Sr, one of Canada's outstanding divers and winner of a gold medal in the 1950 British Empire Games in New Zealand had married Irene Hartzell, a champion at synchronised swimming. Their child, young George, was not allowed to water-ski until he could swim 46 m *50 yd*.

George's interest in water-skiing never waned. Every chance he got he was out on the water with his ironing-board with his father towing by running along the beach.

He had his first real skiing adventure behind a boat when he was six, quickly learning the tricky idiosyncrasies of the lake – it is about 145 km *90 miles* long but very narrow, which means that the waters are mostly choppy and the ardent skier can usually use his boards only first thing in the morning or last thing at night.

One of David Nations' earliest Training Cadres at Ruislip.

Athans put up with it because he had to, and until he was nine messed about on skis, just for fun. But then he started getting proper teaching – in slalom and tricks from Fred Schuler, who ran a Kelowna marina.

'Fred was the only one around Kelowna who really knew anything about the sport. He spent countless hours teaching me the fundamentals and everything there was to know.'

When he was eleven, George entered his first competition in Kelowna 'buoyed' with confidence and won every event in his division. The big turning point came in 1965 when the Kelowna Aqua Ski Club packed Athans off to the Canadian National Water Ski Championships.

'I came first in the Slalom event and it was there that my future in water-skiing was really shaped. Clint Ward, an Air Canada pilot, National water-ski champion, and coach-manager of the National Water Ski Team, spotted potential in me and took me under his wing. I came to Montreal and trained and practised at Hudson and in Sherbrooke. I was the number two of the national team and this qualified me for international competition.'

That came in 1966 at the North and South American Waterski Championships in Mexico. At the age of fourteen, giving away some four years to the next youngest competitor, he finished third in Slalom. 'That certainly got my hopes up. For the first time I felt I could make it to the top.'

In Britain, Jeannette Stewart-Wood was fitting in her University studies with her training programme at Ruislip and Rickmansworth. Since 1962, David Nations had held training courses, inviting people from the growing number of clubs to his training base at Ruislip: 'My idea was to teach people to coach others and to get a pattern and a standard of regular teaching. I realised that the only way we were going to train and promote talented young skiers was to establish good enthusiastic coaching

all over the United Kingdom. There is no payment for this sort of thing – they just did it for the love of it. Such wonderful people as Peter Hill, Brian Scoffam, Peter Pearl, Don Downing, David Walling – not to mention Bob Kelly in Scotland, Clive Jenkins in Wales, Tony McCleery and John Glover in Northern Ireland, and so many others – were preparing British water-skiing for a strong position in years to come, a long-term investment of fifteen years and more.'

In May 1966, 46 members from 22 clubs gathered at Ruislip, showing how the concept had grown since 1962 when 23 people had turned up – or even in 1957 when Nations had begun a small course for about five people. Now Jeannette, Robin and others were able to give demonstrations of world class quality, to the men who would be helping to find the talent in their own localities.

That July, Jeannette went over to Callaway Gardens to do battle with the world's top skiers in the US Masters Invitational Tournament. She was the first Briton ever to be honoured with such an invitation. Once again, she came face to face with Liz Allan and 'Leapin'' Linda Leavengood and acquitted herself passably well.

But in October at the Group 2 Championships at Vereeniging, South Africa, Jeannette beat Sylvie Hulsemann in Slalom, 38½ to 38 buoys, and set a new European Jumping Record of 31·54 m *103 ft 6 in*, executed in immaculate style. That was somewhat better, but her most important challenge was yet to come, in 1967, for which 1966 had only really been a warm-up.

It was in the January of 1967 that David Nations' old friend, Donald Campbell was sadly killed when his *Bluebird K7* jet hydroplane took off from Coniston Water at 515 km/h *320 mph* to crash back violently into its murky depths. Campbell had been more involved with promoting water-skiing than most skiers realised. In 1958 he had coasted the *Bluebird* up and down Ruislip

Lido at a modest 48 km/h *30 mph* to help raise funds for the Variety Club of Great Britain, and although no skiers had dared to take a tow, the run had been watched by an amazing crowd of 25 000 spectators.

It was perhaps ironic that also in 1967, Lord Wakefield of Kendal, the man who had originally footed the bill for Campbell's *Bluebird*, became the new President of the 100-Club strong British Water Ski Federation. Unknown to many, his Lordship had been involved in water-skiing since 1945, when his daughter had gone skiing round Lake Windermere, using a lengthy pair of pre-War Mediterranean skis, and a re-engined 40-year-old motor-launch called the *Lindy Loo*.

With Masters Invitational Tournaments already established in Groups I and III, it was perhaps inevitable that a European Masters be organised by one of the Group II countries. Together with W. D. & H. O. Wills, David Nations decided to take the initiative and arrange for the most exciting skiing yet to be seen in Britain. Invitations were sent out to eight European countries, the USA and Australia to come to Ruislip on 10/11 June.

For that summer's weekend, seventeen skiers had arrived from Britain, France, Holland, Italy, Luxembourg, Sweden, Switzerland, West Germany and the USA. Ron Marks of Australia was unable to come due to injury, but blonde Liz Allan arrived with the Colonel – she had been training hard for her battle with Jeannette.

The BBC and many of the Press were there in force.

The only contest held on the Saturday was the Men's Tricks, which was duly won by Christian Raisin of France, who executed 31 tricks in the 40 seconds – Britain's Paul Adlington came eighth.

Sunday began with the Women's Slalom, won by Liz Allan with 40 buoys, and Jeannette coming fourth. Women's Tricks went to Sylvie Hulsemann, who rather surprisingly beat World Champion tricks-mistress Dany Duflot. Luigi Zucchi, the one-eyed lad from Italy's Lake Maggiore (better known as 'Roby' from the robot-like way in which he used to walk as a small boy), won Slalom in superb style.

But the overseas domination was shattered in dramatic fashion with the Women's Jumping. Jeannette was the first to go:

'To me the most important thing is the beauty of the jump and the total feeling of lift and of soaring – the feeling of the cut, and of the spring and of what you're doing on the ramp, then in the air, then the landing.'

Her distance was 32·39 m *106 ft 3½ in* – while the World Champion Liz Allan could only manage 29·49 m *96 ft 9½ in*. But almost three nail-biting hours elapsed with checking and re-checking before the judges finally confirmed Jeannette's distance as 9 cm *3½ in* more than Liz's World Record. Unfortunately WWSU rules stated that for a record to be set, a jump must be 20 cm *8 in* more than the previous best – she was denied the record by a mere 11 cm *4½ in*.

In the Men's Jumping, Cypress Gardens' 23-year-old Joker Osborn jumped 41·40 m *135 ft 10 in* which was just too good for the European record-holder, Pierre Clerc of Switzerland, while Scotland's Jack Fulton jumped 36·27 m *119 ft* and came fifth. Over-all titles, hard fought, went back to Florida, with Liz and Joker. Jeannette was runner-up, but to the British crowds she was Queen of the Lido.

Again, along with Australia's Colin Faulkner, she was invited to compete at the US Masters – and continue her jumping duel with Liz Allan. Nine girls and twenty men competed, and one of the highlights was Alan Kempton's trick somersault off the ramp. Kempton went on to take the Over-all including a 45·11 m *148 ft* jump.

Another highlight was the Women's Jumping. On the first day Liz jumped 31·70 m *104 ft*, followed by a 30·17 m *99 ft* jump from Jeannette. On Day Two, Liz and Jeannette both did 31·39 m *103 ft*, but Jeannette won on form and was then only 1·5 points behind her rival. On the third and last day Linda Leavengood and Jeannette made 31·09 m *102 ft*, while Liz Allan did 30·78 m *101 ft* – but Jeannette just managed to win on her beautiful form. Liz and Alan Kempton won the Over-all, but Jeanette's victory was highly praised by 'Bo' Callaway.

The chance was now approaching which both Jeannette and Britain had waited for two years – the challenge of the World Championships.

At that time, Nations was also training two other Worlds competitors – Tito Antunano and Deirdre Barnard. He had been visiting Acapulco over many years to judge the annual event. Tito and his father became friendly with him and his wife Elaine, and David gave lessons to Tito whenever he was out there – also keeping in touch by post. Three months prior to the World Championships, Tito asked if he could come and train at Ruislip, with the ambition of an Over-all title alongside Jeannette. Deirdre Barnard, the daughter of South African cult figure Dr Christiaan Barnard, was also staying with Nations and training hard on Ruislip Lido.

At the US Nationals held on Town Lake, Austin, Texas, durable Chuck Stearns, won Slalom, Jumping and his seventh National Over-all title, a feat that could well stand for all time in the annals of Men's water-ski competition. Chuck once said: 'Before I took up skiing, I used to go to the beach a lot and we had a gang of kids that used to compete against the other kids. We had the toughest gang and I was their leader. It's always been that way with me; I like competition in anything.'

In sharp contrast to the 25 US Nationals, two countries held their very first National Championships that year. The Venezuelan Nationals were held by the newly formed VWSF with 35–40 competitors, with the Women's Championship going to 13-year-old Maria Victoria Carrasco. The Czechoslovak Water Ski Federation's President Jaroslav Malik and his Vice-President Ladislav Nemes, had organised the first CSSR Nationals in Bratislava. Their first champions were Frantisek Stehno (Men's Over-all) and Nalepova Hana (Women's Slalom and Over-all).

In 1966, René Daumas Nemoz, as President of the Mexican Federation, had organised the first Group I Championship in Tequesquitengo. Now in 1967, on the initiative of the Colombian Water Ski Association, and its President Oscar Botero Mejia, the first South American Waterski Championships were held at the Los Lagartos Club in Bogotá. Colombia came first with a team of Andres Botero, Daniel Vargas, Diego Roblendo, Manuel L. Villegas, Matilde Roblendo and Matilde Mejia. Venezuela were second and Peru third.

Late that August, David and Elaine Nations and the British team went out to Canada. David recalls: 'It was the trip of a lifetime, with so much excitement and hope attached to it, and we fully expected to see Jeannette take

Dr Christiaan Barnard driving the Boesch motorboat at the Ruislip Lido, with his daughter Deirdre enjoying her ski-run behind.

at least one gold medal. We had given so much, trained so hard and now we had arrived at the threshold of world triumph.'

It was usual after a long trip, such as the one to Canada, for the skiers to have a few days free before the start of official practice, to acclimatise and get over the effects of travelling. The British team used this chance to go and see the Montreal Expo.

The 10 000 acre Lac des Nations, Sherbrooke, Quebec created by damming the Magog River, promised to give good calm conditions. The £35 000 Chalet de Ski Nautique clubhouse with its eight huge 12·80 m *42 ft* skis mounted criss-cross fashion over the roof had been built specially for the tournament in the Jacques Cartier Park by the city of Sherbrooke, as part of the Quebec Centennial Celebrations. The 86 skiers from the 25 nations competing, stayed together at the modern and beautifully equipped University where old friendships were renewed and many new ones made.

The Opening Ceremony on Sunday saw a flag-ski parade of countries followed by a water show and aerial display, and that evening the Merrymen from Barbados made sure that the reception was a gay affair. The next three days were divided up to give skiers the chance to train on the course, and the next two and a half days after that saw the Eliminations.

Tito Antunano, who had been training hard at Ruislip, appeared to be well on his way to the Men's Over-all crown with a Slalom victory and a close second to America's Alan Kempton in Tricks. Despite American Mike Suyderhoud making a 148 ft jump, Tito was in the points lead and had the ability to keep this easily with his usual good jumping distance – but he timed his cut too late, caught his fin on the jump and took a very nasty fall, to be taken to hospital. He came back for the finals, to nail down his Slalom and Tricks successes and come seventh in Jumping – and end only 81 points behind the dedicated Suyderhoud of San Anselmo, California.

Despite a rainy Sunday, attendance at the four-day meet topped 50 000. An additional 30 000 000 were expected to watch the highlights of the action on television in the US, Canada, Europe and several Pacific countries. Tournament Director Clint Ward's 'troops' were everywhere with most of them tuned in on a $50 000 network of multi-channel radios. The order of the day was 'instant' everything, and it was carried out to the letter by twenty runners, more than 150 bilingual assistants, interpreters and typists, using twenty cars, 70 telephones (in addition to the radios), and $50 000 worth of Xerox duplicating equipment.

Interest now centred on the three-cornered battle between Liz, Linda and Jeannette. After the Slalom, Liz led by one buoy from Jeannette and Linda equal second. Then came the Jumping.

Jeannette remembers that: 'On the first day in the

World Water Ski Union President, André Coutau, with Canada's Clint Ward, preparing for the 1967 World Championships at Sherbrooke.

Jumping, my legs were like jelly. I just could not cut, which meant no speed off the ramp and my spring was wasted. The second day I cut so hard I nearly killed myself – and then I couldn't spring. It was really tough!'

But she finished first in Jumping with 29·57 m *97 ft* to Liz's 29·26 m *96 ft*, and on points Liz came third to Linda.

It was then realised that with a narrow lead of 400 points, Jeannette had the slim chance to win the Overall, but that she had to do this with Tricks, which were her greatest weakness. In Tricks, there were still four or five girls who could beat her – everything became very tense.

Under the intense pressure, the two American girls faltered. Liz Allan fell on her toe side-slide during her second run, while Linda Leavengood was only able to score 2800 points. But Jeannette could also fall.

She went running to David Nations who was sitting in the stand. There were still four to five people to go, but the best people – Dany Duflot, Elaine Borter and Sylvie Mauriol – had already gone because of the seedings. As Jeannette was so low in her Tricks, she was not due to go until towards the end.

She asked him if she could leave out two tricks that she was a little unsafe on, because the position looked so good for her to possibly grasp the title. He told her, 'No, you do exactly as you were trained. You leave *nothing* out. Just go and do your programme, then you'll have more points than anybody else!' He knew she had the ability.

Jeannette Stewart-Wood then went out on the Lac du Nations course – and brought off two magnificently steady and beautifully executed trick runs.

Nations recalls: 'Elaine and I just ran to her. There were no words because we knew. But we still had to wait for the final totting up – waiting also for the unexpected. Then we heard. She had scored 2900 points and was Over-all Champion of the World. The little girl who had started with us ten years ago, had beaten the cream of the best in the World – and we cried for joy.'

A public presentation was held on the lakeside and winners of each event in turn were handed their medals, Olympic style, while the flags of their countries were raised behind them. Later in the evening, after the banquet there was a further presentation ceremony plus speeches. Jeannette was congratulated by two men, who had also achieved much in water-skiing – André Coutau, who had just retired from his Presidency of the 42-strong World Water Ski Union he had founded so long ago, and Ralph W. Samuelson, the Guest of Honour at these Championships. Those who took first places received additional medals and all the winners received pieces of Eskimo sculpture. This was followed by the farewell ball.

As the British team flew back to London, the water-skiing world talked about Jeannette's ability to understand scientifically the technique of jumping, then to turn it into 'poetry in motion'.

Not long after his arrival back in London, David Nations received a letter from the USSR Water-ski

Jeannette Stewart-Wood – World Champion on her return home from Canada in triumph in 1967. The banner was obviously prepared in haste.

President Yuriy Gagarin, congratulating the British Federation on winning two World gold medals. 'He was so delighted and expressed how in the eyes of Soviet skiers we were heroes because by our performance we had beaten the USA. He also made a present of the badges of all the water-ski clubs in the USSR. It was a great gesture.'

And as for Jeannette: 'From now on I could have peace of mind – or so I thought.'

But something happened the following year which made her change her mind about retirement. David Nations takes up the story:

'In the early days, I encouraged everybody – paying for travel, board and lodgings, putting up people at hotels – in order to tempt them to come and ski in this country where we boast a climate with ten months of winter and two months of bad weather. But when you had skiers of ability, the cost of upkeep and of keeping drivers and equipment was beyond the possibility of what one could individually afford. It soon became apparent that very much more sponsorship was needed.

'In the early 1960s, Elaine and I had met Mr and Mrs Harborne Stephens of the *Scottish Daily Express*. I remember how, after dinner at Lochearnhead, Harborne

was rather bemused to think that this sport could ever attain any prestige and distinction. I told him that it was my primary aim to produce a world champion.

'Somewhat cynically Harborne commented: "It's a warmwater sport – you're not even successful in Europe and you can tell me this?" Then I so emphasized the point that his wife chided him for being so cynical and told him to take note of what I said.'

They became very good, close friends and Harborne Stephens eventually became Managing Director of the *Daily Telegraph*. This national newspaper was well known for covering minority sports and took on ours, with Bob Burrows (today head of BBC Sport on Radio) pioneering a form of reporting ideally suited to water skiing. When Harborne Stephens saw Jeannette become a champion, he decided to back water-skiing in a big way – with a five-figure sum of money, the *Daily Telegraph* sponsored the 1968 European Championships in Britain.

The situation of a World champion, sitting back and watching the European title taken from her grasp on home ground, without some semblance of a fight, was one which someone of Jeannette's nature simply could not accept.

9 The global ski

With literally hundreds of manufacturers now experimenting and specialising with every piece of water-skiing hardware, it might well have been wondered how much bigger the sport would grow, and how many stretches of water were left which had not seen the surf and spray of skis.

Many weird and wonderful things had been done on water-skis. Months-old children had skied supported in their parent's arms. Old men and women, blind people, even one-armed and one-legged people had skied. People had been married on skis with the priest reading the Wedding Service from the boat.

Out in the South Atlantic, after Dr Mackay's departure from St Helena in 1968, his boat and skis became the property of Graham Sim, who began to introduce the sport to some of the local men and women.

The sport was fast growing in Thailand, the most active skiers and organisers being Piboon and Pairat Bencharit, owners of the South-East Asia Trading Co., and Kasem Burokumkorit. One of the best trick skiers was Somsaki Sueyyongki of Roi Et in northeastern Thailand. A slalom and trick tournament took place at Pattaya Beach that May, with Paiboon Bencharit winning Tricks while Slalom was won by 13-year-old Nantana Javewong and Ek Silapamongki. The contest was such a success that they decided to make it an annual event.

In the Philippines, Romualdas Vildzius was promoting the sport along the coasts of Luzon and Mindanao.

On the North African coast, in Morocco, the sport came to be enjoyed more and more both on the Mediterranean and on the Atlantic shorelines. The local waterskiing experts were not merely content to practise their sport on bays, estuaries and lakes, but also skied from Mohammedia to Casablanca or across the Straits of Gibraltar – exploits which no longer seemed phenomenal, but were still tests of skill and endurance. The leading clubs on the Atlantic coast were the Royal Motorboat Club of Rabat-Sale, Casablanca, Agadir, Kenitra and Skhirat; on the Mediterranean coast, Smir and Al Hoceima offered opportunities for skiers.

By forming a Junior section of the Barbados WSA, pioneer families such as the Leacocks, the Goddards, the Johnsons and several others living on the Island had already begun to train their children to become good skiers.

In India, near Kashmir, Indians began to ski on Lake Dall, encouraged by the enthusiasm of Maganlal Radia of Bombay.

The 1968 Group I Championship was held on El Juncal ('The Rushes') Lake in Colombia, watched by many thousands of Colombians. Competing in the somewhat choppy water conditions were the USA, Canada, Mexico, Colombia, Bermuda, Argentina, Chile, Venezuela, the Bahamas and the West Indies. Ricky McCormick won the Over-all and Tricks and Mike Suyderhoud the Jumping for America, while Canada's

George Athans won the Slalom. Vailla Hoggan won Women's Tricks to prevent Liz Allan from making a clean sweep.

Meanwhile, back at Florida Cypress Gardens . . . four performances continued to be put on per day, of what was now the longest continuous running show in the world, with its very able Director, Dick Pope Jr at the helm. Many stars and public figures were drawn to the beautiful Aqua maids and the now magnificent gardens – Lee Marvin, Johnny ('Tarzan') Weissmuller, James Dean, the Shah of Iran, Victor Borge, Bette Davis, the Duke of Bedford, the Duke and Duchess of Windsor, Debbie Reynolds, Henry Fonda, King Saud of Saudi Arabia, King Hussein of Jordan, June Allison and many others. Television personalities like Dave Garroway, Joey Bishop, Bud Collier, Mike Douglas and Johnny Carson had made television shows at the Gardens.

By now the Cypress Gardens format was probably the most copied in the world. In Britain, there was Pam Horton's Ski Circus. Pam had formed the first-ever travelling British Water Ski Circus in 1964, made up of members from her club. Initially the main object was to perform shows at Theale to raise club funds in order to purchase equipment. Then more lakes were discovered whose owners welcomed the idea of a ski show to entertain the public at weekends. Such shows were staged at Dudley, London, Gloucester, the City of Birmingham's Festival of Sport, Lord Hertford's Ragley Hall (to raise funds for Coventry Cathedral) and others, some of which were televised.

Compared to the half-hour Cypress Gardens Show, which included fourteen individual acts, Pam Horton's Ski Circus was 45 minutes long with 20 acts – and particularly topical the 'Water Beatles' rode on a large disc. One of the star skiers was Jon Pertwee.

Still in the limelight, Jeannette Stewart-Wood had been presented, among other things, with a gold Maple Leaf from the British Water Ski Federation, and a 12-in silver statuette of herself in flight, made by Garrards & Co. Ltd of Regent Street, the Crown Jewellers. This was from David Nations as a reward to Jeannette for becoming a World Champion.

Among several competitions which took place that year – the annual Oxford versus Cambridge (Varsity) Water Ski fixture, was won, like the Boat Race, by Oxford, although Cambridge still led 2–1. At the 1968 British Nationals, sponsored by Coca Cola, and held on the Edgbaston Reservoir, near Birmingham, 17-year-old Gail Brantingham emerged as the most impressive newcomer.

She approached David Nations afterwards and asked if there was a chance of her ever reaching the same heights as Jeannette Stewart-Wood had done. Though at Leeds University, she indicated her willingness to work as hard as was necessary, and Nations agreed to help her with coaching and finance.

Another enthusiast arrived at Ruislip about the same time, but with a somewhat different background. He came to Nations at Ruislip and asked for a lesson. 'You never know who you're talking to when everybody is in

Water-skiing clowns, always a strong feature in the Cypress Gardens Show.

Buster MacCalla, one of the real stylists of water-ski jump-in the 50s and 60s. In 1959 he won the World Jumping Title at Milan and was later director of the water-ski show troupe at Cypress Gardens.

trunks. This gentleman said he could ski all right on two skis but not on one. I asked him what sort of craft had been towing him and he replied they had been destroyers.' It turned out to be the Commander of the Home Fleet, Admiral Sir Charles Madden. Soon after this Sir Charles, always willing to help, even became involved with jetty marshalling at the Wills Internationale that July.

A small injury received in a car accident prevented

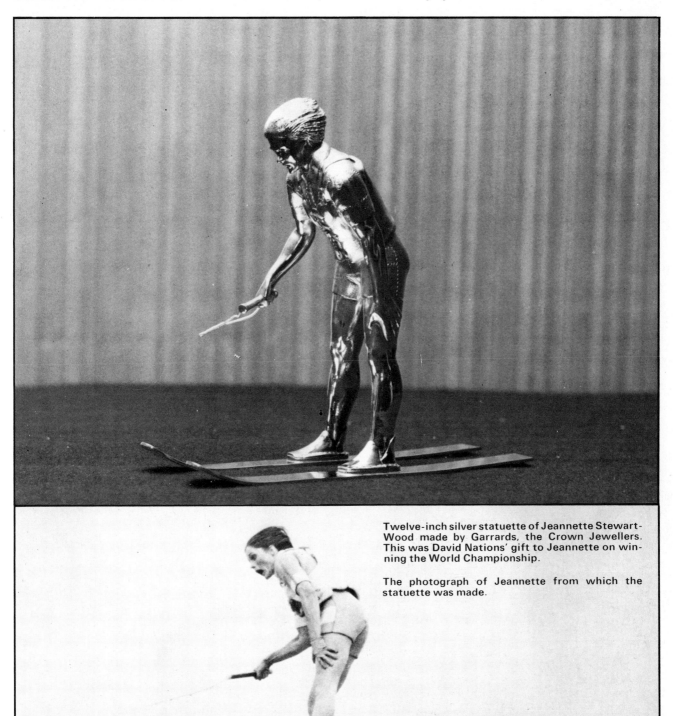

Twelve-inch silver statuette of Jeannette Stewart-Wood made by Garrards, the Crown Jewellers. This was David Nations' gift to Jeannette on winning the World Championship.

The photograph of Jeannette from which the statuette was made.

Jeannette from competing at this Internationale, together with Deirdre Barnard who was recovering from a knee-cartilage operation, and Elaine Borter who had suffered a skiing accident.

Nevertheless, this Wills European Masters was an unqualified success, with Mike Suyderhoud demonstrating the style he had used for his Record 48·76 m *160-footer*, with a 46·63 m *153 ft* winning jump, followed by the Group 2 Jumping champion Pierre Clerc with 40·23 m *132 ft* and Group 3 Jumping champion Colin Faulkner. Christian Raisin won Tricks, while Roby Zucchi won the Men's Slalom and Over-all. Barbara Cooper-Clack won the Women's Slalom and Over-all, while Sylvie Hulsemann won Jumping and Tricks, with Sylvie Maurial (France) and Connie Dane (Holland) also being placed. That evening Lord and Lady Verulam gave a party for competitors, judges and organisers at Gorhambury, their stately home.

Romain Grimstead, Lady Verulam, had recently made a documentary film with Robin Beckett on water-skiing, again sponsored by Wills, entitled 'Quest for Gold'. It was given an award at the Montreux Film Festival for the Best Sporting Film.

Having recovered from her car accident, Jeannette made a come-back for the 22nd European Championships at Bedfont, Middlesex. She was 'not skiing for myself, but for the British team'. She competed only in the Slalom and the Jumping, as with virtually no training behind her, trick-skiing was out of the question.

Nineteen countries competed and Zdenek Hovorka became the first Czechoslovakian ever to compete in the Championships. The Men's Over-all and Slalom were won by Roby Zucchi of Italy, while Jacques Tillement won the Tricks and Pierre Clerc the Jumping; Robin Beckett came seventh Over-all. In the Women's Division, Luxembourg's Sylvie Hulsemann was prevented from making a clean sweep when Jeannette made a magnificent and final leap of 27·92 m *91 ft 7 in* against Sylvie's 22·55 m *74 ft*. The prizes were presented by the BWSF's patron, the Earl of Snowdon and the band of the Royal Marines beat the retreat.

A further British landmark came when 14-year-old James Carne brought back two gold medals in Jumping and Over-all from the European Dauphin Championships. When James had joined David Nations, aged ten, this little 1·07 m *3 ft 6 in* boy, who suffered from a bad chest and winter colds, used to trek regularly right across London on buses and trains just so he could train at Rickmansworth. James Carne's brave enthusiasm would pay off in his winning no less than eight European golds in the next four years as a Dauphin, following this up with two golds as a Junior skier. It was the first time a British boy had achieved such international success. His strength was his beautiful jumping – in the same class as Jeannette – and eventually at seventeen he would break the European Jumping Record with a superb 47·85 m *157 ft*.

Under the Presidency of Eric Dolk, the sport in Sweden boomed to the point where the Swedish Federation could boast 50 clubs and 2000 members, with its water-skiing magazine *Pa Vattenskidor* (*On Water Ski*) ably edited by Christer Widing.

Left to right: Luke O'Reilly, Paul Adlington, Romain Grimstead (Lady Verulam), Dr Christiaan Barnard, David Nations, Mike Allington and Robin Beckett.

Nicholas Frangistas of the famous Greek water-skiing family.

In Yugoslavia, official competitions were now well under way, often held on Lake Zbilj, under the direction of Ljubljana WSC President Mitja Vaupotic. 'Belgrade's Best Skier Trophy' was already becoming a much-coveted prize for Czech, Austrian, Swiss and Yugo-slavian competitors. In similar fashion the Greek Federation began to organise contests between Leban-ese, Egyptian, Persian and Greek skiers – the ancient Graeco-Persian wars had now been resumed on the water!

The sport flourished in the USSR, where tournaments were held by the Belorussia SSR Water Ski Association, and the Sarapul Water Ski Club established an annual invitational tournament at Sarapul, Udmurtia. For this skiers from all over the Soviet Union practised on the Kama River for the team trophy – a Ural HiFi record player – which was won by the Moscow team. The National Championships saw 81 men and 39 women competing at the Dinamo Stadium – winners came from the Army Water Ski Club and the Aurora Club. Vladimir Filin jumped 33·53 m *110 ft*. A USSR versus CSSR con-test took place at Tbilisi, in which Vladimir Filin was the best Soviet man, jumping 37·26 m *122 ft 4½ in* and Miss Necajewa won the Women's jumping with 24·08 m *79 ft*. But the main honours went to a Czech, Zdenek Hovorka, who won the Slalom and Over-all, with another Czech named Veit, taking the Tricks title. The Czech girl, Alice Kalinova, won the Women's Over-all, Tricks and Slalom.

For the Northern European Championships, held at Bedfont, Middlesex, England, teams came from Czechoslovakia, West Germany, Sweden, Holland, Finland, Scotland, Ireland, Wales and England. England won the team title with a staggering display – British records being set in all three events. In Jumping young Paul Seaton and James Carne landed in the low 40 m's *130 ft's*, while Scottish skier Jack Fulton jumped 44·78 m *146 ft 11 in* to win the event. The Men's Slalom was won by Heikki-Olamo of Finland, and Sweden's Lars Bjork won Tricks and Over-all.

Here we can resume the story of the British girl, Gail Brantingham of whom, David Nations writes: 'Throughout the winter of 1968/69 and the following summer, Gail would come down from Leeds University to train with me at Ruislip. She really had ability and guts and I believed in her. To emulate Jeannette's success in jumping was her dream. Anything less, for Gail, was going to be very hard to accept.'

With the World Championships coming before the European competition in 1969, the only way that she could qualify for the World ratings – in two events, Jumping and Slalom – was in the British Nationals at Halstead, Essex. She won the Jump and her next competition was for the World Titles in Copenhagen, Denmark.

The XIth Championships, held on Lake Bagsvaerd, in August, attracted entries from 22 countries, as well as an eight-strong fact-finding mission from the Soviet Union. Throughout the contest a strong east wind unfortunately created poor, roughwater, skiing conditions.

Nevertheless Mike Suyderhoud retained his Over-all title, Spain's Victor Palomo took the Slalom and Australia's Bruce Cockburn won the Tricks – the first time that Spain and Australia had ever won titles. A 14-year-old American, Wayne Grimditch, of Lighthouse Point, Florida became the youngest competitor then to win a World title, when he jumped 42·82 m *140¼ ft*.

Then, for the first time in the 20-year history of the Championships, Liz Allan became the first skier, male or female, to make a clean sweep. But as Liz recalls: 'I felt it was too easy, there was no competition – I missed Jeannette Stewart-Wood at that contest. All the same, it was quite something to see England's Gail Brantingham jumping the second farthest distance in the world and winning a medal alongside me.'

In fact, in the whole history of the sport, Gail Brantingham is probably the only girl ever to win a silver medal in only the second competition of her skiing career.

Since the start of the Championships, the USA had now won 54 gold medals out of a possible 80. Much had changed since 1949 – for example, the Tricks event.

The WWSU now recognised 74 tricks, among which were water turns such as the 180° Front-Back, 180° Back-Front, up to a 720° Front-Front, 720° Back-Back, Front-Back Stepover, Back-Front Toehold and a similar sequence of wake turns – and trick Number 24, the Somersault (for which 400 points were awarded). Then there were Miscellaneous Tricks such as the side-slide, and side-slide toehold. The pioneers of the sport would have been amazed.

It was at the Copenhagen Championships that Canada's George Athans had almost clinched the Over-all; he had done so well in Slalom and Tricks that all he needed was a 39·62 m *130 ft* jump to win the big apple. He felt sure he had it in the bag, because he'd jumped over 45·72 m *150 ft* several times before. But unfortunately George's jump was drawn at the end of what had previously been a calm day – just in time for a rare late afternoon wind to spring up and make the water choppy. Athans jumped less than 36·50 m *120 ft*, and to his despair the title slipped away.

On his way home, Athans travelled together with British coach, David Nations, who gave him the friendly advice that in future he must change his ideas that world

David Nations with the Russian Delegation at the World Championships, Copenhagen, in 1969.

Victor Palomo jumping in a typically Spanish setting.

sites were always smooth. Conditions had turned the Copenhagen lake into a sea, and he had to practise under bad conditions as well as good. Athans vowed that he would do this.

At the European Championships, held at Canzo, near Milan, Italy, Gail Brantingham followed through, and as Ruislip team mate Ian Walker won the silver medal for Jumping.

What would the new decade of the 1970's produce?

At the beginning of the 1970's, in the peak season in Australia, almost 1000 boats could be counted towing skiers in all directions, on the 97 km *60 miles* of the Hawkesbury. Among the foremost competitive water skiing families, including the Faulkners, the Thurlows, the McPhersons and the Nevilles – the Cockburn family (pronounced 'Coburn') was the most effective. Sandy Cockburn was the driving force behind his three children – Bruce (18), Lesley (17) and Graeme (15).

Sandy had started his children training around the many bays of Lake McQuarry, a saltwater lake, 32 km *20 miles* from Newcastle, which opened into the Pacific Ocean and was notorious for its sharks. Sandy would arrive at the school gate every afternoon with the boat in tow and they would all go down to the lake. Lesley did not initially like skiing, but was made to do it. As she recalls: 'I used to ski and cry at the same time, but I persevered.' Bruce and Graeme showed the potential, particularly Graeme at first – but in the long run it was Bruce, a bit slow in the first instance, who learned the correct way to do things.

One of the Cockburn's friends has recalled that these children only had one pair of skis between them. On occasions, Bruce had gone and jumped and broken the bindings. Before Graeme could take his turn they had to get nails and screwdrivers out and slam the fitting back on. But Sandy was a strict instructor – they trained and trained – and they even used to train during the winter by moving around the lake to another area called Vale Point, which has a big powerhouse which pumped out warm water. They also used to shift around the lake because of trouble with fishermen – every time they put down a slalom course the fishermen would come and chop it up.

Lesley Cockburn adds: 'I think my parents thought that if we all did the one sport, it would bring us that much closer. We're inseparable now, doing everything together. I consider my brothers to be my best friends, and very seldom have an argument with them. We've developed our own special style in trick-skiing. Very few people use our type of trick-skis. In 1967, when they first brought in the shorter length of trick skis, by pure luck, the ski Dad made up split. So they put braces across it and it gave the effect we wanted on the bottom of the ski.'

Bruce is the experimenter and innovator in the family and he developed things with such tricks as the inverse tow 180°, which led to the toe back-back and the toe-wake back-back.

In the 1969 Australian Nationals, Bruce Cockburn won the Trick-skiing and Over-all titles, while Graeme won the Junior Boys' Tricks, Slalom and Over-all titles and was second in the jump. Lesley took the Women's New South Wales titles for the Trick, Slalom and Jump events.

At the 1970 Moomba Masters, Bruce, by now a World champion, won the Tricks, while American Ricky

McCormick won the Jumping with 44·50 m *146 ft* and also took the Over-all. Slalom was won by Colin Faulkner. In the Women's Tricks and Slalom, Lisa St John was successful, and Australian Kay Thurlow won Jumping and Over-all. The Cockburns were to continue winning events for some time to come.

Just across the Tasman Sea, the New Zealand Water Ski Association, by 1970, controlled eight regions with 40 separate clubs and an associate membership of 2200 – holding seven or eight national competitions a year, several of which were held in Orakei Basin, by the Auckland Club. The New Zealand champion for several years was Willy Coughey.

In South Africa, the National Champions over the past decade had been Mike Plotz, Chonky Hampson, Collard, Rumbak and Van de Merwe (Men's Division), and Barbara Drimie, Johanna Keuning, Deirdre Barnard and G. Friedman (Women's Division). The South African Waterski Association was now divided into four zones: Southern Transvaal, Northern Transvaal, Western Province and Natal.

California was once called a country in its own right and now alongside the US Nationals and Masters, the 'Cal' Cup was put up for a competition, staged in July at Berkeley Aquatic Park, with Yapp Suyderhoud, Mike's father, as a promotional director.

The first South African Team to go to Europe. Alf Korving, Mike Plotz, Barbara Drimie and Johanna Keuning.

Britain's Ian Walker went out to train at Jim Mc-Cormick's school at Tampa, Florida, to improve his tricking for the season. Walker, who was on a trainee management course in the furniture industry was also in the States in connection with his studies. Meanwhile Gail Brantingham continued to train at Ruislip, alongside two other protégés of David Nations – Sylvie Maurial from France and Willi Stahle from the Netherlands. Nations has recalled:

'Sylvie Maurial was to spend five years training with with me at Ruislip, hardly ever returning to her native France, except to qualify for her place in the French team. She was very timid and everybody in Europe knew how she used to squeak when she went over the jump, shivering and near petrified – it was for me to make jumping her best event.'

'Fred Stahle had telephoned me from Holland about his daughter Willi, who had some ability in tricks, but desperately needed to improve her slalom and jumping. So I was to instruct Willi for three years. Both she and Sylvie went through the rigorous training we employed for everybody else and it was evident that they both had the makings of World champions.'

The Winter Competition at Rickmansworth saw the appearance of an 11-year-old from Lincolnshire named Mike Hazelwood (whose farmer-father introduced him to the sport at the Lincolnshire Speedboat Club when he was eight). He jumped 20·12 m *66 ft* and although only 15 years old came second to James Carne, who won with 33·83 m *111 ft*. During that summer Hazelwood and Jack Fulton joined Nations for training at Ruislip. Of Mike Hazelwood, David Nations recounts: 'He was so small and thin that I said to his father "Don't you feed him? He's obviously got talent and he'll make good, but you've got to build him up. He's got to do exercises."' Mr Hazelwood pointed out that Mike was at a St James's Catholic Choir School, Grimsby, where they didn't do exercises. Something had to be done and the priest in charge of the school at Grimsby was contacted to point out how imperative it was for this boy, who had exceptional talent, to do exercise.

When Nations stated that he would go as far as to say that Mike Hazelwood had the potential of winning gold medals for Britain, the good Father answered:

'Mr Nations, how could you say that? Are you God?'

In fun, back came the reply: 'In British water-skiing? They say I am!'

With that the ice was broken and he allowed Mike Hazelwood to go twice a week for physical training and boxing lessons in Norwich. From then on he was to come under a very dedicated and strict training regime.

But Hazelwood still had some way to go before he would catch up with Ian Walker, who had returned from Florida to take part in the Wills Internationale at Ruislip, where he came a very, respectable fourth. Mike Suyderhoud fell in Tricks to finish third behind the two Australians, Colin Faulkner and Bruce Cockburn, but won Slalom and Jumping, while Jacques Tillement won Tricks, and Colin Faulkner won Over-all. Ruislip trainee, 20-year-old Sylvie Maurial, made a clean sweep over Sylvie Hulsemann (now Mrs Gutenstein) who was attempting a surprise comeback after two years in retirement.

But Ian's finest hour came during the 1970 European Championships, held on Lake Segrino, Canzo, Italy –

another very fine water-skiing site – when he won the first gold medal by a British *Senior* Man in 24 years, with a 42·98 m *141 ft* jump.

The following year, 1971, Liz Allan ('the greatest gal that ever put on a pair of skis') married Bill Shetter ('George'). Before long he had become her trainer on Lake Killarney, and the new Mrs Shetter was once again winning the Women's Over-all at the US Nationals on White Sulphur Lake, Columbus, Ohio. Mike Suyderhoud again won the Men's Over-all, although Ricky McCormick tricked best and the powerful Kris La Point won Slalom.

Also living beside Lake Killarney was a Mrs Cook (formerly Willa Worthington, one of the greatest women skiers of all time), who had been very busy managing a chain of restaurants. For five years, Willa had been suffering from arthritis in her hips. Then she decided on the suggestion of a friend, to begin skiing again. Buying a modern pair of skis, within three months she had learned seventeen new (to her) tricks, had learned new slalom techniques and was again jumping 18·29 m *60 ft*. Her arthritis vanished and she began to compete in the Senior Women's Division.

Cypress Gardens, where Willa had skied and developed the Aquamaid costumes, was the setting of NBC TV's production 'Ed McMahon and his Friends Discover Wet at Cypress Gardens' with Special Guest Star Bob Newhart.

Since the Johnny Carson Show, the stadium and photographers' stand, always such an important part of the Pope presentation, had been rebuilt. An 800-seat stadium was constructed in concrete, steel and wood, of cantilever design, at a cost of £200 000, while the new photo pier was a 300-seat stadium built in octohedron-tetrahedron design.

It was from these two fine stadiums that spectators were able to watch McMahon, Newhart, the Aquamaids and Champions, Zany Aquatic Clowns, Daredevil Skydiving and the exciting precision boat driving team, the Johnson 'Super Stingers'. It was also in 1971 that, organised by Jean Marie Muller and backed by the French Government, a World Cup International was hosted by Tahiti in the South Pacific – land of flower-garlands and grass skirts. The hospitality was superb.

But perhaps the most imaginatively conceived ski show of the 1970s was to appear six years later, in front of the Atlantis Starlight Theatre at the Sea World, South of Orlando in Florida. This was to see a daily performance, woven around famous comic-strip Superstars skiing on a 17-acre lagoon – 'Batman and Robin', 'The Flash', 'Green Arrow', 'Captain Marvel', 'Wonder Woman and Superman' had their skiing feats made difficult by such villains as the Crook, Riddler, Penguin, Joker and Mr Freeze. Skilfully organised and backed by Mercury Marine, and realised by a staff of 37 under the supervision of Chuck Gordon, the Atlantis show would soon be holding its own with the Cypress Gardens Show, not that many miles away from each other.

On the other side of the Pacific, encouraged by Mr R. Sasakawa, Chairman of the Japanese Water Ski Association, Professor Hsu Fu-teh of Taiwan, Republic of China, formed a National Committee, which was to culminate, the following year, in the foundation of the Amateur Water Ski Association of the Republic of China, with 7 clubs and 28 teams, almost immediately

Canada's George Athans.

approved by Group III President for affiliation to the WWSU.

The Spanish Nationals took place that year at San Sebastian on the north coast. World champion, Victor Palomo, was forced to retire from skiing after these Championships at Arcos de la Fronte because of a severe leg injury caused by falling off a motorcycle. He was to do much good work in training national teams for the future, but it was a real tragedy that he was unable to compete at the twelfth World Championships, which were held in his home territory on the crystal clear waters of Lake Bañolas, near Gerona.

About four days before the Championships were due to begin, there was virtually nothing on the site, but backed by the Spanish Government, work went on around the clock building the judges' tower, cement pontoons, etc. – not to mention transplanting four full-size trees – to create a fantastic piece of 'Spanish Architecture'.

There were 115 competitors from nineteen nations. Mike Suyderhoud, US Captain and defending World champion, lost his Over-all title to George Athans, whose rough water training programme had paid off. Mike salvaged his international prestige by picking up the top prizes in Slalom and Jumping. Liz Shetter had decided to sit this one out in favour of marriage and the pursuit of her college studies. Nevertheless, the Women's Over-

all crown was retained by the US, thanks to the steady skiing of Christy Lynn Weir in all three events of the preliminary round – Christy also won a gold medal in Jumping, while her team-mate Christie Freeman became the 1971 queen of the World Slalom skiers. Ricky McCormick won the gold for Trick-riding. The only event to elude the US skiers was the Women's tricks which was won by David Nations' protégé, Willi Stahle of the Netherlands. Perhaps the most dramatic and unfortunate incident was when a Spaniard mis-timed his cut and did two vicious somersaults on the ramp, to the horror of the thousands of spectators.

In spite of wind and rough water conditions that plagued much of the competition, many of the winning performances were the best ever recorded at a world tournament – Suyderhoud's perfect slalom pass with 9·8 m *32 ft* off the line, and three buoys with 10·67 m *35 ft* off, plus his 48·43 m *158·9 ft* jump; Christie Freeman's perfect pass with 9·75 m *32 ft* off the line, and one buoy at 10·67 m *35 ft* off. Ricky's 5567 point trick run was fantastic and had the judges completely baffled. Despite the availability of instant replay motion pictures, they required several hours to agree on his total pointage.

On the social side, with the Championships hotel situated 56 km *35 miles* away on the coast at Bagur, and with the judges and some competitors enjoying themselves pleasantly till late in the discotheque, the prospect of making the journey to the tournament site every dawn, was considerably enhanced when the Spanish Air Force laid on a fleet of helicopters to fly them to and fro.

At the WWSU Congress, the Union now recognised 48 countries. Franco Carraro resigned as President and Alan Clark of Australia was elected.

The Israeli Team.

One of the spectator countries at the Worlds had been the Israelis, and David Nations notes:

'Water-skiing in Israel is the story of one man's dream – that of the first Baron Sieff. In the days of peace he had first thought of developing Israel into a combined St Moritz/South of France type of resort to attract the tourists; to be able to snow-ski on the Mount Hermon heights and then come down in under 30 minutes to be water-skiing in temperatures over 70° F on Lake Tiberias (the Sea of Galilee).'

When Baron Sieff died his son Sir Marcus Sieff, the Chairman of the Marks and Spencer chain store in England, asked Nations if he would help in this project. At Bañolas in 1971, among the first few Israelis who had come to see World Class skiing were Izzi Marshawsky and Maurice Greenberg. When they were told about the plans they were terribly enthusiastic.

So in 1972, Nations went out to Israel with his business partner, Freddy Strasser, and Marcus Sieff. They donated skis and equipment and had a ramp built while lectures and seminars were conducted for all those interested. An Association was formed and Nations was asked to become President, and Strasser the Vice-President.

The Government was asked to assist in the idea of promoting tourism and an excellent site was viewed at the end of Lake Tiberias, which would provide wonderful facilities with water sheltered by the mountains. Baron Sieff's dream was becoming a reality because the Israeli Government and the local Mayor of Tiberias backed the project and all development in the area was prohibited.

Many offers of help were forthcoming and it was thought that many European skiers could be induced to come and train in the warm waters of Galilee in the winter months. 'We all got very enthused about it and set up a consortium to raise money and funds and approached big developers and planners back in England to set all this up. I had a series of meetings with Israeli Tourist Ministers. The whole thing was set to roll but it was delayed because of 1973 Yom Kippur War.'

After the Bañolas World Championships, Israel had been invited to send some skiers, young people who could just about ski – the Marshanksy boys and Moshik Ganzi – together with Maurice Greenberg to Ruislip. There Greenberg was taught how to become a technical officer – all about judging and the technical side – while the others were given coaching instruction. This was repeated in subsequent years.

In the Netherlands, which had previously produced Connie Dane, Willi Stahle became the greatest skier that country has yet produced, when she made a clean sweep with four gold medals at the 1972 Group 2 Championships at Temple-sur-Lot. Also, when referring to Dutch water-skiing one must mention Arie de Gans and Marlon van Dijk. But tournament skiing being, of course, only a very small part of the sport, the 25 member-clubs of the Nederlandse Waterski Bond were only a small part of the total water-skiing fraternity in that country.

The same may be said of the fourteen clubs and 900-odd skiers in the Danish Waterski Federation (by now accepted and financially aided by the National Federa-

Despite appalling conditions at the Olympics of 1972 (*above*) the medal ceremony was held.

tion of Sports). Their National champions were Bo Lassen and Lisbeth Grabowski and they could now afford to go away on training courses etc. Niels Vinding has a great challenge ahead of him as President of this Federation.

The year 1972 was regarded as the 50th Anniversary of Water Skiing. The Minnesota Historical Society honoured Lake City as its birthplace with an impressive historic marker on the shores of Lake Pepin. A crowd of 40 000 people stayed to see the Centennial Parade as Ralph Samuelson rode in the place of honour on the Centennial Float, 'competing for attention with some pretty glamorous girls'. Soon after this, Ralph and Walter Bullock, the man who had piloted the Curtiss flying boat which had towed the young Samuelson across Lake Pepin, were elected to the Water Ski Hall of Fame in Orlando and the Aviation Hall of Fame. 'It just shows you,' laughed Samuelson, 'if you do something crazy enough, you'll be famous some day.'

Other landmarks that year included 17-year-old Wayne Grimditch breaking the Men's Jumping Record with 51·51 m *169 ft*, at the US Masters, while already holding the Junior Boys' and the Boys' Jumping Record at 40·84 m *134 ft*. He became the only one ever to hold all three records simultaneously.

At the Moomba Masters Tournament in Melbourne, Australia, Graeme Cockburn and Kay Thurlow won the Over-all crowns – the third in a row for Kay Thurlow, although Lesley Cockburn's Tricks victory prevented her from taking the 'grand slam'. Wayne Grimditch won the Jumping there with 46·50 m *152½ ft*.

But perhaps the most important step for water-skiing in 1972 was its inclusion as the Invitation Sport at the Olympic Games in Kiel, West Germany, alongside the scheduled sailing contests, with the competitors housed in the Olympic village. This virtually acknowledged that the sport had come of age and could stand alongside other sports, some of which were over two thousand years old. But it had only been achieved after fourteen years of diplomacy, behind which Switzerland's André Coutau had been the tireless, leading light.

The first overtures had been made in 1958 to members of the International Olympic Committee (IOC) and the Presidents of the National Olympic Federations. Coutau relates:

'It was in Tokyo at the 1964 Olympic Games that we first put forward the Union as a candidate, knowing that we would not be accepted as a whole federation, because the number of Federations (21) able to participate in the Games was limited. We wanted to be known as an International Federation for the Sport with the hope that the question would be reconsidered. During 1965 we had various contacts with the IOC President, Avery Brundage, and IOC secretaries, who gave us valuable advice. At Tokyo our first request had been received, and then reviewed at the Congress of Madrid, in October 1965. Since then we had followed up our endeavours and contacted Mr Taher, an important member of the IOC, and several contacts were made with his secretary, Mr Jonas. One objection which was made to us was that Part 6 of our Constitution was in opposition to the rules of the IOC. This needed a modification of the constitution, which would be presented at the next Congress of the WWSU at Surfers Paradise in October 1965. The Group Presidents gave their agreement at this Congress.

'Then in January 1966, we prepared an illustrated brochure of 28 pages edited by Mr Franco Carraro and Mr Varella. All the members of the IOC and the Olympic Federations received a copy (in total 600). Mr Diacakis, President of the Greek Federation, published privately an essay entitled 'Echo from Olympia', in which he studied the Olympic possibilities of water-skiing and the external mechanical forces necessary to practise it. He quite justly compared the towboats to the chariots and horses of antiquity and to the sailboats used in today's modern games. These publications strongly aided our cause with the IOC.

'In Lausanne, we also personally contacted Mr Brundage, the Olympic President, who listened with interest. Our request was duly examined at the IOC Congress at Rome in April 1966. Then, on 12 June 1967 we were finally told that our request had been accepted by the Olympic Congress in Teheran. The WWSU became an Olympic Federation, with one reservation: the sport could not take part in the Games. Within the Olympic framework of 21 official sports there was always the chance that this condition might change. After five years of struggle, the German Water Ski Federation persuaded the Olympic officials to choose water-skiing as one of the two "non-participating" sports customarily demonstrated at the Games.'

In very rough water, the 35 skiers took part. Roby Zucchi won Slalom, while Ricky McCormick won Tricks and Jumping. And in the Women's events Holland's Willi Stahle won Tricks, Liz Allan Shetter won Slalom and Sylvie Maurial won Jumping. Ian Walker came eighth in Tricks and ninth in Slalom, while Karen Morse came sixth in Jumping. The victors were presented with the identical gold, silver and bronze medals that were presented in the official Olympic sports – the only difference being that these medals were not included in the unofficial tables of medallists by country. But it was at least a move in the right direction.

Another significant achievement of the period was the creation of an artificial lake in the middle of a desert, specially designed for water-skiing by and for Doctor Jack Horton, his family and friends. Horton's father had spent nearly two years searching California's Mojave Desert, before picking a site near Newberry Springs, a small community 27 km *17 miles* east of Barstow. The lake was to be 201 m *220 yd* wide and 804 m *880 yd* long and it took nine months for an excavation contractor to dig and seal the bottom with clay and native Bentonite, and another nine months to well-pump the lake full to a general depth of 1·68 m *5½ ft*, with two basins 2·13 m *7 ft* deep.

Calm water and ideal tournament conditions could be maintained to a major degree by turnaround islands at either end which virtually eliminated wake problems. Additional protection was afforded by a half-mile windbreak of evergreens which would grow to a height of 15·24 m *50 ft*. The slalom course was put in permanently (measured with steel tapes) on the lake bottom before the lake was filled. Clouds are few and rain is extremely rare in the area, while mountains surround the site. The Lake abounded with more than 20 000 catfish (the fish with whiskers) which the Hortons were to raise commercially and sell as 'fingerlings' at the side of the lake. Naturally, it was not long before Dr Horton had organised a meeting which he called the Horton Lake Over-all Super-Masters three-day tournament.

The XIIIth World Championships, held at the exclusive Los Lagartos Club near Bogotá, Colombia, South America, raised doubts in some minds. All competitors were booked into the Tecandama Hotel some 25 minutes' drive through slum poverty areas to the beautifully lush, fully equipped country club with its two swimming pools, golf course, tennis courts and beautiful lake. The main problem was acclimatisation because, with the lake 2438 m *8000 ft* above sea level, medical officers advised the use of oxygen at the starting jetties to help competitors breathe more easily. Another problem was the unusual pattern of weather. From a cold morning of track suits and anoraks, by eleven o'clock the weather was hot enough for swim trunks and bikinis. Also it rained almost every day at lunchtime for at least an hour-and-a-half and then by about four o'clock in the afternoon it had turned cold again.

The man whom everybody was talking about was George Athans, who was known to train for only four months every summer, with tough snow-skiing to keep him in shape during the Canadian winter. As well as studying Communication-Public Relations Studies at Sir George Williams Concordia University in Montreal, George found time to help design skis for Sea Gliders of Canada.

In between the changeable weather, 'Gentleman George' and America's Lisa St John won the Over-all competitions, Ricky McCormick and Liz Allan-Shetter won the Jumps, Athans and France's Sylvie Maurial won the Slaloms, and Wayne Grimditch and Venezuela's 19-year-old Victoria Maria Carrasco won the Tricks. The agility and beauty of the Carrasco trick-run had been rumoured throughout the world, but this was the first opportunity most enthusiasts had had to see it, and, needless to say, this pretty girl with the radiant smile, caused a sensation with her high point score.

The Colombian hosts took the competitors on trips to the Gold Museum, to see emeralds, and a magnificent cathedral carved out of a salt mine.

One of the happiest competitors to return home to her native France was the beautiful Sylvie Maurial, who wrote to her English instructor and mentor as follows: 'Dear Mr Nations, all I want to tell you again and again is THANK YOU. This world title that I won in Bogotá is due to you and the work that we did together in Ruislip. All the falls, the tears, the cold, the disappointment has been rewarded with your help. My parents and myself missed you so much on that day, to share our happiness.'

Although Russia was still not competing in the World championships, they had certainly progressed. In the period from 1967 to 1974, leading Soviet water-skiers had taken part in twelve International meets with the national teams of Czechoslovakia, the German Democratic Republic, Poland, West Germany, France and Finland. In the first eight meets the Soviet skiers had eight wins, were runners-up seventeen times and came third twenty-three times. In the last two contests they won top honours eighteen times. The skill of such skiers as Anatoly Radushinsky, Inessa Potes, Vladimir Filin, Galina Litvinova, Victor Melnik, Tamara Retskaya and Olga Zorina was reaching top international level.

In 1974 the USSR Championships were held for the first time in a specialised water-ski stadium at Dnepropetrovsk in the Ukraine. When it was completed, the stadium had three aquatories, well protected from wind and waves, separated by artificial islands – remarkably reminiscent of Dr Horton's lake.

At this time, the World Record Jumping still remained the province of the Floridans. At the US Nationals, held

Below: **The XIIIth World Championships at Bogota, Columbia.** *From right to left:* **J. Y. Parpette (France), J. M. Jamin (France), P. Seaton (GB), J. Battleday (GB), J. Carne (GB), M. Hofer (Italy), P. Clerc (Switzerland), Finsterwald (Switzerland)**

To Mr Nations, and
Ruislip water ski club !
for all s ouve vrew - Thank you -

Sylvie Maurial

Sylvie Maurial at the World Championships in Bogota.

at 'Bo' Callaway's Gardens, not only did Liz Shetter make a clean sweep, but also set a new Record jump of 38·10 m *125 ft*. She has described her feelings when jumping: 'When I'm out of control I hit the ramp, I get nothing out of it. When I have a hellacious cut, all in control, my arms in, body together, and I hit the ramp and spring. It's like – if you ever remember as a kid, when you've got a rope on a bucket of water and swing it around your head, you feel this centrifugal force, keeping the water in the bucket – this is what you feel when you come off the top of the ramp. The boat and the rope and the air and everything just pulls the hell out of you, your arms and your body, and you're just being lifted straight up and out. That's what I feel going up and then out and then slowly down. I guess the most exciting part is just when you leave the jump, just as you come right off the top and reach your highest point, then when you come down and stand. I'm trying so hard for the feeling that I'm going so much further than I've gone before.'

Kris La Point, with his superbly co-ordinated legs and arms, won Slalom for the fourth year running, while Russ Stiffler won Tricks for the first time.

Meanwhile a very successful International tournament was held – in excellent conditions with wonderful hospitality – by the young Jordanian Water Ski Federation in the Bay of Aqaba.

In 1975, Alan Clark, the President of the 50-strong World Water Ski Union stated: 'International organisation is growing at a speed which keeps pace with the growth of the sport. We just cannot find out how many millions of people throughout the world ski regularly. But if you care to look at the statistics of water-ski manufacturers, I reckon you'd finish up with something like 40 to 50 – maybe 80 million skiers in the world today. Twenty years ago it was a bit of a hill-billy recreation. It is now a very highly technical and skilled sport.'

US Government researches have predicted that participation in water-skiing in the States would increase more than 300 per cent by the year 2000, i.e. 30 million skiers. By 1975 the current figure stood at an estimated 14 million Americans.

Back in the USSR, Boris Olshevsky of the TASS News Agency, wrote that: 'Water-ski sections are functioning in 52 towns of the USSR and their number keeps growing. Fifteen thousand people go in for the sport seriously. The cities of Rybinsk and Dnepropetrovsk have water-skiing stadiums and the construction of similar facilities is underway in Balakovo, Riga and Minsk.

'Water-skiing is practised in the leading Soviet sports societies among them Dynamo, Trudovye, Reservy, Spartak, Zenit, Trud, Avangard, Gantiadi, Vodnik, Daugavka and Krasnoye Znamya. Soviet industry produces high-quality gear – skis, bindings, suits and tow-ropes.

'Anyone who is physically fit can become a water-skier by joining a club. The membership fee is 30 Kopeks a year for which he can use club gear and get expert training.

'The USSR Federation supervises the development of the sport, co-ordinates the activity of locally-based organisations, works out regulations for competitions, arranges national championships and international meets, and trains coaches and judges. In the near future water-skiing sections will be opened at the Institutes of Physical Culture of Moscow, Leningrad, Volgograd,

Kiev and Minsk for the purpose of training specialists. The Federation intends to join the World Water Ski Union soon with a view to taking part in World and European Championships.'

In the People's Republic of Communist China (where the population is some 700 000 000 people), Hsu Te-Tsin of the All China Sports Federation has stated that there water-skiing is just beginning to develop.

While in neighbouring Taiwan, Professor Hsu Fu-teh reported: 'The ski population in this country is around five thousand, and looking forward to growing.'

Of the Czechoslovakian scene, Engineer Ladislav Nemeš has reported: 'Nowadays the Czechoslovak Water Ski Federation has 55 clubs with 2350 members and 1010 active competitors. During the last season 44 tournaments were organised in our country. We now have 30 Boesch motorboats and 70 boats with Wartburg, Crescent or Mercury motors with 50–100 hp. Our champion, tricks-master Frantisek Stehno, is a national hero.'

In Australia, the New South Wales Water Ski Association alone could boast 4000 skiers, while membership of the Australian Water Ski Association was estimated at about 15 000.

However, Britain still remained the second largest Federation in the Union in terms of membership, boasting 125 clubs and some 85 000 skiers. France had 130 clubs, Italy 80 clubs, Norway 7 clubs with 200 members, Finland 36 clubs, Austria 20 clubs, Sweden 70 clubs, Germany 50 clubs and Poland 5 clubs.

In terms of tourism, water-skiing could never have been more popular. For example, the Club Mediterranée, which opened its first holiday tent village in 1950, had begun water-ski instruction and runs for its guests at Corfu in 1953 with 'Artoff' Reffay as instructor. By 1975, the Club had 87 villages, in 18 of which there were 520 ski-instructors taking about 100 000 Club members for ski-runs. These villages could be found all across the world – at Buccaneer's Creek (Martinique), Mauritius (in the Indian Ocean), Thalassa (Roumania) and Sveti-Marko (Yugoslavia).

Yugoslavia, to take a popular example of water-ski tourism, could offer almost 644 km *400 miles* of Adriatic coastline for skiing, south from Umag down to Ulcinj, while Lake Zbilj near Medvode, Zagreb, Bosanski Brod, Velika Gradiska, Skopje and Lake Dojran were only some of the inland stretches of skiable water available to tourists.

Out of all these skiers, Wayne Grimditch still proved himself the World's Greatest jumper, when he reached 52·42 m *172 ft* at Horton Lake Open, and then went on to achieve something that raised him to a legendary level.

For a long time it had seemed that 54·86 m *180 ft* was an impossible target. To jump about 50 m *170 ft*, with the boat travelling at 57 km/h *37 mph*, a skier must position himself for his counter-cut (the first of his two cuts), go slightly to the incline, pull out very wide on the counter-cut, stay in the position, then cut in with the hard edge, right the way past the boat driver's position; leaning in well away, the skier nearly comes to a stop, almost brakes, and then is pulled from a 'frozen' position to the ramp and with a tremendous kick off the ramp to land 'with legs like fire hydrants'.

On Sunday 12 July 1975, the US Masters at Callaway Gardens, Wayne Grimditch lifted the record to exactly

Mobjar Music,
Yugoslavian National
Champion in 1973.

54·86 m *180 ft*. As he relates: 'Usually on a good jump, everything goes fairly easily and that's just about how I felt. It was very easy. I had a good cut and then a good spring and from then on it's just maintaining your own form. But it has to do with a lot of practice and building up strength beforehand, and a lot of concentration and things like that. For instance, we usually video-tape my jumps then analyse them in slow motion.

'There are a lot of times in practice when you don't do well, a lot of people get down and really upset over it. A lot of times when I do poorly in practise on Lake Ida, I just don't worry about it. Positive thinking is important. Progressively building each time and not going beyond your limit.

'It's a great feeling on a good jump – just floating and hanging in the air like that. It's really tough to describe the sensation but it's enjoyable. I guess the sensation is just prolonged a little bit more!'

It was a sad irony that nine days after Wayne's jump, while the record was still in the process of homologation, England's Paul Seaton jumped 53·80 m *176 ft 6 in* at the British Nationals. If the Masters had been scheduled one fortnight later, this would undoubtedly have counted as a World Record – as it is, it was a new European and British Record.

Britain in 1975 was at another peak of its water-skiing history. After almost thirty years of tireless effort to bring the sport to the country, to develop it to what it was, and to bring back honours, David Nations went to Buckingham Palace where he was awarded the Order of the British Empire (OBE) by Her Majesty Queen Elizabeth II. In accepting the honour he felt that:

'After so many years, recognition was given to me but, as far as I was concerned, it was more because they had recognised water-skiing as a serious sport.'

At the Britain-versus-France International sponsored by Old Spice at Ruislip Lido that July, Paul Seaton, recently returned from training in Florida, won the Over-all, Tricks and Jumping, while Mike Hazelwood set a new National Record for Slalom of 26 buoys through gusting wind and driving rain. England beat France by 1254 points and Jean Marie Muller took his team of Naudinat, le Prince and Sommer home for further training.

For Paul Seaton, Mike Hazelwood, James Carne, Karen Morse, Ann Pitt and Jack Battleday, and the team captain, Ian Walker, the task ahead was a challenging one: to compete successfully in the XIVth World Championships to be held on their home-ground, at Thorpe Water Park, Surrey, England.

10 The World Championships: 1975

On board the Roman Galley, Britannica, at the 1975 World Championships at Thorpe Water Park, England. *From left to right:* Alan Endsor (Leisure Sport), Dennis Howell (Minister for Sport), Kevin Desmond, David Nations, OBE, Terry Catliffe (Leisure Sport).

In 1970, Ready Mixed Concrete Ltd had formed a new subsidiary company, Leisure Sports Ltd, with the objective of providing centres for recreation in beautiful surroundings where the general public could watch top sportsmen in training and competition and be encouraged to learn and develop new sports and interests. One of the prototype centres is the 500-acre Thorpe Water Park in Surrey, 30 miles outside London, England, which includes some 300 acres of water, extensively and naturally landscaped to provide special facilities for various types of watersport – including an embanked arena designed to give optimum conditions for water-skiing.

The primary purpose of the Arena, developed to competition requirements, would be to serve the XIVth World Championships, which Leisure Sport had decided to host in September 1975. With almost five years to go, it might well have seemed that the company directors and the British Water Ski Federation had plenty of time on their hands.

However, as if the problems of preparing for a World Championship were not enough, halfway through the development of their facility, Leisure Sport were faced, in 1974, with the first major setback. They had gone ahead after receiving outline planning permission for the site, only to find that the details of their plan had not been accepted.

David Nations was approached, in his capacities as a Government Officer for the Water-Space Amenity Commission (representing the eight million people who use the water for recreation purposes in the British Isles) and also as Chairman of the Water Recreational Division of the Central Council for Physical Recreation. With the backing of this new and future-thinking government agency, devoted to the development of water sports, and after many meetings with the local authorities, the Leisure Sport directors were able to go ahead, using the 28-day rule which allows certain facilities to be used without detailed planning permission. The Championships would be held.

But this and other delays meant less and less time in which to have the complex in readiness. Nevertheless, in so far as equipment for the contest was concerned, it would be as modern, fast and accurate as possible.

At the first World Championships, jumping-distance readings had been made using a calibrated cord, fixed permanently from one side of the ramp. Several boats, with judges, were moored alongside this cord and would estimate distances.

Later a reading by two viewfinders was introduced and gave better results, with skiers approaching the ramp head-on. But when they began to cut and reach farther distances, a new system of angular measurement was introduced in 1964, which gave exact lengths using three viewfinders, placed at about 10–20 m *32–65 ft* and up to 40 m *131 ft* from the ramp. They measured the angle of point of impact on a fixed protractor, the three angles being plotted on a 'Master Chart' giving the point of impact. Later still, each position had been equipped with two viewfinders placed one above the other, and their average taken. Despite the wider and wider cut, with the jump-lengths increasing, this system always worked well.

The challenge was then tackled by Longines of Switzerland, who measured by three positioned cameras filming the jumps across a calibrated grid, to fix the exact point of impact of the skier's heel with the water. Film needing time to develop, the viewfinder system was the quicker, although often both systems were used together so as to give immediate results as well. It was soon replaced by three fixed video-tape cameras, the tape immediately examined on a calibrated TV screen – and the impact frame, showing the skier's distance, being examined within 75 seconds.

For many years, all calculations had been made by hand and Johnny Morris recalls: 'At first we used slide rules. The first six places were probably right, while the others . . .! It used to take us all night and was frustrating for both skiers and spectators.'

'After using a Bodenia electric calculator at the 1959

British Nationals, we toured the computer companies, only to be refused help, with the exception of de la Rue Bull (now Honeywell) who gave us their support absolutely free, providing telephones, programming and instant results. The first computerised results' service took place at the 1969 Wills Internationale at Ruislip, and with the Longines jumping measuring system, produced results to ·01 of a metre *½ in*.

For the XIVth Worlds, the computer was programmed for the site, the measurements and the positions of the three closed-circuit cameras. In the control room, computer terminals would take input from the three cameras, to link up by satellite to American computer 'super centres' several thousand miles away at Cleveland, Ohio, and Rockville, Maryland. Results (to 0·001 metre accuracy) would be available within minutes of the final competitor finishing each event.

There were several other sophisticated schemes for this contest. For Slalom, Longines had put an electronic contact into the starting gates of the course of six carefully measured buoys, to control the boat speed, which cut out at the end of the course. The boat speed was so precise that a tenth of a second had become the difference between a given run and a re-run.

While these details were being worked out, in triplicate, yet another threat reared its ugly head. Because of racial discrimination in South Africa, the British Government told Leisure Sport quite categorically that unless they banned that country from the tournament, it would have to withdraw the £15 000 it had contributed towards the cost of the Championships. As a member of the WWSU, South Africa was fully entitled to compete. With only weeks to go, the Executive Committee of the WWSU voted 7–3 to allow Leisure Sport to make their own decision. Inevitably they followed Government policy and South Africa did not take part.

About a fortnight before – and it couldn't have been later – a grandstand for 5000 people and the Judges Tower were still under construction on either side of the Arena, and flagpoles were being put up round one embanked end of the course, where the grass seed was beginning to grow.

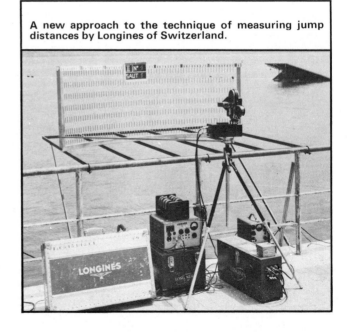

A new approach to the technique of measuring jump distances by Longines of Switzerland.

At the same end, was the symbol of Thorpe Water Park, a 3·66 m *12 ft* high golden fibre-glass statue of a nude Britannia, with shield and trident, and flanked by four lions. Henceforth that end became known as the Britannia End, while the other end was known as the Start Jetty.

For a welcome change, the British Isles had been blessed with a hot, sunny and prolonged 'Indian Summer', and it was under blue skies that Her Majesty's Minister of Sport, Mr Denis Howell, travelled out by motorboat to board the raft that carried the statue of Britannia – and with a fanfare of trumpets – to unveil her naked beauty to the world.

The opening ceremony back at Leisure Sport's HQ at Eastley End House had the national teams of 22 countries assembled around a circular lawn setting of their flags. Then, to the accompaniment of the Royal Marine Band, in an Olympic-like ceremony, they all marched past the reviewing stand where they were presented with medallions by officials of the host country. Minister Howell spoke of the implications of International Sport:

'At its top level it is the means by which many thousands can measure their progress through the media of television and the newspapers which, of course, create tremendous interest in events like this. It means that they too might take up this sport of water-skiing and perhaps achieve the personal satisfaction of representing their own country. There is no honour to compare with this, in my opinion. No honour compares with representing your country at sport. It is the highest distinction.'

On Monday and Tuesday, practice took place, and the competitors discovered that they had the finest site in the history of the sport – tailor-made to their requirements. Liz Allan commented: 'A skier's dream is perfect water conditions and we've certainly got them here. There are about three or four perfect sites in the world that I've been to in my career – this sure is one of them!'

Wednesday, 3 September, was the first day of competition and there was the inevitable tension in the air, with amongst other things the Australian team arriving nearly too late to compete. The excitement of the Men's Jump with a field of 63 in the eliminations, was dampened, as indeed was the morale of the British team and the Championships themselves, by the unfortunate injury to the popular Paul Seaton. On his second jump, he landed badly, snapping three ligaments and damaging the cartilage of his left knee, and was carried off to the nearby Chertsey hospital.

With Thursday and early Friday taken up by the eliminations, the finals were watched by at least 15 000 spectators, not to mention worldwide television coverage of recorded highlights.

First came the Women's Jumping, in which six of the eight finalists bettered their qualifying distances with Liz Shetter getting it all together to make a crowd-electrifying leap of 37·55 m *123 ft 2 in* to capture the gold medal. Liz commented: 'God, I always feel the acclamation of the crowd – before I landed, I literally felt this tremendous murmur which turned into a roar of cheering.'

Britain's Karen Morse got off the second best jump, a new European Record of 35·75 m *117 ft 3 in*, but it still left her out of the chase for the silver and bronze medals, which were taken by Australian team-mates, Kay Faulkner and Lesley Cockburn (making their own personal best ever landings).

In the Women's Slalom Final, Liz won again, while Sylvia Terracinao hung on to second place, and Canada's Pattsie Messner was the only skier to improve on her first day's performance and moved up from eighth to finish, remarkably, in third position.

After a nasty jumping spill earlier in the day, in which she had injured her hamstring, Maria Victoria Carrasco went out on to the water and once again won the gold medal in Trick-riding, just ahead of her sister, while Australia's Kay Faulkner moved ahead of Liz to take third place.

At 24 years of age Liz Allan Shetter now added a fourth World Over-all title to her other three and stated:

'Now I'm going to retire while I'm still ahead. I've been skiing for fourteen years and it gets harder to practise all the time.' Watching these finals were a host of pioneers from water-skiing's past, some still actively involved. From America, Bill Clifford and Bill Barlow Sr and the US team manager Lex Carroll, who began skiing in 1946. From Europe, André Coutau, Philippe de Backer, Lanfranco Colombo and Claude de Clercq – as well as Jean Jacques Finsterwald, Jean-Marie Muller, Ivan Cantacuzene and Frans Stevens. From Australia, the WWSU President Alan Clark, and from Indonesia Colonel Andi Matalata. England's pioneers were represented by Carl Erhardt, Peter Felix, and Mrs John Williamson (*née* Jeannette Stewart-Wood) now expecting a baby.

Perhaps the one Englishman who might have appreciated a World Championship contest in England, who once claimed to be the first World champion, and who could certainly have appreciated how far competition had developed since his era, was sadly not present. Captain d'Arcy Rutherford had died in Canada in 1968, virtually forgotten.

For Claude de Clercq it was a revelation: 'Several seconds after sitting down, I saw the trick-run of the Venezuelan girl, who won the title. I had not seen the sport for very many years and I was absolutely overcome during her exhibition. I had tears in my eyes. I did not think, despite everything that had been told me about skiing during recent years, that it was possible to arrive at such perfection, such continuity, such rhythm.'

The final day of these Championships arrived. It was a Saturday, the weather was warm and bright and over 20 000 people had turned up at the Arena to watch the world's best men skiers in action.

The Jumping saw eleven of the twelve finalists improve their distances of the first round. Ricky McCormick set the pace with the longest jump of the tournament – 52·25 m *171 ft 5 in*, but it only gave him fourth place because of his eliminations score of 47·10 m *154 ft 6 in*. Wayne Grimditch and Bruce Cockburn battled for first place, with Grimditch at 49·85 m *163 ft 6 in* and 51·85 m *170 ft 1 in* and Cockburn with jumps of 49·05 m *161 ft* and 51·30 m *168 ft 4 in*. Finally Wayne won the gold by 1·35 m *4 ft 5 in* with Mike Suyderhoud taking the bronze. Although Britain's James Carne reached a personal best of 49·70 m *163 ft 1 in*, he could not match the others and slipped to eighth place.

The Slalom Final was probably the most exciting event of the Championships. There had been many historic close slalom battles – Cash versus Khoury at Cypress Gardens in 1957 to name just one – and this was to be one of them, Bob LaPoint, perhaps an even stronger

XIV World Water Ski Championships 1975, held at Thorpe Water Park, England. *Left to right:* André Coutau, Philippe de Backer, Jean-Marie Muller, Sylvie Maurial, Lanfranco Colombo.

skier than his brother Kris, and still improving, came into the course on his 11·25 m *37 ft* pass and bit off an horrendous cut at the first buoy which threatened to make him airborne. Hanging on somehow, even though far off balance, he headed for the second buoy unbelievably making it and streaked for buoy No. 3 which he ran over in a wild spill. He scored 32 buoys for a two-round total of 60, giving him the overall lead. There were only two skiers left to follow him – Roby Zucchi and Kris LaPoint.

Next came the graceful Zucchi – once reputed to have gone through a slalom course with a blindfold on – and who now had to improve on his personal best from the previous day of 29 buoys. As he entered the course for his penultimate run, the crowd counted each buoy – you could hear them do it. Now came the sixth shortening with the rope now only 11·25 m *37 ft* – less than half the width of the course! As he made his last run, the crowd roared – then, on committing himself to a hard hook turn at the first buoy, he too was catapulted off balance across the course to take a head-over-heels tumble at the second buoy – to the groan of the crowd – scoring a quarter point under world rules for 31·25 buoys and a two-round total of 60·25 for a quarter-point lead.

The Arena went deathly quiet as Kris LaPoint entered the course. He ran the early speeds smoothly and confidently, but then inexplicably and to the utter amazement of all, fell at the third buoy on the fourth 13-m *43-ft* pass to score only 20·5 and a two-round total of 53 buoys.

When he heard he had won the gold medal, Roby Zucchi was back on the terraces beneath the Judges' Tower:

'*Ho vinto una gara di quarto di una buoy*' (I've won a contest by a quarter of a buoy!) I'm really happy because it is my first World title. I'm so happy for Italy.'

In the Tricks Final, although Suarez fell at the end of his first run, for his second, this precocious Caracas schoolboy performed a deepwater start rope-on-toe backwards, then casually flipped round, still without the use of hands into a forward position and continued his risky antics until he fell again. Although out-tricked by Russ Stiffler (5550 points) and Czechoslovakia's Franta Stehno (5280 points), Carlos's total point score gave him overall victory by 980 points and the Men's Over-all Championship title.

Under the new WOPS Over-all scoring, the nifty little tricker had racked up enough points with a ninth in Slalom and an eighteenth in Jumping to stand alongside Liz Shetter, while Ricky McCormick came second. But in the opinion of many, 'Tricky' Ricky had been the best all-rounder at these Championships. He was bitterly disappointed that the World Over-all title was denied him for the fourth time.

While the US skiers again won the team title with 12 226 points to Australia's 9608, their take-home gold was reduced to only four out of the possible eight gold medals – proof of the water-skiing coming of age of many other countries.

XIV World Water Ski Championship 1975. The United States
Team.

XIV World Water Ski Championship 1975. The Australian
Team.

XIV World Water Ski Championship 1975. The Venezuelan Team.

XIV World Water Ski Championship 1975. The Canadia Team.

XIV World Water Ski Championship 1975. The British Team.

XIV World Water Ski Championship 1975. The Italian Team

XIV World Water Ski Championship 1975. The Italian Team

Carlos Suarez (Venezuela) and Liz Allan (USA), the Over-all World Champions, 1975.

At the conclusion of the Championships, the white-tyred barge carrying Britannia and her lions, was towed across to the Grandstand and became the setting for the award presentations. Britain's Sports Minister, Denis Howell, had been so impressed by Thorpe Water Park that he had offered to cancel his other engagements so as to wind up the proceedings and present the prizes. To cheers from the thousands of spectators, and the world's skiers, he stated: 'We are willing to stage the World Championships here at Thorpe Park as soon as we are allowed to do so again.'

The following morning as various jets flew competitors with their medals and disappointments to the four corners of the water-skiing world, some of them had already set their sights on the XVth Worlds in 1977.

11 Great Britain ahead

Mike Hazelwood, one of the world's greatest skiers, proudly wears the medals he won during 1976.

Britain's three top skiers in 1976. John Battleday, Mike Hazelwood, and Philippa Roberts holding the European Cup.

Above: Karen Morse, European Jumping Record Holder.

The year 1976 began with two very tragic retirements.

After becoming World Champion twice, US Masters champion, and Canadian National Champion ten times in the Senior Division, George Athans was honoured by being named to Canada's Sport Hall of Fame. This and many other honours, made Athans one of Canada's foremost sportsmen. He had written a manual of water-skiing with Clint Ward, *Water Skiing*, the sales of which were to rise beyond 20 000. But George's very unpleasant jumping accident had severely injured his knee. He was unable to appear in England, and in 1976 he decided to pull out of competitive skiing and devote his time to 'less dangerous sports such as squash'. But then as he had said in an interview in 1974, George Athans doesn't see himself 'selling water-skis when I'm 30'.

Then there is the British and European champion Paul Seaton, whose accident at the 1975 Worlds at Thorpe was regretted by all. Although Paul's operation was successful, his rehabilitation programme was not and he has now begun to devote himself to training younger skiers at the Princes Water Ski Club in London. Then, on the other hand, the year witnessed two cases where physical injury was magnificently overcome.

Back in 1974, Mike Hazelwood, the Lincolnshire potato-farmer's son suffered a serious back injury, which meant him having a surgical operation to fuse part of his spine. Despite his being told by two specialists that he might never ski again, David Nations sent him to the

Below: Britain's year of victory, 1976. The three most coveted trophies at Rickmansworth Water Ski Club. *From left to right:* European Junior Team Trophy, European Cup (1976), European Championship Team Trophy.

British Team Orthopaedic Surgeon, the very eminent Mr Tony Cattrell (also working with the British Olympic Fencing team) who told him the only way to overcome his disability. This was physical exercise of the toughest order, whereby he had to build up one full inch of pure muscle. For five months, at Ruislip, this 16-year-old who had once wanted to be a boxer, put in five to six hours of weight training and cross-country running – but with some gentle water-ski practice. He then went to see Cattrell again, only to be told:

'So you've built up one inch of muscle. Well done. Now we'll see what you're made of, because if you're really going to survive, you've got to go and build *another* inch.'

Which is precisely what this long-haired Lincolnshire lad did. So it was that in the 1975 British Nationals, although he had not jumped for all of ten months, Mike's first mark was one of 45·72 m *150 ft*. From there on he did not look back and by the 1976 Season, the 18-year-old 'muscle-man', who spends his spare time playing squash, driving an Escort Mexico or helping on the family farm, was ready to do battle with the top skiers, include his sparring partner John Battleday and James Carne.

Skiers like Frantisek Stehno and Roby Zucchi might be specialised in Tricks or Slalom, but Mike Hazelwood's ambition has always been towards a good Over-all performance and in this he shone brilliantly by taking top Over-all honours in all the major events in 1976. During the European Cup event, held by the Lorraine Water Ski Club in France, Mike shattered the European Jumping Record with a mark of 54·76 m *179 ft 8 in*, just 10 cm *4 in* short of the current World Record. At the Leisure Sport Masters he was only a quarter buoy behind the current World Record in Slalom – and one or two tricks short of the Figures Record at the Group 2 Championships. He was also victorious in Slalom, Jumping and Over-all at the Old Spice International on Ruislip Lido, and the Northern European Championships. But perhaps Mike's greatest triumph came in September at the 30th European Championships, hosted by Italy at Milan's Idroscalo.

Seventeen nations sent 75 skiers to this contest. Despite Zucchi winning Slalom 'on home ground' by a margin of only 29 points and Stehno excellent in Tricks, Mike won Jumping and, at eighteen years of age, clearly showed his dominance by being the youngest skier ever to win the senior event of the year. John Battleday took the silver in Over-all, the two of them nearly doubling the points of their nearest rivals.

After this contest, the grandfather-cum-trainer of the inimitable World Tricks specialist Carlos Suarez, approached Hazelwood and told him that, in his opinion, there were only two skiers in the running for the World title the following year – Mike and his grandson.

It might well be asked, what about the Americans? In the 1976 Leisure Sports Masters Tournament at Thorpe

---

BRITISH WATER SKI FEDERATION
Summary of Medal Achievements – 1976
(compared with previous years)
In Tournament, World and European Championships

	Gold	Silver	Bronze	Total
1967–1972	31	18	7	56
1973	13	6	13	32
1974	14	10	7	31
1975	15	6	9	30
1976	20	16	8	44

Team Awards

1973

European Junior Championships	1st
Northern European Championships	2nd
European Championships	2nd

1975

European Dauphin Championships	1st
European Junior Championships	1st
European Cup	1st
European Championships	1st

1974

European Dauphin Championships	1st
European Junior Championships	1st
European Cup	1st
European Championships	1st

1976

Northern European Dauphin Championships	1st
Northern European Junior Championships	1st
European Junior Championships	1st
European Championships	1st
European Cup	1st

Above: 1976 European Over-all Junior Champion, Philippa Roberts.

Below: Ann Pitt of Great Britain. European Gold Medallist 1975.

Water Park, in competition with the American Champion and runner-up in Miami – Chris Redmond and Ricky McCormick respectively – Mike won the Over-all. He has also won ten out of a possible twelve gold medals in competitions, the other two being won by current World Champions, with Mike taking the silvers – such a series of performances is at once internationally recognised as the mark of *the* finest all-round skier in the three disciplines. His personal progression has become a golden spearhead that in the dim light of a national Economic Depression, has held high the victory flame of British sporting achievement.

Praise is also due to 'the eternal second' Jack Battleday – and to Karen Morse for winning her gold in Jumping and retaining that coveted title in Europe. Also to 15-year-old Philippa Roberts, who at the European Juniors at Vilvoorde (Belgium) in July won three out of four gold medals, as well as a silver, and mention must be made of Kathy Hulme who won a slalom gold and two silver medals in the Junior Girls Division of the Northern European Championships.

Britain's skiers reached a total of twenty gold medals in European competition during 1976 and took the team prize in all the major championships.

And for David Nations it has been the culmination of twenty years' dedication, and the reward for so much hard work and heartache in the cause of British water-skiing. Mike's success in particular, is not so surprising, after the thousands of man-hours given to training him to a peak. It has been a natural progression, fully expected. Now countless requests from all over the world are looking for the secrets of British success and the sport looks to Mike Hazelwood and the others as future global victors.

In September 1976, Nations received a communication from a photographic agency stating that HM Government's Central Office of Information had ordered 430 copies of a photograph of Mike Hazelwood, together with an extended caption concerning British water-ski achievements. These prints were to be circulated by the COI to Embassies and Agencies throughout the World. In fact that is the largest order that the COI make and is known as a 'main and general' order as opposed to a purely sports order. This seems to reflect the importance that they place on Britain's achievements in water-skiing.

The same week, Australia sent Hazelwood an invitation to compete at the 1977 Moomba Masters in Melbourne. But Mike, knowing that he had to keep his training programme going, and in a less cold, rainy climate than the one which the British winter was beginning to promise, had already left for the USA, anxious not to let any time go by, to ski in the warmer temperatures of Florida, in readiness for his greatest challenge yet – the 1977 World Championships.

There were other significant landmarks in water-skiing during 1976. For example, during the European Junior Championships at Vilvoorde, Belgium, in mid-August, a strangely moving slalom contest took place – for severely handicapped invalids. There were about six competitors, and each one was lowered into a 'sledge-ski'. By using his (or her) bodyweight they passed through the first, third and last buoys of the slalom course.

Elsewhere, the American Water Ski Association were getting plans under way to have a new National Headquarters building, built alongside Florida State Route S-542 between Walt Disney World and Cypress Gardens. It would cost $200 000, which was being raised through the AWSA reserve funds and through private donations. One of the main features of the Headquarters would be a Hall of Fame in the north wing, with space for thousands of artifacts and memorabilia that would give tangible evidence of the history of the sport. As the indefatigable Bill Clifford stated in the US *Water Skier* magazine:

'Hold those Museum Pieces – Readers with water-skiing items that they wish to donate for the museum, please do not ship any equipment or historical documents until notified by the headquarters office that space is available.'

Even farther afield, prior to the death of legendary Chairman Mao Tse Tung, Mary Glen Haig, MBE, of the CCPR (Central Council for Physical Recreation), who was visiting Peking with Lord Rupert Nevill, JP, DL (British Olympic Committee) was asked by Hsu Te-Tsin of the All China Sports Federation whether it was possible to send David Nations to train their coaches.

Over the past five years, the British Services in Hong Kong had formed two water-ski sections attached to their sailing clubs, enjoying the sport in the warm seas with their bays around the Colony. The Aberdeen (Hong Kong) Boat Club which also ran a flourishing water-ski section under E. C. Cannon for a number of years, had faded out when many of its members moved on to other parts of the world. Then in 1976, an Australian in the outboard engine industry called Ian Noakes discussed with Jim Laversuch (Water-ski Secretary of the Stanley British Services Boat Club) the idea of forming a properly constituted Hong Kong Water Ski Association. This was duly arranged under the auspices of the Hong Kong Yachting Association, the Government-registered controlling body of all watersports in Hong Kong; with a slalom course, two jumps and – to start off with – several privately owned ski-boats; water-ski carnivals and contests were organised for the ever-increasing numbers of Cosmopolitan members, culminating in October 1976 in the South-East Asian Water Ski Championships being hosted by the Hong Kong Association.

But most significant of all was the USSR's entry into the WWSU. Since 1975, Britain's Peter Pearl, Secretary-General of Group 2, had been corresponding with a personal friend in the Soviet Union, sending him details about the WWSU, its rules and methods of competition. It had been the Soviet intention to compete without joining the Union, but Peter Pearl told his friend that such a state of affairs simply could not be allowed. If they joined the Union, they could compete as much as they liked under WWSU rules.

In February 1976 a letter was written at the Soviet Ministry of Sport and Physical Culture in Moscow and by June, four months later and after official approval from the Supreme Soviet, this letter arrived for Pearl in London. He sent off his reply the following day. In August, at the European Cup Final in France (which was also won by Mike Hazelwood, incidentally), 25–30 Soviet water-skiing representatives turned up – among them Vladimir Savelyev (Secretary-General of the USSR Federation), Mikhail Guterman (President of the Technical Committee) and Victor Sanadze (of the Georgian region). They talked long and hard with Pearl

Above: Elton John, together with David Nations, Mike Hazelwood and Philippa Roberts.

Below: Sandy Grey, the blind British girl water-skiing on one ski — an unprecedented achievement.

Above: The new home of the American Water-Ski Association.

Below: William D. Clifford, AWSA Executive Director since 1958, the force behind the growth of American water-skiing.

XIV World Water Ski Championships, 1975, Thorpe Water Park. *From left to right:* John Wigglesworth (New Zealand), Sondre Wigglesworth, Bill Barlow Jr (USA), Neville May, Graham Young (Australia),Mrs Reg Barnes (Canada), Reg Barnes (Canada), Brian Scoffam (GB), Wolfgang Möhler (Germany), Peter Pearl (GB), Clint Ward (Canada), Elaine Nations (GB), David Nations (GB).

and other WWSU officials and were specially impressed by the over-all friendliness among officials and skiers. In Milan, on 17 September, the Administrative Committee of Group 2 voted the USSR a temporary member, subject to ratification by the next WWSU Congress in 1977.

With, for example, the Soviet Men's Jump Record standing at 44·40 m *145¼ ft* and the Women's Record at 32 m *105 ft* (only a little less than the European mark), it was the beginning of a new era in the sport. Virtually a whole continent was about to fully enter international competition. It would only be a matter of time before the 'client' states of Poland, Bulgaria, Romania, etc., also applied for membership to Group 2, now the largest of the three Groups in the World Water Ski Union. For as Peter Pearl has said, 'With such unity, it is our responsibility to build bridges across political differences and use the friendly philosophy of water-skiing to do this.'

With great pupils in Mike Hazelwood and John Battleday, a superb water-skiing Arena at Thorpe, an International diplomat in Group 2 Secretary-General Peter Pearl, and a completed book on the history of the sport, David Nations might now look back and feel that the three decades in the sport had been worthwhile. But 'DN' never looks back – only forward to the work of the British Sports Aid Foundation (fully backed by a host of influential people – such as pop-star Elton John) – and the challenge of preparing a male champion for the XVth World Championships.

1977 began nostalgically when on 22 January, the AWSAs first permanent home, a shiny new building, hard by a cattle pasture and a new Catholic church, was officially dedicated. Surrounded by wall displays of early skis and photographs of the sport, Bill Clifford who headed the highly successful fund-raising drive for this structure, could now host 350 guests, including Ralph Samuelson as the Guest of Honour and such pioneers as Dick and Julie Pope, Dick Pope Jr, Chuck and Betty Sligh, Don and Dottie Ibsen, Lee Sutherland, Willa Worthington Cook, Lew Withey, Glenn and Johnette Kirkpatrick, Nancy Stilly Hains, Stew McDonald, Marv Rothenberg and so many of the top American skiers. But as Bill Clifford stated: 'The job is only partly accomplished. We need now to concentrate our efforts on raising the necessary money to make the Water Ski Museum and Hall of Fame an actuality.'

In the middle of March, at the Moomba Masters, Melbourne, Australia, Mike Hazelwood showed himself to be unquestionably the World's top skier. While England's cricketers were the underdogs at the Centenary Test Match, less than a mile from the ground, 100 000 people lined the banks of the River Yarra to watch Hazelwood take the Over-all, so beating five former world champions – Wayne Grimditch, Mike Suyderhoud, Ricky McCormick, Bruce and Graeme Cockburn – as well as Chris Redmond, currently ranked top in the United States.

In the words of Max Kirwan, President of the AWSA: 'Mike ski'd them out of sight!' He broke the European trick record with a total of 6440 points so completing his hat-trick of European records in the three disciplines – also winning the slalom event, and jumping 47·85 m *157 ft*. Thus the Moomba Records could state that this was the very first time a Briton had won the supreme Over-all on the Yarra. Out of the great satisfaction of winning against such formidable skiers – the cream of the world – Mike could now face the forthcoming World Championships, to be held on the Idroscalo, Milan in September – with a quiet confidence.

Walking on the Water had come such a long way – so much further than Samuelson, Waller, Pope, Petersen, Rutherford or the other pioneers could ever have conceived possible. One can but wonder how much further it will go . . .

Mike Hazelwood, European Over-all Champion seen here jumping (*right*) and (*below*) showing fine slalom technique.

12 Faster, higher, stronger

Long Distance and Endurance Skiing

On 29 April 1933 Captain d'Arcy Rutherford of London, successfully aquaplaned across the English Channel, towed by a Chris-Craft motorboat; he took 1 hr 20 min to accomplish this. Several years later D'Arcy water-skied across that same stretch of water – 42 km *26 miles* – in 65 minutes.

The following table shows some of the early attempts at distance or time records.

able to train because his boat had been rammed a few weeks before the race, he had to be satisfied with preparations he could not test. He stayed with the mono-ski tactic borrowing a pair of fisherman's waders taped to his blue jeans. 'I started dry and stayed dry,' he recalls.

Eating rare steak for nourishment, drinking three cases of Pepsi to fight thirst, and using a battery-operated telephone to navigate the boat during the night, Shackleford remained on his single ski for 35 hr 15 min, covering

Year	Skier(s)	Distance	Locations	Time/Comments
1941	Franz Steinhardt	193 km *120 miles*	Lake Michigan	—
194–	Charles R. Sligh	81 km *50 miles*	Lake Macatawa	*36 mph*
1950	Dick Cowell	227 km *141 miles*	Portofino to Cannes	Mono-ski 5 hr 45 min
1952	Bruce Parker and Evelyn Wolford	315 km *196 miles*	Nassau to Miami	2nd attempt 8 hr 12 min
1953	Frank Beddor Jr	367 km *228 miles*	Minneapolis to New Orleans	9 hr 10 min Downstream
1954	Carl Mahler	—	San Francisco to Stockton	3 hr 33 min Mono-ski
1955	Dolores Kipple	315 km *196 miles*	Miami to Nassau	Mono-ski 10 hr 15 min
1955	Joseph Balcao and Hubert Miller	444 km *276 miles*	Stockton to San Francisco via Sacramento	9 hr 40 min
1957	John Musser	1151 km *715 miles*	Lake of the Ozarks	23 hr 23 min

The next of these human dynamos was a wiry 1·80 m *5 ft 11 in* character from McKellar Lake, Memphis, Tennessee, named Marvin G. Shackleford. It all started in 1958 during the World's Water Ski Marathon Championship on McKellar Lake. This was designed as an endurance contest in the old *laissez-faire* style, with a winner-take-all prize of $1000. Once the competition began, it didn't end until every contestant – save one, the winner – had collapsed. With only a summer's water-skiing experience, Marvin Shackleford circled round the course for 1007 km *626 miles* and won the prize. But Marvin was not satisfied. He regarded it merely as a prelude to what he was going to do the following year: ski 1609 km *1000 miles*.

The second McKellar Lake Marathon, in 1959, was a fiasco. The night before, a heavy rainstorm washed tons of earth and floating débris into the lake, creating an aquatic obstacle course. Seven hours and 274 km *170 miles* into that race, Shackleford crashed into a submerged object and his dreams of 1609 km *1000 miles* were frustrated once again.

Attempt No. 3 was not going to fail. Remembering the 1958 race where he had been asked – after 23 hours – by tired officials to quit so that they could get home to their families, 'Shack' asked one of the marathon organisers to provide officials who could last as long as he did. Un-

more than 1290 km *800 miles*. The only unforeseen difficulty came when a photographer cruised up during the night and popped a flashbulb in Shackleford's eyes, blinding him for most of one lap. Otherwise, things went swimmingly until, at the 1316 km *818·2-mile* mark, he ran over a sandy corner of Treasure Island and fell into the water on the opposite side – an unusual short cut he didn't remember taking.

Fatigue unquestionably played a major role in this unscheduled detour across dry land, but Shackleford also laid some of the blame on well-meaning friends. 'I could have gone another 293 km *182 miles* easy. It was only six more hours. But some of my friends got to worrying about me and decided to help me out by giving me some kind of pills. They just knocked me silly. The papers all said I went to sleep, but it was just the opposite. Oh, well – I'd rather they said I went to sleep than that I was a junkie.

'The next-to-last guy and I skied side by side for a long time,' he recalls with some poignancy. 'I remember he had tears in his eyes, he said, "Man, I got to go," and he fell. The last five guys before me were taken straight to the hospital, but I was feeling fine. Not tired at all.' As if to prove it, Shackleford was out on the lake bright and early the next morning – water-skiing.

When allowed to stop for a breather, skiers have gone

ever farther. On 22–23 August 1958, Ray de Fir of Portland, Oregon skied a total of 1609 km *1000 miles* over the Colombia River between Portland and Astoria. In 1960, American Larry Degraff made a mono-ski run of 3220 km *2001 miles* from Augusta, Georgia to Houston, Texas; 644 km *400* miles of this run were on the open sea through the Gulf of Mexico and the rest of the journey was completed by making use of the intra-coastal waterway. Then in 1971, the Australian Harry Luther skied a total of 5010 km *3114 miles* from Spain to Cervia, Italy, in 10 days 5 hr.

For those who might be interested, to ski the whole distance of the River Nile in Egypt, you would have to travel 6670 km *4145 miles*. While to ski round the world (in 80 days perhaps) – with the necessary training, planning and finance – you would only have to ski a total of 40075 km *24901·5 miles*!

Racing and Record-breaking

For several years before the War there was held a very successful annual aquaplane race from the isthmus at Avalon to Hermosa Beach, California – a race which was indeed a test of endurance for both man and boat. Usually only 10–20 per cent of the starting teams ever finished, the others dropping out due to boat trouble or because the aquaplaner just couldn't hold on any more. The last race prior to the War, held 20 June 1941, was won by Bob Brown, towed by Don Berry, with a time of 1 hr and 51 min. After the War, in 1946, this endurance run was resumed with aquaplaner Ed Stanley of Orange winning it handsomely.

The Long Beach Boat and Ski Club was formed in 1947 and almost immediately took over sponsorship of this race, renaming it the Grand National Water Ski Race. In 1949 the contest became a round trip run. Starting at Hermosa Beach pier, the skiers raced to the isthmus, circled a turn boat and returned non-stop to the pier. A skier was disqualified if at any time he or she touched the boat or anyone in the boat. Ed Stanley of Orange was the winner of this first round trip race with a time of 1 hr 41 min.

The following year Long Beach became the starting and return point. Many a racing skier in the Catalina Channel used to spot king-size sharks, and although the schools of porpoises were harmless, they weren't too comforting to skiers as they played tag with skiers and boats. Bill Williams, a Californian was for a long time referred to as 'Mr Catalina' by skiing enthusiasts on the West Coast, because he was the spark plug for the races, and chairman for a number of years.

Chuck Stearns, that 'winningest of winners' (a member of the LBBSC) holds the distinction of having won the event nine times out of the twenty-six times it has been presented, while another member Jane Mobley Welch has won the women's class seven times.

In all, the race teams (skier, driver and observer) traverse 93–96 km *58–60 miles* of gruelling open ocean, a severe test of both man and machine. Race teams originally came from only the local area (California) and several close-by western states (Oregon, Nevada and Arizona), but for the past several years competitors have come from as far afield as Australia, New Zealand, South Africa, Germany, Italy and France. Additionally, between 90 and 100 race teams have started in the past two

races (with approximately 80 per cent of them finishing the race).

The Long Beach Club also sponsored the annual 121-km *75-mile* Lake Mead Water Ski Race on the borders of Arizona and Nevada, the fastest and longest race in the US. There was also a 160-km *100-mile* water-ski race at Big Bear Lake, high in the mountains above Salt Lake City, Utah.

In Australia a race was established in the early 1950's called 'The Bridge-to-Bridge'. In the estuary of the Hawkesbury River, at the sea end, there is the Brooklyn road-and-rail bridge while 110 km *68½ miles* upstream there is the Wilberforce Bridge. The race was originally for powerboats alone and as two 1957 competitors recalled: 'I thought I had a good chance of being first into Windsor, but not far from Jack Murray's Beach at Sackville I was too darned busy keeping out of the way of water-skiers . . .' 'Some of the water-skiers were troublesome, particularly around Sackville, where an accident could easily have occurred. Next year, I think some better way of clearing the river should be instigated – otherwise someone is likely to get killed.'

As it turned out, instead of driving the skiers off the Hawkesbury, in time the skiers were to adopt the Bridge-to-Bridge race for themselves. As one of the competitors of the very first unofficial race, Sandy Primo, has recalled: 'We would often get up at the crack of dawn when the Hawkesbury was just like a mirror, and ski 80 km *50 miles* before breakfast, and think nothing of it. Then we had a sort of bet on and we wanted to see who could make the Bridge-to-Bridge first – but skiing. In that first race there were about eight boats and skiers taking part and the prize was a few kegs of beer at Billy McLachlan's place.'

The problem they used to have was that at certain points on the Hawkesbury, there were cable-drawn punts for ferrying the river – one at Wiseman's, one at Sackville and a couple more. They had to stop at each of these ferries, because if the propeller of the ski-boat caught on the cable it used to rip the stern out.

The first official contest was organised in 1961, when there were thirty entries divided into only two classes – Outright and Women. It was run from Brooklyn Bridge through to the Windsor Bridge, although in the years that followed, with the increasing Maritime Services Board restrictions, both start and finish venues had to be changed. Judges were placed on the ferries to allow 'time out' for boats obstructed by them and buoys were placed on sharp corners along the river to prevent competitors cutting corners. These changes led to faster and more accurate times.

In 1965 a Junior Class was introduced along with side valve country and single outboard classes, and *Turbofire*, driven by J. Reeson, with T. Pilz as observer, and with skiers D. Herring and Phil Reeson, covered the 110 km *68 miles* in 1 hr 12 min – an average of 80 km/h *50 mph*. In 1967, 82 boats towed 366 competitors from Bridge-to-Bridge. Each of these boats was allowed to start at one-minute intervals, in their various classes, for safety purposes. In 1968 a Sub-Junior section was added, then in 1969 Juniors were divided into boys and girls and in 1970 Sub-Juniors were similarly divided.

The 1975 Bridge-to-Bridge had a record number of entries totalling approximately three hundred and twenty. Each of these boats has a crew of four people plus a trailer driver. This totals sixteen hundred competitors, probably the largest contested event in the world, and with officials, judges, families, friends and spectators, it becomes quite an occasion.

British Water Ski Racing began when the Whitstable Water Ski Club got together with a Sandgate Beach Club owner to organise and publicise a mass-crossing of the English Channel (La Manche) from Sandgate to Cap Griz Nez and back.

In 1966 a meeting took place at the Mandeville Hotel in London, at which 30 clubs were represented and a Racing sub-committee of the BWSF was formed. A copy of the Californian Racing Rules was obtained from Chuck Stearns, who was staying in London at the time, and its clauses modified to local conditions and safety regulations.

Alan Taylor remembers: 'We also knew that racing had taken place in Belgium three or four years before that, on the Scheldt at a place called Rupelmonde. In the following year, knowing of the Scheldt Trophy race, I and two or three others from the Whitstable Club went over and had a look at this race and began to see what could be built up in Europe – and we invited a Belgian team to compete in the first official cross-Channel race.'

So on 29 May 1967 the Whitstable Club, and the Varne Club, organised the first cross-Channel race. A total of 56 teams, including the one from Belgium, took part in the 68 km *42 mile* run from Greatstone, Kent, to a trawler marker-boat three miles off Cap Griz Nez and back. Boats were allowed to take up to three or four people to ski in relays. The skis were ordinary standard slalom skis for speeds of around 48 km/h *30 mph*; the tow-rope had to be between 22·9 m *75 ft* and 30·5 m *100 ft*. For the purposes of identification, all competitors were provided with an orange or white rubber skull cap – and there was a requirement for crash helmets. This last took the form of canoeing helmets, ice-hockey helmets, American football helmets, and even a somewhat heavy motorcyclist's helmet.

The only skier in the Bridge-to-Bridge who has broken the hour record three times.

Below: A Bridge-to-Bridge Ski-boat roaring down the Hawkesbury.

The committee received Entry No. 47 from a team describing itself as the Sunny WSC, which had as its entrants the powerboat ace Tommy Sopwith, Jocelyn Stevens, Tony Richardson – and a Mr A. A. Johnson. In reality A. A. Johnson was no less than the Earl of Snowdon, patron of the BWSF, attempting to keep his identity from the Press. But somehow the news leaked out and this race was given complete, and dramatic, coverage.

Conditions were good and the 56 teams set off *en masse*. Then the weather changed very rapidly. Boat No. 7 from the Gosfield WSC, then lying in fifth place, was swept down on to the trawler marker-boat, so the skier had to let go of the rope, which wrapped itself round the anchor cable. When the rope tightened, the boat was flipped over, throwing the crew out. They were quickly picked up by the trawler crew, but by doing so, the trawler had to leave its station to take the survivors back to shore. Consequently when the pursuing boats got there, they searched up and down the French coast, looking for the trawler. They included the Earl of Snowdon, who was dramatically lost to the Press for possibly a couple of hours!

More than 20 of the 56 teams who competed, failed to finish the race at all, due to a gale which whipped up 1·83 m *6 ft*-high waves. The winners were members of the Chasewater Power Boat Club, of Solihull, Warwickshire, who completed the course in 3 hr 15 min. The Snowdon team came in fourth at 4 hr 10 min. Red-eyed from salt, the Earl commented: 'I had no idea we had been posted missing. The last marker buoy before the French coast, where we were supposed to turn, must have been out of position, because we couldn't find it. The really rough bit was when we left the French coast. It was so bad it was almost impossible to ski.' He was presented with a cigarette box and a share of the £10 prize.

In 1968 the BWSFRC organised the first British Championship series – Chasewater, followed by a race off the coast at Greatstone, the cross-Wash race at Hunstanton, a race off Hartlepool in North-East England, a circuit race off Penarth in the Bristol Channel, another across the River Medway, and a cross-Channel race. The champion was John Boardman of the Varne Boat Club.

Elsewhere in the world, two other types of ski-racing were initiated. The 130 km *80-mile* trans-Adriatic Sea Water Ski Crossing from Pula in Yugoslavia to Cervia in Italy was instituted. In Arizona, the first water-skiing relay race, a battle between two six-man teams, was held on Lake Havasu, on the lower Colorado River. This was a 29 km *18-mile* race, in which the skiers used hoops 40 cm *18 in* in diameter in place of batons and passed at speeds above 80 km/h *50 mph*. Most of the exchanges were almost letter-perfect and the winning team was captained by Chuck Stearns.

In 1969, the British Championship series was increased to eight races and was won by Brendan Bowles of Penarth and Barry. The most important innovation in 1969 was the introduction of the European Water Ski Racing Challenge.

In fact, a form of racing had gone on in Europe since 1951 – ski-natation. One warm spring day in 1932, Fortune Altari and his brother Antoine finished snow-skiing with some friends on the Coll de la Cayolle, France. It had been extremely hot work and when they got down again to Nice they rounded off the day with a swim. Inevitably, for them, the dip turned into a race, and thus was born the idea of a combined snow-skiing and swimming competition, both events to be held on the same day. By the following year the Altari brothers had presented a cup and there were 53 spectators. The race increased in popularity every year until in 1950 the event received official recognition by the International

Lord Snowdon stacking his mono-ski in the boat after the 1967 Cross-Channel Water Ski Race. Tommy Sopwith looks on.

Ski Federation. In 1951, on the initiative of Madame Gould, of the Provençal Hotel Juan-les-Pins, the lowland half was developed to include a water-ski slalom as well as the swimming; the competitor with the best overall result, walked away with the 'Combine d'Azur' trophy.

From 1956 onwards a snow and water-ski slalom was held at Sestriere, Italy. The snow slalom in the morning on the Alpette run, and the water-skiing on Lago Avigliana – a slalom on either two skis or a monoski.

Alan Taylor continues: 'Having formed the British Racing Committee, we already had our links with Europe, through conventional skiing, and as we gave a lead to them, they began to organise their own races. There were three International Grand Prix in 1969, held in Holland, Belgium and Britain. Because we were so used to skiing in rough water conditions, almost immediately we did well in the European smoother water conditions. Billy Rixon of Seasalter Alberta WSC managed to turn the tables on his rival Brendan Bowles, to become the first European champion, with Brendan and John Boardman tying for second place. With such results, Europe listened and looked to us for leadership.'

It was also in 1969, in May, that the first water-ski races ever to be sanctioned by the American Water Ski Association were held on Lake Hollingsworth, in Lakeland, Florida. In all, 16 boats pulled 29 skiers on the two-day programme. The Men's Unlimited feature race of five laps around the 2·7 km *1⅔ mile* course, was won by Jack Lewis behind the SK dragboat *Tears 'n Yer Ears*, driven by Joe Whitley.

Since then the racing scene has mushroomed to the point where there are now eight International Grand Prix – Italy, Spain, Austria, Germany (and recently France) have joined the original three – Belgium, Holland and Britain. The European title has only been won by either Britain or Italy – the present score is Britain 5, Italy 3. A British skier has competed in the Australian Bridge-to-Bridge race, while several Australians have competed on European rivers. For the last two years an International Ski race has also been held in South Africa.

There has been no competitive contact with the Americans as yet, although the National Speedboat and Water Ski Association in California has invited Britain to send some racing skiers out to America, where they have undertaken to provide a boat to tow them.

The French have begun to experiment with a course combining speed-skiing, slalom and jumping on a timed trial basis – a lot of fun but the main difficulty is that you can only ever have one competitor on the circuit at a time. Perhaps the strongest aspect of ski-racing is the atmosphere and excitement of the mass-start. Perhaps the future will see mass starts with teams from the 50 federations of the World Water Ski Union taking part – but this will not occur without much-needed sponsorship.

At Vichy, in 1976, on the initiative of Jean-Marie Muller, France held her first international race. Now moves are afoot to hold a World Racing Congress at the XVth World Championships in 1977, with representatives from the three groups hoping to iron out their rules differences, and bring the challenge of a World Waterski Racing Championship, even closer to reality.

The Water-ski Speed Record

Probably the major exhilaration that comes from planing on the water, is that the very closeness of the skier to the water gives a more marked sensation of speed. This section tells the story of what happened when man took that sensation to its logical conclusion.

In 1915 *Harper's Weekly* magazine wrote: 'The best run, the best thrills, are obtained (with aquaplaning) at speeds from 19–32 km/h *12–20 mph*. Faster than that one's wits are bewildered by the rush of air and spray. And, we say most fervently, at 40–48 km/h *25–30 mph* or more it hurts to hit the water when you are spilled off.'

It is interesting to note that at this time, the fastest powerboat in the United States, *Miss Minneapolis*, had been timed at 106 km/h *66 mph*.

By 1921, the powerboat ace Gar Wood of Detroit had driven his *Miss America* to a new World Water Speed Record of 129 km/h *80 mph*, so that when Ralph Samuelson was towed behind the Curtiss MF flying-boat across Lake Pepin, he was travelling at the fastest speed then possible on the water.

Probably because of their broader planing area the aquaplanes were limited in the speeds they could achieve. It was reported that: 'Some of the more courageous of the players of these novelty water sports now ride aquaplanes behind seaplanes going 80 km/h *50 mph*. At times, when the gust of the propeller is very powerful, the aquaplanes take off and go three or four feet into the air.'

In the South of France, Monsieur George Ducros was reported to have achieved 109 km/h *68 mph*, while Captain d'Arcy Rutherford had also made short runs of 113 km/h *70 mph*. He once fell at 100 km/h *62 mph*: hitting the water, crouched low, he rolled and skidded as though 'on a greased slide'. On losing speed he got a ducking and found that there was only one casualty – he lost his pants!

Sometime in 1938 the American, Bruce Parker, used an aeroplane to skim the water at 96 km/h *60 mph*.

During this period, in the 1930s, the World Water Speed Record for powerboats was being improved from 158–228 km/h *98–142 mph*, but Speed King Sir Malcolm Campbell's chief mechanic, Leo Villa has recalled: 'To the best of my knowledge nobody ever approached Sir Malcolm with a pair of skis and asked for a tow.'

As has already been mentioned, the first post-War European Championships at Evian in 1947 included a speed contest with every competitor asking for the maximum speed of 80–90 km/h *50–56 mph* from the speedboat. Claude de Clercq took the fins off his skis, oiled the bottoms, then skied in a rigid 'Egg' position, so gaining extra but significant seconds over his rivals.

But as yet, there was still no official organisation to ratify a World Water Ski Speed Record. The Swiss Michel Vuillety is reported to have clocked 150 km/h *93 mph* in 1947 and claimed the title. But who was to say that Jon Pertwee, precariously skiing well over 96 km/h *60 mph* behind a shark-spotting seaplane on the Hawkesbury River – or Lance Macklin skiing behind the 130 km/h *70 mph* rooster-tail of Gianni Agnelli's speedboat on the Bay of Villefranche – did not also have a claim?

Then in the mid-1950s, the Los Angeles Boat and Ski Club held a World Record Mile Ski Run Championships at the Desert Shores resort, Salton Sea, California. The intent and purpose was strictly to establish once and for all a permanent speed record that would be recognised all over the world. The trials were over a surveyed and

Above: Sally Younger in 1969. The Womens' Water Ski speed record holder.

Below: Chuck Stearns, the World Water-Ski Speed record holder.

measured mile and timed by official timers. Skiers did not have to qualify but had to furnish their own mode of power. Any mode of power meant that aircraft could be used, but at no time could the craft be airborne nor could the skier be pulled by a ski line with a ten-degree lift. It was optional whether one or two skis were used. According to the rules, the skier entered the traps, both ways, with a flying start. If he fell, the boat then had to continue and proceed to the beach, with the skier being picked up by the nearest patrol boat. In the Senior Divisions, Barbara Spanier made 77 km/h *47·9 mph* and Chuck Stearns 95·3 km/h *59·2 mph*. Although rather low, at least these marks had been officially recorded.

The first great official record-breaker on the scene was Harold W. Peterson of Los Angeles, California. 'Butch' Peterson began water-skiing in 1948 at the age of 7 and entered his first ski race three years later. In 1955, aged 14, he had been clocked through the mile traps at 91·7 km/h *57 mph*.

With the ski record, there came a point where officials had to decide whether to keep the speeds low based on a mile course, or to give them the chance to rise on a quarter-mile spring basis, thereby relating to the increasingly popular dragboat racing which was enjoyed in California.

Beginning in 1956 through to 1963, Butch Peterson established progressive quarter-mile Water Ski Drag Records of 93, 129, 135, 139, 171, 182 and 188 km/h (*58, 80, 84, 87, 106, 113* and *117 mph*) at the Oakland Marine Stadium, California. In the final year he also recorded an unofficial run of 201 km/h *125 mph*. 'I fell because of rough water conditions and spent many long weeks in hospital. A number of my friends have asked why I have continued a sport that almost cost me my life. My answer is that, firstly, this accident made the challenge even greater and I had my own emotions to master, and secondly, speed skiing in all its forms is the greatest fun of all for me. I wouldn't think of quitting.'

It should be added that it took a real man to achieve these records. Butch Peterson was a graduate of the University of Southern California, where he played varsity football and was a member of the wrestling team. By 1968 he had won 1100 ski trophies scoring six victories in the 121 km *75-mile* Lake Mead Basin Race, as well as the Long Beach-Catalina-Long Beach race twice, setting a record run of 1 hr 13 min in 1963.

So if the record was to be broken, it would have to be done by such a man as Peterson. That man, already a legend in Classic skiing, was Chuck Stearns. On 17 December 1966, again at the spectator-packed Oakland Stadium, towed by the 850 hp Chrysler-powered drag-hydroplane *Golden Komotion*, driven by 'Dragboat King' boatbuilder Rich Hallett, Stearns hit the traps at 192·3 km/h *119·5 mph*.

'I guess you would have to say it was one big thrill. Travelling at over 160 km/h *100 mph*, a speed skier has the problem of the front of his ski sucking in. He has to lean way back on the ski. If you lose the pull forward, then you have nothing to lean against and you have to get forward. That's what happened to me when I went 192 km/h *119 mph* and set a new record. The boat let off too fast and when this happens the boat slows in a hurry because of the drag. So the tow-rope slacked into the water and I no longer had any tension. I had to turn the rope loose and kind of balance myself. When I did, I

was thrown forward as the front of the ski sucked in, and I went into a forward flip.'

Three years later, on 11 January 1969, the superbly conditioned Californian returned to the Stadium with a new outfit.

Liz Allan Shetter has described the atmosphere: 'It's really exciting – the same sort of atmosphere as with a car race, with thousands of people around – but the dragboats scream even louder than the cars.'

The day started out with a 15-year-old girl, Sally Younger, attacking the Women's drag speed mark of 138 km/h *86 mph*, held by Jane Mobley Welch. Sally's ambition was to hold 145 km/h *90 mph* through the 40-m *132-ft* course, but her driver Bob Nordskog, boosted the speed of his SK-type boat *Sizzling Viking* well above the 145 km/h *90 mph* without realising and Sally created a new record of 149·1 km/h *92·68 mph*.

The atmosphere electrified the 7000 spectators as Chuck, wearing a bright blue wetsuit, a jump jacket and a red crash helmet of his own design, took a few warm-up runs behind Nordskog's boat, to help official timer Otto Crocker in co-ordinating his speed equipment. Chuck then switched to Ray Caselli's Chrysler-powered Hondo hull *Panic Mouse*, which had a drag run of 238 km/h *148 mph* in the books. A nitro-methane alcohol-burner, this 1000 hp (plus) rig had actually been de-tuned to lower its top speed to nearer the level Chuck was seeking. Chuck took the course on a 3-m *10-ft* ski at the end of a 67-m *220-ft* towline, the crowd roared, *Panic Mouse* screamed and the skier made it through the traps at a speed of 195·2 km/h *121·29 mph* but fell outside the course, while the dragboat was still accelerating. He was not injured and his official speed was given as 196·5 km/h *122·11 mph*.

In January 1970 the following announcement appeared: 'Long Beach Boat and Ski Club Presents – Chuck Stearns World Water Ski Drags – Chuck challenges anybody in the world to drag against him to beat his existing record of 196·5 km/h *122·11 mph*. This from a standing start in 5½ seconds.'

But unfortunately that very month, Stearns was painfully injured in a water-ski race at Parker Dam, Arizona, when he struck a submerged tree trunk while travelling at about 129 km/h *80 mph*. Despite suffering seven broken ribs and a punctured lung doctors estimated that he would return to skiing in two months. In June of that year, Sally Younger raised her own Women's Record to 169·17 km/h *105·14 mph* at Pennis, California.

But how much faster could a man ski on the water? In 1971 Danny Churchill took up Chuck Stearns's challenge at the Marine Stadium and pushed the mark to 202·24 km/h *125·69 mph*. Soon after this, Churchill was offered $300 for a run at a dragboat meet and $500 if he broke the record. They had been experimenting with parachutes, so that if the skier fell, he would be pulled straight on to his back and just slide. The parachute was fixed on the skier's shoulders, while the ripcord ran down his arm and attached to the end of a finger, so that as soon as the ropes came out of the skier's hand, his finger straightened and pulled the ripcord. This seemed okay in theory.

It is reckoned that Churchill was skiing in excess of 209 km/h *130 mph* when he fell forward and somersaulted, still hanging on to the rope, his head almost touching the water. As the parachute was letting out one of its strings got caught under his leg and ripped right up through his body.

Churchill was in hospital for almost two years and totalled $150 000 in medical expenses, not all of it covered by insurance. He suffered terrible internal injuries but he is back skiing now – but nothing fast. In spite of all this, there are still men preparing to beat Churchill's record – if not break the 200 km/h *130 mph* barrier. One of these is the Australian record-holder, Geoff Burgess who says:

'Unless the money was there, I wouldn't just go out and do it for kicks. You don't want to do what Danny Churchill did. If that hadn't happened, sure guys would have been going for 225 km/h *140 mph* then 241 km/h *150 mph* until someone hurt themselves. But something like that, sobers you up.'

Kiting

'How would you like to hitch a winged aquaplane with a long rope behind a swift speedboat, balance this sort of glider on the surface of the water as you move along at 72 km/h *45 mph* and then rise with it 2–2·5 m *6–8 ft* in the air?' So read a popular magazine article, published in the late 1920s.

Dick Pope Sr has described the sensation in his book *Water Skiing* thus: '. . . after scores of newsreels, my good friend Harrison Fraser, the aviator, built a wing with an area of 1·6 sq m *18 sp ft* and mounted it above my aquaplane. My brother Malcolm took me out on the lake for a test run on this strange contraption. It was quite a sensation as I pulled back on the ropes and felt the aquaplane gradually lift off the water. The urge to

fly like a bird lies dormant in almost everyone, but here was the realisation of a marvel of the ages as I flew on my magic carpet 60–90 cm *2–3 ft* above the water.'

In September 1929, Gar Wood, the legendary pilot of the *Miss America* racing hydroplanes used his speedboat to tow a pontoon-equipped glider, piloted by Oscar Kuhn, from the waters of Gross Pointe Municipal Park, Detroit. A wire cable 129·5 m *425 ft* long was attached between the aircraft and boat. The glider easily took off at 40 km/h *25 mph*, then at 50 km/h *32 mph* the glider was released and coasted down from 61 m *200 ft* to a perfect landing. This was the first time the experiment had been carried out in the US. The English glider-pioneer, Lowe Wylde, was to carry out the same experiment in 1931 on the Welsh Harp lake in North London, only this time there were floats on the wingtips and under the fuselage.

It was not until 1951, that Vernon Cary and Paul Opdyke, from the Sacramento River, California, participated in their first kite flying on water skis at the Sacramento State Fair. Their kite 3 × 3·6 m *10 × 12 ft* in size, weighed 6·4 kg *14 lb* and was made of muslin stretched over a frame of specially reinforced aluminium tubing. Four previous models had ended in disaster at the bottom of the river, their framework bent and buckled from pressure they could not withstand. But No. 5 – the red kite – logged over 25 minutes of flying time over 30 flights. At the Fair, the kite rose to an altitude of 7·60 m *25 ft* and travelled about 91·4 m *100 yd* in the air. After an appearance in the newsreels and on TV, Cary was swamped with correspondence from skiers all over the world.

Other pioneers of water-ski kiting, were George and

Dick Pope experimenting with the original water-ski kite in the 1920s: take off.

Tony Baird of Everett, Washington, George Quinn of Canada and Doug Levershaw of Australia. In 1956 Quinn made a mono-ski take-off on Lake Okanagan, British Colombia, and flew up to 42·7 m *140 ft* with a spruce and canvas kite weighing 18·2 kg *40 lb*.

It was Doug Levershaw, a show manufacturer from Melbourne, Australia, who introduced his brand of kiting to Cypress Gardens in 1956. The kites, some 4·26 m *14 ft* long and 2·4 m *9 ft* wide, were flat in design, bearing the appearance of an oversized child's toy. The flyer would hang on to the cross-bar as if he were 'chinning' the bar. The length of time a flyer would remain in the air would depend on his physical strength in terms of 'hanging on'.

The first kites were not aerodynamically designed, so the height of the flight was mainly determined by how hard a flyer pushed off as he skied over the ski jump.

Alan Clarke, one of the Australian pioneers, has recalled: 'A fellow named Doug Levershaw, brought a kite back from Cypress Gardens in 1957, an ordinary flat-winged thing. He came up to ski with us – Billy McLachlan, Jack Murray and I. Funnily enough, we could never understand why he didn't get up and show us. Well he just brought this kite with an ordinary ski-rope – there was no question of hooking it on. We had the ski-rope round the bar of the kite, that was all. Jack Murray had been an Olympic wrestler and was a bit heavy, so he went kangaroo-ing up and down the river for a bit, because the boat would only do about 40–48 km/h *25–30 mph*. Bill got up and he flew for about 91·4 m *100 yd*; then I got on and I was a bit lighter. I went round a corner and got a cross-wind and finished up in a tree.

Well, I thought, if that's kiting, you can have it mate!'

Flat kites improved with time, and Ken Tibado, a young skier from Lake Wales, Florida, directed his talents to building and flying flat kites. Tibado's Kites were advertised as 'the World's Most Thrilling Ride' with the kite flyers soaring to heights of 23 m *75 ft*. Fortunately, most kite flyers were not foolish enough to try for much more height due to the unstable nature of the flat-wing kite design.

The first World Kite Championships were held in late 1957. Tibado won the event and kite flying came of age at Cypress Gardens. Improvements were made and trick flying was added to later tournaments with the addition of a harness. Instead of the flyer hanging on to the cross-bar, he now used a 'swing harness' to support his weight and thus could stay up for longer periods. The pendulum action of the swing made for more stable flights and lessened the chance of accidents.

Alan Clark takes up the story again: 'In 1959, when they held the World Water-skiing Championships in Milan, Bill McLachlan and I were joint team managers. A week after the Championships, we went to the Leonardo da Vinci Museum together, and saw a model of a kite. After we went home for several years we just yapped about it on and off until Bill found a couple of young aeronautical engineers, and they built the Aqua-Delta. This was a kite with pontoons and a joy-stick. You sat in a little seat and didn't have to ski with it. This was in about 1962/63.

'Because I'd done a bit of test-flying during the War, we started playing around with it. It was a little bit too heavy with floats and seat, so we took it up to 91 m *300 ft*

137

and I became one of the first guys to freefall one of them.'

Another Australian, Sandy Primo, recalls: '1964 saw the beginning of organised water-ski kite flying in Australia with the formation of a kite club in New South Wales and another in Victoria. Later they merged to be known as the Australian Water Ski Fliers' Association.

'At this time I was skiing with Ray and Betty Leighton, and we also included flat-back and Aqua-Delta kiting. One day we had a visitor, John Dickinson from Grafton, New South Wales, who told us of an invention of his which would interest us. He wasn't a water-skier and didn't know how to ski, but asked if we would mind trying out his invention. He then assembled a kite, now world famous as the Delta Ski-Wing. The whole framework was made out of wood, and his wife had made the sail out of canvas. Leighton was the first to try it out and then the others did.'

Not satisfied with an ordinary flat kite, which without power had the gliding angle 'of a brick', John Dickinson, this quiet methodical insurance man, decided to put into practice some theoretical designs for the Delta-Wing, first proposed by Dr Francis M. Rogallo and patented in 1951. The Rogallo kite's altitude could be varied by changing its pitch.

Before long Dickinson had been put in touch with another Australian, an auto-electrician called Bill Moyes from Waverly near Sydney. From there on 'Moysie' started making frames out of aluminium piping and things started happening. In 1967, only six weeks after he began flying, Moyes astounded aeronautical experts when he flew his wing to 319 m *1045 ft* over Tuggerah Lake, becoming the first man to exceed 305 m *1000 ft* in a man-carrying kite and gained the world altitude record. He also glided down in a free-fall to land exactly where he had planned – to the inch. Early in 1968 on Lake Ellesmere, New Zealand, behind a high-powered speedboat, on a 3050 m *10 000 ft* wire cable, he increased that to 874·8 m *2870 ft*. Then in 1969, Bill made an heroic, but stormy and finally unsuccessful attempt to fly from Sydney to Brisbane, a distance of 805 km *500 miles*.

In 1967, Freddy Strasser, who had first learnt to kite at Juan-les-Pins and then, on the advice of his business partner David Nations, had gone out to train under Ken Tibado at Cypress Gardens, became the first British National Kite Champion at Cirencester Water Ski Club, beating nine competitors, including Tony Richardson and Graham Stevens.

By this time, Bill Bennett, who worked with Moyes, had brought the first water-ski Rogallo kite to the US. Dave Kilbourne, a water-skier/kiter, met Bennett and provided the boat on several demonstration flights in San Francisco Bay. Bennett also flew his kite 183 m *600 ft* above the Statue of Liberty and landed gently and with precision on a lawn in front of the 97·5 m *320 ft* statue. In early 1970 Bennett introduced the kite to Cypress Gardens, by climbing up to 610 m *2000 ft* behind the towboat, releasing the towline and after several fantastic manoeuvres, making a perfect landing on the beach. Of course, the Gardens soon introduced this new

The faithful old Albatross driven by Rosemary Brigham tows George Adlington, the first water-skier to experiment with kiting in the British Isles.

act to the regular water-ski shows. Visitors were thrilled when the flyers would release and go into free flight from heights of only 91 m *300 ft*.

Meanwhile Bill Moyes had further developed his wings till they became capable of high speed. This enabled him to tow by aeroplane, which is just what he did on 15 October 1971 at Amery, Wisconsin, behind a Super Cub. He reached an altitude of 2624 m *8610 ft* above the airstrip, which gained him another world record. By 1972 the altitude record for water-tow had been broken by an American, so Moyes returned to Lake Ellesmere on 14 March and flew to a height of 1448 m *4750 ft* under the boat tow, an astounding achievement in the eyes of expert flyers elsewhere. He used a 110 km/h *70 mph* Hamilton jetboat, carrying a winch mounted across the gunwales. 'At a signal, they gunned the boat and I slid across the grass on a pair of trick skis and

across the water still dry. I discarded the skis as soon as I was airborne and settled down to a prone position in the harness and frame to reduce drag . . . I was secretly hoping for a mile high (1609 *m 5280 ft*), but I couldn't budge the needle of the altimeter.'

Also in 1972, the first US National Delta Kite Championships were held at Cypress Gardens. Up until this time, rules for kite tournaments were written for the towed, flat-wing kites. For example, there was the slalom, on a course similar to water-ski slalom, but of six buoys (or water spouts) plus gate buoys over 4267 m *14000 ft* each, 15·2 m *50 ft* outside the centre to be rounded airborne on a 36·60 m *120 ft* rope. New rules for the Delta were now written by the Chief Judge, Harry Robb, as the tournament progressed. It was the most exciting event ever held at Cypress Gardens. A great new sport competition was born. Paul Solovsky, a

Bill Moyes, the Water Ski Altitude record holder.

native of Minnesota won the first National Delta Wing title, and was selected to go to Nice, France to demonstrate the flying technique. But after arriving there, only one week after winning his title, Solovsky died in a tragic kite accident.

Improvements were constantly being made to these kites. Safety was uppermost in the minds of all flyers and rules were added almost daily to prevent future accidents.

During the American summer of 1972 Bill Moyes had a nasty accident during a flight in North Dakota and fell 91 m *300 ft*, breaking his pelvis. Only six weeks later he competed in the North American Championships and won against America's and Canada's finest, even though he could only walk on crutches.

On one occasion Canadian champion skier George Athans wanted to check on Howard Hughes, said to be in the top floors of Bayshore Inn, Vancouver. He was towed out in the bay, dragged aloft, and made two passes at the hotel to see if he could catch the billionaire recluse doing something. The first time up, the rope snapped before release at 152 m *500 ft* and he had to crash-land into the sea. At the second attempt the winds were too high and he couldn't get close enough.

Unfortunately the fatal accidents continued. In 1973, the Austrian water-ski champion, Bernd Rauchenwald was tragically killed in a kite accident at Nurburgring in Germany, while in Belgium, Dr Veys, the father of Jean Veys the ski champion, also met his death in a similar accident. In fact, there were so many fatal and near-fatal accidents with delta kites, which brought a tragic note and dangerous reputation to the sport, that the World Water Ski Union decided to ban it as a sport division of water-skiing.

Nevertheless kite-flyers, who have now separated from the Union, continue to carry on in their own way.

Barefoot Skiing

The following description, dated 6 March 1947, appears in the book *Water-Skiing* by Dick Pope Sr: 'Shifting his weight to the left foot, which was skimming over the surface, and with his toes turned up, he (Downing Dick Pope Jr) kicked off the freeboard and instantly placed his right foot on the water, shifting his weight to the right side for equal weight distribution. Downing held his breath – and what followed seemed to be a miracle, if not to Downing, certainly to the boat driver. His feet seemed to dig in momentarily and quickly planed to the surface. He found himself leaning farther back than usual, and his knees were bent even more than his normal skiing stance. When he took his first breath, he knew the danger of falling was over. For Downing it was a far greater thrill than anyone could imagine, since he had been the first one to ski on the soles of his bare feet while skimming along the top of the water at a speed of 56km/h *35 mph* or more. He relates how he looked down at his feet with his toes turned up. He wiggled them slightly, and it tickled. Despite the excitement, Downing was soon tired. It was a greater strain than any other type of skiing he had known. The next question was how to stop. Two choices were available. One, he could just let go of the rope and fall backward. Two, he could pull in on the rope, flip forward while tucking his knees and chin into his chest, and somersault forward.'

Pope adds that the first girl to perform the barefoot act was Charlene Wellborn, also on Lake Eloise. Before long the barefoot trick had been incorporated into the Cypress Gardens Show.

Throughout every Federation affiliated to the WWSU, there will undoubtedly be those who claim that they were the first to ski barefoot in their country and, of course, this will be disputed. Nevertheless, the very knowledge that barefooting was possible, gave many others the confidence to 'try their feet'.

It was not until 19 September 1954, that anything was done to officially ratify a World Barefoot Record – and then it was in Switzerland, by a young Frenchman called Bernard Collier. That Thursday morning, with André Coutau officiating and the water-ski champion Pierre Jaegar driving the boat, Collier set out from the Eaux-Vives jetty on Lake Geneva, with the intention of covering the 7 km *4.4 miles* to Bellvue, on a 44 m *145 ft* rope. He was only able to cover 4950 m *5415 yd* – a run of 4 min 45 sec – before he was toppled by the waves. Now he had set an inaugural record, it was up to someone else to beat it.

Back at Cypress Gardens, a couple of skilful skiers had thought up two novel types of take-off: Ken Tibado became the first to make a barefoot beach take-off in 1956, while the following year Joe Cash originated the deep-water take-off. In time, start methods were to become quite important in this breakaway discipline.

One country where barefooting really began to catch on was Australia, again on the Hawkesbury River. The reason for this was simply a need for variety in their skiing. Water-skiers on that river always had problems with floods – whenever they tried to put down a slalom course, it was swept away in half an hour, and this was also the case with attempts to anchor a jumping ramp. So the Hawkesbury pioneers – in particular skiers like 'Woggy' Wright of Yarwonga, the Purnell family, Peter Forrest, Erwin Lusigger, Ray Leighton and John Hollands – became quite proficient in barefooting, travelling up to ten or twenty miles in perfect conditions.

In 1962, on the initiative of Jimmy 'Flea' Jackson, the

The earliest barefoot sequence ever taken of Dick Pope Jr at Cypress Gardens, 1947.

AWSA formed a Barefoot Club consisting of those who had skied continuously for at least one minute on their bare feet before an official observer. Jimmy was Member No. 1. Within months, the New South Wales Water Ski Association had also formed an Australian Barefoot Club with the same rules – and a Barefoot Badge became a much coveted emblem.

The following year an Australian became the first barefooter to skim up a special masonite jumping ramp at Manly Dam. He was Geoff Nicholls. Nicholls designed this smaller-than-average ramp, built it himself and jumped 5–6 m *15–20 ft* landing on his backside. Unfortunately not long after he also had the distinction of becoming the first barefoot jumper to have a serious accident. The other barefoot performers of the time thought Nicholls was totally mad, but somehow barefoot jumping caught on.

It was also in that year that a new American record of 33 min barefoot was set by Don Thomson of Lee's Summit, Missouri. Then in the summer of 1964, Thom-

142

Vaughan Bullivaunt of New Zealand. A superb exponent of the barefoot art.

son won his third National Barefoot championship in a row, with a run of 31 min on Lake Eloise, Cypress Gardens.

The first barefoot contest in Britain appears to have been held at Lochearnhead, Scotland when Lance Callingham won by staying on his soles longer than anyone else.

In barefooting competitions the judges were often to tell the skiers to go out and execute some trick, which they would then literally write-up into a rule, using what they had just seen.

In January 1965, Paul McManus ski'd barefoot continuously for *59* minutes behind Bill McLachlan's *Miss Evinrude* on the Hawkesbury River, timed by the Australian BWSA.

In 1966, to promote the barefoot art, a group of twenty Australians went on a world tour to display their talents and spread goodwill to Hawaii, Mexico, the USA, the UK, India, Japan, Hong Kong and Singapore. Their demonstrations included wake crossing (with double score for crossing on one foot), jumping out of two skis, jumping off a disc, rope-on-neck, 180° jump-around and jumping over the 20 cm *2 ft* high ramp. Also in 1966, Harold Miller beat Paul McManus's Endurance Record by almost a full minute. This was again increased to 67 minutes over 58 km *36 miles* by the American Stephen Z. Northrup in 1967.

By 1968, membership of the AWSA Barefoot Club had grown to 1300. That year, McManus set a backwards barefoot record of 33 min 19 sec, while elsewhere a barefoot jump of 13·10 m *43 ft* had also been recorded.

The barefoot speed record began at 96 km/h *60 mph*. Then Wayne Jones of Australia pushed it up to 121·55 km/h *75·55 mph* followed by compatriot Garry Barton who pushed that mark up to 125 km/h *77·7 mph* at Berkeley Aquatic Park, California. In setting this record, Barton reached a maximum of 138·4 km/h *86 mph*, which gave him among other things, second degree burns to the bottom of his feet. At these speeds, Barton was literally skimming on top of the water and had only 2·5 cm *1 in* of his heels for a planing surface. On 28 March 1972, John Taylor increased the record to 140·7 km/h *87·46 mph* on Lake Ming, California. On 18 August, with very hot feet indeed, Gordon Eppling increased that to 159·13 km/h *98·9 mph* at Long Beach, California. Another American has done 177 km/h *110 mph*, but only after he had injected his feet with morphine to kill the pain!

One of New Zealand's crack water-skiers, Vaughan Bullivaunt, also became a superb barefooter, performing in the shows at Cypress Gardens. Despite a crippling, near-fatal accident at the Gardens, Bullivaunt – thanks to the efficiency of rescue craft and surgeons – was soon back on the water and continued to innovate on his bare feet.

The Barefoot Endurance Record was also getting longer and longer, having been regained by Paul McManus with a run of 2 hr 37 min, and he had also increased his Backward Barefoot Record to 39 min.

Meanwhile in competitive terms, the start methods were many: Running off the end of the jetty, deepwater start, beach start and tumbleturn start. Garry Barton, the Australian National Open Barefoot Champion for four consecutive years, was the first to show that backward deepwater and backward beach starts into a backward barefoot position, were not impossible.

Most tricks, one-foots, one-foot reverse, toe-holds, toe-hold reverse, rope-in-teeth, rope-on-neck, tumbleturn, tumbleturn reverse, side-slides, backward-toe-on-foot, 180°, 360° turns – were possible on bare feet. Garry Barton was the first to execute a toe-hold 180° turn back-front and first to recover from a rope-on-toe and complete the backward rope-on-toe opposite foot.

With a 61 cm *2 ft* ramp, a jump of 16·46 m *54 ft* had also been recorded in Australia.

A major landmark came in September 1975 when, at the World Water Ski Union Congress in London, a set of rules for barefoot competition was finally accepted and official contests could then get under way. On 21/22 August 1976, the very first European Barefoot Championships took place at Princes Water Ski Club, near London's Heathrow Airport, England.

Disciplines involved were – Final Start Methods, Wake Slalom, Tricks, Jumping and Over-all; there was no division between the sexes. In that year of water-skiing triumphs Britain shone again. Mike Thomas became Individual European Champion, while the four other disciplines were won by British skiers and the eight-strong band also carried off the Team Prize with 11 350·6 points – over 5000 points ahead of their nearest competitors Germany, Netherlands, Spain, Belgium, Italy, and France. In view of the fact that this was the first barefoot competition to be held under World Rules, Keith Donnelly (Northern Ireland) could claim that his 13·25 m *43·5 ft* jump was a World Record.

With an International contest in the record books, it would only be a matter of time before a World Barefoot Championship was organised – and yet another move towards this came when the dynamic Franz Kirsch of Germany was elected as the new President of the World Barefoot Commission. Dick Pope Jr (Downing) would perhaps have smiled at all this, as he recalled a day back in 1947 when . . .

Opposite: **All the excitement and action of skiing barefoot and backwards.**

Techniques

Right: Incorrect: pulling yourself up using the arms.

Centre: Correct: position for beginner to stand up on land. Observe loose rope.

Far right: Correct: skiing position for beginner using the legs only to stand up.

Josephine Crane, instructed by David Nations.

THE FIRST SKIING LESSON

I believe that water-skiing is a sport for people of all ages.

Initially, during the first stage of learning how to water-ski, it is important to accept the fact that your arms must act only as an extension of the rope – a necessary attachment for being pulled along by the boat so that you have the motivation to plane on the surface of the water and ski.

In the early years of the sport, people were taught to use their arms to help themselves up in basic water-ski lessons, but nowadays this is considered as the very misguided method which caused so many people to fail and flounder in the first lessons. This false premise of considering the rope as a means for pulling yourself up, will soon put you in a position where your skis shoot forward in front of you and you fall flat on your back. This very common and disappointing first experience in water-skiing has been the greatest discouragement to so many people throughout the world – their first ski lesson had been a failure.

Land Lesson

At this early stage of learning to ski, you must then start with a simple movement. Place a pair of skis on a flat land surface parallel and even with each other. The skis will be easier to put on, and will fit better, if you first wet your feet. Push your foot forward into the binder as far as possible, then pull the rear section of the binder up around your heel.

Stand in a comfortable position, legs about 30 cm *12 in* apart, shoulders and head in an upright position. Keeping your arms straight and with the handle of the towing line in your hands, make them a continuation of the rope. You should be sitting on the skis just behind your heels with your arms fully extended, parallel to your skis, with your knees between and almost touching your elbows. Now, begin a sequence of knees raising and bending, because what you are trying to simulate is pushing your body off the water; as later, when in the water, you will be ready to understand the way you have practised this bent knees position – you want to stand on the water – you've got to try and push with your knees and legs, attempting to make your skis 'touch bottom', as you will be pushing your skis down into the water, as deep as you can. This action will push your body up.

It is very important to understand how to control your head and shoulders: your back is almost straight, with just a slight lean forward. Bending of the knees must not be accompanied by the head and shoulders moving or shaking backwards or forwards. Come up slowly and in control. Stay on your toes with your knees bent, then as you come up, get on your heels and stand with your legs firm, do not allow them to wobble, keep a resilience through your legs and through the whole structure of your body. Remember that when you get on the water, because the speed of the boat will show a marked contrast to where you were simply standing still on the land, any movement you make will be accelerated and exaggerated. If you get your Land Lesson right, it will be so much easier when you enter the water.

Before entering the water, it is very important for you to wear a water-ski life-jacket, no matter how good a swimmer you are, because it will give you stability and ability to float in the water when you fall, and also help you to conserve valuable energy.

The ability to feel confident in the water is also most important. A beginner should be given time to stay in

the water with his skis on, just floating and getting a good position in the water, skis parallel – to get his balance. It is so important to have your skis parallel and body balance right *before* you take your first tow. Practise swivelling around in the water, with swimming movements, until you feel able to control your body position and skis.

One can even suggest, as we do with children, trying this out in swimming pools, where they can learn in shallow water, which is warmer and more reassuring.

If, to your complete satisfaction you have understood the Land Lesson and feel at ease in the water, then you will be prepared and ready to be pulled off by the boat.

Grasp the tow handle firmly and make certain that the tips of your skis are above the water and evenly spaced apart. The tow-line is guided between the skis and the slack is taken out of the rope, but you must have proper balance in the water before the signal is given by the instructor to the boat driver that you are now ready. A gradually increasing start is best for beginners. This will enable the beginner to check and control balance and position.

Remember that you are in a sitting position, in the water, with your arms fully extended forward and your knees between them.

As the boat picks up speed, you should repeat the action you learned on the land. Pushing with your knees and legs, you should rise slowly from a sitting position. Remember it is vital that you do not 'pull' the rope in towards you by bending your elbows – or attempt to pull the handle up towards your chest or over your head. Just use your arms as an extension of the rope, as previously explained.

The distribution of weight is balanced directly over your feet. Do not try to stand completely upright, keep the knees bent instead. Remember, your knees act as 'shock absorbers' and help you to maintain the balance you need over water movement.In case you lose control and fall, then it is best to quickly let go of the handle. If you are wondering what is the best way to stop, just let go of the rope and spread your arms out to your sides for balance. Your speed will decrease rapidly, and if your balance is correct you will slowly sink into the water, resting comfortably on your skis. If you feel unstable, or in an emergency, get ready to sit down in the water, on the rear of your skis, as quickly as possible.

The reason a beginner falls is generally due to excessive movements, like suddenly pulling or snatching the rope in, or letting the head and shoulders move backwards or forwards sharply or sitting down on your skis, and allowing them to spread or cross each other. There are so many cases when while learning to ski, the skier 'feels' he is going to fall when doing one of the above movements. It is wiser not to panic, but instead to try hard to keep in mind all of the earlier lessons on the land. Stay in control and there is no reason why the beginner should not ski on the first lesson.

The First Ski Run
Once you get up on the water with good balance, you should concentrate on maintaining this position with as little movement as possible, skis parallel – arms straight out and inflexible – knees bent and with your head and shoulders in an upright position.

During the Land Lesson you were told of the physical sensation of the difference between the straight and bent arms and the importance of understanding the use and control of the rope. Then when you have learnt to stand up on the water and can ski with confidence, we can start to change the inflexible arm position and teach you how to pull in those hands, just two or three inches or centimetres at a time, in-and-out, in-and-out, so that you can now understand this movement of staying in full control, not pulling on the rope hard and jerking yourself into the backward, 'flat-on-your-back' arc. Always remember that technical ability, gradually and slowly learnt is always a 'buoy ahead' of enthusiasm, even though you need a mixture of both.

Next, at the same time as moving in-and-out with your hands, the direction of the skis is controlled by the turning of your foot. This is an ankle movement. Now one foot exerts a little pressure and moves towards the other, then you will begin to virage. If you want to go left, push on your right foot, and if you want to go right, push on your left foot, using your legs this way with a slight inclination of pressure, so skiing from side to side inside the wake.

With sufficient practice and good control you should be ready to cross the wake. Understanding and knowing how to change your weight turn with your skis into the direction of the wake you are about to cross, keep your knees bent and use them as shock absorbers at all times in this movement. You can then turn your skis at a right angle and re-cross the wake and continue through to cross the other wake whilst always keeping your body in good position. Continue doing this from side to side.

When a skier has the ability to do this and is then in full control of the skis, then viraging and skiing on two skis will soon give the skier the pleasure and satisfaction of success in the sport of water-skiing.

Starts on One Ski
These should not be attempted until you can perform viraging and wake-crossing correctly and with confidence and ease.

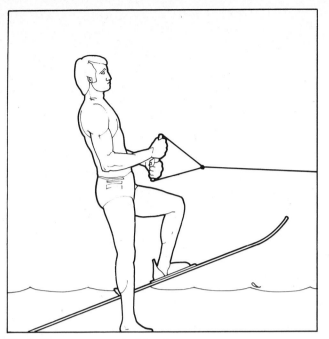

Fig. 1. Scooter start: position A.

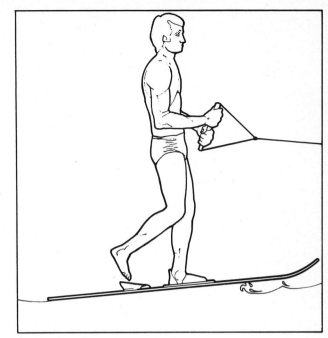

Fig. 2. Scooter start: position B.

Scooter Start

Most people find this the easiest to learn. It should be tried from a beach or the side of a lake where the bottom is firm and sloping. The skier stands on his free leg with the water reaching almost to the knee. The front leg should be well bent and held in front of you with the ski resting at an angle in the water. Because it is difficult to keep your balance it helps if you can rest your back against a jetty or if someone can offer you support from behind. With one hand on the handle, hold a few coils of rope in the other, and play these out as the rope tightens. This makes it easier for you to tell when it is coming taut and prevents it dragging on the water and jerking straight. When it becomes taut step forward on to the ski and pull

in on the rope keeping your body under control until you are water-borne and secure. It is helpful to drag the free foot through the water behind you as this will act both as a brake and a keel, helping to prevent your leaning forward, and giving you a straight direction through the water.

Deep Water Start

The position you assume in the water can best be learnt on land. Try sitting on the edge of a table with the knee of your ski leg tucked right up to your chest, the free foot dangling under the table. Put your arms on either side of your knee and stretch your shoulders forward as far as you can so that they are over the foot. If you keep your

Fig. 3. Deep water start: one foot free of binder.

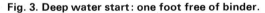

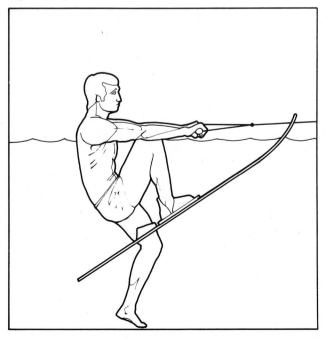

Fig. 4. Deep water start: both feet in the binders.

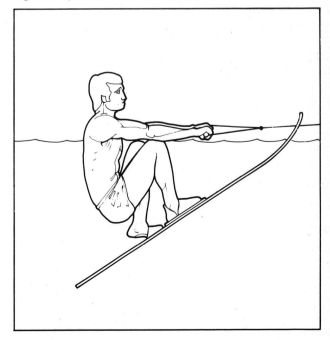

weight forward like this it makes it much easier for you to be pulled up onto the water surface. Keep your head up and look straight ahead. When you are in the water a life jacket, or buoyancy aid, should help you to float comfortably while you are concentrating on the position. To help you keep your balance in the water let one hand paddle gently until the rope begins to come tight. The passenger in the boat should let this out for the skier so that there is a firmness in the rope all the time. This will help you to hold your position. When you feel the pull from the boat, pull in hard against it and push down simultaneously with your foot, stretching your body straight. Let your free foot drag behind you. This is not easy to learn and will require all your concentration and strength until you have mastered it.

Some skiers feel happier if they keep both feet in the bindings for they feel able to press down harder on the ski this way. However with one foot locked behind the other, certain difficulties arise: it is hard to keep the weight forward and at the same time to put equal pressure on both feet, and because your body weight falls naturally to one side it is hard to keep balanced, especially as you do not have the free foot to steady you. These problems can be overcome if you forget about trying to point your ski directly at the boat. Let it point instead to one side and when the boat starts off, pull away to that side.

Jetty Start
This start is very similar to the scooter start. Sit right on the edge of the jetty, with the ski in front of you resting on the water, with the knee bent and your weight back. You should play the rope out yourself. When it comes taut you simply stand on the ski and pull firmly back.

If both feet are in the bindings you should press down hard on the back foot. If the back foot is free you may find it helpful to lift it up on to the edge of the jetty, so that you can push off with it when the boat pulls. As you take off, let it drag in the water to give you extra balance.

Fig. 5. Jetty start.

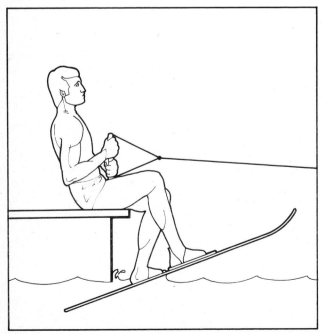

NB – The driver's role in all these one-ski starts is very important. If he drives away too fast and suddenly, the skier will be unable to hold the pull and will be jerked forward. If the boat is too slow it will be hard for the skier to counter the backward drag of the water. The driver should watch the skier carefully and pick up speed gradually and as necessary.

SLALOM SKIING

To progress from two skis to a slalom ski is to discover a whole new world of experience on the water, for one ski offers greater manoeuvrability, and with this the possibility of more speed, better control, freedom of movement and grace.

The process of learning can be broken down into several simple stages. It is essential to master the correct technique at each stage. If you try to learn too quickly, your progress will be hindered and your eventual standard of slalom skiing is likely to be limited. The boat speed should always be such that the skier rides comfortably and securely on the water.

We must first determine on which foot you have most stability – in other words, the one which you will have in the front binding of the ski and which gives you the best balance. An ordinary pair of skis should be used at first; do not use a slalom ski at this stage, and remember to wear a life-jacket or a ski belt.

Ski in the centre of the wake and with the boat speed sufficient to allow you to plane comfortably. Try to lift one ski at a time in a series of 'walking' steps, by slightly pulling in your arms up to your sides, and by raising one knee at the same time. Remember to lift the toe of the ski to keep the tip upwards, at the same time raising the whole ski out of the water. Then repeat with the other leg.

Incorrect: simulating the wrong position for raising the ski.

If the skier feels unsteady, the ski can be quickly replaced on the water to regain balance. It will soon be found that there is more stability on one foot than on the other. Practise on this foot and try skiing with the other ski held off the water for as long as possible.

Correct: simulated position for raising the ski.

Above: Removing the foot from the binder.

Below: Slowly putting the foot down behind and near to the front binder.

At this early stage of learning to slalom, keep your arms and skiing leg locked. Stay in the centre of the wake for stability and only when encountering waves should you bend the skiing knee, but don't pull your arms in sharply or hard – keep them extended. When this movement has been mastered, then the raised ski can be kept off the water. When good body control and balance can be maintained, the moment will have come to cast off the raised ski.

It will be found helpful to practise this lesson by casting off the ski on land, before doing so on water. At the same time, it may also be helpful to familiarise yourself with the grip of the handle used in slalom skiing. Get someone to hold the rope taut throughout this land lesson. The hand is held in an almost perpendicular position (see Fig. 5) – one hand above the other. Adjust the binder of the ski you intend to drop, so that it fits loosely. Keep your arms straight, back straight and head up, whilst slightly bending the knee. Pressure should be put on the ball of the foot and the heel raised. Do not lift the ski, but slip the foot out of the loosened binder. When doing this movement, the ski will just slide backwards. Keep practising this position until you feel confident of your balance. Now try this on the water. Remember what you did on land. Get your position right first, keep your head up, arms and back straight, and now with the ski ready for casting-off on the water, bend your knee slightly and slowly ease your heel out of the binder, followed by the rest of your foot. The ski will leave you and you will be on one ski. If you start to wobble, do not panic, keep the free foot raised in the air and re-steady your position.

The most common fault is that the skier usually tries to jerk or pull hard on the rope – when the balance is best controlled by keeping the arms and the skiing leg straight,

151

Correct: the skiing position on slalom ski. Observe the way in which the handle is held.

the body evenly balanced and all movements done slowly.

Keep your ankle and leg fairly rigid. This will stop the ski wobbling from side to side. Once you can ski with confidence in this position, you are ready to place the free foot on the back of the ski.

Keeping the foot up, slowly move it round behind your front leg. When lowering the free foot to the back of the ski, remember to keep it completely unweighted to prevent you toppling, then lower it until your toes touch the ski surface behind your front binder. Begin to transfer the weight gradually on to the heel of your back foot

Fig. 6. Correct: pulling with the waist, shoulders and head going back – elbows in.

and bend the knee of your back leg so that most of your weight is now on your back foot.

If the ski wobbles and you feel you may fall, lift your leg and return to your first one-ski position. Then try again.

When you can ski comfortably in slalom position, with your arms straight, you can begin to practise bending and straightening your elbows – slowly – taking care not to jerk. At the same time, maintain rigidly your body, head and shoulder positions. Do not raise your hands – if you do, your shoulders, head and body weight will go backwards and you will fall. It is very important that this

Fig. 7. Incorrect: pulling with shoulders and head coming forward into a crouched position.

exercise should be repeated until you are able to do it with confidence, remembering that the pull must always come from a backward position and your chest, shoulders and head must never be allowed to get into that fatal forward position. I have found this fault in so many skiers, who have allowed themselves to be pulled into a crouched position with their head down, which completely changes the weight of the body, so that the ski dips down and the skier falls forward. It is so important that this should be understood at this early stage of learning to slalom ski. It will become clearer when working in the slalom course and at faster speeds.

Another tendency to be carefully avoided is the one that some skiers have of bending their body and dropping their shoulders just as they are turning.

As soon as you have control of your slalom ski, it is vital that you understand the importance your arms will play if you are to become a good slalom skier.

Staying inside the wake, let us say the skier is going to ski to his right from point A to point B (see Fig. 8). It is important to realise that your pull must be rationed, pulling a bit at a time all the way through, so that you reach point B at the end of your pull.

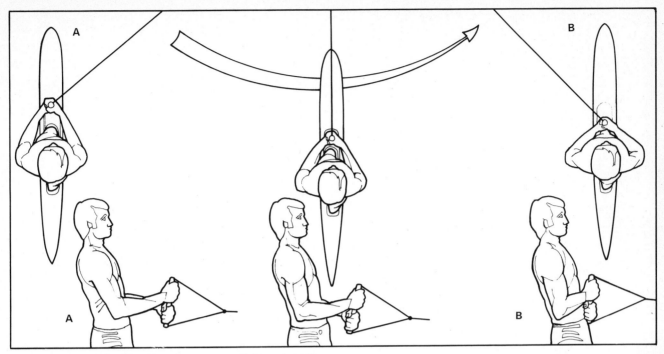

Fig. 8. Correct: using hands and arms to pull from A to B.

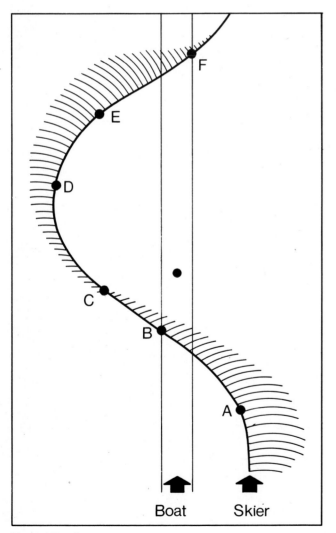

Fig. 9. Viraging.

It is very common for skiers at this stage to use up the whole of their 'pull' in the first metre or two of the distance from A to B. You must not allow your pull to be dissipated and wasted in this way. It is, after all, not a long pull, since your elbows are held against your waist at the beginning and your hands can only move into your body by the end of the pull. At the same time, you have maintained your good basic slalom position.

As you reach point B, extend your arms out again so that your elbows have returned to their original position and you are ready to turn and repeat your gradual pull to a point in direct line with A (see Fig. 8).

It is also your arms which provide the means whereby you can gauge the strength of the boat's pull and how much force you should exert against it. The power from the boat differs according to the actual speed of the boat and at different points of your path as you virage.

Your arms feel that altering strength of the pull and know how much energy to exert against it. Rigid arms have no such sensitivity. As you will see when we discuss the use of arms at the turn, it is largely their movement that enables you to both alter your weight distribution over the ski and to obtain the rhythm essential for effective viraging.

It is important to remember when you pull in, to keep your hands down towards your waist (or the body's effective centre of gravity). If you pull in above this point, your body will become unbalanced and your weight will no longer be directly over the ski, with the result that the ski will lose its edge and may slide away under you.

You should now be ready to try to ski on an ordinary slalom ski with a rear binder. Cast off as usual, and put your back foot into the rear binder at a slight angle for better balance. At this point you should understand how to ride over waves and bumps. To reduce the size of wave you will encounter when the boat turns back on its path and crosses its own wake, the driver should approach that wake at a sharp angle.

Above: Philippa Roberts seen here pushing on the keel and turning round the buoy.

Below: The blond, Terry Van der Merwe (SA) displaying skill and precision in slalom skiing.

Mike Hazelwood with his weight at the back of the ski leaning sideways and pushing around and away from the boat.

You will then only have to encounter a few short waves. If the boat drives alongside its previous wake or crosses it gradually, the waves you meet will be elongated and rolling and more difficult to manage. On meeting rough water, all you need do is to flex your knees slightly and concentrate on keeping body and arm control positions and your weight back. The driver can help further by reducing speed slightly as you meet any unusual waves for you will be lower in the water and have more stability. When you have managed to do this in a good slalom position, remember that the same principles of body movement and weight distribution apply whether you are viraging freely on one ski or through the slalom course. All that differentiates between the two are the specific methods of timing and positioning that enable you to utilise your one ski technique to attain the greatest efficiency through the slalom course.

A virage has two main stages – (a) travelling across the water, and (b) turning. To understand what you must do in each stage it is helpful to look first at the action of the ski itself in the water.

Across the wake the ski is leaning on one edge, the bottom surface inclined toward the boat. As it does this, two things are happening. Firstly, the edge of the ski cleaves through the water and, acting rather like a keel, gives it direction. Secondly, as the ski banks, it pushes water away towards the boat, and, as it does so, exerts a

force that counteracts the forward pull of the boat, which allows it to assume a different path. The greater the lean of the ski the greater is the surface area pushing away in the water. As this increases, so also does the amount of resistance to the forward pull and the angle of lean one can achieve away from the boat.

Since the boat will constantly be trying to pull the skier and ski into a straight line behind it, you must exert pressure mainly on the back of the ski if you are to turn it round away from the boat and maintain an angle in the water.

If you look at Fig. 9 (p. 153), the amount of spray thrown up signifies the degree of pressure that is being exerted by the ski in the water. At the beginning of the pull across the wake (from A to B and E to F in the diagram) the pressure is at its greatest as the ski has most angle in the water to carry it across the wake.

As the ski changes direction round the turn it must move from one edge to the other. At the start of the turn (B to C in diagram) it begins to flatten. As it does so, pressure against the forward pull of the boat is reduced and it straightens in the water. At point C it is flat and coming round to face the boat. The lack of spray at this point signifies the fact that there is no sideways force at this moment. If you are to achieve an unbroken turn the ski must move smoothly and continuously from one edge and begin to turn in the opposite direction as the back is

155

pushed round and pressure is again exerted against the boat pull.

The first thing to realise is that your weight must be mainly over the back of the ski. Looking at a slalom ski you will see how the binders are placed for this purpose. Remember the position of leaning back on the back foot. Your weight must be back for two reasons. Firstly, because, as previously discussed, the ski is turned round in the water by the pressure on the back of the ski. Secondly, since the boat is constantly trying to pull the skier forward towards it, if the ski is not effectively kept between the skier and the boat the skier has no surface on which to resist the forward pull.

Not only must your weight be to the back of the ski, but it must also be pressing away from the boat. If you simply lean back you will do nothing more than push water away towards the boat and you will continue in a straight line behind it. It is only if you lean sideways away from the boat simultaneously, that you will edge the ski and obtain direction through the water.

To maintain an edge in the water all your weight must be behind the ski, as nearly as possible directly resisting the forward pull. For this purpose your body will be effectively in a straight line pressing down on the ski.

If you allow the boat to pull the top part of your body to it, as it will in effect be trying to do, you will automatically become more upright and the pressure of the body on the ski will be down on to the water rather than in direct resistance to the boat pull. The result will be that the ski will flatten and lose its edge and angle through the water. If you become too upright the ski will no longer be between you and the boat, and you will have no surface on which to offer resistance to it. The result will be that all the pull from the boat will be taken by the arms, which in themselves cannot match the tug from the boat, and you will be pulled forward.

At the second wake, you should stop pulling and as you come off the wake you should start straightening for the turn. To do this you let your arms out gradually and begin stretching in towards the boat. Your body will then

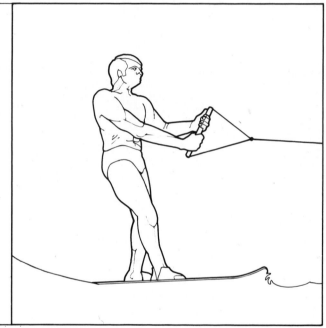

Fig. 10. Demonstrating the position of the hand when reaching for the handle.

Above left and right: Correct. *Below:* Incorrect.

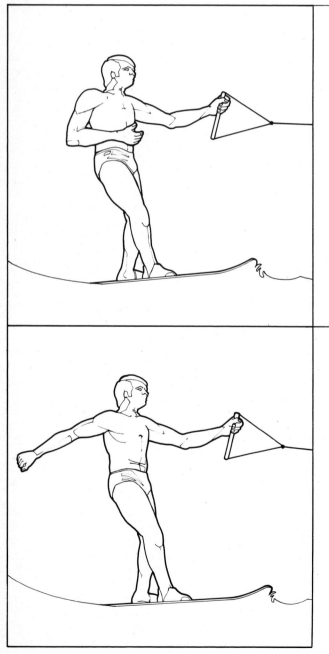

move upright, and as it does transfer your weight on to the front foot, so unweighting the back of the ski which up to now has been pressing the ski round. The ski will flatten, but since you are leaning in towards the boat it will immediately move over on to the opposite edge and go into a turn. At the mid-point of the turn pull in with your arms, at the same time leaning back on the rope away from the boat and forcing the ski round with the back foot.

While learning to virage you should keep both hands on the handle all the time, at the turn stretching both of them out towards the boat. Only when you can virage confidently and correctly should you consider taking one hand off the handle as you turn. The reason for releasing the outside hand on the turn is that by doing so you can reach farther and more easily towards the boat. The longer your reach the greater will be your lean and the quicker your turn. You can demonstrate this for yourself on land by stretching your arms out to one side of your body, firstly with two hands together and then with just one. With the second movement you will be able to stretch farther, less awkwardly.

The second hand leaves the handle at the moment when you have come off the second wake and are starting to reach out towards the boat. As you stretch the inside hand you must remember not to swing or throw the free arm out behind you but to keep it close to your body ready to reach for the handle as you begin to draw it back again. At the mid-point of the turn pull in on the rope with the inside hand, as you do so meeting the handle with the second hand and completing the pull with two hands. It is important to observe this arm movement carefully for it is essential to effective viraging and yet so often disregarded. Most skiers tend to extend the inside arm at the start of the turn and leave it outstretched all the way round the turn until point E on Diagram I, when they put the second hand on the handle and pull in. They rely solely on the lean of their body, and of their ski in the water, to bring the ski round in the turn, and because of this have little control over the speed or angle of the turn. Turning technique can be improved considerably if the arms are used more effectively and if you feel as though you are actually pulling yourself round the turn. They should never remain in an outstretched position and you should start to pull in immediately your inside arm has obtained its full reach at the mid-point of the turn. You should not wait until the second hand is on the handle to start the pull but, as described, begin pulling in with the one hand letting the second meet it, as you do

so. If you start the pull here you will come out of the corner with more speed and force, for your weight will be transferred to the back of the ski more quickly. Because you are continuously applying power you will also have greater stability on the water. If you remain still on the turn, relying solely on the edge to bring you round you will be for the moment exerting the minimum of resistance and will be more easily unbalanced by any unevenness in the water or boat pull. By using your arms in the manner described, you will in effect be accelerating out of the turn and the ski will come round as cleanly and smoothly as a car does if its driver applies the accelerator coming out of a bend. If no extra power is exerted the turn will be less effective and controlled. In a similar manner, if a car rounds a corner at a constant or slackening speed the back will tend to swing round.

Before you consider attempting the course, you should be able to virage at speed, rhythmically and maintaining balance and good form. The slalom course consists of six buoys set diagonally in the water with a series of gate buoys in a straight line down the middle, through which the boat passes, while you pass through the gates at either end and round each of the six buoys in turn. The distance between the gate buoys at either end of the course from the first and sixth buoys respectively is such that you have in effect little more water space on the first or last buoy than on any of the others. You should remain on a flat ski until you are capable of making the course successfully at speeds up to 41–45 km/h *26–28 mph*.

Wayne Grimditch reaching to meet the handle with his second hand.

Sylvie Hulsemann (Lux) returning to both hands on the handle.

When first attempting the course, the speed should be slow and such that you feel secure but are planing comfortably. On your first attempt you should ignore the gates and not even try to round any of the buoys but virage inside them. As you approach the course you should pull out before reaching the gates until you are travelling in an imaginary line about a metre inside the first buoy. As you come alongside, you should turn and pull across the wake to the second buoy turning inside it and continue in this way through the course. You may find that your turn and pull are too slow at first and that you gradually fall further behind.

This is not important. What is essential is that you keep your rhythm and control. As you repeat the exercise you will become accustomed to the strength of pull and speed of turn necessary to virage neatly within the course. Once this has been achieved, you must adopt the same procedure, this time going round the buoys. The extra distance you must cover will mean you need to pull harder. If you find you miss a buoy, you should ignore it and pull for the next, again concentrating on maintaining the viraging movement and good form. If, when viraging freely you have been used to releasing one hand on the turn you can continue doing this when making your first attempts at the course. If, however, the effect of having to virage near or round the buoys is to make you lose balance and swing your free arm wildly, it is worth while practising at this stage with both hands on the handle at the turn and skiing like this until you have

achieved the necessary smoothness of movement. When you can ski through the course successfully at a speed of up to 49 km/h *30 mph*, you should consider the specific methods necessary for effective slalom.

The boat travels the length of the course in a straight line, maintaining a constant speed. However, because you are viraging through the course, you have to cover more than double the distance of the boat over the same

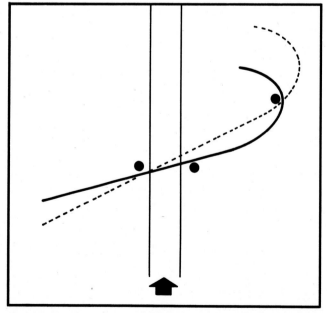

Fig. 11. The approach position, going through the gate and turning on the first buoy. —— good approach, turning round the buoy. - - - - bad approach.

158

length. As a result you must average a much greater speed and are, in effect, involved in a race against time and the boat – a race made more difficult because of the buoys around which you must manoeuvre at the same time. You have to learn to round them in such a way that the least possible time is lost.

The gate and the first and second buoys are the points of greatest importance. Lose time here and you will be fighting to make up lost ground through the rest of the course. Once you start fighting you will find yourself taking risks that only jeopardise your chances of success. Also, if you set up a good rhythm and begin pulling well and positioning yourself accurately on the first turns you will establish a pattern of movement that you should be able to maintain through the rest of the course. One of the secrets of good slalom is in achieving this rhythmic pattern.

It is important to pass through the gate in such a way that you have maximum time in which to position yourself and turn on the first buoy. See Fig. 11 for the correct angle to assume. If you make a bad approach, you will ski close to and past the buoy. If you make a good approach, you will be ready to turn well before you reach the buoy.

To achieve the necessary angle through the gate, pull well out to the far side of the wake, and as you near the course, watch only the gate buoy farthest from you. Aim to ski through the gate so that you just clip the inside of this buoy. Concentrating on the one buoy will help you to achieve a good direction, for it is easier to focus on a single point. You should leave the pull until the last minute, until you feel you must go if you are to make the gate. In this way you will achieve a good angle and pull.

James Carne, positioned early on the approach, breaking and transferring edges.

You should pull hard through both wakes before you start to brake and prepare for the turn.

The intention on the turn should be to round the buoy so that the least amount of water space possible is lost on the far side of it. Water lost is time lost. If you are still turning when past the buoy, you are losing precious moments when you should already be pulling for the next buoy. Ideally you should turn before the buoy so as to pull past it under power for the next. To achieve this you must first be early on the approach, and second be positioned wide of the buoy. You must be early so that you have time to brake and transfer edges because otherwise, if you brake and change edges early, you will find yourself turning before the buoy, and only if you are sufficiently wide is it possible to pull past the buoy. It may help to think in terms of turning round an imaginary buoy a metre or so (a few feet) outside and in front of the actual one, this being something you pass almost accidentally.

It is essential to achieve a good position for the turn as this is the only way to ensure safety and efficiency. If you are too close to the buoy or too late you will have to effect the turn from an awkward angle, and, in your efforts to achieve this, will be obliged to move in ways that involve risk.

For example, if you are too close on the buoy as in the diagram you will have to travel in a straight line for a while in order to pass it and will find you have slack rope. Slack rope occurs when a skier travels in the same direction as the boat but at a greater speed. You will have

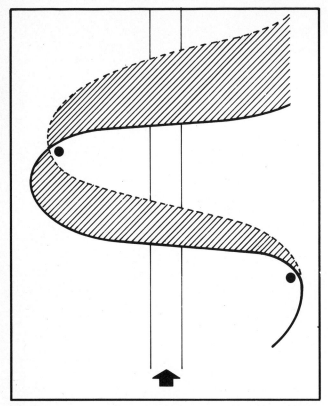

Fig. 12. Rounding the buoy, not diagonally, but at right angles.

greater speed because you have just been pulling and are insufficiently wide to be able to start braking. You will be on a flat ski, travelling straight, because you have no room to start leaning in on an edge. Since you have to pass the buoy before you can turn, you will want to turn quickly to make up lost time and as your ski is not edged and assuming the direction of the turn, your movement on the turn will be the more abrupt and dramatic. The situation is made worse because the rope may be slack and you will have nothing firm against which to pull and lean. In an approach like this, you are likely to fall in on your shoulder and your ski may slide away from under you.

If you are late on your approach, in order to turn quickly, you will find yourself 'hooking' the buoy – that is, turning round it very sharply and close. Risk arises because in a very short space you have to completely change the direction both of your body and your ski, and since you have had little or no time in which to brake you will be doing so at speed, with the likelihood of slack rope. The tendency again will be for you to fall as above. If you find yourself badly positioned for a buoy, it is best not to try to round it quickly but to wait momentarily until you feel the rope taut and have time to brake and slow down before you make the turn. You can concentrate then on making up time on the pull where you are in a position of far less risk.

It is very important to guard against the tendency that many skiers have of using their body weight to take them round the turn, ignoring the use of their arms. This is a tendency that is inherently risky and which becomes more so when used in an attempt to turn quickly from a bad position. If you throw your body into the turn, you will be insensitive to the value and strength of the pull from the boat which only your arms and hands can

gauge. Remember this varies at different times. If you lean over without simultaneously gauging the pull, and the rope is at that point slack, you will almost inevitably fall on your shoulder. It is to a considerable extent the use of the arms that is essential for the achievement of a safe, smooth, controlled turn. If ever you need to turn more sharply than usual, you can best accomplish this by pulling in quickly on the rope, which has the effect of pulling you round.

Your aim should be to achieve the perfect turn on each buoy. Almost without exception, skiers find they have a good and a bad side for turning, depending on which foot is forward on the ski. If you ski left foot forward, your natural turn will be on buoys 1, 3 and 5, and vice versa. Do not allow yourself to be defeated by your bad side but try to practise until you are unaware of the difference, remembering that the better your position before the buoy, the more easily you will achieve the turn.

Understanding how to pull correctly is very important. The object of the pull is to take you across the wake in the shortest possible time so that you are in a good position for the turn. If you look at Fig. 12, you will see clearly the angle to be assumed. Your direction across the wake should be 'square and right-angled', rather than diagonal so that you feel as though the bottom of the ski is parallel to the back of the boat. If you achieve a good turn and pull past the buoy, your ski will already be directed at a good angle. The pull and the turn are complementary, the efficiency of the one depending on that of the other. Only if the pull is correct will you be properly positioned for the turn and vice versa. You can never be early enough on a buoy, and when you are late or in difficulty, it is on the pull that you are best able to make up time. Many skiers, however, are unaware of their potential pulling power, and they should concentrate on pulling hard all the time, whatever the boat speed. It is useful to think in terms of pulling the back off the boat. At the same time remember that the pull must be exerted in a controlled fashion. If it is violent or rough you will tend to over-pull or to lose your edge, and, on a flat ski, leave the water over the wake, so losing balance, and your sensitivity to the pull from the boat. You will find yourself falling or out of control before the turn. The best slalom is always the smoothest.

Once you can make the course at a certain speed (55 km/h *34 mph* for women and 58 km/h *36 mph* for men) it is usual to start shortening the rope progressively to 18·25 m *60 ft*, then to 16 m *52½ ft*, 14·25 m *46¾ ft*, 13 m *42½ ft*, 12 m *39¼ ft* and finally to 11·25 m *37 ft*.

On short rope you will experience a harder, more abrupt pull from the boat. The reason for this is the greater angle you have to pull through as you cross the same distance from one side of the course to the other (see the diagram). With the greater angle the forces from the boat through the rope increase, with the result that there is more tension in the boat pull. This gives the skier greater acceleration and a higher speed potential. If your acceleration is not controlled, you will have more speed at the turn. This will increase the problem of slack rope if you do not ensure you are always on an edge, or allow yourself at any point to come on to a flat ski and assume the same direction as the boat. Because of these differences, your reactions must be faster and, although your basic technique will be the same as on long rope, certain aspects of it will need exaggeration.

You will have to lean much farther back on the ski if you are to cope with the greater force of the pull from the boat, concentrating on keeping your ski and your body between the boat and the point where its pull is felt. That is at the shoulders and on the arms, because it is through the body and the ski pressing on the water that resistance is offered to the boat pull. If you do not do this, you will find you are taking the effect of the boat pull with your arms and they alone have insufficient strength to hold it. As a result you will be tugged forwards. If you adopt an exaggerated lean, however, and hold your hands in hard at the point of pull, you will find you can hold it with surprisingly little effort.

As the rope is shortened, you have greater acceleration, and need not pull so long to achieve the speed necessary to take you across the wake. You will need longer time to control the speed before the turn. You should pull with maximum power as you come out of the turn until approximately the middle of the wake and avoid the tendency, once you have stopped pulling, to straighten up. For if you do this, the ski will lose its direction and you will lose the effect of the pull and fail to travel wide enough on the buoy. Maintain your lean and the angle of the ski in the water until you have cleared the second wake, are on a good approach and in the correct position for braking and turning.

Because everything happens at greater speed on short rope, and because of the increased tendency for slack rope to occur, it is harder to correct and make good a bad approach on the turn. Accuracy of positioning and movement are essential. If you pull as above, you should

reach the point of turn on a tight line and this should minimise the risk of incurring slack.

The only significant difference in technique on the short rope turn results from the different direction in which the arm must be extended. On short line, the direction of the boat pull is at a greater angle to the body, and the arm has to reach out to the side rather than forward to the boat. Because of this, the weight distribution on the ski will also be different. You will not be able to move forward on the ski and your body lean will instead be accentuated in a sideways direction over the edge of the ski. Your weight must remain on the back foot at this point or you will not be able to keep the ski between your body and the boat, and will fall forwards on your side. At the point of turn, pull in hard and press the back of the ski round so that it comes round and you are leaning well back against the boat pull.

At this stage, you should pay particular attention to your style of approach through the gate, because if you pull too long, you will have too much speed on the first buoy and shoot right past it. The technique to adopt is similar to that employed when pulling between buoys. You should aim to achieve the same angle towards the first buoy but at a controlled speed. To do this, you should not pull so wide to the far side of the gate on approach as you have been accustomed to do when on long line, but leave the moment when you start to pull just as late so that you have a good angle across the water. Pull hard to approximately the centre of the wake and then stop, but maintain body lean and the direction

Mike Suyderhoud in position, ready to accelerate.

of your ski in the water until you are in a wide position before the buoy, ready to brake and turn.

You will find that on the first shortening of the rope the length of pull you should adopt through the gate and across the course is fairly similar to that on the long line. The differences between skiing on long and short rope only really become significant on the second shortening. Slaloming on a short rope does, of course, demand great skill and precision. The line up and entry through the gate buoys must be perfectly timed because, as the rope is further shortened, the speed at which you travel requires you to brake almost immediately after your initial pull.

Skis
There are various types of slalom ski, these being designed to be useful at different speeds and at different stages of performance.

Basic Slalom Ski
This is flat-bottomed and square-edged. It rides high in the water, planes easily, and is best for beginners and for use at speeds up to approximately 46 km/h *28 mph*. All other designs are intended to increase the efficiency of the ski on the turn and across the wake and generally to give it greater holding power at higher speeds.

Bevelled Edge
This enables the ski to ride lower in the water and so give it more security. Also, because the edge is rounded and smooth, movement from one edge to the other is facilitated.

Important Points to Remember
1. A flat slalom ski should be used at the early stage of learning to slalom and until you are able to go through the course at a comfortable speed.

2. As you virage you should avoid pulling far outside the wake and should start the turn immediately you leave the second wake. If you pull farther out you will pick up too much speed and will have less control on the turn.

3. It is essential to concentrate on achieving a rhythm and to maintain correct body position and control. Your body should move as a whole, its only movement being forwards and backwards on the ski as you begin and leave the turn, and towards and away from the boat as you straighten and set an edge.

Some Common Mistakes
1. As you come out of the turn and pull on the rope, there is often the tendency to pull your body forward to the boat rather than away from it. The effect is for you to come forward on the ski, to lose an edge and possibly fall over the front of the ski.

2. Very often if you are concentrating on keeping the weight back you will forget that you must at the same time lean away, and in coming out of the turn you will find all your weight on the back foot and yourself travelling in a straight line to the boat, losing the angle of the turn.

3. It is too easy for you to find yourself taking all the boat pull with the arms, again forgetting to lean away and resist the pull. The result will be that you have a lot of body movement, the ski may lose its edge and you will achieve no real direction through the water.

4. Many skiers fling their free hand as they make a turn. If they concentrate on maintaining a correct body position, rhythm and control this should not happen. Very often the free arm is used wildly because you are unbalanced. Also if you are using your arms in the manner described earlier you should not have time to let your free hand far from the handle.

5. Another common tendency is that of over-pulling. If you pull or lean away too violently for the boat pull you may fall in on your shoulder as you come out of the turn. Or even if you manage to hold your position you may be jerked upright again and come forward, losing an edge and tumbling over the front of the ski.

Kris LaPoint, pulling with maximum power.

JUMPING

Basic Jumping
If you have decided to learn water-ski jumping, you should first make sure that you are fit enough – both physically and mentally – to participate. But having said this, in my experience, it is generally easier to take a skier over the jump and get him to land, than to teach a skier to turn and take the first and second buoy in slalom, or to do a 180° turn in tricks. Contrary to general opinion, I have not found that this is the most difficult discipline to teach skiers to master – rather, in its initial stages, the easiest. I have taught thousands of people to jump in their first lesson over the ramp. As long as the basic lesson is clearly understood and followed, there is no reason for the beginner to feel that jumping is the most difficult, or even as some may feel – the most 'terrifying'. This is not so. The immense pleasure and satisfaction gained when the skier learns to jump, is immeasurable. Travelling through the air, in control of your body and landing successfully, is something which can be learnt quite easily and safely if the rules of the lesson are carefully followed.

In order to prepare yourself for the ramp, you must first learn to jump off the water, maintaining control over the body and skis. In the initial stages of this preparation, I would advise that the skier does not use the heavy jumping skis, but practises with a good pair of doubles – and it is compulsory to wear a proper lifejacket.

It is important that the skier stays in the centre of the wake, holding the rope handle, in an almost perpendicu-

Fig. 13. Wake jumping.

lar position with the elbows held in to the waist. The feet and knees should be about 30 cm *12 in* apart, the knees should be bent a little more with the body in an half-sitting position, keeping the head up and hands down. With your skis parallel, maintain a firmer muscle control in your legs and at the same time, keep your toes up. Straighten your knees to spring off the water. Do not allow the fronts of your skis to dip downwards when you

are in the air because they will catch the water and you will fall.

When practising these jumps, it is very important that the leg movements should be synchronised. The most common fault is to bring one leg up at a time as you jump off the water. Keep them together and parallel, with the tips up. Remember to keep your elbows pressed to your waist and hold your forearms rigid so as to be sure that you do not throw your hands up towards your head. Practise this exercise in the wake, until you are able to maintain good control and clear the water.

Maintaining the same position, move towards one of the wakes, making sure you keep both skis parallel, about shoulder-width apart. On approaching the bottom of the wake, bend the knees a little more in order to get a good spring off the top of the wake as you cross it. Keep your head and shoulders upright, elbows bent and hands in, and again keep the tips of the skis up.

When you are able to jump the wake consistently, pull away from the outside of the wake, then turn your skis at a right angle and repeat the jump back over the wake. Never make your approach parallel to the wake, always turn into it. Practise wake jumping until you are jumping both wakes in good control. Now you should be ready to go over the jump itself for the first time.

Setting the jumping ramp at the lowest possible height – about 9–12 cm *3–4 ft* – you will nevertheless encounter a considerable impact as your legs, and, in particular, your knees, absorb the force of the angle of the ramp. In order to prepare yourself for this new experience, there is another land lesson that I have found to be helpful.

Assume your jumping position on land and get some-one to stand behind you with their forearms over your

Showing the approach to the jump in the correct position.

163

The correct position for jumping off the ramp.

shoulders and hands clasped across your upper chest. At a given signal, get him to strongly push down his forearms in an attempt to make your jumping position collapse. You will find that your knees are particularly valuable both here and on the ramp. The idea of this land lesson is for you to become accustomed to resisting this 'crushing' sensation and maintain your position in spite of it.

The boat approaches the ramp at a speed suitable to the weight of the skier, and moves to the right-hand side of the ramp, while the skier pulls out to the left-hand side. In my experience, skiers need plenty of time to line up for the ramp and to concentrate on their land lessons and body position. Remember you must keep your hands low, your elbows tightly against your waist, head up, knees bent and 'freeze' in this position. When you reach the ramp, do *not* pull. Your instinct will be to do so because you are now at a different angle on a new and slippery surface and you will want something to clutch! But do not pull – instead concentrate on your legs, do not let them spread or collapse, keep your head up looking towards the top of the ramp. By this time you will be over the ramp and in the air – keep the same position and remember to keep the tips of your skis up – as in wakejumping. On landing, your knees will probably buckle, so resist this and stand up. At the same time, you will find that there is a tendency to get some slack rope on landing, so be prepared for the jerk and don't allow it to snatch the handle out of your grasp.

Continue this lesson until you are landing consistently

Fig. 14. Incorrect position on the ramp.

and in good control. Your next step will be to maintain the same body position and same approach to the ramp, but with a slightly increased boat speed of about 3–5 km/h *2–3 mph*. When you are able to adapt to this increase, the ramp can be raised to 1·50 m *5 ft* and you should continue to practise at this height.

Jumping Technique

Once you feel comfortable, travelling over the ramp in a straight line at speeds up to 49 km/h *30 mph*, you can begin to think about 'cut' and 'spring'.

Girls will expect to remain on the 1·50 m *5 ft* ramp at speeds no greater than 49 km/h *30 mph*, but because under the present rules men jump at 1·80 m *6 ft*, they may be rushed into assuming they should start to use the 1·80 m *6 ft* ramp once they can stand up efficiently over the lower ramp.

A difference of 30 cm *1 ft* in height may not appear significant, but on experiencing it you will soon realise how considerable, in fact, it is. To graduate to the higher ramp before gaining expertise and experience on the lower is to take unnecessary risks, to minimise rather than increase your chances of deriving pleasure and satisfaction, and probably to frustrate your chances of progress.

The men would be well advised to remain at 1·50 m *5 ft* until they can cut and spring confidently and efficiently at speeds up to 55 km/h or 58 km/h *34 mph or 36 mph*. If they then decide they want to go on to the 1·80-m *6-ft* ramp they will find their level of capability and the know-how already accumulated will facilitate the transition and enable them to obtain new enjoyment with the minimum of difficulty.

The purpose of the cut is to increase your speed, that of the spring to launch you in flight, and the combination of the two to increase your distance and pleasure. Cutting entails travelling across the wake of the boat to the ramp, increasing speed in the process, so that maximum velocity is attained just before reaching it. Springing involves straightening the leap on impact with the ramp and lifting off into the air. The success of both the cut and the spring is entirely dependent on the effectiveness of the other.

Much, if not all, of the speed obtained by cutting will be lost if your body collapses on hitting the ramp. Likewise, if you have no speed in addition to that provided by the boat, all the effort you may put into the ramp by springing will serve only to take you up in a high arc without significantly increasing your distance over the water. The two techniques are complementary and their efficient co-ordination should at all times be the jumper's goal. As long as one movement remains weaker it will frustrate the potential of the other. Generally, a well-timed and executed combination of the two will achieve greater distance for the skier, than an exceptional cut and poorly performed spring, or likewise, a weak cut and superlative spring.

In learning to cut and spring, the important aspects to grasp are timing and correct body positioning and movements. Power can be increased later. For the sake of clarity, the techniques of cutting and springing and methods of developing them will be described separately.

It may be helpful to distinguish two types of cut, the 'progressive' and the 'constant'. The aim of both will be to attain maximum velocity at point X as shown in Fig. 15, so the increase in speed in both will be progressive to this point. The difference is only in the degree of effort that is applied in either cut. In the progressive cut, you will be cutting within your limit and the amount of energy you exert will increase progressively in the same way as your speed. In the 'constant' cut you will be at your limit and will have to apply all your strength and

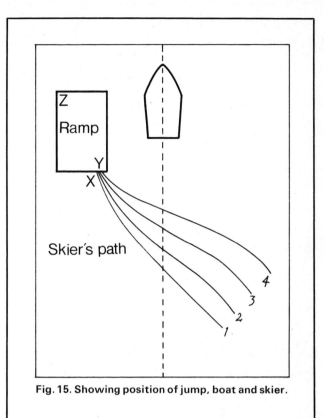

Fig. 15. Showing position of jump, boat and skier.

power from where you start to cut to position X, if you are to reach this position. The effort you are exerting throughout will be constant, though your speed will be increasing all the time.

The limit of the skier is the point at which you are most stretched, but also know both what to expect and what is expected of you. It is only beyond this point that an element of unknown risk is introduced.

According to your experience, your limit may be at 1, 2, 3 or 4 on the diagram or at any point in between. It may not necessarily be even from outside the far side of the wake. In the early stages of learning it may be from a point inside the wake. Your limit will be continually pushing on up the line from 1 to 4 as you grow in strength and skill. When you are cutting at your limit, your cut will be like that employed in slalom, a race between the boat and yourself. An attempt to cross the necessary distance in the shortest possible time, but with one major difference, the intention of attaining the greatest speed, not losing it, at the farthest point.

At any stage before your limit, you will have no need to extend yourself in the same way, as you will have more time in which to get to X. Because you have more time, you cannot apply full effort at the beginning or you will reach the other side of the wake too early for the jump, and in waiting to meet it will lose any of the speed you may have attained in your approach. You should fix your eyes on point Y on the ramp and calculate the amount of power you need to exert to reach X at the appropriate moment.

To learn how much energy, and how much increase in energy, is needed for a progressive cut from any given position, and to learn at what point your cut is approaching the 'constant' stage, involves practice and is essentially a matter of judgement and experience. However, there are certain factors you can and must know. These

European Over-all champion 1976, Chantel Escot (Fr), leaving the ramp with the handle down to the right of the body towards the boat.

are boat speed and positioning and the point from which you start the cut, whether inside or outside the wake and how far out. Only if these are consistent will you be able to assess correctly the nature of your cut and the effect your increasing strength and skill has on it. You will learn when to normally begin your cut from your position in relation to the boat and the jump. You should try not to use landmarks as these are of no help if you ski at any time on a different stretch of water. You may not be able to specify what points to use to sight your line of cut, but should find you recognise them easily enough when actually in action.

Before going on to describe the process of learning, it is important to clarify two further factors. Firstly the significance of point X on Fig. 15. This is the point at which you cease cutting. You will notice it is a short distance away from the ramp itself. It is essential to understand from the beginning that you never cut directly on to the ramp, but must always allow sufficient time and space in which to alter your body position from that required both to ride the jump efficiently and safely and for an effective spring. The distance needed is never more than about a metre. If longer, you would lose speed. Its length is decided by your skill and your speed on

approach. For the top competitive skier, the space will be minimal and the time only a brief moment, but they will still exist and prove essential to the success of your jump.

Secondly it is important to bear in mind that it is the two quarters of the ramp that you use, crossing from the corner of one to the opposite corner of the other, from Y to Z on Fig. 15. By aiming for a point on the ramp about one metre inside the edge, you are giving yourself a safety margin in which to allow for mistakes, a margin you lose if you direct the line of your cut from corner to corner of the jump. Safety, and the confidence this gives, are both prerequisites for good jumping.

It will be helpful for you if the boat is driven at the same distance from the ramp throughout the early learning stages.

You need a fair stretch of water between the boat wake and ramp when cutting, so that you reach your quickest speed and prepare yourself for the jump in the smooth water outside the wake, not while you are still coming through it.

Between 46 and 49 km/h *28* and *30 mph*, is a good speed at which to learn cutting, though a particularly light skier may feel more secure at a slightly lower pace.

Fig. 16. Crossing from one corner of the ramp to the opposite in good form.

When you first learn to cut, you will be aware of two new points. The initial stages of learning are designed to accustom you to these. Firstly, you will be assuming a different direction from the boat before and on the ramp and in the air and, as a result, the line of pull from the boat will alter. Until now you have been travelling straight over the ramp and receiving an almost direct pull. As you cut, however, you will swing across the boat wake, as you do so moving in an arc around the back of the boat which is continued as you go diagonally up the ramp and through the air.

You will feel the rope pull to the right of your body and the effect of this at first may be to overbalance you in that direction. To counteract this, you must concentrate on keeping your body and shoulders square and your weight evenly distributed over your skis as you hit the ramp and travel through the air. It will help if you keep looking straight ahead, not at the boat. As you leave the ramp, you should push the handle down and to the right of your body towards the boat. As you land, maintain the same body position, flex your knees and pull your hands in just below the waist. Keeping your body on balance and under control in this way is chiefly a matter of concentration and confidence.

The purpose of the first cut is not to gather speed, but to get used to the line of direction and movement a cut entails. Instead of moving out of the boat wake and lining up directly behind the ramp as you used to do when going straight over, you should stay just outside the left-hand boat wake on your approach. Then, leaving a comfortable amount of time, pull over steadily until you are opposite point Y. You should adjust your weight so that it is even over both skis and move up and over the ramp on a slight diagonal, concentrating, as explained above, on keeping good body control. You must practise this until you are leaving the slight cut to the ramp later and achieving a controlled continuous movement towards and over the jump, allowing enough space to correct your weight distribution before the ramp without breaking the flow of the movement awkwardly. Then repeat

the same action but starting from inside the wake. At this stage concentrate only on accustoming yourself to the movement the cut involves.

The second factor you must learn to cope with in learning to cut is an increase in speed. To obtain confidence it is helpful at this point to start increasing the boat speed in stages up to an extra 6 km/h *4 mph* at the same time practising the movement described above. This is the easiest and quickest way for you to familiarise yourself with the speeds you will find yourself generating with a cut. After gaining confidence at speed, you should drop the boat speed again and continue practising your cut, now moving more vigorously and feeling the increases in velocity you yourself can create. Once you have an efficient cut from the middle of the boat wake, and before you start moving over the wake to the right and widening your cut, you should learn how to spring and give your concentration to co-ordinating it with the cut you have developed.

As you widen your cut you may need to begin to cut earlier until you become used to the great distance you must travel. You must remember that your primary consideration in developing a cut is to learn how to time the application of power in relation to your distance from the ramp so that your greatest speed is reached just before riding over. When still on the 'progressive' stage and within your limit, because you will be exerting energy gradually, you must take care that you do not develop a lazy cut. A cut must always have force and vigour to be effective. If you are always positive in action the more positive will be your thoughts, and alert concentration is crucial for all effective skiing – and especially in jumping.

You can realise the full potential of the cut and achieve your greatest possible acceleration in three ways. Firstly, by starting your cut at the maximum distance you can attain from the ramp. You will have reached this by cutting hard to the left of the boat first (Point A in Fig. 17), when you have then pulled out to the

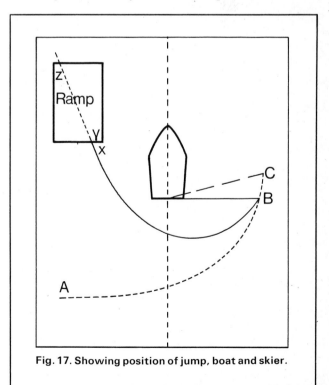

Fig. 17. Showing position of jump, boat and skier.

right of the boat and are level with the rope pylon, point B. Secondly by allowing the boat to move as far as possible in its path alongside and past the ramp before you start your cut. The farther the boat is along its path the shorter is the time available for you to travel round the arc you make from one side of the wake to the other. This distance will remain constant if your starting position and the distance of the boat path from the ramp also remain constant – because you have less time to complete the same distance your speed must increase.

Thirdly, by instructing the boat driver to drive in a line farther from the ramp. The effect of this will be to increase further the distance you must travel to reach the ramp. Most skiers in the advanced stages of jumping take the boat just inside or just outside the 14-m buoy. Some will take it a farther distance outside or through the middle of the two buoys. Few take it further out than this. Where you take the boat at any stage in your development is an individual matter and it is for you alone to decide which position is most effective for you. As the boat moves farther from the ramp the space between its wake and the ramp obviously increases. It can be advantageous and also comfortable, to have as much space as is possible on the smooth water after the wake in which to complete the most crucial part of the cut.

The correct position for the beginning of the full cut is point B on Fig. 17. This is the point at which the skier is alongside the rope pylon and travelling at the same speed as the boat. While moving at the same speed you will experience no strain on the rope. Because you have no speed of your own, the boat must overtake you. As it does, the rope will again become taut and as it does, you can pull away on it in the direction of your cut.

If you reach no farther than position B, and at this point have to sight your line of cut and change edges before starting to pull, you will find that the time this takes will result in your dropping back rapidly and 'drifting' behind the boat, so losing precious cutting space. If you attempt to prevent this loss of water by leaning away hard on the rope, the water you save will still be lost in the time it takes for you to swing over from one edge to another. The awkwardness of this movement and its distraction will prevent you giving all your concentration to the cut itself.

To eliminate this difficulty, you should aim for point C on the diagram before starting your cut. Between points B and C you have more forward speed than the boat. Because there is no strain on the rope you cannot yet begin your cut. As a result you have time in which to sight the cut and prepare for it. As you reach C with your own speed and no need to pull on the rope you should be coasting on flat skis and in an upright position, looking for point Y on the ramp. As you are already upright when you begin to think of setting your edge, the amount of movement is less than if you had to change immediately from one edge to another. Because of this, and because you have the time it takes to drop back from C to B in which to set your edge, your action can be smooth and careful and all your concentration can be on the pull for which you are preparing. When you reach point B, you should be completely ready and waiting to pull away in your cut. In this way no time or precious water is lost.

As you learn to use the area of water from B to C, one major difficulty will present itself, that of slack rope. The rope becomes slack because the skier is travelling in the same direction as the boat at greater speed. Controlling the rope is largely a matter of concentration, and of sensitivity to the changes in its pull. Slackness can occur as soon as he passes point B. The problem is increased when you start to set your edge and lean in towards the boat. As you come past B towards C and move into a planing position, you have two things to think of: keeping the rope tight while you coast and anticipating the need to maintain its tautness when you start to drop back and prepare for the cut.

There are three ways in which you can help yourself. By keeping your skis directed slightly to the right of the boat so that you are always moving away from it, by using the speed you have to move your skis out to the right arching your body in toward the boat and, if necessary, pulling slightly away from the boat. You should try to avoid the latter as it increases the movement you must make in setting your edges for the cut. As you reach B on the way to C you should let go of the handle with the right hand while extending and stretching the left arm straight out to the side towards the boat. You should use your arm to gauge the tightness of the rope and to help you feel how you must move to keep it tight.

To keep a good distance from the boat and a corresponding tautness in the rope when you begin to lean in for the start of the cut, you should have stretched your skis and body as far away from the boat as possible on reaching point C. As you then set your edges you will be able to pull in a little, enough to take up any resulting slack without reducing the length of your reach too much. The more reach you have as you turn in to the cut, the more power you will be able to exert at the start of the pull.

Two particular styles of beginning the cut can be distinguished. In the one, you keep a fairly upright position as you drop back from C to B and only as you begin your cut lean over quickly, pulling in sharply to bring yourself into the turn. In the other you assume a position approximating that used in a slalom turn, leaning in and reaching forwards as well as sideways towards the boat well in advance of the actual turn. To do this it is especially important for you to have stretched your skis and body as far away from the boat as possible before beginning to set your edges.

To be able to reach point C you will need considerable speed. You obtain this by a process of double cutting, which means you not only cut through both wakes on your approach to the ramp, but also to attain the appropriate position for the start of the cut for the ramp. You should begin the first cut from point A, which is well outside the left-hand wake opposite the jump and pull hard through the wake and with increasing force to just before point B from where you will begin to straighten up on your way to C. Some skiers find it helpful to lift the right ski as they move upright. Because of the reduced ski surface on the water there is less drag and you move more easily and quickly to the end of your cut. On one ski, you will also have greater cleavage through the water, better direction and a feeling of increased security.

The feet and skis should be comfortably spread, about 30 cm _1 ft_ apart, so that you feel balanced and secure.

It is most important to keep the weight behind both skis when cutting so that maximum pressure is exerted on the water, in order to hold a good edge and achieve an

Liz Allan Shetter, Over-all and Jumping champion of the world, 1975.

effective angle across the boat path. You should pull away from the boat so that your shoulders and upper body are behind the line of the skis. Both feet should be pressed towards the boat. You will feel greater force on the right leg because it is the first point of resistance to the pull from the boat. The arms must be bent and the hands held in to the body, just below the waist. If the arms are allowed to straighten, the body will be pulled too far upright over the skis. If this happens, and if the left ski falls behind or beneath your shoulders, you will lose power, your edges and direction through the water.

You should concentrate on maintaining a good position through the wake and not let yourself be distracted by its tendency to unsteady you. If you cut through it on a good edge, you will have greater security in the water. If you ride it on flat skis you will 'jump' it, will risk losing balance and certainly lose power and speed. You should hold your position right up to point X, when you prepare for the ramp. You must remember that you should have timed your cut so as to attain the greatest velocity between the wake and point X. If you are cutting 'progressively', you should feel yourself exerting maximum effort at this stage. If you are cutting 'constantly' you should be maintaining the same length of cut you achieved before and through the wake.

Your lean should be directly away from the boat, with your weight evenly distributed over your feet. You must pull back on your skis. If your weight is even on your feet you will be exerting force through the length of the ski, not just on the back, and so will achieve greater power. Also, you must be standing squarely on your skis when you reach point X. If you have been leaning back on your cut, the movement required to obtain the correct position at this point will be greater than if your weight is already squarely behind the skis.

The correct body position for the spring includes head up, knees bent, weight squarely distributed over the feet, the hands held in a few centimetres or *inches* from the body and just below the waist. It is crucial that they should be in and that they should not have become extended during the cut. If they are stretched out before the ramp, when you hit it you will almost inevitably be pulled forwards in the air, and you will not be in a position to obtain an effective spring.

To appreciate the importance of this position you should try adopting it on land and springing up into the air. If your weight is too far over your toes, you will topple forwards and not achieve any height. If your weight is too far back on your heels the same will happen in reverse. Only if your body is squarely positioned will you spring with height and power. You will feel most of the force on the balls of your feet. This is what should be felt when on the water. You should not however, be misled into thinking that to obtain a good position you should rest on the balls of your feet and lift your heels. Experience on land should tell you such a position is insecure and will tend to make you come too far forward and both reasons will cause your spring to lose strength. Your knees should be comfortably, but not excessively, bent.

If you are bent to a point where you are almost doubled up, the movement, when you try to spring, will be slow and require a great deal of strength and achieve less, or certainly no more, height than a spring from a slightly straighter position. If, on the other hand, you

adopt too upright a position you will obtain little or no power. The correct stance is midway between the extremes. By practise on land you should ascertain where it is and how flexed your knees should be.

When you spring, you will notice that the effective movement is in straightening your legs. You may have the tendency to drop your shoulders and upper body but if you consider this you will realise it does nothing to increase your impetus and a great deal to disturb your balance and control. When springing correctly you should feel your feet pushing powerfully into the ground and force being exerted through the length of your legs as they straighten sharply. As they straighten, your body should stretch upwards and experience a feeling of lift. Every muscle should be taut and as you go up you should breathe in. This gives a sense of lightness. You should not let the upper body feel like a dead weight over your feet and legs, but try and feel power travelling up from your feet through the whole of you to your shoulders, lifting you up. You must think only of going up, never of coming down again, so that you maintain your 'lifted' position and tautness until you reach ground again.

The sensation can best be described by likening the movement of the skier to that of a piece of elastic when you stretch it and ease it again. If you held the slack elastic upright and pulled both ends you would simulate the feeling when as a skier, from a bent position you push with your feet and stretch your body upwards. If you then released the elastic by letting the lower end come up you would simulate the feeling when the skier's feet and legs, having pushed down, lift with the upper body.

If you imagine the sensation and try to achieve it the mechanics of the movement will come more easily. The feeling of the spring will be harder to obtain on land than when you are actually jumping, but if you continue to practise off the water you will speed up the process of learning considerably.

Because you are on the ramp for only a fraction of a second, if you do not think to spring before you hit it you will have come off the end before you are able to either start or complete it. You should always think to begin the springing movement on impact. If you watched a jumper in slow motion you would see him starting to push into the ramp as he hits it, continuing to press and straighten all the way to just before the end when he lifts off and climbs up into the air in an arc. If he does not complete the movement on the ramp you will see his leap flicking straight in the air and he will achieve no significant height. In a similar way his spring will have no effect if the movement involved is finished too soon and if his body is already fully stretched before he reaches the point of greatest inclination on the ramp.

The speed of spring must correspond to the speed with which you travel over the ramp. A spring must always have force but if your speed over the ramp is slow the process of pushing into the ramp must be the more gradual, and its completion timed to take place just before the end of the ramp. The snappiness of the spring increases with the speed of the boat and of your speed as you reach the jump.

Different body positions during flight have been advocated at different times. Of these 'banking' and bending forwards are the most familiar. In both you usually let go of the handle with your left hand, putting it on

Bob LaPoint jumping in good form.

your hip or leg for the sake of style. In banking you lean towards the boat and let your skis swing out to the left. In bending forwards you reach down, dropping the upper body so that the handle comes near or level with the skis.

The merit of either technique for improving distance is questionable. Distance is achieved as a result of the height and speed you have attained. Both are created by your work before the ramp. By keeping both hands on the handle very close to the body, the pull from the boat will help you to achieve extra distance. By reaching in or down to the boat you cannot increase the distance of your skis from the water level, you can only lower your hand and shoulders towards it. If you hope, by reaching, to delay the moment when you feel the pull of the rope, any time you may save will most likely be lost in the movement that is required for you to right yourself again. It is also possible that activity while in the air may disturb the flight and decrease rather than increase its length.

Even more important. if on your approach to the ramp, you are thinking of banking or bending and or reaching down, this is likely to detract from the energy you put into going up off the ramp. Also, if you are going to reach down or to the right you may anticipate this in your movements before and on the jump and, as a result, your weight may not be even over your skis and you will not obtain equal or maximum power when you press your feet into the ramp. The effect may also be to overbalance you with the right shoulder dropping and your feet sliding away to the left. For these reasons it is almost certainly better for you to concentrate on keeping your body squarely positioned before and on the ramp and in flight, springing up with all the force you can attain, holding a controlled position through the air and feeling the sensation of lift until you reach the water. The effective work will have been, and should have been, done before you leave the ramp.

As you push your feet into the ramp and rise up off it the handle should simultaneously be pushed down and to the boat.

The shoulders and upper body should continue to lift as you do this. The purpose of pushing the handle down is to keep your body balanced over your feet and skis. If you pull up, your weight will go back. You push the handle to the right because the pull of the boat is from that direction and by taking it there the skier will not be pulled round in the air.

Some skiers let go of the handle with their left hand as they push it down. Recently it has become popular to keep both hands on. Letting go with one hand was thought to increase your reach and to help you to keep your body straight in the air by eliminating the need to stretch the left arm across the body and the possibility this could have of overbalancing the skier to the right. The supposed advantages of reaching have already been disputed. If the result of letting go with one hand is to encourage you to think of reaching towards the boat it will cause the worst effects already described.

The two-hand style is advocated to try and prevent this. With both hands on the handle, you have a feeling of greater compactness and are less likely to anticipate reaching down in the air. Because of this you may find it easier to think of keeping the left shoulder down in the cut on the crucial approach to the ramp. Since you will be taking the boat pull all the time across your body with the left as well as the right arm you will be encouraged to keep your left shoulder forward, level with the right one on the ramp and in the air, so maintaining a square body position. With two hands on the handle your body will feel more constrained and lightly held. This feeling should help produce a corresponding sensation of control and potential power.

Some skiers find it useful to wear the new armstrap to keep their arm from being pulled in towards the boat.

Different styles in themselves have no ability to determine your movements, but their very feel can be of influence. There is no reason why, holding the handle with one hand, you should be less controlled than a skier holding it with both hands. Faulty positioning is prevented only by concentration and thought. Accepting this, you should adopt whatever style you feel is most advantageous to you individually.

A good landing can only be achieved if you attain and hold a correct position in the air. It is a reflection of good form and adds the final polish to a good jump.

Champion jumpers in action. *Top left:* James Carne (GB). *Top right:* Moshik Ganzi (Isr). *Centre left:* Mino Cazzaniga (It). *Centre right:* Mike Hazelwood (GB). *Bottom:* Wayne Grimditch (USA).

TRICK SKIING

To understand trick skiing, it must be appreciated that a great deal of self discipline – and patience – is needed, together with the determination to learn that the basic tricks have to be consistently and immaculately executed.

There is no short cut. You must understand that it is only by adopting absolute single-mindedness in this particular discipline that you can become a trick skier of any standing. Many skiers have a terrible impatience when learning tricks. I understand, of course, that this stems from their enthusiasm – which is great – but such enthusiasm cannot take the place of understanding technique. This takes time, but the end result will be that the skier will learn to trick well, and sooner. As with all three disciplines, the most important point to make is that the skier must always understand the value of practising tricks in a controlled body position – and must be prepared to work for this.

A skier should take time until able to do the basic tricks on two skis – the side-slides, the 180° turns, 360° turns and their reverses – with the realisation that every other trick to be learned and executed, contains one or all three of these movements. When you can control these tricks effectively with a fluency of style which demonstrates a mastery of your tricks skis, you will then be ready to progress further. I have always felt that after first mastering the basics on two skis, the skier should not go on to the more advanced tricks, such as steps and wake tricks etc., but instead should start the same basics on one ski and be prepared to follow the same principles as those for learning on two skis.

Fig. 18. Various positions on the disc.

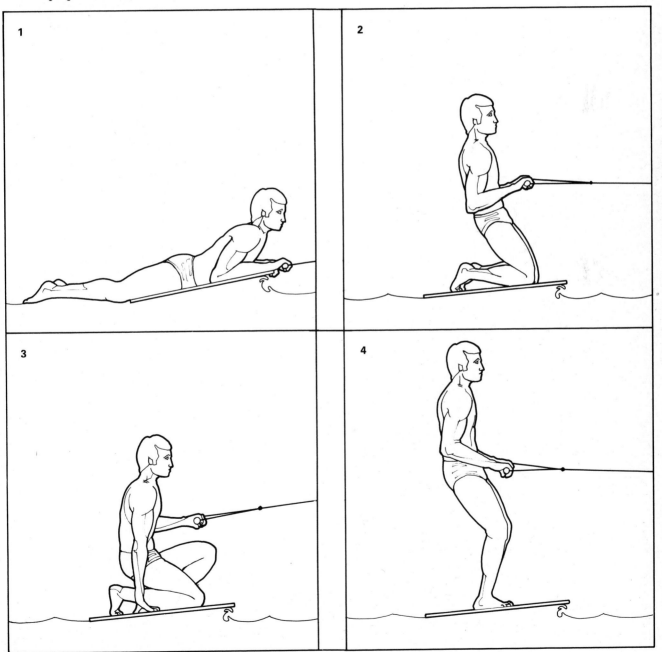

To become a good trick skier, of whatever standard of ability you have set for yourself, you must understand the importance of complete and perfect basic control from the beginning.

A Lesson for the Beginner in Tricks

Some may find it easier to understand the basis of trick skiing with its turning movements, by first practising on a disc – preferably a heavy one for stability.

Standing on a disc in the same way as explained earlier for your land lesson (see page 173), you should ski with a full-length rope in the centre of the wake, to get the benefit of flat water. Starting in the water, get the upper part of your body lying on the disc with your hands holding the handle at the top edge of the disc.

As the boat starts to pull you slowly out of the water to a planing speed, you should begin to pull one knee on to the disc, followed by the other, keeping your body weight slightly to the back so as to keep up the leading edge of the disc.

From this knees-bent position, start to stand up, using one hand on the rope and the other on the disc as you position the first leg to stand up, following it with the other leg – with your weight equally placed on the disc – for balance. On encountering waves, bend your knees even more so that they act as 'shock absorbers', controlling the disc.

Viraging in the wake, from side to side, to get the feel of the disc, will be helpful. This may be followed by turning the disc slowly into the side-slide position, body leaning away from the boat keeping the leading edge of the disc up slightly – then reversing this procedure.

If you fall off and go under the water while practising – remember to put your hands up above your head as you surface, to protect yourself from a floating and possibly spinning disc.

Skiing on a disc will help you learn how to turn and make it easier for you to start on trick skis.

To start with a good basic position, go out on a pair of trick skis – with your knees slightly bent, body straight and head up. It is important that you keep your hands down at waist-level, arms slightly bent and close to the body all of the time. If your hands are out, the tendency is for your shoulders to bend forwards, which must be resisted. You should always be able to keep your stability provided you remember to keep the handle in close to the body.

Just allow yourself to go out and feel the movement of the skis – remembering that this is the first time you are using skis without fins to act as stabilisers. From the start, your skis will wobble in a side-to-side movement. Tighten the leg and ankle position; with a little practice this should improve and you will be ready to virage slowly from side to side until you can control the movements.

Once you feel you have mastered the initial 'wobbling', you will be ready to begin your first basic trick – the Side Slide.

Side Slide (Two Skis)

In general, if you ski with your left foot forward on a slalom ski, you will find it easier to attempt to turn to the left on trick skis; right-foot-forward skiers will normally find it easier to turn to the right.

REMEMBER 3 Cardinal Rules for Trick-Skiing.

(1) Retain a good body position.
(2) Keep the handle close to your body.
(3) Always remember to lean away from the boat.

Side Slide (Two Skis) Water Turn

Stay in the centre of the wake, using a full-length rope, and keep the handle low and near to your body, with your knees bent and head and body straight. Now turn both feet about 25° quickly to the side, at the same time releasing one hand to follow in the direction that your skis are turning, then return to the front position, immediately bringing the free hand back to the handle and looking towards the boat. Remember to keep control of your body all the time. Repeat this, but then turn the skis more to 45°, keeping your position stable: practise this until you are able to attempt a 90° position.

During this process, skiers will find they are moving towards the wake. The reason for this is that there is too much weight on one leg. Do not pull yourself to the side – your body weight should be equally distributed. Just allow yourself to be pulled by the boat: it is a feeling similar to being on the losing side in a 'Tug-o'-War'. Another reason for moving towards the wake is that you are turning too slowly and not getting to the 90° position.

With sufficient practice, you will find that you suddenly break through that 'barrier' where you just cannot quite seem to get your skis to turn towards the 90° position. This will need a quicker turn, using your feet, knees and legs right through to your hips.

After that, you must be able to maintain the 90° posi-

Simulating the basic position for tricks.

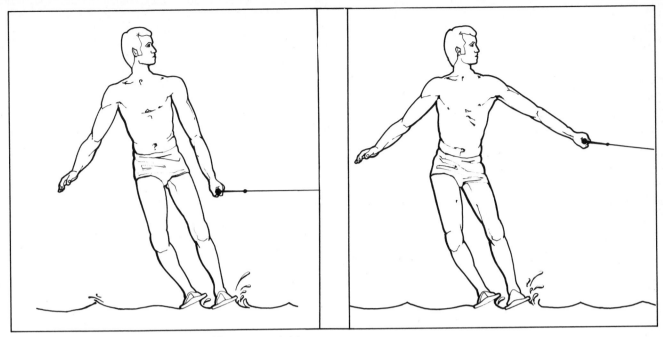

Fig. 19. Correct basic position, *left*, and incorrect, *right*.

tion and to side-slide in the middle of the wake for long stretches at a time, thus getting used to the feel of this position. When you have mastered this, you can now begin doing the reverse side-slide, by literally using the same method of instruction *in its reverse sequence*. This will also apply to later tricks, where their reverse is not explained in detail.

180° Front-to-Back (Two Skis) Water Turn

The 180° Front-to-Back is simply a continuation of the side-slide movement. As you have learnt the technique to go into the 90° position, you will find this will enable you to understand and work on the 180° Front-to-Back trick, much more easily.

Again, keep your hands low and close to your body before you start to turn. If you are turning to your left side, leave the handle with your left hand, whilst the right hand keeps the rope taut. With your knees bent and your head up, turn through the 90° towards the 180° position, whilst instantly bringing your free left hand near the buttocks to catch the handle as soon as possible.

It is very important that you understand this free hand position and what it means to be able to do the 180° turn. Your free hand must be in place by your buttocks *before* your turn is completed, so it will be ready to receive the handle being pulled round by your right hand. So many skiers – not understanding this – have taken a great many falls, requiring much longer to master this movement.

Remember, this is one of the most important lessons in learning trick skiing – to be able to return your free hand to the handle, which will always allow you to maintain a proper skiing position. Without doing this, the boat will simply pull you back and around to the front position. At this stage, a longer handle can help you a great deal.

In doing this, remember that at the beginning of the turn you are holding the handle with your palms 'down', but when you reach the back position, the palms are in

Below: Stephen Lawrence demonstrating a good backward skiing position.

175

the 'up' position, with the body slightly forward, head up and leaning away from the boat, weight more on to the balls of your feet.

At a later stage, this trick can be executed with either one or both hands for greater speed, but at this stage, *two* hands are maintained in a back position. This enables you to have your first experience of actually skiing backwards. This initial experience of backwards skiing is very important as it teaches you to maintain and control your balance. This balance is essential to know and to understand at an early stage – you should be able to hold the backwards position for long stretches at a time, before progressing any further.

180° Back-to-Front (Two Skis) Water Turn
After a 180° Front-to-Back, you should watch the wakes and keep yourself in the middle, between the two of them. Look up and with a turn to the right, let go of the handle with your left hand and turn to the front. Your body should be in the same position as for Front-to-Back, with the right hand keeping in the handle all the time so that just as you finish the turn, you can return that free hand to the handle. Your body is again leaning away from the boat, as you return to the front position.

360° Front-to-Front (Two Skis) Water Turn
When you are able to do both 180° turns and their reverses correctly and separately, then practise the 180° turn and stop, skiing in a good back position then releasing your right hand, pivoting both feet with your left shoulder turning and forcing your body round to the front position.

This should be practised with just a slight pause in the 180° position before coming round, progressing gradually by stopping less and less – still maintaining good body control – until you can accomplish the complete 360° turn without stopping. The most important point to remember is to keep the rope close to your body, which will make the hand-to-hand turning easier. Do not rush this. The skis should always be fairly close together, a shoulder-width apart.

360° Back-to-Back (Two Skis) Water Turn
To perform the Back-to-Back 360° is the same, technically, as the Front-to-Front, the only difference being that you are starting and finishing in a backwards position.

Wake Tricks (Two Skis)
It must be understood that *all wake tricks* not done in mid-air, will not score – in other words you must be in the air and *off* the wake for the trick to be scored and points awarded.

In my experience, I have found that it is so very easy to learn wake tricks by first understanding that the body has to get used to a sideways movement towards the wake, as opposed to the tricks so far described, where you have been skiing in a direct line behind the boat.

Practise moving gradually from the centre of the wake to just *inside* that wake, stopping to perform a normal 180° turn. Keep repeating this towards the wake again, but in stages, stopping less and less, until you do not stop at all. This will help your body to get used to the different direction of moving at a right angle – instead of on a straight line, while you are still able to perform the trick correctly. It is really doing it in stages, then putting it all

180° Front-to-Back Wake Turn.

together. Learning it this way will make the final understanding so much easier. Remembering this system all the way through when learning all wake tricks, will help immensely to shorten the time you take to understand and perform them.

180° Front-to-Back Wake (Two Skis)
Explaining this as a Left Wake turn, you should start in the middle of the wakes and cut to the left wake. When you are on the top of the wake with the handle in, push down hard on your knees, simultaneously releasing your hand and turning your body to the left.

The rope must be kept in very close during the turn, because after landing it will be easy to catch the handle immediately with your free hand. The whole turn must be done in the air, and you must spin enough to land completely in the back position. Landing is on a slightly bent knee, although your body and head are still up. You must have speed enough on the wake to land on the flat water outside the wake. If you do not 'time' the top of the wake correctly, you will land on the side of the wake with the danger of sliding down on one side and falling in.

After landing, you must lean away from the wake, to prevent the boat from pulling you back into the centre of the wakes.

180° Back-to-Front Wake (Two Skis)
This trick, like most Back-to-Front tricks, is easier to perform than the Front-to-Back, because the skier finishes the trick skiing forwards.

Go outside the wake, turn into a 180° back position, lean gently in to the wake, watching the wake on your left side and wait until you reach its top. When on top, push down with your legs to spring off and start to spin to the front. Your left hand leaves the handle simultaneously to your right hand keeping in the rope. Now turn your body straight in the air, to a full front position, landing in the middle of the wakes with your left hand catching the handle.

360° Front-to-Front Wake (Two Skis) (Helicopter)

This trick is a key to many future tricks, such as 540° and 720° wakes. It can be executed either using a wrapped, or a hand-to-hand position.

The Wrapped Position

To learn this trick, you should position yourself inside the wakes, so as to practise wrapping and turning, before attempting the trick, using the wake.

The wrapped position.

To learn to 'wrap', start with both arms outstretched, pull the handle sharply towards your body, where then one hand is released while the other hand holding the handle is passed around the back. Immediately the handle is in this position, your free hand reaches round the back to grab the handle, whilst your other hand is now brought forward to hold the rope, so preventing you from being spun round to the front, prematurely. You are now ready to begin turning. This is done by releasing your hand from the rope and turning the shoulders and

skis around 360° to return to the full front position, where you can then place your free hand back on the handle. Having practised this technique inside the wake, you are now ready to go *outside* the wake, again wrapping but this time performing the trick in the air, using the wake. Standing about one metre outside the wake in the wrapped position with the weight on the balls of your feet, you then lean into the wake and on reaching the top, release your hand and push up on your legs, spinning your body to the front position. You must keep your hand in close to the body throughout the turn, and you must immediately replace your free hand on the handle on landing.

Having executed this wrapped technique, the other method is to pass the handle from hand-to-hand as with the 360° Water Turn. Again the trick is more easily performed from the outside of the wake, landing on the flat water inside.

360° Back-to-Back Wake (Two Skis)

This trick can either be done using the hand-to-hand technique – or wrapped.

Hand-to-Hand

The surface 360° Back-to-Back should have been practised and perfected before you even attempt the Wake Back-to-Back. To attempt this trick, stand outside the wake and turn backwards, then lean in towards the wake and perform a simple wake turn, landing in a forward position between the wakes. Now execute a surface 180° Front-to-Back. You will find that trying to do the whole trick in one movement is harder, so the easier method is by breaking the trick down into two parts; you then have more time to control your balance and feel the movements. This procedure should be repeated until the whole trick becomes continuous without stopping in the front position.

Wrapped

To perform the trick wrapped you should use the same technique as for the hand-to-hand procedure, the difference being that you turn yourself into the rope before starting the trick – this will make you turn automatically and more easily.

540° Front-to-Back Wake (Two Skis)

A 540° is simply two tricks: a 360° turn, and a 180° turn. Start in the same way as the wrapped 360° Front-to-Front Wake, only the cutting, spinning and jumping-up is now harder and faster.

Learn the trick by doing the 360° turn and the 180° turn on the water behind the boat, as with the wrapped 360° turn – then and *only then* attempt to do the trick using the wake. Wrap outside the wake, as already described for the 360° wake. Then do a normal 360° wake, land and do a surface 180°. Repeat this until the movement is continuous and you can perform the whole trick in the air, landing backwards.

On reaching the backward position, you should return your free hand to the handle quickly and with your head and shoulders up, lean hard against the pull of the boat.

540° Back-to-Front Wake (Two Skis)

As with the Front-to-Back 540°, the Back-to-Front 540° is simply a continuation of another trick ie a 360° Back-

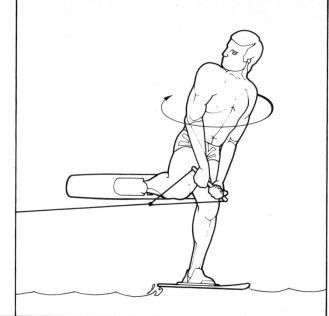

Fig. 20. Back-to-Front Stepover (two skis). *Top left:* back position. *Top right:* half turned position. *Bottom:* coming into front position.

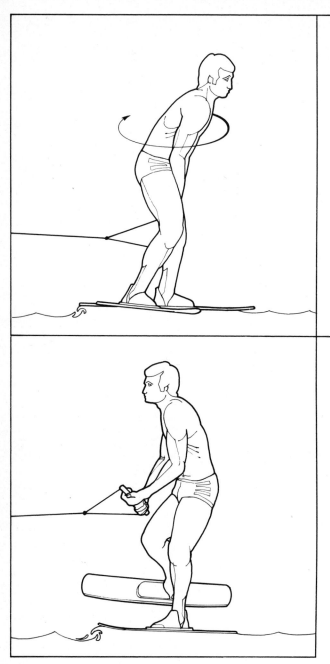

to-Back, plus a 180° turn. You should again learn it in stages, as explained with the 540° Front-to-Back Wake.

Skiers have found that this trick can be learnt more easily by starting with a wrapped back position, rather than a normal back skiing position.

Stepover Tricks

When practising your first step trick, you must pay a great deal of attention to keeping your shoulders very straight, head up and maintaining the correct balance. This has to be controlled by not stepping too hard or too fast over the rope, or rather by being able to balance this movement. The stepping and turning movements must be done simultaneously.

Many skiers who have the problem of learning step tricks would find it so much easier to understand if they realised that they cannot just lift their free leg over, without at the same time turning their ski – and that it is of no use just turning their skiing leg without co-ordinating the step-over at the same time.

Back-to-Front Stepover (Two Skis)

This is the easier of the two, 180° surface steps to learn, as with all other tricks the movements and procedures should first be learnt on dry land.

Standing in the back position, bend your knees and hold the handle in between your legs, below knee-level; the weight is then transferred on to your single, skiing leg. From this position, you are now ready to do the stepping-over and turning movement. Keeping the hands and rope low, by bending your knee you begin to lift the ski over the rope whilst simultaneously turning your body and ski, round towards the front position.

This movement continues until you arrive at the full front skiing position. On arriving at this position, it is very important that the rope remains low and the weight falls on the front of your feet to prevent you from sitting down and falling backwards.

Throughout the stepping and turning movement, the skiing leg must remain strong and firm and must not be allowed to collapse on the water; to make the trick easier the rope should be at its full length and kept as low to the water as possible from the boat.

Front-to-Back Stepover (Two Skis)

As with the Back-to-Front Step, the movement should again be practised on dry land. The techniques are the same as for Back-to-Front Step – that is – the rope must be kept low, stepping and turning movements must be simultaneous and the standing leg must always be kept strong. Both steps can be performed at a later stage by using one hand only – this method of using one hand is an aid to learning the *wake step*.

Back-to-Front Wake Stepover (Two Skis)

It has been found that the Back-to-Front Wake Stepover is easier to learn than the Front-to-Back. You should first be competent at performing both surface steps before attempting the wake step.

Go outside the wake and get into a 'rope-between-the-

James Carne performing Front-to-Back Wake Stepover (two skis).

legs' position, then lean into the wake and on reaching its crest, push hard down with the skiing leg, then step and turn (as already described for the surface step).

When doing this trick, only one hand should be used to hold the handle, thus enabling you to stand more upright and in better control of your balance. However, on reaching the full front position, you should return your free hand to the handle.

Front-to-Back Wake Stepover (Two Skis)
The stepping and turning are the same as for the water turns, but the speed and timing whilst doing the wake step are vitally important. The turn should be performed from the top – or crest – of the wake, thus allowing the skier to land in the flat water outside the wake.

If the skier attempts to turn *before* the top, very little height will be produced to do the trick, and you will also land on – or down – the side of the wake, often ending in a fall. If the turn is performed too late, you will again fail to produce the lift required to perform the trick in the air.

On landing you should resist any undue bending of the legs as this will allow the boat to pull you off balance, when in a back position. Instead, keep your head and shoulders upright with your body leaning away from the ankles against the pull of the boat. Leaning OUTWARDS away from the wake, will allow you to remain away from the wake, giving you time to regain your position and balance. The free hand can then be placed back on the handle.

360° Front-to-Front Wake Stepover (Two Skis)
This trick is a combination of a Step 180° and an ordinary 180°. Correctly performed, it is executed as a continuous 360° movement in the air, using the wake. But the beginner should treat the trick as two separate parts. Then, after practice, join those two parts together without stopping.

Assuming that you can perform a competent stepover and 180° with good body control, the two tricks should be done initially on the water between the wakes, one after the other, first stepping Front-to-Back and then turning Back-to-Front in a continuous direction throughout the movement.

Begin by using the wake from the outside position, coming in. Approach the wake slowly, in a good upright position, holding the rope low with both hands. On reaching the top of the wake, pull the handle sharply towards your body, at the same time stepping and turning. As the body turns, release one hand, but keep it close to the side of your body, ready to change hands on the handle to help you complete the full 360° turn. On landing forwards, the free hand is then placed back on the handle.

360° Back-to-Back Wake Stepover (Two Skis)
As with the Front-to-Front Wake Step, the Back-to-Back should be learnt in the same way – that is, first as two tricks on the water and then as *one trick* using the wake. When landing in a back position, your free hand

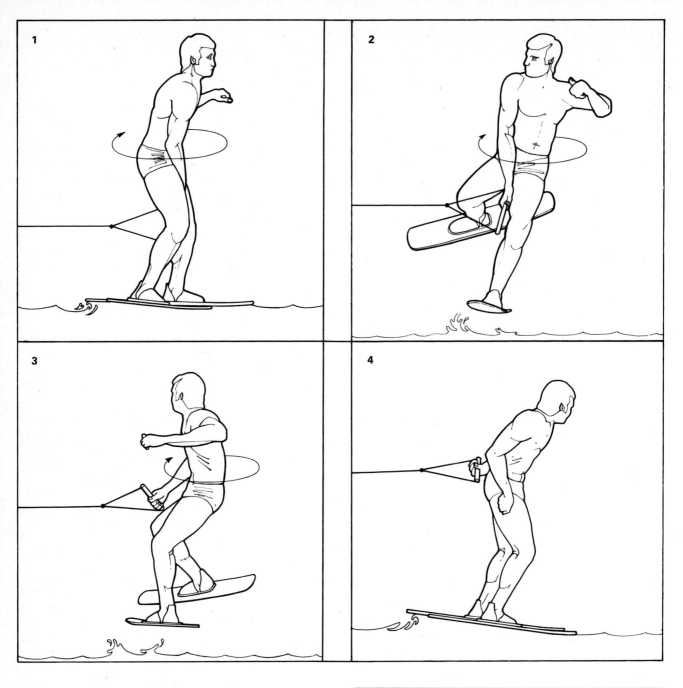

catches the handle behind you as soon as possible. All the time, your body must be upright, with head up, remembering to keep the rope close to your body. Speed to the wake is important to get the height and to enable you to land in the middle of the wakes.

The Single Trick Ski

The front binder of the single ski should be placed 2–3 cm *1·1½ in* farther forward than that of the second ski, to allow room for the back foot. The back foot binder should be placed as close as possible to the heel of the front binder, at an angle which allows the heel of the back foot to rest near the centre line of the ski.

Performing tricks on one ski requires that much more balance and control, and therefore relatively more time to perfect. However, when a trick is learnt properly on one ski, it can sometimes be executed with more speed and ease than on two skis. The boat speed required for one ski is slightly faster than when you are skiing on two.

Fig. 21. Back-to-Back Wake Stepover (two skis).

Side Slide (One Ski)

On one ski, repeat the same basic lesson as on two skis, always remembering to keep a good body position, especially with your knees slightly bent and the handle close down and in to the body. It does not matter if your whole body is turning or not, as long as the leg and the ski are turning to a right angle or 90° position.

As with your first lesson in side-sliding on two skis, it is good to turn only about 25°, then to 45° for a short time, repeating this in-and-out position all the while. Then after more practice, try for a 90° turn as you did on two skis. As you do this, hold the position for a longer period each time in the middle of the wake. The handle

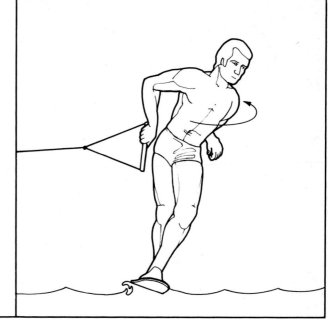

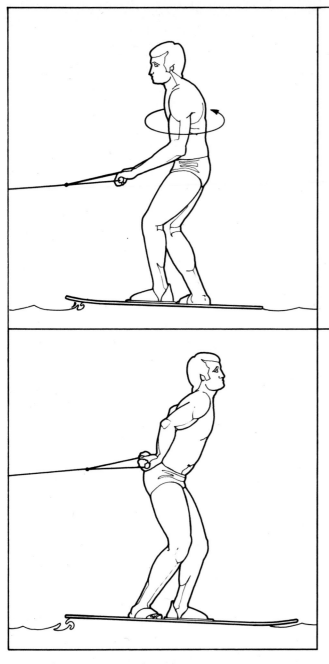

can be held with both hands, or with one. You should be looking towards the boat while you are side-sliding. When you have mastered this, you can begin doing the reverse side-slide by the same technique, always remembering to lean away and to keep the leading edge of the ski up and clear of the water.

180° Front-to-Back (One Ski)
Again as explained earlier for two skis, the principles for 180° turns should be followed just the same. You must start this trick with a slightly bent knee, looking forward, and with a straight body. After the 90° turn, let go of the handle with one hand while turning to the back. Your free hand keeps the rope close in to the body and, when you arrive in the back position, return the free hand quickly, so as to catch the handle with both hands.

Once in the backward position, the body should lean away in a straight line from the ankles, slightly more than when on two skis. This position should be held for a period of time to enable you to get used to the feel of skiing backwards again – this time on one ski.

As a useful exercise from this position, virage slowly inside the wake – this will give you confidence and the feel of the single trick ski.

180° Back-to-Front (One Ski)
Having mastered the Front-to-Back turn, the Back-to-Front 180° can now be attempted. You should be in a good position before trying the turn, with your handle held in close to the small of your back. When ready, you should release one hand, pivot your body, and leading with your ski, turn round to the front position, quickly moving your free hand in and back to the handle.

360° Front-to-Front (One Ski)
Having learnt the 180° Front-to-Back and Back-to-Front and their reverses, the 360° turn is very simple to accomplish. Turn Front-to-Back, pause, regain your position, then continue in the same direction back to the front position. Repeat this process until the turn becomes continuous, by making the pause period shorter and shorter. It is important to understand that it is not necessary to spin or turn too fast, as many skiers are inclined to believe. Turning slowly but continuously, will allow you to maintain better control and balance throughout the turn. (See photograph on page 182.)

360° Back-to-Front (One Ski)
The technique for doing this trick is the same as explained for doing the Back-to-Back trick on two skis. The only difference being that the balance on one ski is that much more critical than on two skis.

Karl Heinz Benzinger (Ger) executing a 360° Front-to-Front (one ski).

180° Front-to-Back Wake Turn (One Ski)

Using the correct length of ski line to produce the best wake definition, and having experienced the wake turn on two skis, you are now prepared to attempt the turn on one ski.

Starting behind the boat, move slowly towards the top of the wake; on reaching this point, do not at this early stage attempt to push the body into the air, but simply perform an ordinary 180° turn on the water. Continue to turn the ski slightly past the 180° position – to compensate for the outward directional movement of the body. Without doing this, the ski can easily 'catch an edge', resulting in a fall. Practise this until you have gained confidence and control. Now attempt to achieve height off the top of the wake, by pushing down hard with both your legs. By doing this, you will eventually complete the full turn clear of the water.

180° Back-to-Front Wake Turn (One Ski)

From a backward skiing position outside the wake, you can now start to do a Back-to-Front wake turn. Lean slightly into the wake, watching its position by looking down and back so as to judge correctly the point at which you will make this turn. Reaching the top of the wake, release the handle with one hand and turn your ski and body round into a forward position, again being careful not to produce too much clearance by pushing down with your legs. Only at a later stage, after continual practice, should you try to perform the trick off the water. Throughout this turn, your head and shoulders must be kept up and the handle kept in close to your body. Remember not to bend forward when you are landing.

360° Front-to-Front Wake Turn (One Ski)

For this trick, starting outside the wake, wrap the rope as for a 360° Front-to-Front Wake on two skis. About one metre outside the wake, start to cut slightly towards the top of the wake. Reaching the top, the hand should be released from the rope and your body should spin to the front position. Whilst spinning, the rope must be held in close. At the same time, as you land, catch the handle immediately with both hands. Keep your head up and land with your weight on both feet. It is very important to turn with a straight body and the rope in. So many skiers lose the landing and fall, because in turning, they do not keep their shoulders straight and level. It is so easy whilst turning to drop your shoulder and body position, then land at a sideways angle, which is just the sort of stance to make you fall.

As with two skis, this trick can be performed by also using the hand-to-hand technique. The procedure for learning this is the same as for that on two skis.

180° Front-to-Back Stepover (One Ski)

Before attempting this trick, you should be able to do the two-ski step-over, as much of the principle of stepping on two skis still applies when working on one-ski steps. A full-length rope should be used, the body should be held in a well-balanced position with the back leg off the ski and bent up with the knee near and close to the rope.

As you start to turn towards the back position, the bended leg is passed over the rope. This movement is continued round and through into the back position, the free leg does not touch the water at this early stage, because if it did, a drag would be set up which would result in loss of balance or even a fall. Instead, the free leg is held clear of the water, until complete balance is attained. Only then should the free foot gently touch the water to make the trick complete.

Throughout the whole turn, as with the two-ski step, the skiing leg must remain firm, as it is this leg which controls the complete movement, and the handle must be kept at all times close to the body.

180° Back-to-Front Step (One Ski)

Once in the back-stepped position, the skier is ready to try the return to the front position. Many skiers find this trick the easier of the two steps to learn, as they can finish the trick in a forward skiing position.

Again the movements are similar to the two-ski Back-to-Front Step. As the body in turning is approaching the front position, the weight should be brought slightly forward over the skiing foot. A very good way to practise this trick is to just step *under* the rope and back, to get used to the movement. Falls will inevitably result if the free foot is 'kicked' hard over the rope, as this will lead to loss of balance and cause you to overspin.

180° Wake Stepover Front-to-Back (One Ski)

The skier should have mastered the one-ski Surface Stepover before attempting this wake step. The trick is attempted from a starting position inside the wakes. You should be standing with your back foot off the ski, in a raised position, knee close to the rope, and with the handle held close and low to the body.

In this position, you then move slowly to the *top* of the wake where a normal surface 180° Stepover is performed

– leaning away from the wake once you are in this position, will prevent the boat from pulling you back to the centre. Again, as when learning the Surface Front-to-Back Step, care should be taken not to 'overstep' too hard, or place the free foot in the water until complete balance is maintained. Repeat this technique until you are confident. Height is gained by pushing off the top of the wake with the skiing leg, until the whole trick is performed in the air. It is very important, especially on landing, that the skiing leg is not allowed to bend and that the body maintains a good position, and leans away from the boat. To assist balance on landing it is sometimes helpful to replace the free hand back on the handle.

180° Wake Stepover Back-to-Front (One Ski)
As with the Surface Step, the Back-to-Front 180° is the easier of the two tricks to learn. Once in a backward position outside the wake with the rope between your legs, you should move slowly inwards towards the top of the wake. The free leg should be up and out of the water, ready to be lifted over the rope, immediately you start to turn to the front. On turning to the front you must keep the rope low with one hand, whilst the free hand is kept close to the body, ready to take the handle in the front

position. As before, the trick should be learnt using the wake but not trying to gain too much height at this early stage, as this makes the landing more difficult.

360° Back-to-Back Wake (One Ski)
Start this trick the same way as for the two-hand backward position on two skis, as this method tends to help with the spinning movement. The trick should first be attempted from the outside position, moving inwards, and the same technique as used on two skis should be adopted. If difficulty arises from attempting the trick from the outside wake position, then it should be attempted from *inside* the wakes. With all tricks involving a backward-landing position, the beginner will face difficulties. A positional 180° to the front often helps you to control and maintain your balance when learning these difficult tricks. However, having mastered the trick, retaining the backward position is good practice, giving you time to prepare for another trick which would start from a back position.

540° Back-to-Front Wake (One Ski)
At first, you should attempt this trick *behind* the boat, by turning into the rope, to a back position.

Skiing backwards in this position, you should then allow yourself – assisted by the pull of the boat – to be pulled round through 540°, back to the front position.

Using this technique, the hand need only be released

Lars Bjork, Swedish and European champion, executing a Back-to-Back Wake (one ski).

Carlos Suarez, World Over-all and Tricks champion 1975, during a 180° Back-to-Front Step (one ski).

once from the handle and replaced after reaching the front position. Having practised this movement on the water, you can then attempt the trick using the wake. It is easier for the beginner to try this trick from inside the wakes to the outside. It is also an advantage to have mastered the Back-to-Back 360° Wake, because the 540° Wake, like the 540° Front-to-Back, is again a continuation trick.

Because the backward, wrapped starting position is difficult to hold, the timing and execution of this movement is very important. To attempt the full 540° turn from this wrapped position, is at first difficult, and so an ordinary 180° wake turn should be practised, until the timing and co-ordination is perfected. This, incidentally, assists when learning the 360° Back-to-Back Wake trick. The turning movement, from 180° through 360° is con-tinued until finally completed in the full 540° turn. Speed gained by cutting at a sharper angle to the wake will then give the height necessary to complete the whole turn in the air.

540° Front-to-Back Wake (One Ski)
This trick is a combination of two separate tricks, a wake 360° and a 180° turn. Once again, it is more easily learnt on the water behind the boat, so as to get used to the movement and 'feel' of the trick. After practising this, you should then attempt the complete trick, using a wrapped starting position outside the wake. Now continue as for a normal wake 360°, landing in a forward position, then turn 180° to the back position on the water. The whole movement is repeated until the trick becomes continuous from front-to-back, and executed

Fig. 23. 360° Front-to-Front Wake Stepover (one ski). (See page 186.)

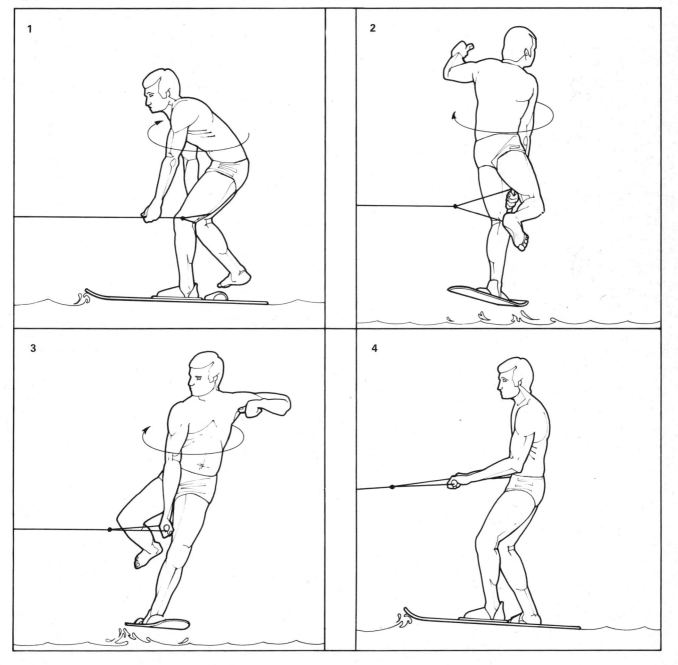

clear of the water. The height needed to perform the trick totally in the air, is gained by 'cutting' at a more acute angle towards the wake, which results in more speed. The co-ordination of speed and timing on the wake are of tremendous importance for all 'multiple turn' tricks. Your body and head are again in that upright position.

360° Front-to-Front Wake Stepover (One Ski)

This trick can be done in a wrapped or a hand-to-hand position and should first of all be learnt by doing the trick on the water behind the boat and not on the wake.

To execute the hand-to-hand 360° Front-to-Front Step, the skier does an ordinary 180° Step Front-to-Back and then continues to do the 180° turn from the back position to the front. It is very important to always keep the handle close to your body throughout the trick. Having become used to this movement on the water, you can then go outside the wake and perform the trick from outside, coming in. As with the 360° Wake, pull the handle in towards your body, perform a Front-to-Back Step Wake, land, and then do a Surface 180° and turn back to the front position. This movement is repeated until the whole trick is done in the air as a continuous movement. It is most important to keep the skiing leg only *slightly* bent throughout the turn and remain in this position for landing in the front position. If the knee is allowed to bend too much, you will collapse backwards and fall.

With the wrapped position, you again learn the trick on the water behind the boat and not on the wake. Pass the rope around the outside of your skiing leg, with your free foot held up and off the ski, and slightly bent in the air. One hand is held between your legs to take the handle, whilst the free hand is held on the rope to stop the boat spinning you around before you are ready.

When ready to turn, you release your free hand from the rope and with the help of the boat, start turning and stepping around to the front position. As with the hand-to-hand, it is important to keep the rope close to the body and to keep the leg slightly bent throughout the turn.

Once perfected, you can then proceed to use the wake and perform the trick in the air. Many skiers find it is very helpful to use an elastic knee-bandage to prevent the rope rubbing into their leg.

360° Back-to-Back Wake Stepover (One Ski)

This trick is a combination of the 180° Step Wake Back-to-Front and a Front-to-Back 180°, therefore the two tricks should be learnt and perfected separately, before trying the full 360° Back-to-Back Wake Step-over. The learning procedure should be the same as for all wake tricks and that is by doing the trick in two parts, on the water then *continuously* on the water, and lastly on the wake.

Again, do not attempt to get too much height off the wake at the early stages. It is difficult to try and maintain a backwards-landing position and so a positional 180° turn immediately on landing will help you to maintain your balance and control. Only at a later stage should you try and hold the back skiing position.

It is important to stand in an upright position with the shoulders held back as much as possible towards the boat, before attempting this trick.

The handle must be kept in close to the body, with the

Mike Hazelwood (GB): Back-to-Back Wake Stepover (one ski).

one hand, throughout the turn, and you must also maintain the 'lean away' from the boat throughout the turn, especially on landing.

As the tricks become more complicated, sometimes comprising two complete turns in the air, and often including one, or even two step-overs, the learning procedure becomes more and more of a personal and individual process. However, although individual styles and capabilities may effect the final execution of the trick, the basic methods of learning any of these complicated turns, remains the same. By first separating and mastering the individual sections of the whole trick and then progressing from practising on the water to the wake, the learning time for the trick will become that much shorter. By using this method, the 'feel' of the trick can be experienced at a much slower speed, with much more control than might ever be gained from trying to perform the trick from the start, using the wake. Some of these multiple-turn tricks will be found easier to perform starting from a wrapped position, whereas a hand-to-hand technique is favoured by others. Conversely, turning off the wake can also be used to advantage where the normal rotation method is found to be unsatisfactory. This category of tricks includes the 540° Double Step, 720° etc.

Toe Hold Tricks

When attempting any Toe Hold Tricks it is advisable to have a quick-release attachment on the rope, to prevent being 'dragged' after a fall.

It is also important that the person releasing the rope is fairly experienced and understands the techniques of toe tricks, thus knowing when – and when not – to pull the release.

The beginner should not choose a toe-hold strap which is small and tight, as this can be an added danger in the event of a fall. Rather, the toe-strap should be slightly larger and made of a 'soft' material.

Above: Frantisek Stehno (Cz) preparing for a 180° Toe-Hold Front-to-Back. *Below:* Sylvie Terraciano (It) during a 180° Toe-Hold Wake Front-to-Back.

180° Toe Hold Front-to-Back

The trick should be learnt using a full-length rope – with the quick release attachment as already mentioned. Skiing on the flat water in the centre of the wakes, before attempting to turn, you should first become familiar with being towed along in a forward position using the toe-strap.

The foot should be placed in the toe-hold so that the strap rests across the bridge of the foot, with the toes pointing 'upwards' rather than forwards. A series of viraging should then be performed slowly from wake to wake. Having practised this, you can then position yourself in the middle of the wakes, in preparation for the turn.

Your body should be held with the head and shoulders upright, your hands held at shoulder height and your skiing leg slightly bent. From this position, you can now start to turn your body backwards. The ski and body must turn simultaneously and the foot holding the rope must be kept close to the skiing leg throughout the turn, remembering to keep the 'lean away' position from the boat.

On reaching the back position it is important to keep your head and shoulders well up to help control the balance and prevent you falling forward and down. It is vital that the observer in the boat must be fully attentive to the possibility of an instant fall and thus be prepared to immediately release the skier; this should avoid any possibility of the skier being injured by being dragged by the boat.

Having reached the back position, you should not attempt to turn forward at this stage, but rather keep skiing in this backwards position in order to gain your confidence and learn how to ski backwards in control. At a later stage, the ski can be weighted by pushing down on the skiing leg before making the turn, helping to make the ski turn more easily.

180° Toe Hold Back-to-Front

This trick is harder to learn than the Front-to-Back. The key to the whole trick lies in the correct backwards starting position.

You should again be skiing on a long line inside the wakes with your head and shoulders upright and back towards the boat as much as possible. The toe handle should be held in close to the skiing leg. You should then start to turn towards the front position keeping the towing foot close to the body. On reaching the front position, the body should be brought forward from the waist, whilst at the same time the towing leg should be lifted upwards until balance and controls have been achieved. Only then should the hands be brought forward to take the handle off the foot. At a later stage, the ski can be 'unweighted' by pushing down on the skiing leg before making the turn, helping to make the ski turn more easily.

180° Toe Hold Wake Front-to-Back

Having learnt the surface 180° Front-to-Back Toe Hold, you can now proceed to learn the Toe Hold Wake. In the early stage of learning this trick, it is helpful to just move from the centre of the wake towards the inside of the wake, and at this point, stop and do the 180° Front-to-Back again as a surface trick. This will give you the

'feeling' of going towards the wake in this sideways movement and practising the 180° turn which, when perfected, will enable you to do the complete trick off the wake.

Starting inside the wakes in a well-balanced position, bent slightly forward from the waist, you should move towards the wake and on reaching the top, turn to the back position. When in that back position, your towing leg should not be allowed to be pulled too far away from the skiing leg, but held in close until control and balance has been achieved.

At this early stage, once again, it is not important to try and gain height off the wake, it being more significant to learn the movement. Once this has been achieved, then you can proceed to push off the wake with your skiing leg, until the complete turn is performed in the air. To prevent you from being pulled back into the wake, it is important that you should lean slightly outwards and away from the wake.

180° Toe Hold Wake Back-to-Front

Skiing in a backwards Toe Hold position outside the wake, with your towing leg held close to your skiing leg, and your body and shoulders kept in an upright position, you are now ready to learn the Back-to-Front Toe Hold Wake.

You should ski slowly towards the top of the wake, trying to make the back – rather than the side – of the ski touch the wake first. On reaching the top of the wake, you should turn into the forward position.

It is now very important that you bring your body slightly forward from the waist and lift up your towing foot, to help in gaining control after the turn.

As the movement becomes more natural, you can now try and gain height by pushing down on the skiing leg, as you reach the top of the wake. Throughout the learning procedure, you should move only slowly to and from the wake, to prevent any undue sideways movement.

Toe Hold Side Slide

You should learn this trick using a long rope and skiing on the flat water inside the wakes. Standing in a good, firm position, with your skiing leg slightly bent and the handle held low, you can now turn into the side-slide position. It is important not to 'jump' into the side-slide position, but to just turn the ski quickly in and out sideways, then immediately back to the front position. Balance is critical throughout the movement. Only by repeating this quick sideways-and-return movement, will you slowly build up the complete side-slide position.

Turning the towing foot sideways at the same time as the ski is turned, and pulling the handle down towards the skiing foot, will help keep the leading edge of the ski up and prevent it from catching in the water.

It is good practice to hold this side-slide position for stretches at a time.

Toe Hold Side Slide Reverse

Care must be taken when learning all Toe Hold tricks which involve *turning into the rope*. The observer handling the quick release must always be alert in the event of a fall.

Patrice Martin (Fr) in good style, performing one of his many sequences of toe tricks.

Keeping the handle in close to the skiing leg is the 'key' to learning all Toe Hold Reverse tricks. Therefore, before attempting the reverse Toe Hold side-slide, you should practise skiing on a full-length rope, and simply practise pulling the handle 'in and out' towards the knee of your skiing leg, without turning the ski.

You can now start to practise turning towards the side-slide position. At this early stage, you should only try to turn about 45° and not to the full 180° position – to enable you to get used to this different movement. When turning into this 45° position, it is very important to keep the handle very close to the skiing leg, otherwise the ski can easily catch an edge, often resulting in a fall.

To help in keeping the handle in this position, the toes should be turned outwards, rather than pointed upwards. Only after having turned to the 45° position with control can you now attempt to pass through the 45° into the full 180° side-slide position. To do this you should turn harder from the beginning to overcome the opposing pull from the boat.

Throughout the whole movement, you should keep your body in a controlled position, with the skiing leg again slightly bent to lower your centre of gravity, with head and shoulders kept in an upright position to help maintain good balance.

180° Toe Hold Front-to-Back (Reverse)

Having learnt the reverse toe-hold side slide technique, the reverse 180° turn is just a continuation of this movement.

As with the reverse side slide, you should be skiing inside the wakes, using a full length rope with a safety release. Stand in a well balanced position, with your skiing leg slightly bent, and your body, head and shoulders in an upright position. Allow your towing foot to be pulled about one metre away from your skiing leg, then brought in sharply, until it touches the knee of that skiing leg. Only when the toe-hold is near your knee, should you begin to turn round to the back. Your body must be kept in an upright position throughout the turn, with the lean away from the boat coming from your ankles and not from your waist.

180° Toe Hold Back-to-Front (Reverse)

This trick is the easier of the two 180° reverse turns to learn, but the Front-to-Back 180° turn has to be learnt first, so as to arrive in the correct wrapped starting position for the Back-to-Front turn – trying to wrap the rope from a backwards skiing position will prove too awkward to attempt.

Having arrived backwards from the 180° front skiing position, the turn back to the front becomes almost an automatic movement, through the pulling action of the boat. It is only necessary to maintain a good upright skiing position throughout the turn and to keep the toe-hold close to your skiing leg. On arriving at the front, your weight should be brought slightly forward over your skiing foot to help control your balance.

360° Toe Hold Front-to-Front

Before attempting this trick, you should have first achieved the Toe Hold 180° and Toe Hold Wake 180° turns. Learn the trick using a full-length rope (complete with safety release), skiing inside the wakes. Wrapping the rope correctly before the turn is very important, and quite difficult in itself. You should take enough slack rope to enable the handle to be passed around the outside of the skiing leg, where it is then placed on the free foot, which is by now held just behind and slightly below the knee.

One hand, or two, can now be kept on the rope, to prevent the boat from pulling you around to the front position before you are ready. The weight of the body should be kept over your toes, rather than the heel of the skiing leg, and the rope kept as low as possible, without disturbing your balance.

Once in this controlled, wrapped position, the hand or hands can be released from the rope. You should *not* turn immediately on doing this, but should wait until the pull of the rope falls on your towing foot, before turning. If this were not done, 'slack' would appear in the rope and tighten again just as you were reaching the back position, often resulting in a fall. Having now felt the

TRICKS

David Nations
instructing Patrice
Martin, European
Dauphin Overall and
Tricks Champion
(1976), at Ruislip
Lido in the Spring of
1977.

Above: Toe Hold 540° Front-to-Back

Right: Toe Hold 360° Back-to-Back.

(See page 192.)

Right: Toe Hold Side-Slide.

(See page 188.)

Right: Toe Hold Side-Slide Reverse.

(See pages 188–9.)

Toe Hold Side-Slide.

'Patou' during a Toe-Wake Trick.

pull on the towing foot, swing your ski and body slowly round to the front position, pushing down hard on your leg throughout the turn and remembering to keep your towing leg close to your skiing leg. Your body should be held upright until you arrive in the forward skiing position, where again, as with the start of this trick, your weight should be brought forward on to the front of your skiing foot.

Turning into a 180° Front-to-Back position and pausing to regain balance, and then continuing to turn round to the front position, can help in the learning of this trick. This pause period can slowly be reduced until eventually the whole turn becomes continuous.

360° Toe Hold Front-to-Front (Reverse)

Both the Toe Hold 360° Front-to-Front turn and the reverse 180° Front-to-Back and Back-to-Front turns, should be learnt before trying the 360° Front-to-Front Reverse. As when attempting all Toe Hold tricks, the beginner should use a full-length rope with a safety quick-release.

The trick is made up of two separate tricks, namely a surface Front-to-Back 180° turn, continued by a surface 180° Back-to-Front reverse turn, and should be learnt by doing both tricks with a pause in between. The beginning part of the trick is therefore relatively easy. It is only the reverse part of the 360° turn that proves difficult.

Starting in a front Toe Hold position you should turn into a backwards 180° position, but instead of keeping your towing foot close to your skiing leg, it should be allowed to be pulled away about one metre. Having your towing foot in this extended position allows you to pull the rope in hard, so enabling you to turn much more easily round to the front skiing position. On arriving in the front position, your body should be brought forward to enable you to take hold of the rope with both hands to prevent the pull of the boat from immediately spinning you round again to the back position. The trick should be repeated until the whole turn becomes continuous.

360° Toe Hold Back-to-Back

This is a combination of two separate tricks, namely the Back-to-Front Reverse 180° and the Front-to-Back Surface 180° turns. These two tricks should first of all have been perfected, before attempting the full 360° Back-to-Back turn.

Again it is necessary to use a full-length rope to gain the benefit of the flat water behind the boat – not forgetting the safety release. You should not try the complete movement from the start, but instead perform the trick, pausing in the front skiing position to regain your balance and control, and then continue round into the back position. With practice, the whole 360° turn will become continuous. The important points to remember are to always keep your body upright and to always keep the Toe Hold close to the skiing leg.

These Toe Hold tricks, like the normal tricks, become more complicated as you progress. From 360° Toe Hold turns, then 540° and 720° turns, you then go on to execute them all, using the wake. At this stage of trick skiing, different techniques will help different skiers' styles, and the complexity of variation seems almost endless.

BAREFOOT SKIING

Barefoot skiing in Britain is run under the newly approved World Rules, and administered by the Specialist Committee of the British Water Ski Federation. An official barefoot team of six or eight members is sent to all the major European barefoot events and since 1974 the British Barefoot team have been European Champions. The qualification to join the Barefoot Club is to ski in a barefoot position for one minute, under the eye of an approved official. In the case of a cadet member or a woman, to ski for half a minute. Membership of the Club has risen to about 180 and is rising fast, but qualified members are still at the stage where they have a distinct feeling of belonging to an élite corps. Any good mono skier can learn to barefoot in a very short time, and given competent tuition, most skiers could achieve the art in one session.

The Step Off One Ski

Use a 75-ft line with a normal handle and the slalom grip. Wear a life jacket, preferably under your suit. Not strictly necessary for the step off, but you may as well get used to it for the more advanced starts. Also a beginner should wear a helmet with ear flaps or a rubber hood whilst learning. Injuries are rare, but you will be taking a few hard smacks whilst learning, and you should protect your eardrums.

Use a normal ski but with a strap of the Reflex type design. If you wish you may remove the front rubber, leaving only the heel piece plus strap, but this is not necessary. Leave the rear rubber bridge in position. Place your front foot on top of the front rubber and clip on the strap. Proceed with a normal deep water start but press down really hard with your front foot as the rope tightens.

The ski will feel strange at first, but you will soon begin to feel at home. Instruct the driver to pull you up normally and settle at about 49 km/h *30 mph*. A right foot forward skier should move out to the right of the boat and a left foot forward skier to the left hand side. For brevity, the following instructions apply to a right foot forward man or woman. Simply reverse if you belong to the left foot forward fraternity. You are now on the right hand side of the wake. Make sure your rear foot is very loose under the rubber bridge, and withdrawn slightly. Crouch down and unbuckle the strap. Signal the driver to increase to 58 km/h *36 mph* and move to the hard clear water, just outside the wake. Place your rear foot *firmly* on the water about shoulder width away from the ski, but about 23 cm *9 in* in front of the foot still on the ski. Keep your body upright but a little back, and look at the boat or at the horizon, not down at the water. Full weight on the free foot in a confident manner, raise the foot still on the ski and quickly bring it down on the water. See page 141. Be determined and hang on at this point. Many a novice manages the step off, and is so surprised by success that a fall results. Hang on and stay still. Do not wobble about adjusting your position. Get used to success slowly.

However, one important factor will be common throughout your further learning, and that is never to forget those vital *basic* lessons of position, and rope handling. For without applying these techniques, the learning and mastery of any new trick becomes that much more difficult and time-consuming.

SUGGESTED
WEIGHT TRAINING

These exercises are designed primarily for men to strengthen muscles and ligaments basically used in water-skiing. Each exercise fulfils a different purpose. For example, exercise No. 2 is for the abdominals which are so necessary when rounding the buoys in slalom.

No two physiques are the same, so the weights should be adapted in relation to the strength and size of each individual. With progress, you should increase weights without excessive strain.

Before beginning a series do a general warm-up of toe touching, side-bending, and loosening up as necessary.

1. Squatting. Heels on wedge-shaped block approximately 3–4 cm *1–2 in* high. Two sets of 25 repetitions each working up to 4 sets: total 100. Thighs should be parallel to the ground and no lower. Do not bounce off the knees.

2. Abdominal Raise. Try working up to 50 repetitions in one set. To start do 5 sets of 10 repetitions each. If you have any difficulty, put your arms and hands alongside your body, or try it on a flat bench.

3. Step-ups with bar across shoulders. Weight up to 20 kg *45 lb*. Three sets of 15 repetitions, alternating sets for each leg.

4. Pull-ups hanging on bar. Working up to 5 sets 10 repetitions each. *Full extension on lowering*, which means unlocking your arms otherwise muscle becomes shortened.

5. Curling. Arms upwards weight to be determined by user. Five sets of 10 repetitions each. Arms again at full extension on lowering.

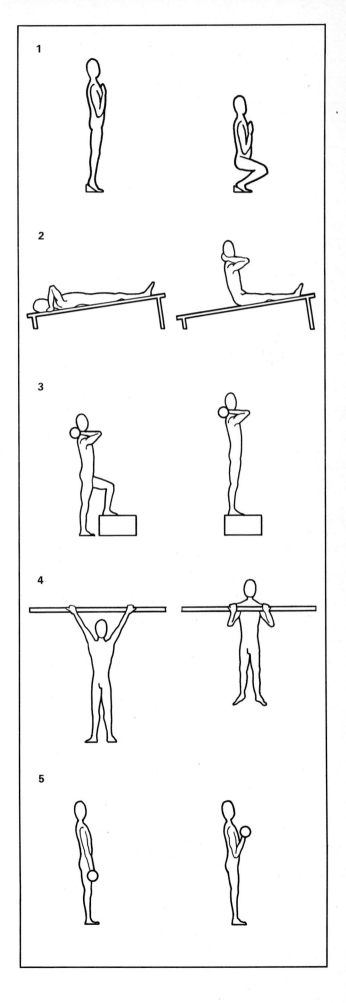

THE THREE COMPETITIVE
DISCIPLINES OF TOURNAMENT WATER SKIING

Tournament waterskiing as a competitive sport is divided into three separate disciplines—Slalom, Tricks and Jumping. Following World Rules, the skier with the highest points in each event over two rounds, preliminary and final, is the winner. In addition the most points achieved by a skier in either the preliminary or final round are added together to give an overall score. The skier with the greatest number of points is the overall winner.

Slalom

A slalom course (Fig. 25) consists of an entry gate at either end, through which the skier must enter and leave the course. The six buoys which the skier has to negotiate,

are positioned alternately at set distances from the centre of the boat path. The boat passes through a series of guide buoys. This is set out on 1976–77 Rules laid down by the World Water Ski Union.

The tow boat is driven through the course at a set speed. The skier negotiates the entry gate, the six buoys and the exit gate.

Having completed a successful pass the boat turns around and the speed is increased by a predetermined amount up to a specified maximum: for men 58 kph *36 mph* and for women 55 kph *34 mph*. When the maximum speed has been reached, the tow line (normally 18·25 m for competitions in Europe) is shortened by predetermined lengths to 11·25 m, then by $\frac{1}{2}$ m. A pass ends when

Fig. 25. Official slalom course.

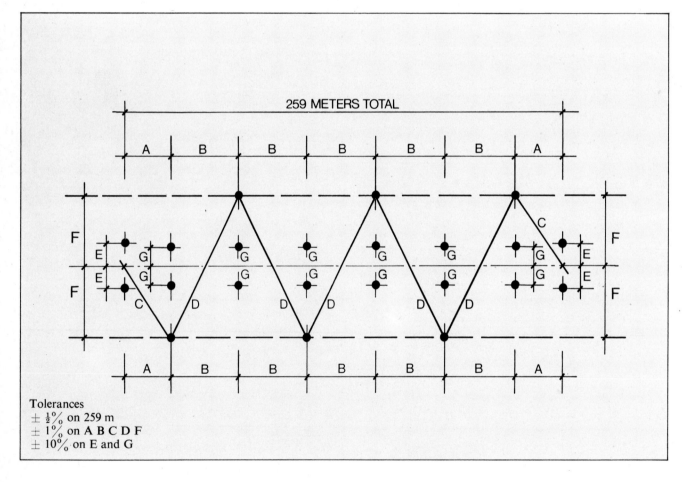

259 METERS TOTAL

Tolerances
± $\frac{1}{2}$% on 259 m
± 1% on A B C D F
± 10% on E and G

Dimensions

259 m		*849 ft 8·8 in*
A = 27 m		*88 ft 7·0 in*
B = 41 m		*134 ft 6·1 in*
C = 29·347 m		*96 ft 3·4 in*
D = 47·011 m		*154 ft 2·8 in*
E = 1.25 m		*4 ft 1·2 in*
F = 11·5 m		*37 ft 8·8 in*
G = 1·15 m		*3 ft 9·3 in*

Allowed ranges on dimensions

259 m overall	257·705 m–260·295 m	*845 ft 5·9 in–853 ft 11·8 in*
A (27 m)	26·730 m–27·270 m	*87 ft 8·4 in–89 ft 5·6 in*
B (41 m)	40·590 m–41·410 m	*133 ft 2·0 in–135 ft 10·3 in*
C (29·347 m)	29·054 m–29·640 m	*95 ft 3·9 in– 97 ft 2·9 in*
D (47·011 m)	46·541 m–47·482 m	*152 ft 8·3 in–155 ft 9·3 in*
E (1·25 m)	1·125 m–1·375 m	*3 ft 8·3 in–4 ft 6·1 in*
F (11·5 m)	11·385 m–11·615 m	*37 ft 4·2 in–38 ft 1·3 in*
G (1·15 m)	1·035 m–1·265 m	*3 ft 4·7 in–4 ft 1·8 in*

a skier either misses a buoy, passes over and sinks a buoy, fails to pass through either set of entry/exit gates, or falls.

Each buoy rounded scores one point, and ¼ and ½ points are awarded if the skier partially rounds a buoy, as set out in Fig. 26.

Seniors, Juniors and Dauphins also have their own maximum speeds.

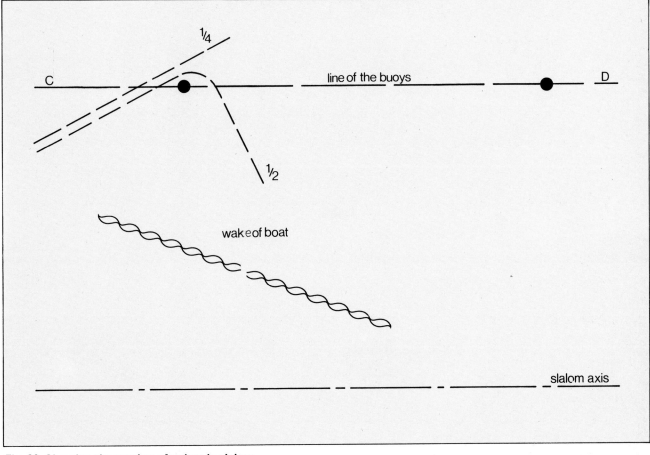

Fig. 26. Showing the scoring of points in slalom.

Tricks

Each competitor has two, 20-second passes in which to perform as many tricks as possible. A trick course is marked by two sets of buoys at either end of the course, which is approximately 200 m long (see Fig. 27). The timing of the 20-second run begins when the skier makes his first movement towards a trick in the approximate area of the entrance buoys, and the end of the run is signified by a loud, audible device. The speed of the boat, which is set by the skier, and the path of the boat, are regulated by boat judges.

The tricks allowed in competition are set down in a schedule and a points value is given to each one according to its definition. A panel of judges decides whether the trick was performed correctly and according to the Rules. Tricks may be filmed, when possible, by a video camera from the tow boat, as an aid to the judges. A pass ends when the 20 seconds has elapsed, or when the skier falls.

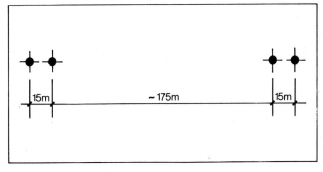

Fig. 27. Official trick course.

The second 20-second pass is taken in the same manner in the opposite direction to the first.

Trick values

Description		WATER TURNS					WAKE TURNS			
	No	2 Skis Basic	2 Skis Reverse	1 Ski Basic	1 Ski Reverse	No	2 Skis Basic	2 Skis Reverse	1 Ski Basic	1 Ski Reverse
Side slide	1	20	20	70	70		—	—	—	—
Toehold side slide	2	—	—	150	—		—	—	—	—
Wrapped Toehold side slide	3	—	—	230	—		—	—	—	—
180 F-B	4	30	30	60	60	15	50	50	80	80
B-F	5	30	30	60	60	16	50	50	80	80
360 F-F	6	40	40	90	100	17	110	110	150	150
B-B		40	40	90	100	18	160	160	210	210
540 F-B		50	—	110	—	19	240	240	310	310
B-F		50	—	110	—	20	250	250	320	320
720 F-F		60	—	130	—	21	260	—	320	—
B-B		60	—	130	—	22	300	—	350	—
180 F-B Stepover	7	80	80	120	—	23	110	110	180	—
B-F Stepover	8	70	70	110	—	24	110	110	160	—
360 F-F Stepover		—	—	—	—	25	200	200	260	260
B-B Stepover		—	—	—	—	26	200	200	260	260
540 B-F Stepover		—	—	—	—	27	270	290	370	370
F-B Stepover		—	—	—	—	28	240	240	370	370
F-B Double Stepover		—	—	—	—		—	—	450	450
B-F Double Stepover		—	—	—	—		—	—	450	450
180 F-B Toehold	9	—	—	100	110	29	—	—	150	180
B-F Toehold	10	—	—	120	130	30	—	—	180	180
360 F-P Toehold	11	—	—	220	300	31	—	—	300	350
B-B Toehold	12	—	—	250	280	32	—	—	330	380
540 F-B Toehold	13	—	—	400	400	33	—	—	500	—
B-F Toehold	14	—	—	400	—	34	—	—	500	—
720 F-F Toehold		—	—	500	—		—	—	—	—
180 F-B Toehold Stepover		—	—	—	—	35	—	—	290	—
B-F Toehold Stepover		—	—	—	—	36	—	—	320	—
360 F-F Toehold Stepover		—	—	—	—		—	—	350	350
Somersault		—	—	—	—	37	450	—	450	—

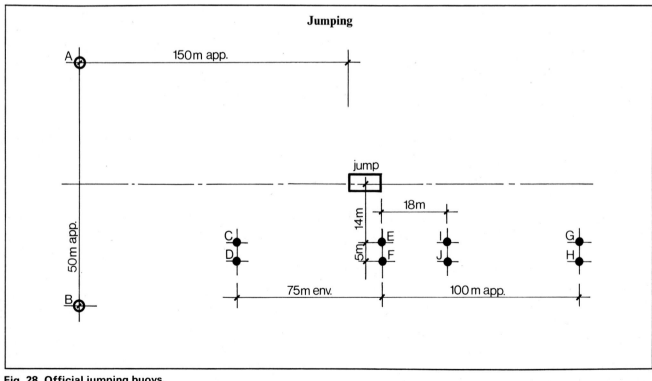

Fig. 28. Official jumping buoys.

The jumping ramp is an inclined plane approximately 4·30 m *14 ft* long and 3·70 m *12 ft* wide. The length under water is 1 m *3 ft* approximately. Under present WWSU Rules the front edge of the ramp is 1·80 m *6 ft* high for men and 1·50 m *5 ft* high for women. Other heights are used by Seniors, Juniors and Dauphins. There is a safety apron on the right hand side of the ramp.

The boat takes a parallel course to the side of the ramp and between 14 and 19 m *46 and 62 ft* distant from it, at a maximum speed of 58 kph *36 mph* for men and 49 kph *30 mph* for women, and again other agreed speeds for Seniors, Juniors and Dauphins.

The skier enters the jump course which is approximately 250 m *820 ft* long, passes up and over the ramp, lands and must maintain skiing position to a ride-out buoy which marks the end of the course. If the skier falls, a jump must be registered for each fall. Each skier has three attempts at the ramp and the longest distance is the one that scores.

WATER SKIING
DO'S AND DONT'S

Water-skiers
DO know how to swim and always wear a lifejacket.
DO always check your equipment, wing nuts, loose binding, splinters and sharp metal.
DO understand and use approved signals between skier and observer and driver.
DO keep clear of solid obstacles – jetties, boats, mooring buoys, rocks, banks, etc.
DO watch the water ahead of you at all times.
DO avoid falling forward – sit down, or if falling sideways, curl yourself into a ball.
DO always throw away the handle on falling.
DO come in slowly to land and run parallel to shore.
DO hold up your hand or ski to signal all is well after falling.
DO use an approved lifejacket when skiing.
DO recover skis quickly, they will help you to keep afloat.

DO NOT shout 'Hit it' to the driver until rope is taut and your ski tips are up.
DO NOT wrap rope around any part of the body (fingers, hand or foot).
DO NOT place any part of the body through the bridge (neck, arm or leg).
DO NOT ski in shallow water.
DO NOT ski at night.
DO NOT ski directly ahead of, or to the side of, another boat.
DO NOT attempt fast landing directly towards the shore – sit down if coming in too fast.
DO NOT ski in waters unknown to you.
DO NOT jump from a boat whilst it is moving.

Ski Boat Driver
DO have a competent observer at all times in the boat watching the skier.
DO make sure observer understands water-ski signals.
DO have a rear-view mirror.
DO wait for the skier's signal and his ski tips above the water before starting.
DO give him a smooth and steady pull on take-off.
DO steer clear of other boats and floating obstacles.
DO return immediately to pick up the skier.
DO always carry an extra lifejacket in the boat.
DO NOT drive directly towards a skier in the water.
DO NOT turn sharply and put the skier in the water, gradual wide arc turns are the rule.
DO NOT take the skier aboard without shutting off the engine first.
DO NOT drive the boat through swimming or restricted areas.
DO NOT operate boat sitting on the side; sit in the seat.

First Aid
It is strongly recommended that all participants in water-skiing (instructors, club coaches, drivers, observers and skiers) are fully conversant in all methods of resuscitation and general first aid.

Every nation in the World Water Ski Union has its specific safety recommendations. All participants must make it their responsibility to find out, to know and to obey those regulations.

Equipment

THE EVOLUTION OF
SKI DESIGN

As has already been chronicled, pre-war water-skis, hewn out of hickory or mahogany, brush-varnished, then fitted with heavy metal and leather foot-binders, nearly always dwarfed their rider, being heavy and unwieldy.

During the five years after World War II, Phillippe de Backer and Claude de Clercq of Belgium, spent a great deal of time tackling that very problem. De Clercq recalls:

'At this period, I made the acquaintance of an extraordinary joiner who was very friendly to water-skiers. This was a Monsieur Poncelet who during the 1914–18 War had made wooden propellers for Major Crombez and my father, both of them aviators.

'He made hundreds of pairs of water-skis for us, charging for little more than the cost of the wood. A ski lasted sometimes two minutes, sometimes a quarter-of-an-hour, then we would cut it ourselves, plane it, change it, break it and then tell Monsieur Poncelet how we wanted the next pair. We abandoned the idea of grooves, and cut the fins, which had previously run the whole length of the skis, down to half their size. We shortened and widened the skis, tried out various types of wood. To jump further than 20 m *65 ft*, the skis had to be reinforced and conceived differently – with their front ends very light and their back ends very supple. We also replaced the leather bindings with a synthetic rubber design. I think that we in Belgium brought about much in the development of tricks and jumping skis, although all the improvements in slalom ski design indisputably came to us from America.'

Very soon after this, by 1951–52, skis had been developed in the United States, which were aptly nicknamed 'banana skis' – apt because many was the time that a skier slipped up on one!

In 1958, after fourteen years' countless experiments on Lake Eloise with every shape and width of ski, Dick Pope Jr felt ready to go into the manufacture of 'Cypress Garden Skis'. He too had discovered that, for instance, if you fitted two runners, instead of giving directional control, they only created an air pocket. A single runner was better. Then someone took about $7\frac{1}{2}$ cm *3 in* out of the rise in the ski, understanding that the lower ski rides much more easily over the wake, in addition to the old ski being much more prone to breakage on impact with the jumping ramp.

The Cypress Gardens Men's Jumping skis, which Dick decided to market, were 1·83 m *6 ft* long by 17 cm *6$\frac{3}{4}$ in* wide, while the Women's Jumping skis were 1·73 m *5 ft 8 in* long and 18 cm *6$\frac{3}{4}$ in* wide.

The single slalom ski which Bud Leach had produced, back in the 1947 Nationals, had been square-backed and square-edged, which although offering more manoeuvrability than two skis, still had its limitations in the turns.

A group of historic skis – from the 1930s to the 1960s.

David Nations with his first pair of water skis manufactured in Munich before World War II by Sportberger, Rofschwaigs.

Experimentation led to the rounding of the back of the slalom ski, which permitted better digging-in at the turns, with the same amount of exertion by the skier. Then the edges of the ski were rounded, lessening the tendency of the ski to skid in the turns, and the binders moved further forward to increase acceleration on the turns.

With the continual sophistication of trick-skiing, trick skis were the shortest at 1·4 m *54 in* with ends curved for turnarounds.

It was around 1960 that the *concave* ski was introduced. At 58 km/h *36 mph*, skiers had reached the point of no return to find themselves cavitating and skidding on the turns, so in the search to find something that would give grip, the skis had to be given an unequal surface – and concaving was the answer.

Legend has it, that Mike Amsbury was going round the tournament scene in America and winning all the slalom events, to the envy of other competitors. So they decided to take a look at his ski and found that it was a bit warped with age, causing the bottom to be somewhat concave – and so not long after this . . . !

To trick with even more manoeuvrability, trick skis were being shortened, bevelled, and rounded off as much as the technical regulations would allow, while to give more spring, some skis were braced back at the tips. In the US, the major manufacturers were Cypress Gardens Skis Inc, Northland, AquaSport and Hydro-Flite, while in Europe the popular marques were Reflex (France), Britt (Switzerland), Freyri (Italy), Kneissl (Austria), Elan (Yugoslavia), Polsport (Poland), and Skeemaster and Lillywhites (GB). It was a long way from Toshe et Lahuppe at Juan-les-Pins in the pre-war era!

In 1965, a major breakthrough was made in ski-construction, when an American company named Saucier made use of Space Age 'spin-off' technology to make snow skis from epoxy fibre-glass. It was not long before the US concern of EP brought out honeycomb-structured aluminium and fibre-glass skis, which not only came out of the same mould, but were lighter, more controllable and virtually unbreakable. They were to help towards even greater jumping records. Also helpful were the new jumping ramps, which from teak rollers, via plywood and wax, were also receiving the fibre-glass or aluminium treatment.

For trick skis, with the rules relaxed (finally) to permit skis 25 cm *12 in* wide and as short as 1 m *3·3 ft*, little wonder that trick scores were climbing towards the 5000 plus points mark. The introduction of the bevel-edge had been a major breakthrough. Ricky McCormick, for so long an outstanding world class skier, remembers his early experience with bevelled edges as being one of chance. He skied on the same pair of trick skis for many years and they had to be re-finished from time to time. As his older brother, Jim, sanded the skis, the edges gradually and inadvertently became more rounded. Rick did not recognise the effect of the change until he bought a new pair of trick skis. When he tried them, he could not perform as well as he could on his old ones. Jim reasoned that the edges were the difference and altered them to match the edges of the old ones. This do-it-yourself attitude was responsible for many innovations in the sport.

In 1974, the minimum length of trick skis was further reduced to 91 m *36 in*. The McCormicks merely cut the

ends off their skis to meet the new tolerance, paying little attention to the square design that resulted. But there was no one design for trick skis. In the official Technical Rules, set out by the WWSU for 1976–77 (Rule 10.03): 'Maximum ski width shall not exceed 30 per cent of the overall length' just about sums the situation up.

But as David Nations has explained: 'The standard of competitive skiing has improved to levels we never dreamed of in the 1940s, and ski design has had to keep pace. This has sometimes been done by ski-manufacturing companies – such as Reflex – working from constant supervision and feedback with the champions.

'For example, in 1976, Paul Adlington, a former British champion as well as a fully experienced coach and driver at Ruislip Lido, was working with top skiers, feeding the information back to Michel Valeton at Reflex in Grenoble, France. It was similar to my friend Claude de Clercq and Monsieur Poncelet experimenting in the late 1940s only a much finer critique and much larger worldwide scale was envisaged. The technology of the raw materials used in ski construction is ever-changing, involving combined 'sandwiches' of rubber, fibre-glass epoxy resin and alveolated aluminium – the latter a spin-off from the same metallurgy which has produced parts of the Anglo-French Concorde supersonic airliner. Composition wood involves pieces of pine-ash, mahogany and ABS, while polyethylene and injected plastics are also incorporated.

'Contrastingly, trick skis have now become fractionally longer and wider, to assist with toe tricks, and stiffer, to give more lift off the wake. The intricate formula for slalom design has to be an integration of thickness, edges, tapering, and weight displacement along the ski. Who knows the shapes and construction methods that will be developed before the 1980s?'

We have come a long way from Ralph Samuelsons' original pine boards, to be sure.

THE EVOLUTION OF
THE SKI BOAT

If water-skiing had been developed in the 1870s, there was an 26·52 m *87 ft* steam launch, named the *Sir Arthur Cotton*, officially clocked at 39·60 km/h *24·61 mph* on the River Thames, England, which could have given some brave Victorian a tow! And at the beginning of the century, there were some pretty nifty petrol-engined launches – Daimlers, Wolseleys, Thornycrofts (GB) and Elco or Speedway in the US, which were probably used by early aquaplaners.

Even though the cost of petrol in those early pioneer days was only a fraction of what it is today, efforts were being made then to find a less costly fuel. Crude oil, kerosene and even alcohol had been tried with varying success and there was one device to produce *gas* for marine use with coal as the basic material. The first gas producer was installed in a 16·46 m *54 ft* yacht and successfully drove a four-cylinder 5½-by-8 in engine at 350 revolutions and at a speed of 14·50 km/h *9 mph* at a cost of 6 cents per hour. Peat coal in those days cost $4.50 per ton. Perhaps the increase in the cost of coal was too much, because the gas producer – for the time being – was shelved.

Left: A typical speed boat of the late 1920s as would would have towed the aquaplaners – and even the earliest water skiers.

The Chris-Craft

It used to be said that a synonym for the word 'motorboat' was 'Chris-Craft'. After building his first motorboat in Algonac, Michigan in 1906, Christopher Columbus Smith simply did not look back. In 1927, the Chris Smith & Sons Boat Company's engineers designed and built a successful 250-hp 8-cylinder engine, and constructed machines and jigs for the fabrication of motorboats on a mass scale. By the time of the formation of the Chris-Craft Corporation in 1930, over 1000 boats were being turned off the stocks each year, ranging in size from 4·72 m *15½ ft* to 14·63 m *48 ft*, divided mainly into runabouts, cruisers and utility boats. Prices ranged from $795 to $35 000. The boats were distributed throughout the world by 250 dealers, with Arthur Bray, for example, the Chris-Craft concessionaire in the UK.

The Albatross

In 1949, Archie Peace, who had trained as an aircraft engineer with the Bristol Aeroplane Company, started Albatross Marine Ltd, at Great Yarmouth, England. Before long, he was joined by the Hon. Peter Hives (son of Lord Hives, the then head of Rolls-Royce Ltd) and Mr Bruce Campbell, a former de Havilland test pilot.

As aircraft engineers, they were impressed by the possibility of applying aircraft techniques to boatbuilding and were convinced that great things could be done with aluminium alloy. By 1952, they had built a 3·66 m *12 ft* three-seater prototype, by hand, installing a marinised Ford Anglia engine, and called it the Albatross Sports Runabout.

David Nations recalls: 'I had a phone-call from Bruce Campbell, inviting me down to Great Yarmouth to see this boat. I took Marc Flachard of France, the reigning European champion, then at Ruislip to ski, as my guest. Flachard looked at this boat and exclaimed, "Shoosh! I will pull it from the water, David!" So Bruce Campbell said, "I'll tell you what – it will pull *two* of you off together." We both looked at each other and thought "Let's see this, before we believe it." So we took a double tow and sat there, and damn me, it bloody well pulled the both of us up! So I bought one for Ruislip. It was a brand new machine, which still had its teething troubles.

'They were to base all their modifications on our work. For example, during the water-testing, we would get evaporation, the boat would go for 91 m *100 yd* and then stop. We found out that the carburettor was so near the heat manifolds that the petrol would vaporise, and we were telling them all the problems by phone and they were modifying it back at their yard. Later on, I bought

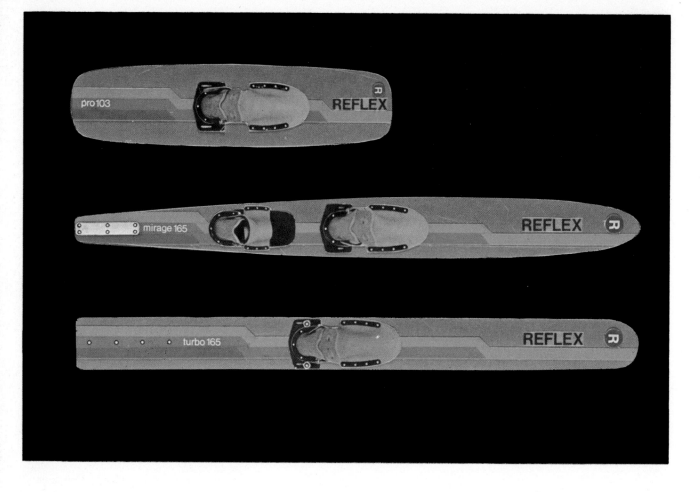

Above: Modern ski designs, 1977. *Top to bottom:* skis for tricks, slalom and jumping.

Below: A rare colour shot of a water skier being towed round the harbour of a west coast English resort by a pre-Second World War motorboat, possibly a Chris Craft.

The superb finish that was the hallmark of Riva ski boats and can be seen in this photograph taken in the 1950s.

Two Riva boats at speed depicted on this stamp with the official Riva postmark on top. Not many boat yards can lay claim to this distinction.

another Albatross, because they were ideal boats for teaching.'

With a maximum speed of 49–52 km/h *30–32 mph*, the Albatross was not only to become the popular workhorse for British water-skiing, but also on the Riviera and in the United States.

Riva

The Riva family first built fishing boats in 1860, when Ernesto Riva established his 'Cantiere' (shipyard) on the banks of Lake Iseo, Sarnico, in Northern Italy. But it was Ernesto's son, Serafino, who began construction of the first mahogany-hulled outboard-engined Riva power-boats, which he raced to victory in the 1920s. Serafino's son, Carlo, took over the Sarnico shipyard in 1949. He returned from a visit to the United States with the ambition of turning out some superbly finished mahogany-hulled luxury motor-launches to be called 'Tritone', 'Ariston' and 'Florida', initially engined with American marine units and later re-designed by Riva engineers. These boats were bought by royalty and millionaires all over the world because their finish expressed the quality of a piece of antique furniture. Because of their success, in 1954 Carlo built a new shipyard on the road to Predore where the custom-building of his launches in seasoned Honduras mahogany and other exotic wood could be speeded up. Increasingly used for water-skiing, the 'Florida' model was soon followed by the 'Super Florida'. Carlo Riva's final creation was the 'Aquarama', and in 1969 the US Whittaker Corporation bought out the company, appointing as managing director, Gino Gervasoni, who for many years had been Carlo's right-hand man. One contest in which Riva 'Super Aquarama' powerboats were the regular victors, was the Cervia-Pola Adriatic water-ski sprint.

Boesch

Although Herr Walter Boesch of Kilchberg, near Zurich, first built his Horizon hydroplanes in the late 1940s,

installing a marinised American Crusader engine with a Chevrolet block, it was not until the early 1950s that the glossy wooden Boesch speedboats were first used for water-skiing in regional and Swiss National contests. At the same time, skiers like Pierre Jaeger were already taking their private Boesch speedboats abroad to international competitions, especially in France. These early Boesch '500s', powered by 6 cylinder 120 hp engines, were replaced in the late 1950s by the Type '560' with its hull bottom modified for water-skiing conditions and powered by a V8 170-hp unit. Two Boesch '500' boats were first used officially at a European Championship on the Worthersee, Austria in 1960 – and for the first time at a World Championship in Vichy in 1963, where four Boesch '560s' powered by 230-hp engines, did the towing. Eleven European Championships and four World Championships saw skiers competing behind Boesch boats – in particular the '510' powered by a 260-hp engine. About 1000 Boesch '510s' were distributed throughout the world, with over 50 per cent modified for water-skiing. The 1975 World Championships in London saw the 300-hp Boesch '580' successfully driven for the first time at an international contest.

Correct Craft

It was in the early 1920s that God-fearing Walter C. Meloon had taken time off after work at an automotive foundry, to build a boat powered by a Ford Model T engine, driving an old aeroplane propeller. By 1925, Walt and his wife Marion, had set up the Florida Variety Boat Company in Pine Castle, Florida, changing its name to the Pine Castle Boat & Construction Company in 1930, and ultimately to Correct Craft in 1938.

From the moment of buying a $50 Meloon 'Punkinseed' powerboat in the late 1930s, to the very first Cypress Gardens Show and all subsequent shows, Dick Pope Sr always used Correct Craft as towboats, although Pope and Meloon rejected a written agreement for one of mutual Christian trust.

Over the years, whether from their Titusville or Pine Castle boat-plants, Correct Craft Inc. built ski-boats under the names of International Skier, Tournament Skier, American Skier, Ski Nautique, Ski Tique, Al Tyll and Skier. Development, for example, saw their earliest lifting ring on the stern of the boat, continually modified until there was a towing pilon positioned just ahead of the engine. Likewise fins were moved all over the bottom of the boat before a satisfactory position was found, suitable for US and Canadian competition conditions.

The Waterjet-propelled Boat

As far back as 1787, a Mr James Rumsey, of the State of Virginia, had carried out experiments in a 5·50 m *18 ft* steam-powered waterjet-propelled boat on the River Potomac – and reached speeds of 6·44 km/h *4 mph*. But it was not until the 1950s that C. W. F. ('Bill') Hamilton of New Zealand, modified the American Hanley Hydro-jet principle and built a waterjet unit in his little work-shop 'half-way up Mt Cook', that would propel him up the fast-flowing rocky rivers which led to some beautiful high country regions near his South Canterbury holding. It was Hamilton's innovation of replacing the under-water propulsion and steering nozzle with a jet directed straight out through the transom *above* the waterline which proved the turning point in marine jet propulsion.

By 1954, the first batch of 40 Hamilton 'Rainbow' jet units were marketed throughout New Zealand, followed in 1956 by the 2-stage and 3-stage axial-flow 'Chinook' unit, which soon came to be marketed in Australia, Canada, the USA and the UK.

In Britain in 1958, Sir George Dowty organised a factory at Cheltenham, England, to build 'Turbocraft', or fibre-glass hulls using the Hamilton 'Chinook' unit, powered by a 6-cylinder Zephyr engine. Donald Campbell took time off from creating World Water Speed Records in his *Bluebird K7* to become a director of

Above: George Adlington prepares the nifty little Albatross for a run in the early 1950s. Notice the 'banana-peel' skis worn by Peter Brown before he bears the icy waters of Welton.

Below: How the Riva boat yard looked about 100 years ago – before expansion!

Dowty Marine, and test-drive – among other craft – a 12·19 m *40 ft* cabin cruiser called *Desi*, powered by three Dowty jets, which was uncontrollably powerful. Noting the steerage and safety potential for water-skiers behind the standard model, Campbell soon invited his old friend David Nations to Cheltenham for trials to test for cavitation and towing efficiency.

But the Dowty Turbocraft proved too expensive and in the end, Dowty Marine went out of business. With characteristic determination, Campbell set to work with Peter Milne, the designer and magazine editor, and with Norris Brothers, his *Bluebird* engineers, producing a less costly item.

In 1960, three Hamilton jetboats had successfully navigated up and down the unpredictable Colorado River and the Hamilton 'Colorado' range of jet-units had been born. In 1966, after some initial failures, the *Jetstar*, a 3·96 m *13 ft* plywood craft, using the Hamilton Colorado Junior single stage jet unit, and powered by an 80-hp Evinrude, had already towed four skiers together round a test-lake in Knokke, Belgium. It had also been put through its paces at 64 km/h *40 mph* in front of an enthusiastic Mr Kilgour of the Malta Dry Docks Company, with the idea of establishing a jetboat plant in Malta, which would eventually turn out 5000 jetboats per year. Sadly, Campbell's tragic death on Coniston Water in 1967 precluded this ambitious project. But the value of the waterjet unit to skiers had been proved through the farsightedness of one man.

All Nations Ski Tow

When he entered a Mercury '28'-powerboat for his first race as a hobby in 1959, Norman Fletcher was professionally designing and marketing model aircraft and boats in a small shop in West Bromwich, Staffordshire, England. The following year he decided to build his own small sports-boat, incorporating a revolutionary lapstrake design, which enabled him to compete on equal footing against powerboats with much greater engine capacity.

When Todds had exhibited the very first fibre-glass hull at a Boat Show in the late 1950s, everyone had scoffed. But the turn of the decade saw the advent of the fibreglass revolution. In 1964, using their model-making experience for forming shapes and producing a good 'finis' Fletcher Marine developed the lapstrake/fibreglass 3·66 m *12 ft* runabout called the Arrow 120 ('Fletcher' means 'Arrow-maker'). That same year, together with Lionel Vizor as navigator, Norman Fletcher raced his *White Tornado*, a standard Arrow 140 production boat powered by a 50-hp Mercury, to win the first Class III Championship, with a spectacular 1800 points out of a possible 2000 – as against the runner-up's 880 points. From 1965 onwards, always testing their designs under the most severe conditions on the Welsh coast, and

The famous 'picture' boat that Correct-Craft built for Cypress Gardens.

Above: Donald Campbell stands in the cockpit of the Dowty Turbocraft and disentangles the ropes that are to pull three skiers. David Nations, *left*, in a wet suit prepares to take the tow with Maureen Lynn-Taylor, women's National champion.

Below: Just one of the successful power boats which Norman Fletcher has built for ski racing contests.

racing standard models for publicity, Fletcher began to forge ahead with the Deep-V design for 14-footers and ultimately 17-footers. The late 1960s saw the rise of British and European water-ski racing and Fletcher powerboats towed winning skiers to victory on many occasions, becoming renowned for their seaworthiness in testing Channel conditions. Variously named 'Arrow Man', 'Arrowbolt', 'Arrowflyt', 'Arrowsport', 'Arrowstreak' and 'Arrowbeau', by this time the prolific Fletcher output was distributed worldwide from a larger factory at Bruntwood in Staffordshire.

At the 1975 London Boat Show David Nations approached Norman Fletcher with the challenge of building the perfect ski-boat for classic competition – robust, of low fuel consumption, requiring very little upkeep, and efficient for slalom, tricks and jumping.

Fletcher has recalled: 'We spent nine months attempting to modify the stock design of our fibre-glass 17-footer, installing a big inboard with an outdrive. But David soon rejected this for the conventional drive as he'd been used to in the Boesch and the Correct Craft.

'But by this time, we had investigated and converted a 225-hp V8 "Blue Water" Mercruiser to run on propane gas (LPG) which would prove far more economical for David, who was regularly running his boats for thirteen hours a day in the summer. He was seriously concerned about a worldwide inflationary problem where the costs of the conventional petrol consumption system were continuing to escalate out of all reasonable proportion. The economic advantages of a ski-boat, which, apart from being equipped to run on petrol, could be designed to incorporate this propane gas system as well, could not be underestimated as regards efficiency and cost-saving

Above: The All Nations Ski Tow moored alongside the jetty at Ruislip Lido with, *left to right,* David Nations, Norman Fletcher and Paul Adlington. *Below:* the cockpit arrangements of this craft.

Above: Water polo was a sporting craze in the 1920s. Notice the outboard engines fixed on the back of the aquaplanes.

Left: the latest Johnson outboard engine at work driving a Fletcher boat — a far cry from the 1920s!

Here, taken from the Zodiac Archives in France, is a very rare photograph of the first inflatable boat ever constructed: the year is 1936.

to any waterski club throughout the world. It was a breakthrough of vital necessity.'

What neither Nations nor Fletcher knew was that they had now surmounted the problems which had shelved the 'pea-coal' gas producing system for motor launches of seventy years before.

Fletcher continues the story: 'As regards the hull, despite the thousands of "man-hours" necessary to create surfaces in the design of a prototype boat and to actually make a plug ready to mould off, we finally decided to start completely from scratch without the influence of either our own "Arrows" or of already accepted ski-boats. At first, we didn't really know what we were catering for, therefore we had to rely on David and Paul Adlington to tell us what they required. But even "DN" didn't always know himself. He knew the benefits he wanted, but he didn't know how to express them clearly to a designer like myself. He was not an easy taskmaster in that he would ring me up at all hours of the day and night – but there was tremendous feedback between us.'

A very conventional boat began to emerge, which in some ways from the pure utilisation of power, was a quite different boat by Fletcher standards. But as soon as they tried to make it more efficient, it lost those characteristics required by the skier. Continually they were stymied by their own knowledge. They had to buy reliable, long-mileage engines from the States – to develop propellers, shafts, tubes, exhaust elbows – they did their own pattern work. Eventually they built the prototype: with a draught of only a few inches and a slight 'V', they gave it more freeboard with a beam of 254 cm *8 ft* and a length of 594 cm *19¼ ft*. Particular care was taken to provide for the comfort of the judges and driver. The driver's seat would be adjustable for rake and height and distance, so that the two judges seats were alongside facing aft. Three of the world's most accurate Speedos were fitted. Two for the driver, and one positioned amidships for the judges.

The first time out on Ruislip Lido, Paul Adlington, who had been driving boats since he was a child, and skiing for almost as long, came back and commented 'Marvellous!' But even then, after building the first production boat, they found that it was not as good as its prototype and had to do a further modification towards perfection. Since 1959, Fletcher had never been faced with such a challenge as this boat.

They worked solidly and produced two boats for the Regional Championships in Nottingham. Those boats had never been on the water until the day before the contest. They ran the engines in through the night, then chose one as the runner and the other as the support boat. That boat ran for thirty odd hours, pulling skiers from the nine regions of Great Britain – and there was not one re-run. No skier managed to slow it up, to pull it across, or whatever. It's the first time, as far as is known, that a first-class competition had been run without one re-run. As Norman Fletcher has said:

'I'm satisfied with this boat if David is, and I know that if he is, with over 25 years' experience in water-skiing, and being a perfectionist, then it has got to be right. We've called the boat the *All Nations Ski Tow*, as an international pun on his name. But we think it will sell to every nation in the World Water Ski Union.'

The Johnson Outboard Engine
In December 1921, almost a year to the day after they had begun building the first model of their outboard motor, the Johnson brothers – Harry, Lou and Clarence – put their first aluminium engine ('The Light Twin' or 'Water Bug') into production at South Bend, Indiana, on the banks of the St Joseph River.

By 1929, the ever-growing Johnson plant had moved to Waukegan, Illinois and begun to produce its first line of 'Sea Horse' outboards ('16' and '32'). Eventually, the millionth unit rolled off the Waukegan assembly line in 1952, the two millionth in 1959 and the three millionth in 1968. The spectacular way Johnson outboards were used at Cypress Gardens has already been chronicled.

For 1977, Johnsons have produced yet another new range of outboards, some especially for the water-skier – the '50', '70' and '75', complete with loopcharging systems for fuel economy, electronic ignition, dual-path water cooling, easy-tilt shock absorbers and exhaust tuning, outboard engineering concepts only dreamed of 50 years ago.

The Zodiac Inflatable
With a 30-year-old reputation for building airships, the Société Zodiac first took an interest in pleasure craft in 1934 when the French engineer, Pierre Debroutelle, created the first Zodiac inflatable boat, shaped ·like a two-seater kayak. By 1936, Zodiac had developed an inflatable catamaran, incorporating parallel buoyancy chambers pointed at each end, together with a centreboard – that could carry an outboard engine at its stern.

In 1937 Zodiac made a survey of inflatable boats for use by the French Navy. It was in Cherbourg, the following year, that a boat was accepted by the Navy as being suitable for supplying bombs and torpedoes to seaplanes. This particular design was the ancestor of the inflatable boat manufactured today – with the 'U'-shaped bow and a wooden transom at the stern.

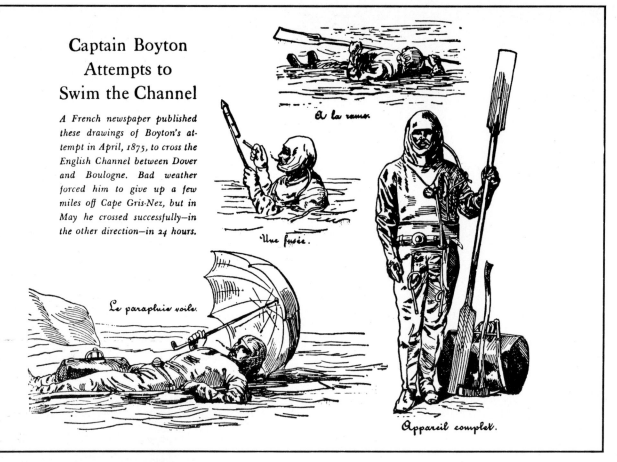

Captain Boyton Attempts to Swim the Channel

A French newspaper published these drawings of Boyton's attempt in April, 1875, to cross the English Channel between Dover and Boulogne. Bad weather forced him to give up a few miles off Cape Gris-Nez, but in May he crossed successfully—in the other direction—in 24 hours.

à la rame.

Une fusée.

Le parapluie voile.

Appareil complet.

Above: **The 'Skisacksuit' manufactured by David Nations, is here worn by Patti Chamoun, wife of the son of the ex-President of the Lebanon in the early 1950s.**

After the war, many fine synthetic fabrics, that were both durable and waterproof, came on the market and Zodiac began using these fabrics for their inflatable craft – particularly a highly resistant, heavy nylon weave coated on both sides with Neoprene (Dupont de Nemours) for air-integrity, and protected outside with Hypalon (again Dupont de Nemours).

Today the company employs 750 people in Rochefort-sur-Mer near La Rochelle on the Atlantic Ocean, where one inflatable comes off the stocks every six minutes, backed up by two further plants in Barcelona, Spain, and Toulouse, France.

The latest range of Zodiacs range from the 3-metre 'Cadet' right up to the 5·30-metre 'Mark IV Grand Raid', although the 3·80-metre 'Mark II Compact', fitted with an outboard of 20–40 hp, can easily tow a water-skier.

THE WATER SKIING SUIT

On the evening of 21 October 1874, a daring American jumped overboard from the SS *Queen*, in a violent Atlantic storm some thirty miles from the Irish coast – and succeeded in gaining shore safely, *warm and dry*. Captain Paul Boyton of the New Jersey Life Saving Service, Atlantic City, had just demonstrated the life-preserving suit invented by C. S. Merriman.

It was made of solid rubber sheeting, and was in two parts, the lower being the 'pantaloons', to which boots

Anna Gerber, British ski champion, skiing on Ruislip Lido wrapped up warmly in her plastic mac top and gloves.

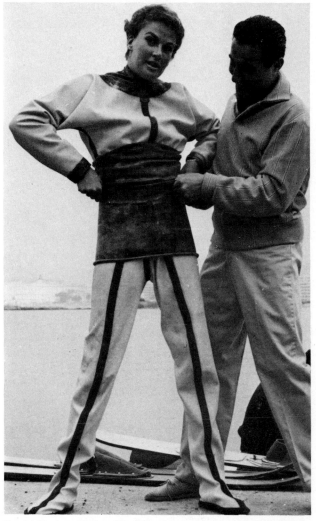

David Nations helps Jilly Morris to try on one of the early rubber suits produced in France, in the early 1950s.

were attached, and the upper the tunic, with sleeves, gloves and helmet connected to it. This 7-kg *15-lb* suit was secured with a watertight joint at the waist and the wearer was rendered buoyant by inflating five air-chambers, the headpiece having a small opening which exposed his mouth, nose and eyes. When out of use the suit was packed away in a rubber bag, weighing about 1 kg *2 lb*. With a little practice, it could be put on and inflated in two minutes. A superb showman, Captain Boyton spent the years 1875–78 colourfully demonstrating Merriman's dry-suit along every major river of Europe and the USA.

Eighty years later, in the 1950s, many enthusiastic pioneers who decided to ski the whole year round, were at once faced with the problem of keeping warm and dry while skiing into the wind on a bitterly cold winter's day. To avoid the deepwater start, many of them learned that if they could make a jump take-off from the jetty, either standing up or sitting down, provided they could coast straight back to the same jetty at the end of their run, they could keep their jumpers, golfing anoraks and scarves relatively dry and their bodies relatively warm. Even so, the depressing thought of plunging into the freezing cold water and turning blue for three hours was certainly not very encouraging, to even the most hardy of skiers.

David Nations, who used to ski in fisherman's rubber waders, has recalled: 'I first got the idea of a protective suit from Siebe Gorman, who were making diving suits for the French Navy. Then a suit came out in France – a natural, closed-cell yellow rubber, developed by the Société Franco-Belge du Caoutchouc Mousse. They had supplied it to a heating engineer from Marseilles named George Beuchat, who made the first one hundred garments. That was in 1951. Patti Morgan (now married to Danny Chamoun, son of the ex-President of the Lebanon) and myself had a couple made – they were very expensive. Then I made a plastic suit with a zip at my own factory as a cheap alternative.'

Peter Felix remembers: 'One day David arrived with a transparent watertight suit, closed at the neck and arms and ankles and said "Boys, this is the answer! Who's going to try it – what about you, Peter?" So they bunged it on me. I tried, fell a few times and without my realising it, it must have torn because it started to fill up with water. When they came to pick me up for the fourth time, I looked more like the Michelin Man and was going under. So that was the end of one early attempt at insulation.'

But it was Oscar Gugen, the Founder of the British Sub Aqua Club, who pioneered and promoted the wet-suit in the British Isles. As he recalls:

213

'I'd been diving amongst the first enthusiasts back in 1928. Even before I started the British Sub Aqua Club, I went to see Heinke and asked them whether they could make a dipped rubber suit with stockinette material. This resulted in their two-piece Delta suit that you roll up at the middle – similar to the Pirelli made for Italian frogmen during World War II.

'We tried these out in 1953 at a place called Laughing Waters on the Rochester By-Pass. It was winter and we were freezing. When we tried to take them off, we almost had to cut them open with knives, because our hands were so stiff from the cold.

'I reflected that until such time as anybody designs a suit, either wet or dry, whichever it is, that you can take off and put on easily and feel comfortable, there is no future in either diving or water-skiing in coldwater countries. So I set out to do just that.

'I didn't like the idea of the roll-up suit, because it was never really waterproof. So we made a one-piece drysuit with a front entry closed by two zips opposite two rubber sausages which we squeezed together with the zips; it was waterproof but it was not really 100 per cent satisfactory. Once I found myself diving in a lake in Austria, and I could not get out of the blooming suit – I had to cut it open because the zip-fastener got stuck through corrosion. So I sat down and thought about some other means of closing it, and invented a closure which was so simple that we took out a patent – I believe in eleven or twelve countries. I remember when I took it down to the Navy in Portsmouth, the Superintendent of Diving said that "Who ever had invented it, must really have been a fool and known nothing about engineering! When I told him that I was that "fool", he replied, "That's right. There you are, because if you had had any knowledge of engineering, you wouldn't have invented something that is so simple and efficient".'

Gugen demonstrated this early drysuit for German TV – it was the very first programme that the German network had broadcast – and took under 30 seconds to put it on.

Alongside this, he also made a 'mid-season' diving suit in natural sponge rubber, which was the fore-runner of the 'wet' suit and cost a princely £11! He continues the story:

'In 1954 I met Tony Richardson who had a friend who owned a gravel pit out at Walton. As it was winter, I brought along a dry diving suit (complete with boots) and we went water-skiing. Richardson bet me a "fiver" I wouldn't stand up. I replied that if he didn't throttle the engine, he wouldn't throw me off! Neither of us won the wager because I duck-dived only to find myself upside down with my feet in the air, drowning underwater. All

David Nations skiing with two handles and wearing fishermen's rubber waders and a windcheater to keep him warm and dry in the early days of the 1950s when no wet suits were available.

The first water ski 'shortie' produced by Oscar Gugen and Typhoon in the 1950s.

This, in the late 1950s, is the top half of the very first two-piece wet suit, complete with its Velco fastener, to be produced by Typhoon.

the air had rushed up to my feet and the only way I could right myself was to open the closure and let the water get into the suit, then struggle like hell to turn downside up!

'Although we created a dry water-skiing suit which was quite successful, I decided that, until we could really perfect the "dry" suit, for the water-skier, the "wet" suit should be the answer.'

Neoprene as an expanded, synthetic rubber, had been pioneered by Dupont/Rubatex in the United States, as a by-product of the chemical industry. What made it so good for divers was that it could not be affected by extreme sunlight, chlorine, oils and saltwater. In 1956 Gugen heard that the Société Franco-Belge de Caoutchouc Mousse had painstakingly developed an expanded cellular material which they called Nepex (Neoprene Expansée).

'The first "wet" suits I had produced for myself and a Mr John Mills, a graduate of the Massachusetts Institute of Technology, USA, were from Rubatex expanded Neoprene, which was an unlined material.

'The first ones we made were bang on. We knew nothing about tailoring. We made a suit that fitted the man as closely as you could fit him – a second skin – then we just glued it, we did not stitch it. We tested them successfully at Kingston Swimming Pool.

'Next we started putting chalk marks on where we thought the seams should run, cut it apart, made a pattern, then another suit, then another pattern – until we eventually came up with the answer. David Nations was extremely helpful. He took suits of ours, tried them, and tested them. We soon found that if we did not line the material, when we took them off, they were torn. Eventually we introduced double-lining.'

By the early 1960s, rubber suits were rapidly becoming available for both divers and water-skiers. Suits on the market were Beaufort, Dunlop, Pirelli, Siebe Gorman, Sirocco, and Tarzan – but basically they followed Oscar Gugen's pioneering results.

As he says: 'We eventually finished with a pattern, which has been undoubtedly the most copied pattern in the world – the Typhoon. We did consider alternative names like "Hurricane", which is another wind, but "Typhoon" sounded better.'

After a full circle of fifteen years, during which he had also pioneered the first water-ski gloves in Neoprene and leather, Oscar Gugen's mind next turned to the second challenge – to perfect that drysuit for the water-skier.

'I would regularly go to firms in search of new materials and when I saw something I liked, obtain a sample and take it back to see what I might create with it. In this way, I found a lightweight nylon, sandwiched with "Butyil" rubber, with its breaking strength on a 50 mm wide strip of 135kg warp and 115 kg weft. This made it one of the toughest materials available, and more important, one which could keep a skier totally dry. So we spent some time making up half a dozen prototypes in our Research and Development Department, which were tested during the winter of 1975/76 and stood up very well.'

Having decided to go ahead with full-scale production, they had to retrain some of their operators to make a new type of suit complete with heavy duty zip, neck seal and cuff seals. But no sooner had they started than it was found that the adhesive was not holding the production suits together. After a conference with the manufacturer, they learnt that they had recently and unwittingly changed the formula for their adhesive – this was sorted out eventually.

Then there was the problem of how to test the drysuits before they left the factory, to ensure total efficiency. They found a good test was if they sealed up the cuffs and neck, over-inflated the suits with air and left them overnight, reading the pressure gauge to see the drop in pressure over twelve hours. If they stood up to that test, a follow up with a leakage test by underwater immersion worked well.

They also developed a pair of water-ski socks to keep the feet dry, but only after overcoming the problem of water seepage through tiny pin-holes in the prototypes.

It takes one minute to put on the Typhoon water-skier drysuit, fitting it over a warm track-suit – and even less time to take it off. Apart from private orders, Typhoon

The prototype dry suit was tested out by Oscar Gugen's son Roger in 1975.

drysuits were almost immediately adopted by the Royal National Lifeboat Institute, the Royal Transport Corps and the Army. Coincidentally, it first went on view at the 1977 London Boat Show, literally a stone's throw from the stand exhibiting the *All Nations Ski Tow*.

Final proof of the drysuit innovation was observed by David Nations in the February of 1977, during a traditional weekend of training at Rickmansworth Aquadrome. It was a cold, winter's day with both sleet and rain falling. Nick Frangistas, the Greek ski champion, had had three hard sessions of slalom skiing at maximum speed with a progressively shorter line – and many falls into the icy water during practice. He was wearing a Typhoon drysuit with his shirt, tie, cardigan, normal underpants underneath – all he did was to wipe his feet, put his trousers, shoes and socks on, then he was ready to leave.

'Nicholas, why do you wear your normal walking-out clothes – why not a tracksuit?'

'I've been skiing so many times like this and I've never got wet. Why bother to change?' he replied.

This was the breakthrough for which we had worked so long – the perfect answer to counteract for once and all the problem of feeling cold, getting wet and having to endure cold-climate water skiing. No longer would there ever be the need for skiers to lave their own surroundings because of colder weather and train abroad in warmer climates. This drysuit had totally removed that barrier and begun a new era in water-skiing.

The drysuit concept may have been pioneered by Captain Boyton in the *1870s* but it is Oscar Gugen who perfected the water-ski model in the 1970s.

SAFETY

Even from the days of aquaplaning, there had been accidents, some of them near-fatal, many of them leaving unpleasant scars. From fear and concern that the same accidents should not be repeated, came the protective design of skiing equipment.

For example, soon after the introduction of the wake cut in jumping, American champion Butch Rosenberg was practising when he misjudged his cut and ran straight into the jump at speed, suffering fatal injuries. From then on the sides of the ramp were covered with what came to be nicknamed 'cowcatchers', after the metal frame fixed to the front of a railway engine to remove obstructions.

Not long after this, with approach speeds and jumping distances getting faster and further, associated with the increasing popularity of water-ski racing, the lifejacket and crash helmet appeared on the scene.

The Lifejacket
In 880 BC King Assur-Nasir-Pal had commanded his Assyrian soldiers to cross a river using inflated animal

Oscar Gugen in 1976, standing next to a skier who is wearing the modified drysuit.

. . . and always wear a life jacket. (See page 197.)

Below: Mike Suyderhoud going up a jumping ramp. Note the cowcatcher in front.

880 BC: Assyrian soldiers cross a river, using animal skins which they continually inflate to keep afloat.

skins – or so a famous stone bas-relief in the British Museum has suggested.

We come forward to 1698 when 'Man preserved from drowning in any kind of Water, by a new light hollow Girdle filled with his breath with conveniences to eat and drink if cast away by Sea. By Francis Cryns, Gentleman Sworn Servant in ordinary to his Majesty, who will endeavour to answer all reasonable Objections. Experimented in several Waters: At Bristol Feb 28 last, by a man weighing one hundred and a half, bound hand and foot; before thousands at Portsmouth March 25th and at Windsor before His Majesty's Court (William III) the 20th of this instant May, by a tall heavy man to the satisfaction of the spectators.'

In 1757 Colonel de Gelacy of France is reported to have devised a cork lifejacket, while in 1763 their Lordships of the Admiralty were seriously considering the use of Dr J. Wilkinson's cork lifejacket for the British Fleet.

By the 1850s the rubber revolution was well on its way and rubber life-preserving 'air pillows' from Mr Mackintosh's factory were taken by Sir John Franklin on his 1824 Expedition to the Arctic. Britain's Thomas Hancock (of 'Vulcanised' rubber fame), Charles Goodyear of the US, the inimitable Captain Paul Boyton, and Herr Paul Raschke, 'a working tailor from Breslau', were just four of the 19th-century pioneer salesmen of the inflatable rubber life-preserving vestment.

When water-skiing became safety-conscious, Mae Wests and other traditional life-jackets were tried, but they only hindered body movement. So it was in the late 1960s/early 1970s that a water-ski jump-jacket (or waistcoat), built of close-cell foam covered with bright yellow nylon, or plastic-coated, began to be used. In their goal towards perfection, manufacturers soon found that these jackets were prone to crack and ultimately break at the shoulders. From this a lifejacket was recently designed out of tough waterproof yachting fabric that is less brittle and more enduring.

The Crash Helmet

Once again, as we see from the bas-relief, the ancient Assyrians, together with the Persians, wore helmets of leather and or iron before the decisive Battle of Marathon was fought on the plains of Greece (490 BC). From then on, whether they were used for battles or jousting tournaments, armour-plated helmets came in all shapes and sizes. More recently, arising from the first skull fatalities in aviation and motorsport, helmets were being designed.

The very first, if somewhat brittle, plastic was Parkesine, a thermoplastic material produced from nitrocellulose, camphor and alcohol by Alexander Parkes of Birmingham and originally manufactured by the Parkesine Co. at Hackney Wick, London in 1866. An almost exactly similar thermoplastic was patented by John Wesley Hyatt of Albany, NY in 1869 and given the name Celluloid. It was perhaps inevitable that some bright

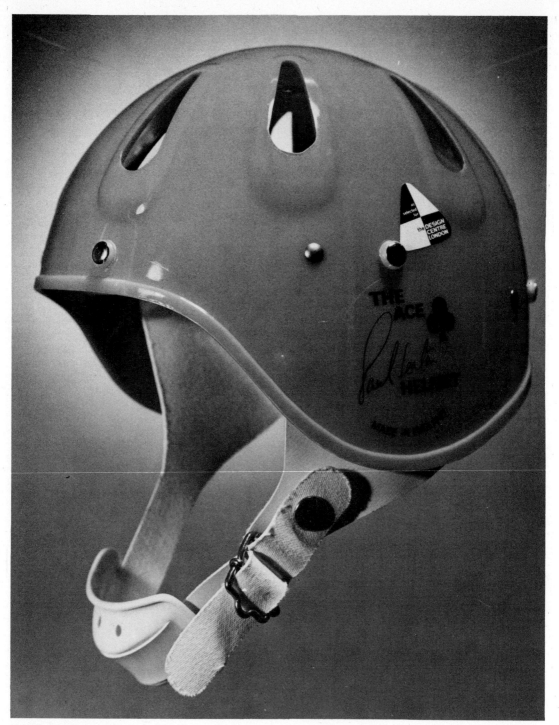

Here is just one design for the water ski helmet. Notice the chin strap and the gaps to let in the water.

spark would eventually develop a reinforced plastic in their laboratory.

Although luminescent (phosphor) wrist-watch dials had been used in the 1914–18 War, it was not until the mid-1950s that fluorescent 'Dayglo' colours – red, yellow, orange, etc. – came to be used in paper and then for plastics and fabrics.

The fluorescent, reinforced-plastic helmet first came to be used by water-ski-racers and jumpers in the late 1960s. At first they adapted American football, lightweight motorcycle, ice-hockey and canoeing helmets. But before

long, a custom-designed helmet had appeared on the market, complete with chin-cup and slits to allow the water to go through in case of a fall. But it was here that a further dilemma arose. If the slits were made too large, the water could rush in with such force as to perforate the ear-drums, but then if the slits were made too small, the skier's deafness could result in lack of balance. The problem is to control the entry-speed of the water, and at the time of going to press, the World Water Ski Union Safety Committee can recommend no helmet that meets this standard. But then history does not stand still.

Results
and Records

For reasons of administration and competition, the World Water Ski Union has been divided into three Groups:

Group I comprises both of the American Continents, including Bermuda and the West Indies.

Group II comprises Scandinavia, Europe, the USSR, Yugoslavia, Czechoslovakia, South Africa, Greece, Iran, Lebanon, Israel, and Jordan.

Group III comprises Australasia and the Far Eastern Countries, including Japan and the Republic of China.

The following tables include results of the major contests for each of these Groups.

THE WORLD CHAMPIONSHIPS

1949: Juan Les Pins (France)

	Over-all	*Slalom*	*Tricks*	*Jumping*
Men:	Christian Jourdan (Fr) Guy de Clercq (Bel)	Christian Jourdan (Fr)	Pierre Gouin (Fr)	Guy de Clercq (Bel)
Women:	Willa Worthington (USA)	Willa Worthington (USA)	Madeleine Boutellier (Fr)	Willa Worthington (USA)

1950: Cypress Gardens (USA)

Men:	Dick Pope Jr (USA)	Dick Pope Jr (USA)	Jack Andresen (USA)	Guy de Clercq (Bel)
Women:	Willa Worthington McGuire (USA)	Evie Wolford (USA)	Willa Worthington McGuire (USA)	Johnette Kirkpatrick (USA)

1953: Toronto (Canada)

Men:	Alfredo Mendoza (USA)	Charles Blackwell (Can)	Warren Witherall (USA)	Alfredo Mendoza (USA)
Women:	Leah Marie Rawls (USA)	Evie Wolford (USA)	Leah Marie Rawls (USA)	Sandra Swaney (USA)

1955: Beirut (Lebanon)

Men:	Alfredo Mendoza (USA)	Alfredo Mendoza (USA)	Scotty Scott (USA)	Alfredo Mendoza (USA)
Women:	Willa Worthington McGuire (USA)	Willa Worthington McGuire (USA)	Marina Doria (Swi)	Willa Worthington McGuire (USA)

1957: Cypress Gardens (USA)

Men:	Joe Cash (USA)	Joe Cash (USA)	Mike Amsbry (USA)	Joe Mueller (USA)
Women:	Marina Doria (Swi)	Marina Doria (Swi)	Marina Doria (Swi)	Nancie Rideout (USA)

1959: Milan (Italy)

Men:	Chuck Stearns (USA)	Chuck Stearns (USA)	Philippe Logut (Fr)	Buster McCalla (USA)
Women:	Vickie Van Hook (USA)	Vickie Van Hook (USA)	Piera Castelvetri (It)	Nancie Rideout (USA)

1961: Long Beach (USA)

Men:	Bruno Zaccardi (It)	Jimmy Jackson (USA)	Jean Marie Muller (Fr)	Larry Penacho (USA)
Women:	Sylvie Hulsemann (Lux)	Janelle Kirkley (USA)	Sylvie Hulsemann (Lux)	Renate Hansluvka (Aut)

1963: Vichy (France)

Men:	Billy Spencer (USA)	Billy Spencer (USA)	Billy Spencer (USA)	Jimmy Jackson (USA)
Women:	Jeannette Brown (USA)	Jeannette Brown (USA)	Guyonne Dalle (Fr)	Renate Hansluvka (Aut)

THE WORLD CHAMPIONSHIPS (continued)

	Over-all	Slalom	Tricks	Jumping
		1965: Surfers Paradise (Australia)		
Men:	Roland Hillier (USA)	Roland Hillier (USA)	Ken White (USA)	Larry Penacho (USA)
Women:	Liz Allan (USA)	Barbara Cooper-Clack (USA)	Dany Duflot (Fr)	Liz Allan (USA)
		1967: Sherbrooke (Canada)		
Men:	Mike Suyderhoud (USA)	Tito Antunano (Mex)	Alan Kempton (USA)	Alan Kempton (USA)
Women:	Jeannette Stewart-Wood (GB)	Liz Allan (USA)	Dany Duflot (Fr)	Jeannette Stewart-Wood (GB)
		1969: Copenhagen (Denmark)		
Men:	Mike Suyderhoud (USA)	Victor Palomo (Sp)	Bruce Cockburn (Aus)	Wayne Grimditch (USA)
Women:	Liz Allan (USA)	Liz Allan (USA)	Liz Allan (USA)	Liz Allan (USA)
		1971: Banolas (Spain)		
Men:	George Athans (Can)	Mike Suyderhoud (USA)	Ricky McCormick (USA)	Mike Suyderhoud (USA)
Women:	Christy Weir (USA)	Christy Freeman (USA)	Willi Stahle (Hol)	Christy Weir (USA)
		1973: Bogotá (Colombia)		
Men:	George Athans (Can)	George Athans (Can)	Wayne Grimditch (USA)	Ricky McCormick (USA)
Women:	Lisa St John (USA)	Sylvie Maurial (Fr)	Maria Victoria Carrasco (Ven)	Liz Allan Shetter (USA)
		1975: Thorpe (England)		
Men:	Carlos Suarez (Ven)	Roby Zucchi (It)	Wayne Grimditch (USA)	Ricky McCormick (USA)
Women:	Liz Allan Shetter (USA)	Liz Allan Shetter (USA)	Maria Victoria Carrasco (Ven)	Liz Allan Shetter (USA)

1977: Milan (Italy)

Men:
Women:

1979:

Men:
Women:

The Cup of the Nations has been won by the American team for ten World Championships in succession since 1957.

BIENNIAL GROUP I CHAMPIONSHIPS

	Over-all	Slalom	Tricks	Jumping
		1968: Neiva, Colombia		
Men:	Ricky McCormick	George Athans (Can)	Ricky McCormick	Mike Suyderhoud
Women:	Liz Allan	Vailla Hoggan	Liz Allan	Liz Allan
		1970: Lake Tequesquitengo, Mexico		
Men:	Mike Suyderhoud	Mike Suyderhoud	George Athans (Can)	Mike Suyderhoud
Women:	Liz Allan	Christy Weir	Christy Weir	Liz Allan
		1972: Montreal, Canada		
Men:	Ricky McCormick	Mike Suyderhoud	Ricky McCormick	Ricky McCormick
Women:	Liz Allan Shetter	Liz Allan Shetter	Liz Allan Shetter	Liz Allan Shetter

1974
(No contest held)

		1976: Canal Cuemanco, Xochimilco, Mexico		
Men:	Carlos Suarez (Ven)	Bob LaPoint	Carlos Suarez (Ven)	Ricky McCormick
Women:	Cindy Todd	Pat Messner	Maria Victoria Carrasco (Ven)	Trudi Speak

1978:

Men:
Women:

Unless otherwise noted all winners above are Americans.

UNITED STATES NATIONAL TOURNAMENTS

	Over-all	*Slalom*	*Tricks*	*Jumping*

1939: Jones Beach, New York

	Over-all	Slalom	Tricks	Jumping
Men:	Bruce Parker	Bruce Parker	Bruce Parker	Jack Schiess
Women:	Esther Yates	Esther Yates	(Not held)	(Not held)

1940: Jones Beach, New York

	Over-all	Slalom	Tricks	Jumping
Men:	Bruce Parker	Charles Sligh Jr Karl Popelik	Bruce Parker	Bruce Parker
Women:	Virginia Pfaff	Virginia Pfaff	Virginia Pfaff	(Not held)

1941: Macatawa Park, Holland, Michigan

	Over-all	Slalom	Tricks	Jumping
Men:	Chuck Sligh	Bud Pichard	Doug Fonda	Chuck Sligh
Women:	Lyda Mae Helder	Lyda Mae Helder	Lyda Mae Helder	Not held

1946: Macatawa Park, Holland, Michigan

	Over-all	Slalom	Tricks	Jumping
Men:	Lew Withey	Bill Telling	Doug Fonda	Chuck Sligh
Women:	Willa Worthington	Willa Worthington	Willa Worthington	Katy Turner
Jr Boys:	Lew Withey	Lew Withey	Lew Withey	Lew Withey

1947: Macatawa Park, Holland, Michigan

	Over-all	Slalom	Tricks	Jumping
Men:	Bob Sligh	Bud Leach	Bob Sligh	Bob Sligh
Women:	Willa Worthington	Dottie Mae Andresen	Willa Worthington	Willa Worthington
Jr Boys:	Dick Pope Jr	Jimmy Andresen	Dick Pope Jr	Dick Pope Jr
Jr Girls:	Sammie Stilley	Sammie Stilley	Sammie Stilley	Sammie Stilley
Doubles:	Bob Sligh and Irene Boer			

1948: Martin Lagoon, Middle River, Maryland

	Over-all	Slalom	Tricks	Jumping
Men:	Dick Pope Jr	Bud Leach	Bob Sligh	Buddy Boyle
Women:	Willa Worthington	Dottie Mae Andresen	Willa Worthington	Johnette Kirkpatrick
Jr Boys:	Dick Rowe	Dick Rowe	Dick Rowe	Jimmy Andresen
Jr Girls:	Liz Sharpe	Janet Andresen	Liz Sharpe	Liz Sharpe
Doubles:	Bud Leach and Evelyn Teagle			

1949: Martin Lagoon, Middle River, Maryland

	Over-all	Slalom	Tricks	Jumping
Men:	Dick Pope Jr	Dick Pope Jr	Dick Pope Jr	Buddy Boyle
Women:	Willa Worthington McGuire	Willa Worthington McGuire	Willa Worthington McGuire	Willa Worthington McGuire
Jr Boys:	Skillman Suydam	Skillman Suydam	Skillman Suydam	Jake McGuire
Jr Girls:	Mary Lois Thornhill	Mary Lois Thornhill	Mary Lois Thornhill	Mary Lois Thornhill
Doubles:	Bruce Parker and Sandy Shard			

1950: Seattle, Washington

	Over-all	Slalom	Tricks	Jumping
Men:	Dick Pope Jr	Dick Pope Jr	Jack Andresen	Dick Pope Jr
Women:	Willa Worthington McGuire	Willa Worthington McGuire	Willa Worthington McGuire	Janette Burr
Jr Boys:	Skillman Suydam	Skillman Suydam	Emilio Zamudio	Skillman Suydam
Jr Girls:	Mary Lois Thornhill	Mary Lois Thornhill	Mary Lois Thornhill	Mary Lois Thornhill
Veterans:	Bill Schumacher	Bill Schumacher	Samuel Zamudio	Bill Schumacher
Doubles:	Rod Andresen and Doris Roswald			

1951: Lake Placid, New York

	Over-all	Slalom	Tricks	Jumping
Mens:	Skillman Suydam	Skillman Suydam	Dick Pope Jr	Jack Flanagan
Women:	Willa Worthington McGuire	Willa Worthington McGuire	Willa Worthington McGuire	Willa Worthington McGuire
Jr Boys:	Emilio Zamudio	Emilio Zamudio	Emilio Zamudio	Emilio Zamudio
Jr Girls:	Mary Lois Thornhill	Mary Lois Thornhill	Leah Marie Rawls	Mary Lois Thornhill
Veterans:	Henry Suydam	Samuel Zamudio	Henry Suydam	Bill Goodhue
Doubles:	Bruce Parker and Evie Wolford			

1952: Minocqua, Wisconsin

	Over-all	Slalom	Tricks	Jumping
Mens:	Emilio Zamudio	Emilio Zamudio	Emilio Zamudio	Alfredo Mendoza
Women:	Marguerite Williams	Evie Wolford	Marguerite Williams	Marguerite Williams
Jr Boys:	Joe Mueller	Charley Lloyd	Joe Mueller	Joe Mueller
Jr Girls:	Laurie Ann Hohl	Carol Ann Duthie	Laurie Ann Hohl	Laurie Ann Hohl
Veterans:	Bruce Parker	Samuel Zamudio	Bruce Parker	Bill Goodhue
Doubles:	Bruce Parker and Evie Wolford			

	Over-all	*Slalom*	*Tricks*	*Jumping*

1953: Long Beach, California

	Over-all	*Slalom*	*Tricks*	*Jumping*
Men:	Warren Witherell	Warren Witherell	Warren Witherell	Alfredo Mendoza
Women:	Leah Marie Rawls	Leah Marie Rawls	Willa Worthington McGuire	Willa Worthington McGuire
Jr Boys:	Buster McCalla	Buster McCalla	Gene Marotti	Charley Emry
Jr Girls:	Sharon Crosby	Sharon Crosby	Sharon Crosby	Tweedle Becker
Veterans:	Samuel Zamudio	Al Fames	Samuel Zamudio	Bill Martin

1954: Laconia, New Hampshire

	Over-all	*Slalom*	*Tricks*	*Jumping*
Men:	Butch Rosenberg	Warren Witherell	Alfredo Mendoza	Butch Rosenberg
Women:	Willa Worthington McGuire	Willa Worthington McGuire	Willa Worthington McGuire	Joan Turbett
Jr Boys:	Charley Emry	Charley Emry	Gene Marotti	Charley Emry
Jr Girls:	Connie Der	Connie Der	Sally Morris	Connie Der
Veterans:	Jack Andresen	Jack Andresen	Jack Andresen	Bill Goodhue
Doubles:	Bruce Parker and Evie Wolford			

1955: Lakeland, Florida

	Over-all	*Slalom*	*Tricks*	*Jumping*
Men:	Butch Rosenberg	Warren Witherell	Warren Witherell	Butch Rosenberg
Women:	Willa Worthington McGuire	Willa Worthington McGuire	Willa Worthington McGuire	Connie Der
Jr Boys:	Chuck Stearns	Chuck Stearns	Chuck Stearns	Bobby Marotti
Jr Girls:	Mary Ann Moenert	Mary Ann Moenert	Vickie Van Hook	Ann Parks
Veterans:	Earl Hollowell	Jack Andresen	Walter Pollack	Earl Hollowell
Doubles:	Jack and Mary Andresen			

1956: La Porte, Indiana

	Over-all	*Slalom*	*Tricks*	*Jumping*
Men:	Alfredo Mendoza	Charley Emry	Warren Witherell	Alfredo Mendoza
Women:	Elaine Roper	Leah Marie Atkins	Leah Marie Atkins	Sandra Lecklider
Jr Boys:	Mike Amsbry	Mike Amsbry	Mike Amsbry	Roger Ray
Jr Girls:	Janelle Kirkley	Janelle Kirkley	Janelle Kirkley	Mary Ann Grass
Veterans:	Jack Andresen	Jack Andresen	Jack Andresen	Bill Goodhue
Doubles:	Jane and Tom Dorwin			

1957: San Diego, California

	Over-all	*Slalom*	*Tricks*	*Jumping*
Men:	Chuck Stearns	Chuck Stearns	Wally Albright	Joe Cash
Women:	Leah Marie Atkins	Leah Marie Atkins	Leah Marie Atkins	Nancie Rideout
Jr Boys:	Roger Ray	Glenn Sperry	Mike Amsbury	Roger Ray
Jr Girls:	Vickie Van Hook	Janelle Kirkley	Vickie Van Hook	Sally Morris
Veterans:	Henry Holmes	Henry Holmes	William Morris	Hal Roberts
Doubles:	Mike Amsbry and Vickie Van Hook			

1958: Callaway Gardens, Pine Mountain, Georgia

	Over-all	*Slalom*	*Tricks*	*Jumping*
Men:	Chuck Stearns	Simon Khoury	Chuck Stearns	Joe Cash
Women:	Nancie Rideout	Nancie Rideout	Nancie Rideout	Nancie Rideout
Jr Boys:	Roger Ray	Roger Ray	Roger Ray	Roger Ray
Jr Girls:	Vickie Van Hook	Janelle Kirkley Vickie Van Hook	Vickie Van Hook	Barbara Cooper
Veterans:	Jack Andresen	Jack Andresen	Jack Andresen	Jack Kililea

1959: Lake Opeechee, Laconia, New Hampshire

	Over-all	*Slalom*	*Tricks*	*Jumping*
Men:	Mike Osborn	Joe Cash	Chuck Stearns	Buster MacCalla Mike Osborn
Women:	Nancie Rideout	Nancie Rideout	Vicki Vance	Nancie Rideout
Jr Boys:	Fred Pendlebury	Fred Pendlebury	Larry Penacho	Penny Baker
Jr Girls:	Vickie Van Hook	Janelle Kirkley	Janelle Kirkley	Barbara Cooper
Veterans:	Henry Holmes	Henry Holmes	Joe Templton	Jim Middlebrook
Doubles:	Joe Grimaldi and Mary Megginson			

1960: Lake of the Isles, Minneapolis, Minnesota

	Over-all	*Slalom*	*Tricks*	*Jumping*
Men:	Chuck Stearns	Chuck Stearns	Chuck Stearns	Chuck Stearns
Women:	Norine Bardill	Norine Bardill	Judy Rosch	Norine Bardill
Veterans:	William Morris Sr			
Doubles:	Joe Grimaldi and Mary Megginson			

UNITED STATES NATIONAL TOURNAMENT (continued)

	Over-all	*Slalom*	*Tricks*	*Jumping*

1961: Town Lake, Austin, Texas

	Over-all	Slalom	Tricks	Jumping
Men:	Mike Amsbry	Jimmy Jackson	Chuck Stearns	Jimmy Jackson
Women:	Janelle Kirkley	Jenny Hodges	Janelle Kirkley	Barbara Cooper
Jr Boys:	Gary Abben	Jonathan Staryk	Gary Abben	John Wiegart
Jr Girls:	Charlotte Bruner	Barbara Lynch	Weslie Walker	Terri Shrader
Veterans:	Henry Holmes	Wally Pallack	Walter Marble	Roy Tye
Doubles:	Candy Smith and Ray Shearer			

1962: Callaway Gardens, Pine Mountain, Georgia

	Over-all	Slalom	Tricks	Jumping
Men:	Chuck Stearns	Chuck Stearns	Al Tyll	Larry Penacho
Women:	Jenny Hodges	Jenny Hodges	Jenny Hodges	Cecele Campbell
Jr Boys:	William Spencer	William Spencer	Ricky McCormick	William Spencer
Jr Girls:	Margaret Poe	Liz Allan	Margaret Poe	Liz Allan
Veterans:	Harry Price	Jim A. Rusing	Walter Marble	Jim A. Rusing

1963: Long Beach, California

	Over-all	Slalom	Tricks	Jumping
Men:	Larry Penacho	Chuck Stearns	Al Tyll	Jimmy Jackson
Women:	Barbara Clack	Janelle Kirkley	Janelle Kirkley	Barbara Clack
Jr Boys:	Dave Holt	Dave Holt	Dave Holt	Dave Holt
Jr Girls:	Liz Allan	Liz Allan	Liz Allan	Liz Allan
Veterans:	Harry Price	Harry Price	Harry Price	David K. Sutton

1964: Webster, Massachusetts

	Over-all	Slalom	Tricks	Jumping
Men:	Joker Osborn	Joker Osborn	Al Tyll	Jimmy Jackson
Women:	Dicksie Ann Hoyt	Janelle Kirkley	Dicksie Ann Hoyt	Barbara Clack
Jr Boys:	Kenny Dabbs	Frankie Dees	Ricky McCormick	Kenny Dabbs
Jr Girls:	Linda Leavengood	Betsy Callaway	Maggy Jorden	Lorrie Hewes
Veterans:	Harry Price	Harry Price	Harry Price	Don Roberson
Doubles:	Bill Pierce and Marilyn Shaw			

1965: Lake of the Isles, Minneapolis, Minnesota

	Over-all	Slalom	Tricks	Jumping
Men:	Chuck Stearns	Roland Hillier	Al Tyll	Chuck Stearns
Women:	Dicksie Ann Hoyt	Barbara Clack	Dicksie Ann Hoyt	Barbara Clack
Jr Boys:	Ricky McCormick	Kris LaPoint	Ricky McCormick	Donald Kreuger
Jr Girls:	Christy Lynn Weir	Christy Lynn Weir	Lisa St John	Linda Austin
Veterans:	Harry Price	David Andrews	Bill Schouten	Keith Sutton
Doubles:	McCormick and Young			

1966: Miami, Florida

	Over-all	Slalom	Tricks	Jumping
Men:	Paul Merrill	Tom Decker	Roland Hillier	Paul Merrill
Women:	Barbara Clack	Barbara Clack	Barbara Clack	Barbara Clack
Jr Boys:	Bobby Boivie	Paul Woodward	Bobby Boivie	Bobby Boivie
Jr Girls:	Lisa St John	Lisa St John	Lisa St John	Joyce Leavengood
Veterans:	Bill Stevenson	Vic Galli	Bill Schouten	Vic Varallo
Doubles:	Bob and Cindy Hutchinson			

1967: Town Lake, Austin, Texas

	Over-all	Slalom	Tricks	Jumping
Men:	Chuck Stearns	Chuck Stearns	Alan Kempton	Chuck Stearns
Women:	Weslie Walker	Stephanie Stephens	Weslie Walker	Barbara Clack
Jr Boys:	Bob LaPoint	Bob LaPoint	Tom Ebbesmier	Wayne Grimditch
Jr Girls:	Lisa St John	Lisa St John	Lisa St John	Becky Lynn
Veterans:	Harry Price	Bill Collins	Harry Price	Jud Spencer

1968: Meyers Lake, Canton, Ohio

	Over-all	Slalom	Tricks	Jumping
Men:	Mike Suyderhoud	Mike Suyderhoud	Alan Kempton	Mike Suyderhoud
Women:	Liz Allan	Liz Allan	Liz Allan	Liz Allan
Jr Boys:	Wayne Grimditch	Bob LaPoint	Wayne Grimditch	Wayne Grimditch
Jr Girls:	Whitney Ballantine	Whitney Ballantine	Janie Peckinpaugh	Paula Clower
Veterans:	Bill Stevenson	Art Smrekar	Al Tyll	Joe Hessell

1969: Berkley Aquatic Park, California

	Over-all	Slalom	Tricks	Jumping
Men:	Mike Suyderhoud	Bruce Martin	Alan Kempton	Mike Suyderhoud
Women:	Liz Allan	Liz Allan	Liz Allan	Liz Allan
Jr Boys:	Steve Binford	Steve Binford	Tom Ebbesmier	Steve Binford
Jr Girls:	Cindy Hutchinson	Cindy Hutchinson	Cindy Hutchinson	Cindy Hutchinson
Veterans:	Jack Horton	Art Smrekar	Jay Keegan	Harry Price

Over-all	*Slalom*	*Tricks*	*Jumping*
1970: Meyers Lake Park, Canton, Ohio			
Men: Mike Suyderhoud	Mike Suyderhoud	Ricky McCormick	Mike Suyderhoud
Women: Liz Allan	Liz Allan	Christy Lynn Weir	Liz Allan
Jr Boys: David Borror	Larry Boivie	David Borror	Gary Hagan
Jr Girls: Lynn St John	Jenny Newsome	Jane Henley	—
Veterans: Bill Stevenson	Bill Collins	David McKim	Cecil Monnier
1971: White Sulphur Lake, Columbus, Ohio			
Men: Mike Suyderhoud	Kris LaPoint	Ricky McCormick	Mike Suyderhoud
Women: Liz Allan Shetter	Christy Lynn Weir	Liz Allan Shetter	Liz Allan Shetter
Jr Boys: Richard Till	Richard Till	Richard Till	David Horton
Jr Girls: Lisa Nock	Lisa Nock	Lisa Nock	Cynthia Jackson
Veterans: Harry Price	Tom Wycoff	Robert Moore	Mickey McDonald
1972: Green Lake, Seattle, Washington			
Men: Mike Suyderhoud	Kris LaPoint	Robert Kempton	Ricky McCormick
Women: Liz Allan Shetter	Christy Weir	Liz Allan Shetter	Linda Leavengood
Jr Boys: Bobby Litwins	Mike Mellenthin Jr	Bradley Wahl	Bobby Litwins
Jr Girls: Pam Folsom	Deena Brush	Pam Folsom	Carrie Pawinski
Veterans: J. D. Morgan	J. D. Morgan	Bill Schouten	Cecil Monnier
1973: Picture Lake, Petersburg, Virginia			
Men: Wayne Grimditch	Kris LaPoint	Tony Krupa	Ricky McCormick
Women: Liz Allan Shetter	Liz Allan Shetter	Liz Allan Shetter	Linda Leavengood
Jr Boys: Jeff Mostellar	Mark Cumberland	Jeff Lampas	Joe Cornell
Jr Girls: Camille Duvall	Deena Brush	Camille Duvall	Camille Duvall
Veterans: J. D. Morgan	J. D. Morgan	J. D. Morgan	J. D. Morgan
1974: Callaway Gardens, Pine Mountain, Georgia			
Men: Ricky McCormick	Kris LaPoint	Russ Stiffler	Mike Suyderhoud
Women: Liz Allan Shetter	Liz Allan Shetter	Liz Allan Shetter	Liz Allan Shetter
Jr Boys: Sammy Duvall	Mark Scharosch	Sammy Duvall	Rick Andresen
Jr Girls: Tish Fein	Tish Fein	Terry Olson	Tish Fein
Veterans: J. D. Morgan	Tom Wycoff	Bob Abbott	Nito Quivetis
1975: Tomahawk, Wisconsin			
Men: Ricky McCormick	Kris LaPoint	Tony Krupa	Wayne Grimditch
Women: Liz Allan Shetter	Cindy Todd	Liz Allan Shetter	Liz Allan Shetter
Jr Boys: Mike Morgan	Mike Morgan	Craig Pickos	Sammy Duvall
Jr Girls: Karin Roberg	Terry Olson	Kris Golden	Ann Weikert
Veterans: Ken White	Ken White	Jerry Hosner	Ken White
1976: Miami, Florida			
Men: Chris Redmond	Bob LaPoint	Tony Krupa	Bob LaPoint
Women: Cindy Todd	Cindy Todd	Cindy Todd	Linda Giddens
Jr Boys: Carl Roberge	Carl Roberge	Cory Pickos	Carl Roberge
Jr Girls: Karen Crosier	Karen Crosier	Karen Crosier	Karen Crosier
Veterans: J. D. Morgan	J. D. Morgan	Jerry Hosner	J. D. Morgan
1977: Berkeley Aquatic Park, California			
Men:			
Women:			
Jr Boys:			
Jr Girls:			
Veterans:			

UNITED STATES MASTERS INVITATIONAL TOURNAMENT

	Over-all	Slalom	Tricks	Jumping
1959				
Men:	Joe Cash	Warren Witherell	Geoffrey Wolfe	Mike Osborn
Women:	Nancie Rideout	Nancie Rideout	Nancie Rideout	Nancie Rideout
Boys':	Larry Penacho	Larry Penacho	Fred Pendlebury	Larry Penacho
Girls':	Janelle Kirkley	Janelle Kirkley	Norine Bardill	Barbara Cooper
Veterans:	Henry Holmes	Henry Holmes	Jack Andresen	Hal Roberts
1960				
Men:	Chuck Stearns	Joe Cash	Geoffrey Wolfe	Mike Osborn
Women:	Janelle Kirkley	Barbara Cooper	Norine Bardill	Barbara Cooper
Boys:	Larry Penacho	Larry Penacho	Larry Penacho	Larry Penacho
Veterans:	Wally Pallack	Sam Ogren Jr	Wally Pallack	Jim Middlebrook
1961				
Men:	Chuck Stearns	Warren Witherell	Geoffrey Wolfe	Larry Penacho
Women:	Norine Bardill	Jenny Hodges	Norine Bardill	Judy Rosch
1962				
Men:	Larry Penacho	Joe Cash	Chuck Stearns	Jimmy Jackson
Women:	Jenny Hodges	Jenny Hodges	Norine Bardill	Barbara Cooper Clack
1963				
Men:	Chuck Stearns	Billy Spencer	Al Tyll	Jimmy Jackson
Women:	Jeannette Brown	Jenny Hodges	Nancy Schnering	Jeannette Brown
1964				
Men:	Joker Osborn	Billy Spencer	Joe Cash	Joker Osborn
Women:	Dicksie Ann Hoyt	Janelle Kirkley	Dicksie Ann Hoyt	Barbara Clack
1965				
Men:	Chuck Stearns	Joker Osborn	Al Tyll	Larry Penacho
Women:	Barbara Clack	Barbara Clack	Barbara Clack	Barbara Clack
1966				
Men:	Roland Hillier	Leroy Burnett	Ricky McCormick	Jimmy Jackson
Women:	Liz Allan	Barbara Clack	Christy Lynn Weir	Liz Allen
1967				
Men:	Alan Kempton	Kris LaPoint	Alan Kempton	Alan Kempton
Women:	Liz Allan	Liz Allan	Christy Lynn Weir	Jeannette Stewart-Wood
1968				
Men:	Frankie Dees	Kris LaPoint	Alan Kempton	Mike Suyderhoud
Women:	Liz Allan	Liz Allan	Liz Allan	Liz Allan
1969				
Men:	Alan Kempton	Frankie Dees	Ricky McCormick	Mike Suyderhoud
Women:	Liz Allan	Stephanie Shackleford	Liz Allan	Liz Allan
1970				
Men:	Ricky McCormick	Kris LaPoint	Ricky McCormick	Ricky McCormick
Women:	Liz Allan	Christy Lynn Weir	Liz Allan	Liz Allan
1971				
Men:	Ricky McCormick	Kris LaPoint	Wayne Grimditch	Mike Suyderhoud
Women:	Christy Lynn Weir	Christy Lynn Weir	Christy Lynn Weir	Barbara Clack
1972				
Men:	Wayne Grimditch	Kris LaPoint	Ricky McCormick	Wayne Grimditch
Women:	Liz Allan Shetter	Lisa St John	Barbara Cleveland	Linda Leavengood
1973				
Men:	Mike Suyderhoud	Kris LaPoint	Tony Krupa	Ricky McCormick
Women:	Liz Allan Shetter	Liz Allan Shetter	Barbara Cleveland	Liz Allan Shetter

UNITED STATES MASTERS INVITATIONAL TOURNAMENT (continued)

	Over-all	Slalom	Tricks	Jumping
		1974		
Men:	George Athans	Mark Crone George Athans	Ricky McCormick	Wayne Grimditch
Women:	Liz Allan Shetter	Liz Allan Shetter	Barbara Cleveland	Liz Allan Shetter
		1975		
Men:	Ricky McCormick	Bob LaPoint	Ricky McCormick	Wayne Grimditch
Women:	Liz Allan Shetter	Liz Allan Shetter	Maria Victoria Carrasco	Liz Allan Shetter
		1976		
Men:	Carlos Suarez	Bob LaPoint	Carlos Suarez	Wayne Grimditch
Women:	Cindy Todd	Cindy Todd	Camille Duvall	Linda Giddens
		1977		
Men:	Ricky McCormick	Kris LaPoint	Tony Krupa	Bob LaPoint
Women:	Cindy Todd	Cindy Todd	Maria Victoria Carrasco	Cindy Todd

EUROPEAN AND GROUP 2 CHAMPIONSHIPS

	Over-all	Slalom	Tricks	Jumping
		1947: Evian (France)		
Men:	Claude de Clercq (Bel)	Michel Vuillety (Fra)	Haering (Swi)	Claude de Clercq (Bel)
Women:	Maggy Savard (Fr)	Marie Beday (Swi)	Maggy Savard (Fr)	Maggy Savard (Fr)
		1948: Geneva (Switzerland)		
Men:	Jean Pierre Mussat (Fr)	Jean Pierre Mussat	Claude de Clercq (Bel)	Jean Pierre Mussat (F)
Women:	Monique Girod (Swi)	Monique Girod (Swi)	Monique Girod (Swi)	Monique Girod (Swi)
		1949: Juan les Pins (France)		
Men:	Guy de Clercq (Bel) Christian Jourdan (Fr)	Christian Jourdan (Fr)	Pierre Gouin (Fr)	Guy de Clercq (Bel)
Women:	Madeleine Boutellier (Fr) Maggie Wuarin (Bel)	Madeleine Boutellier (Fr)	Madeleine Boutellier (Fr)	Madeleine Boutellier (Fr)
		1950: Evian (France)		
Men:	Claude de Clercq (Bel)	Claude de Clercq (Bel)	Claude de Clercq (Bel)	Not held
Women:	—	Jacqueline Marcour (Fr)	Monique Girod (Swi)	Not held
		1951: Genval (Belgium)		
Men:	Claude de Clercq (Bel)	Claude de Clercq (Bel)	Claude de Clercq (Bel)	Guy de Clercq (Bel)
Women:	Jacqueline Marcour (Fr)	Monique Girod (Swi)	Jacqueline Marcour (Fr)	Jacqueline Marcour (Fr)
		1952: Juan les Pins (France)		
Men:	Claude de Clercq (Bel)	Claude de Clercq (Bel)	Claude de Clercq (Bel)	Guy de Clercq (Bel)
Women:	Jacqueline Marcour (Fr)	Jane Emy (Bel)	Jacqueline Marcour (Fr)	Monique Girod (Swi)
		1953: Portschach (Austria)		
Men:	Guy Vermeersch (Bel)	Luciano Mosti (It)	Jean Pierre Galtier (Fr)	Marc Flachard (Fr)
Women:	Marina Doria (Swi)	Liselotte Feuchtinger (Aut)	Marina Doria (Swi)	Marina Doria (Swi)
		1954: Milan (Italy)		
Men:	Marc Flachard (Fr)	Marc Flachard (Fr)	Guy Vermeersch (Bel)	Marc Flachard (Fr)
Women:	Marina Doria (Swi)	Liselotte Feuchtinger (Aut)	Marina Doria (Swi)	Colette Chevrot (Fr)
		1955: Beirut (Lebanon)		
Men:	Simon Khoury (Leb)	Simon Khoury (Leb)	Simon Khoury (Leb)	Marc Flachard (Fr)
Women:	Marina Doria (Swi)	Marina Doria (Swi) Liselotte Schuh (Aut) Jacqueline Keller (Fr)	Marina Doria (Swi)	Marina Doria (Swi)
		1956: Copenhagen (Denmark)		
Men:	Franco Carraro (It)	Franco Carraro (It)	Jean Marie Muller (Fr)	Michel Kandelaft (Fr)
Women:	Marina Doria (Swi)	Marina Doria (Swi)	Jacqueline Keller (Fr)	Marina Doria (Swi)
		1957: Arenis de Mar (Spain)		
Men:	Jean Marie Muller (Fr)	Simon Khoury (Leb)	Jean Marie Muller (Fr)	Maxime Vazeille (Fr)
Women:	Jacqueline Keller (Fr)	Jacqueline Keller (Fr)	Piera Castelvetri (It)	Marina Doria (Swi)
		1958: Juan-les-Pins (France)		
Men:	Jean Marie Muller (Fr)	Jean Marie Muller (Fr)	Maxime Vazeille (Fr)	Jean Marie Muller (Fr)
Women:	Piera Castelvetri (It)	Piera Castelvetri (It)	Piera Castelvetri (It)	Renate Hansluvka (Aut)

EUROPEAN AND GROUP 2 CHAMPIONSHIPS (continued)

	Over-all	*Slalom*	*Tricks*	*Jumping*
	1959: Milan (Italy)			
Men:	Bruno Zaccardi (It)	Jean Marie Muller (Fr)	Philippe Logut (Fr)	Jean Marie Muller (Fr)
Women:	Piera Castelvetri (It)	Piera Castelvetri (It)	Piera Castelvetri (It)	Renate Hansluvka (Aut)
	1960: Vienna (Austria)			
Men:	Bruno Zaccardi (It)	Bernd Rauchenwald (Aut)	Jean Marie Muller (Fr)	Bruno Zaccardi (It)
Women:	Piera Castelvetri (It)	Piera Castelvetri (It)	Piera Castelvetri (It)	Renate Hansluvka (Aut)
	1961: Bañolas (Spain)			
Men:	Bruno Zaccardi (It)	Franco Carraro (It)	Jean Marie Muller (Fr)	Bruno Zaccardi (It)
Women:	Sylvie Hulsemann (Lux)	Beatrice Martelly (Fra)	Sylvie Hulsemann (Lux)	Sylvie Hulsemann (Lux)
	1962: Montreux (Switzerland)			
Men:	Maxime Vazeille (Fr)	Bernd Rauchenwald	Jean Calmes (Lux)	Bruno Zaccardi (It)
Women:	Renate Hansluvka (Aut)	Renate Hansluvka (Aut)	Dany Duflot (Fr)	Dany Duflot (Fr)
	1963: Vichy (France)			
Men:	Maxime Vazeille (Fr)	Bruno Zaccardi (It)	Philippe Logut (Fr)	Gerhard Rainer (Aut)
Women:	Renate Hansluvka (Aut)	Renate Hansluvka (Aut)	Guyonne Dalle (Fr)	Renate Hansluvka (Aut)
	1964: Castel Gandolfo (Italy)			
Men:	Mario Pozzini (It)	Tommy Bernocchi (It)	Tommy Bernocchi (It)	Gerhard Rainer (Aut)
Women:	Dany Duflot (Fr)	Jeannette Stewart-Wood (GB)	Dany Duflot (Fr)	Jeannette Stewart-Wood (GB)
	1965: Bañolas (Spain)			
Men:	Jean-Jacques Potier (Fr)	Tommy Bernocchi (It)	Jean-Jacques Zbinden (Swi)	Jean-Jacques Potier (Fr)
Women:	Renate Hansluvka (Aut)	Sylvie Hulsemann (Lux)	Alice Baumann (Swi)	Renate Hansluvka (Aut)
	1966: Vereeniging (South Africa)			
Men:	Bruno Zaccardi (It)	Bruno Zaccardi (It)	Christian Raisin (Fr)	Pierre Clerc (Swi)
Women:	Sylvie Hulsemann (Lux)	Jeannette Stewart-Wood (GB)	Sylvie Hulsemann (Lux)	Jeannette Stewart-Wood (GB)
	1967: Amsterdam (Holland)			
Men:	Jean Michel Jamin (Fr)	Jean-Jacques Zbinden (Swi)	Jean-Jacques Zbinden (Swi)	Pierre Clerc (Swi)
Women:	Jeannette Stewart-Wood (GB)	Jeannette Stewart-Wood (GB)	Dany Duflot (Fr)	Jeannette Stewart-Wood (GB)
	1968: Bedfont (England)			
Men:	Roby Zucchi (It)	Roby Zucchi (It)	Jacques Tillement (Fr)	Pierre Clerc (Swi)
Women:	Sylvie Hulsemann (Lux)	Sylvie Hulsemann (Lux)	Sylvie Hulsemann (Lux)	Jeannette Stewart-Wood (GB)
	1969: Canzo (Italy)			
Men:	Jean-Yves Parpette (Fr)	Jean-Michel Jamin (Fr)	Roby Zucchi (It)	Pierre Clerc (Swi)
Women:	Elaine Borter (Swi)	Elaine Borter (Swi)	Elaine Borter (Swi)	Elaine Borter (Swi)
	1970: Canzo (Italy)			
Men:	Roby Zucchi (It)	Roby Zucchi (It)	Max Hofer (It)	Ian Walker (GB)
Women:	Sylvie Maurial (Fr)	Willi Stahle (Hol)	Willi Stahle (Hol)	Willi Stahle (Hol)
	1971: Canzo (Italy)			
Men:	Roby Zucchi (It)	Roby Zucchi (It)	Karl Benzinger (Ger)	Roby Zucchi (It)
Women:	Sylvie Maurial (Fr)	Sylvie Maurial (Fr)	Sylvie Maurial (Fr)	Willi Stahle (Hol)
	1972: Temple Sur Lot (France)			
Men:	Paul Seaton (GB)	Roby Zucchi (It)	Frantisek Stehno (Cz)	Paul Seaton (GB)
Women:	Willi Stahle (Hol)	Willi Stahle (Hol)	Willi Stahle (Hol)	Willi Stahle (Hol)
	1973: Brussels (Belgium)			
Men:	Lars Bjork (Swe)	Lars Bjork (Swe)	Frantisek Stehno (Cz)	Paul Seaton (GB)
Women:	Sylvie Maurial (Fr)	Eva Maria Frisch (Aut)	Willi Stahle (Hol)	Sylvie Maurial (Fr)
	1974: Hartebeesport (South Africa)			
Men:	Paul Seaton (GB)	Max Hofer (It)	Paul Seaton (GB)	Paul Seaton (GB)
Women:	Willi Stahle (Hol)	Chantel Escot (Fr)	Eva Maria Frisch (Aut)	Karen Morse (GB)
	1975: Trier (Germany)			
Men:	Paul Seaton (GB)	Christian Sommer (Fr)	Frantisek Stehno (Cz)	Marco Merlo (GB)
Women:	Willi Stahle (Hol)	Willi Stahle (Hol)	Willi Stahle (Hol)	Petra Trautmann (Ger)
	1976: Milan (Italy)			
Men:	Mike Hazelwood (GB)	Roby Zucchi (It)	Frantisek Stehno (Cz)	Mike Hazelwood (GB)
Women:	Chantel Escot (Fr)	Chantel Escot (Fr)	Marlon van Dijk (Hol)	Karen Morse (GB)
	1977: Annenheim (Austria)			

BRITISH NATIONAL CHAMPIONSHIPS

	Over-all	Slalom	Tricks	Jumping
1954: Ruislip Lido				
Men:	Eddie Arida	Eddie Arida	—	Geoffrey Eker
1955: Ruislip Lido				
Men:	David Nations	David Nations Peter Felix	David Nations	David Nations
1956: Ruislip Lido				
Men:	David Nations	David Nations	David Nations	David Nations
Women:	Joan Anderson	Joan Anderson	Joan Anderson	Joan Anderson
1957: Yorkshire				
Men:	Peter Felix	Peter Felix	—	Peter Ruben
Women:	Rosemary Brigham	Rosemary Brigham	—	Sue Adamson
1958: Lochearnhead				
Men:	Peter Felix	Peter Felix	Peter Felix	Jimmy Murphy
Women:	Anna Gerber	Sue Mason	Anna Gerber	Gillian Rowe
1959: Ruislip				
Men:	Lance Callingham	Lance Callingham	Lance Callingham	Lance Callingham
Women:	Maureen Lynn-Taylor	Maureen Lynn-Taylor	Maureen Lynn-Taylor	Gillian Rowe
1960: Sonning, Berks				
Women:	Maureen Lynn-Taylor	Maureen Lynn-Taylor	Maureen Lynn-Taylor	Gillian Rowe
1961: Ullswater				
Men:	Peter Rubin	Peter Rubin	Peter Rubin	Lance Callingham
Women:	Maureen Lynn-Taylor	Maureen Lynn-Taylor	Maureen Lynn-Taylor	Maureen Lynn-Taylor
1962: Killbirnie				
Men:	Lance Callingham	Lance Callingham	Peter Rubin	Lance Callingham
Women:	Fiona Saunders	Fiona Saunders	Fiona Saunders	Anne Wilton
1963: Ruislip				
Men:	Lance Callingham	Lance Callingham	Peter Rubin	Tony McCleery
Women:	Jeannette Stewart-Wood	Jeannette Stewart-Wood	Fiona Saunders	Jeannette Stewart-Wood
1964: Sonning, Berks				
Men:	Robin Beckett	Robin Beckett	Peter Rubin	Robin Beckett
Women:	Anne Wilton	Anne Wilton	Fiona Saunders	Jeannette Stewart-Wood
1965: Skewbridge				
Men:	Robin Beckett	Robin Beckett	Paul Adlington	Robin Beckett
Women:	Anne Wilton	Anne Wilton	Fiona Saunders	Anne Wilton
1966: Princes				
Men:	Robin Beckett	Robin Beckett	Paul Adlington	Jack Fulton
Women:	Jeannette Stewart-Wood	Jeannette Stewart-Wood	Jeannette Stewart-Wood	Jeannette Stewart-Wood
1967: Lochearnhead				
Men:	David Johnson	David Johnson	Paul Adlington	Jack Fulton
Women:	Jeannette Stewart-Wood	Jeannette Stewart-Wood	Jeannette Stewart-Wood	Jeannette Stewart-Wood
1968: Edgebaston Reservoir				
Men:	Luke O'Reilly	Wally Johnston	Paul Adlington	Luke O'Reilly
Women:	Leslie Jackson	Leslie Jackson	S. Johnstone	Leslie Jackson
1969: Halstead, Essex				
Men:	Jack Fulton	Paul Adlington	Robin Beckett	Robin Beckett
Women:	Leslie Jackson	Leslie Jackson	Leslie Jackson	Gail Brantingham
1970: Halstead, Essex				
Men:	Ian Walker	Ian Walker	Ian Walker	Ian Walker
Women:	Gail Brantingham	Gail Brantingham	Fiona Saunders	Gail Brantingham
1971: Princes				
Men:	Paul Seaton	Paul Seaton	Paul Seaton	Paul Seaton
Women:	Karen Morse	Karen Morse	Karen Morse	Diane Kirby

BRITISH NATIONAL CHAMPIONSHIPS (continued)

	Over-all	*Slalom*	*Tricks*	*Jumping*
		1972: Ruislip		
Men:	Paul Seaton	Paul Seaton	Ian Walker	Paul Seaton
Women:	Karen Morse	Karen Morse	Karen Morse	Karen Morse
		1973: Biggleswade		
Men:	Paul Seaton	Mike Hazelwood	Paul Seaton	Paul Seaton
Women:	Karen Morse	Karen Morse	Karen Morse	Karen Morse
		1974: Biggleswade		
Men:	Mike Hazelwood	Paul Seaton	Mike Hazelwood	Paul Seaton
Women:	Karen Morse	Philippa Roberts	Veronica Downing	Karen Morse
		1975: Bedfont		
Men:	Paul Seaton	Paul Seaton	Paul Seaton	Paul Seaton
Women:	Karen Morse	Ann Pitt	Ann Pitt	Jackie Dobson
		1976: Ruislip		
Men:	Mike Hazelwood	Mike Hazelwood	Mike Hazelwood	James Carne
Women:	Karen Morse	Philippa Roberts	Ann Pitt	Karen Morse
				Jackie Dobson
		1977: Kirtons Farm, Reading		
Men:	Mike Hazelwood	Mike Hazelwood	John Buttleday	Mike Hazelwood
Women:	Philippa Roberts	Philippa Roberts	Philippa Roberts	Karen Morse

GROUP 3 CHAMPIONSHIPS

Year	Mens	Womens
1962	—	—
1964	Colin Birmingham (Aus)	Margaret Calvert (Aus)
1966	Rohan Shorland (Aus)	May Ward (Aus)
1969	Joe Csortan (Aus)	Kaye Thurlow (Aus)
1970	Jeff Ecker (Aus)	Lorraine Edwards (Aus)
1972	Bruce Cockburn (Aus)	Kaye Thurlow (Aus)
1974	Graeme Cockburn (Aus)	Sue Wright (Aus)
1976	Bruce Cockburn (Aus)	Kaye Thurlow Faulkner (Aus)
1977		

Moomba Results

Year	Mens	Womens
1961	Wally Morris (Qld)	Rosemary Margin (Vic)
1962	Colin Birmingham (Qld)	Rosemary Margin (Vic)
1963	Chuck Stearns (USA)	Margaret Calvert (Qld)
1964	Not held	
1965	Ron Marks (NSW)	Margaret Calvert (Qld)
1966	Chuck Stearns (USA)	Barbara Cooper Clack (USA)
1967	Colin Faulkner (Vic)	Deirdre Barnard (S. Africa)
1968	Mike Suyderhoud (USA)	Kaye Thurlow (Vic)
1969	Mike Suyderhoud (USA)	May Ward (Vic)
1970	Bruce Cockburn (NSW)	Kaye Thurlow (Vic)
1971	Graeme Cockburn (NSW)	Kaye Thurlow (Vic)
1972	Ricky McCormick (USA)	Kaye Thurlow (Vic)
1973	Wayne Grimditch (USA)	Kaye Thurlow (Vic)
1974	Ricky McCormick (USA)	Kaye Thurlow Faulkner (Vic)
1975	Ricky McCormick (USA)	Liz Allan Shetter (USA)
1976	Carlos Suarez (Ven)	Kaye Thurlow Faulkner (Vic)
1977	Mike Hazelwood (GB)	Kaye Thurlow Faulkner (Vic)
1978		

THE WATER SKI SPEED RECORD

Year		
	Unofficial	
1922	Ralph W. Samuelson USA	32 km/h *20 mph*
1925	Ralph W. Samuelson USA	130 km/h *80 mph*
1947	Michel Vuillety Swi	150 km/h *93 mph*
	Official	
1955	Harold W. Peterson USA	91·7 km/h *57 mph*
1956–63	Harold W. Peterson USA	93 km/h *58 mph*
,,	Harold W. Peterson USA	129 km/h *80 mph*
,,	Harold W. Peterson USA	135 km/h *84 mph*
,,	Harold W. Peterson USA	139 km/h *87 mph*
,,	Harold W. Peterson USA	171 km/h *106 mph*
,,	Harold W. Peterson USA	182 km/h *113 mph*
,,	Harold W. Peterson USA	188 km/h *117 mph*
1966	Chuck Stearns USA	192·3 km/h *119·52 mph*
1969	Chuck Stearns USA	196·5 km/h *122·11 mph*
1971	Danny Churchill USA	202·24 km/h *125·69 mph*

THE JUMPING RECORD

Men

Year	Contestant	Distance	Tournament
1947	Charles R. Sligh Jr	14·94 m *49 ft*	Dixie
1947	Tram Pickett (tie)	18·59 m *61 ft*	Nationals
1947	Buddy Boyle (tie)	18·59 m *61 ft*	Nationals
1948	Buddy Boyle	20·73 m *68 ft*	Dixie
1949	Buddy Boyle	21·95 m *72 ft*	Florida State
1950	Buddy Boyle	22·86 m *75 ft*	Dixie
1950	Jake McGuire	24·38 m *80 ft*	Nationals
1950	Jake McGuire (tie)	25·60 m *84 ft*	World Championships
1950	Dick Pope Jr (tie)	25·60 m *84 ft*	World Championships
1951	Dick Pope Jr	25·91 m *85 ft*	Dixie
1952	Bob Cozzens	26·52 m *87 ft*	Dixie
1953	Bob Nathey	27·43 m *90 ft*	Lakeland
1953	Alfredo Mendoza	27·74 m *91 ft*	All-American
1953	Warren Witherall	29·26 m *96 ft*	Eastern Regional
1953	Alfredo Mendoza	29·57 m *97 ft*	Nationals
1954	Butch Rosenberg	29·87 m *98 ft*	Dixie
1954	Alfredo Mendoza	30·18 m *99 ft*	Dixie
1954	Dick Binette (tie)	31·09 m *102 ft*	Nationals
1954	Butch Rosenberg (tie)	31·09 m *102 ft*	Nationals
1954	Warren Witherall	32·31 m *106 ft*	New England
1955	Jim Rusing	33·22 m *109 ft*	Dixie
1955	Alfredo Mendoza	35·36 m *116 ft*	Dixie
1955	Butch Rosenberg	38·10 m *125 ft*	Nationals
1957	Alan Bromberg	38·40 m *126 ft*	Southern Regionals
1957	Joe Cash	38·40 m *126 ft*	Nationals
1958	LeRoy Herren	38·70 m *127 ft*	S.C. Regionals
1958	Joe Cash	39·32 m *129 ft*	Florida Championships
1958	Joe Cash	41·45 m *136 ft*	Nationals
1959	Joe Cash	43·28 m *142 ft*	Fort Myers Jumping
1959	Mike Osborn	43·28 m *142 ft*	Nationals
1960	Penny Baker	45·72 m *150 ft*	Lone Star Championships
1961	Larry Penacho	45·72 m *150 ft*	World Championships
1962	Larry Penacho	47·24 m *155 ft*	Western Regionals
1964	Dennis Rahlves	48·16 m *158 ft*	Rocky Mountain Open
1968	Mike Suyderhoud	48·77 m *160 ft*	California State
1969	Mike Suyderhoud	49·38 m *162 ft*	US Team Trials
1970	Mike Suyderhoud	50·29 m *165 ft*	Fall River International
1972	Wayne Grimditch	51·51 m *169 ft*	Masters
1974	Wayne Grimditch	51·82 m *170 ft*	Masters
1975	Wayne Grimditch	52·43 m *172 ft*	Horton Lake Open
1975	Wayne Grimditch	54·86 m *180 ft*	Masters

THE JUMPING RECORD (continued)

Women

1952	Mary Lois Thornhill	17·07 m *56 ft*	Lakeland
1953	Willa Worthington McGuire	17·98 m *59 ft*	Lakeland
1954	Willa Worthington McGuire	19·81 m *65 ft*	Dixie
1954	Leah Marie Atkins	21·34 m *70 ft*	New England
1957	Nancie Rideout	23·16 m *76 ft*	Nationals
1958	Nancie Rideout	24·08 m *79 ft*	New Orleans Open
1958	Nancie Rideout	24·69 m *81 ft*	Southern Regionals
1958	Nancie Rideout	27·13 m *89 ft*	Nationals
1962	Barbara Cooper Clack (tie)	28·04 m *92 ft*	Lakeland
1962	Judy Rosch (tie)	28·04 m *92 ft*	Lakeland
1963	Barbara Cooper Clack	28·35 m *93 ft*	Nationals
1963	Barbara Cooper Clack	29·26 m *96 ft*	Winter Park Jumping
1964	Barbara Cooper Clack	30·48 m *100 ft*	Florida State
1964	Barbara Cooper Clack	31·09 m *102 ft*	Masters
1966	Barbara Cooper Clack	32·00 m *105 ft*	Orlando Open
1968	Liz Allan	32·31 m *106 ft*	Florida State
1968	Liz Allan	33·53 m *110 ft*	Masters
1971	Barbara Cooper Clack	33·83 m *111 ft*	Masters
1973	Linda Giddens	36·27 m *119 ft*	Nationals
1974	Liz Allan Shetter	38·10 m *125 ft*	Nationals
1976	Linda Giddens	39·02 m *128 ft*	Nationals

GRAND NATIONAL CATALINA WATER-SKI RACE
(California)

Year	Men	Women
1949	Ed Stanley	Dorothy Mae Andresen
1950	Bob Pitchford	Pattie Showalter
1951	NO RACE	
1952	Fred Lang	Aline Williams
1953	Harry Laughinghouse	Frankie Ramos
1954	Harry Laughinghouse	Norma Brisson
1955	Chuck Stearns	Barbara Greer
1956	Chuck Stearns	Barbara Greer
1957	Ronnie Danlicker	Joyce Gibson
1958	Chuck Stearns 1:21	Joyce Gibson
1959	Chuck Stearns 1:27	Sandy Hawkins
1960	Chuck Stearns 1:30	Marge Lisonbe
1961	Rick Fowler 1:18	Jane Mobley Welch 1:30
1962	Chuck Stearns 1:39	Jane Mobley Welch 2:02
1963	Butch Peterson 1:13:40	Jane Mobley Welch 1:30:40
1964	Rick Fowler 1:19:04	Lavone Bushey 1:33:05
1965	Chuck Stearns 1:14:41	Jane Mobley Welch —
1966	Mike Harker —	Jane Mobley Welch —
1967	Butch Peterson 1:14:29	Jane Mobley Welch 1:27:50
1968	Butch Peterson 1:22:12	Linda Martini 1:33:41
1969	Tim Guckes 1:04:38	Sally Younger 1:21:40
1970	Mike Kennedy 1:09:06	Sally Younger 1:11:40
1971	Chuck Stearns 1:04:50	Jane Mobley Welch 1:13:39
1972	Danny Churchill 1:06:31	Joannie Martini 1:24:09
1973	Jeff Wooten 1:06:48	Tracey Whitney 1:16:20
1974	Tim Guckes 1:04:08	Joannie Martini 1:10:52
1975	Chuck Stearns 1:12:27	Joannie Martini 1:22:31
1976	Craig Wendt 1:9:20	Joannie Martini —
1977		
1978		

BRIDGE-TO-BRIDGE RESULTS (Australia)

Year	Boat	Time
1961/62	Yogi Bear	1 hr 33 min
1962/63	Fleet Funn III	1 hr 18 min 30 sec
1963/64	Patricia	1 hr 18 min 15 sec
1964/65	Fleet Funn III	1 hr 14 min 15·2 sec
1965/66	Turbofire	1 hr 12 min 53 sec
1966/67	Shy Anne	1 hr 21 min 57 sec
1967/68	Drag-on	1 hr 17 min 22 sec
1968/69	Caroline	1 hr 03 min 35 sec
1969/70	Louise J.	1 hr 05 min 56 sec
1970/71	Caroline	0 hr 59 min 26 sec
1971/72	Louise J	0 hr 58 min 32 sec
1972/73	Drag Hunter	1 hr 01 min 55 sec
1973/74	Louise J	0 hr 57 min 19 sec
1974/75	Wahoo	0 hr 56 min 35 sec
1975/76	Al Torque	0 hr 56 min 18 sec
1976/77	Thunderbolt (but fastest time: Harada)	Not known

EUROPEAN SKI-RACING CHAMPIONSHIP

1969	Billy Rixon	Great Britain
1970	Brendan Bowles	Great Britain
1971	Bruno Cassa	Italy
1972	Jonathan Harvey	Great Britain
1973	Billy Rixon	Great Britain
1974	Bruno Cassa	Italy
1975	Enrico Guggiari	Italy
1976	Billy Rixon	Great Britain
1977		

GROWTH OF NATIONAL FEDERATIONS IN WWSU

1955	21
1961	33
1965	42
1967	42
1969	46
1971	48
1977	

PRESIDENTS OF THE IWSU

1946–51	A. Schmidt	Switzerland
1951	G. Vermesch (Vice-President)	Belgium
1951–54	W. Geneux	Switzerland

PRESIDENTS OF THE WWSU

1955–56	W. Geneux	Switzerland
1956–58	D. Pope Jr	USA
1958–60	W. Geneux	Switzerland
1961–62	Bill Barlow Sr	USA
1962–63	G. Fustinoni	Italy
1963–67	A. Coutau	Switzerland
1968–71	F. Carraro	Italy
1972–75	A. Clark	Australia
1976–	J. J. Finsterwald	Switzerland

PRESIDENTS OF GROUP I

Bill Barlow Jr
Clint Ward
Hector Caran-Andruet

Bibliography

The Royal Visit. Dedicated to Sir Abraham B. King (Bart.) and Daniel O'Connell Esq. (Dublin 1821)
Notes and Queries (London 1849 – Bound volumes in British Library)
'Relics of the Past' (*Illustrated London News* magazine 1860)
The Picture Magazine (1894)
Harper's Weekly (USA 1915)
La Nature (Paris 1916)
Popular Mechanics magazine (USA 1924)
'Riding the Bucking Bounding Main', Mayne Ober Peake (*Sunset Magazine* USA 1926)
Ski Nautique, Robert Baltié (Paris 1948)
Water Skiing, Dick Pope Sr (Prentice-Hall USA 1957)
'The Bridge-to-Bridge Classic' (2 pp unpublished letter by L. Griffin)
'The Grand National Catalina Ski Race' (Race Programme 1962)
Let's Go Waterskiing, Thomas C. Hardman and William D. Clifford (Hawthorn Books Inc. 1965)
Un Echo d'Olympie ('Echo from Olympia'), A. S. Diacakis (16 pp published pamphlet 1966)
A Book of Waterskiing, Masanori Komorimiya (Japan 1968)
Water Skiing History of the CWSA, Clint Ward (Published programme 1971)
Nosotros Vosotros Y Ellos, Raquel Kerszberg (Argentina 1975)
Bring on the Empty Horses, David Niven (Hamish Hamilton London 1975)
'Lo Sci Nautico in Italia, Bianca Vitali (5 pp unpublished memorandum)
'Historia de Esqui Nautico in Espagna' (2 pp unpublished memorandum 1976)
'El Esqui Nautico en Colombia' (Programme Notes for World Championship 1973)
'Om Opprindelsen til vannskisporten', Emil Petersen (3 pp unpublished memorandum 1976)
'Origin of Waterskiing in Norway, Jan H. Johannessen (2 pp unpublished memorandum 1976)
'Correspondence with Ralph W. Samuelson' (Inc. 5 pp press release 1975/76/77)
'Note de M. Claude de Clercq à l'attention de M. Kevin Desmond (8 pp unpublished memorandum 1976)
'History of Waterskiing in Belgium', Sid Adriaensen (7 pp published memorandum 1976)
'History of Finnish Waterskiing', P. J. Barck (2 pp unpublished letter 1976)
'Water Skiing in Denmark', Niels Vinding (2 pp unpublished memorandum 1976)
'The History of Waterskiing in Sweden', Christer Widing (2 pp unpublished memorandum 1976)
'A Short History of Czechosloavak Water Ski Sport', Ladislav Nemes (3 pp unpublished memorandum 1976)
'The Origin and Development of Waterskiing in the Netherlands, L. F. de Groot (8 pp unpublished memorandum 1976)
'Der Wasserschilauf in Osterreich, Dr Karl Rauchenwald (4 pp unpublished memorandum 1976)
'Informations concernant La Federation Francaise de Ski Nautique', Odette Muller (3 pp unpublished memorandum 1976)
'Waterskiing in Wales', Clive F. Jenkins (7 pp unpublished memorandum 1976)
'History of Waterskiing in Greece, Chr. Papageorgiou (7 pp unpublished memorandum 1976)
'The Origin and Growth of Water Skiing in Yugoslavia, Hrabroslav Lindic (46 pp unpublished Graduation Thesis 1976)
'Mexican Letter', Rene Daumas Nemoz (2 pp unpublished 1976)
'History of South African Waterskiing', Roy Saint, with Monty Tolkin (10 pp unpublished memorandum 1976)
'History of Waterskiing in Iran', Taghi Emami (1 p unpublished 1976)
'Waterskiing in the Soviet Union', Boris Olshevsky (2 pp press report, Novosti Agency 1976)
'Notes on the History of Waterskiing in Hong Kong', Jim Laversuch (2 pp unpublished 1977)
'German Water Ski Federation', Franz Kirsch (2 pp unpublished memorandum 1977)
'Waterskiing in Poland', Zbigniew Naorniakowski (3 pp unpublished memorandum 1977)
'History of Waterskiing in the Republic of China', Prof. Hsu Fu-teh (2 pp unpublished memorandum 1977)
Back Issues of *Water Skier* (USA) and *Scinautico* (Italy) magazines
World Water Ski Union Archives in Geneva, Switzerland (André Coutau)

Index

Index prepared by Anna Pavord

Illustration references in italics

OTHER GUINNESS SUPERLATIVES TITLES

Facts and Feats Series:

Air Facts and Feats, *3rd ed.*
John W R Taylor, Michael J H
Taylor and David Mondey

Rail Facts and Feats, *2nd ed.*
John Marshall

Tank Facts and Feats, *2nd ed.*
Kenneth Macksey

Car Facts and Feats, *2nd ed.*
edited by Anthony Harding

Yachting Facts and Feats
Peter Johnson

Business World
Henry Button and Andrew
Lampert

Music Facts and Feats
Robert and Celia Dearling
with Brian Rust

Animal Facts and Feats, *2nd ed.*
Gerald L Wood FZS

Plant Facts and Feats
William G Duncalf

**Structures – Bridges,
Towers, Tunnels, Dams . . .**
John H Stephens

Weather Facts and Feats
Ingrid Holford

Guide Series:

Guide to Bicycling
J Durry and J B Wadley

Guide to French Country Cooking
Christian Roland Delu

Guide to Freshwater Angling
Brian Harris and Paul Boyer

Guide to Mountain Animals
R P Bille

Guide to Underwater Life
C Petron and J B Lozet

Guide to Motorcycling, *2nd ed.*
Christian Lacombe

Guide to Saltwater Angling
Brian Harris

Other Titles:

The Guinness Book of Answers
edited by Norris D McWhirter

The Guinness Book of Records
edited by Norris D McWhirter

The Guinness Book of 1952
Kenneth Macksey

Universal Soldier
Martin Windrow and Frederick
Wilkinson

The Guinness Book of 1953
Kenneth Macksey

History of Land Warfare
Kenneth Macksey

History of Sea Warfare
Lt-Cmdr Gervis Frere-Cook
and Kenneth Macksey

History of Air Warfare
David Brown, Christopher
Shores and Kenneth Macksey

**The Guinness Guide to Feminine
Achievements**
Joan and Kenneth Macksey

The Guinness Book of Names
Leslie Dunkling

Battle Dress
Frederick Wilkinson

100 Years of Wimbledon
Lance Tingay